This volume consists of two diaries by William Bamford, an Irish officer in the British Army in the mid-18th century:

The first is 'A narrative of the campaigns and feats of arms of the 35th Regiment (Royal Sussex)'. It covers the regiment's activities during the French and Indian War and includes an account of the siege and capture of Louisbourg in 1758, British capture of Québec in 1759, the French siege of Québec in 1760 and the capture of Montreal, a march to Fort Ticonderoga, Saratoga, and Albany in 1761, a voyage to Barbados in 1761, the siege and capture of Martinique and Havana in 1762, a voyage to Saint Augustine Florida, Charleston, South Carolina, and Port Royal, Jamaica in 1763, and a voyage to Pensacola, Florida and a description of Mobile, Alabama (then part of West Florida), and other parts of West Florida, in 1765, and finally back again to England by way of Havana in 1765. Also included in this section are a copy of a letter from Major General Webb to Colonel Munro dated 4 August, 1757 documenting Webb's refusal to reinforce Bamford's regiment at Fort William Henry, and two anecdotes from 1759 and 1760 regarding Anglo-French battles fought outside Québec.

The second dairy, running from January through December 1776, documents William Bamford's service in the 40th Regiment at Boston after the battle of Bunker Hill, during the winter and early spring of 1776, the British evacuation to Halifax, return to Staten Island, New York, the campaign on Long Island, and the occupation of New York City.

In Part II, between the two diaries, a transcribed letter from Bamford relates part of his career, along with his commission as a captain in the 40th Foot.

I0894077

John B. Hattendorf is the Ernest J. King Professor Emeritus of Maritime History at the U.S. Naval War College, where he held that professorship for 32 years from 1984 to 2016. A former officer in the U.S. Navy, 1964-1973, he holds degrees in history from Kenyon College (A.B., 1964), Brown University (A.M., 1971), and the University of Oxford (D.Phil., 1979; D.Litt., 2016). In addition to his many distinguished contributions to the field of maritime history, he also works on eighteenth century military history. He is the author of *England in the War of the Spanish Succession: The English View and Conduct of Grand Strategy, 1702-1713* (1979) and several entries on several early 18th century British military figures, including the first Duke of Marlborough, in the *Oxford Dictionary of National Biography.* He was editor-in-chief of *Marlborough: Soldier and Diplomat* (2012) and *Charles XII: Warrior King* (2018).

A Redcoat in America

The Diaries of Lieutenant William Bamford, 1757-1765 and 1776

Edited and Annotated with an Introduction by John B. Hattendorf

Helion & Company

Helion & Company Limited
Unit 8 Amherst Business Centre
Budbrooke Road
Warwick
CV34 5WE
England
Tel. 01926 499619
Email: info@helion.co.uk
Website: www.helion.co.uk
Twitter: @helionbooks
Visit our blog at http://blog.helion.co.uk/

Published by Helion & Company 2019
Designed and typeset by Mach 3 Solutions Ltd (www.mach3solutions.co.uk)
Cover designed by Paul Hewitt, Battlefield Design (www.battlefield-design.co.uk)

Original text from manuscripts in the John Carter Brown Library, Brown University; William L. Clements Library, University of Michigan; John Work Garrett Library (Evergreen Museum and Library) part of the Sheridan Libraries of The Johns Hopkins University.

ISBN 978-1-911628-47-7

British Library Cataloguing-in-Publication Data.
A catalogue record for this book is available from the British Library.

Contents

List of Plates

Acknowledgements and Note on Sources

The editor is grateful to the John Carter Brown Library, The John Work Garrett Library of The Sheridan Libraries of the Johns Hopkins University, and the William L. Clements Library for their permission to publish these documents as well as to the reference librarians who assisted in providing digital copies of the documents to prepare this volume.

The editor is particularly grateful to Dr John A. Houlding for his invaluable advice and assistance during this entire project. His patient and prompt answers to the editor's innumerable questions over many months on detailed aspects of military officers' careers made an enormous contribution to this work. The book could not have reached the research standard that it has without his guidance and information.

Information with the biographies of people and ships are in footnotes at the first mention in the text. These notes can be readily found through the index. The information for British Army officers is based mainly on the information in the unpublished database on Georgian Military Officers maintained by Dr J.A. Houlding, supplemented by *The Oxford Dictionary of National Biography*, *The History of Parliament*, the *Canadian Dictionary of National Biography*; Andrews, ed., *The Journals of Jeffrey Amherst, 1757-1763*, Vol.2: *A Dictionary of People, Places, and Ships*, and the appendix to Middleton (ed.), *Amherst and the conquest of Canada*. Information on British naval officers is based mainly on Syrett and DiNardo (eds.), *The Commissioned Sea Officers of the Royal Navy, 1660-1815*. Information on warships derives from Rif Winfield (ed.), *British Warships in the Age of Sail, 1714-1792*; Rif Winfield and Stephen S. Roberts, *French Warships in the Age of Sail, 1626-1786;* Jean-Michel Roche, *Dictionnaire des Bâtiments de la Flotte de Guerre Française de Colbert à nos Jours*, the appendix on "Ships of the line of the Spanish Navy (1714-1825)" in John D. Harbron, *Trafalgar and the Spanish Navy;* Paul H. Silverstone, *The Sailing Navy, 1775-1854*, and the online *Dictionary of American Naval Fighting Ships*. The annotation is from these sources unless otherwise indicated. The works listed in the bibliography provided additional information on particular topics.

Introduction

The preparation of this volume has been a process of discovery. The diary for the years between 1757 and 1765 first came to the editor's attention in the early 1990s, when he was involved with a number of initiatives on the subject of maritime history at the John Carter Brown Library at Brown University in Providence, Rhode Island, USA. That document was intriguing, not only for its selection of hand-drawn maps and illustrations relating to the French and Indian War but for the interrelationships it recorded between the activities of the Royal Navy and the British Army in the mid-18th century. For an historian who focused on the sub-specialty of naval affairs within the broad span of maritime history, this diary presented a revelation in the way it showed routine interactions that seemed to be taken for granted between the army and navy, but which historians of military and naval events have often forgotten as they concentrate on their more narrowly defined service-oriented interests. The Navy's role in escorting troop transports and supporting military operations and the Army's dependence on waterborne transportation on the ocean as well as on lakes and rivers, is a subtle, sub-theme that courses through the pages of the documents that follow.

The diary for 1757-1765 presented a major problem that had to be solved in order to publish the document. Who wrote it? The John Carter Brown Library had acquired the manuscript in 1966. The Library director at that time, Thomas R. Adams, lucidly described the document in the Library's *Annual Report* on its new acquisitions for that year:

> Our most interesting addition is a manuscript diary by a British office of the 35th or Royal Sussex Regiment, It appears to have been written in the field, for it is a notebook with sheets of cheap blue blotting paper bound between each leaf and is designed to fit into a saddlebag. In something over one hundred pages the author records the events of the years 1756 to 1765. We have not been able to discover another English military journal as complete as this one is in its coverage.
>
> The diary opens with the Royal Sussex quartered in Albany. From there the regiment was ordered to Philadelphia to embark for the campaigns which resulted in the capture of Louisburg, Quebec, and Montreal. In September of 1760 the 35th marched south from Montreal to Crown Point and by the end of 1761 was back in New York. There it embarked on transports and sent to the West Indies where it participated in the captures of Martinique and of Havana in 1762. The regiment was then sent to Pensacola where it remained until its returned to England in 1765. The last entry

> suggest the rigors of overseas service in the eighteenth century: "The feeble remains of our Worn out Regiment got on Shore we buried a great Many Men at Sea & some in the Harbour, several were sent to the Isle of Wight dreadfully afflicted with the Scurvy, . . . a Scratch on the leg was almost Certain Death, & the loss of the Joynt at Least in the Islands: . . . we landed scarcely 100 Men. Marched to Chatham Barracks."
>
> The identity of the author of this interesting narrative is not certain. The first eight leaves have been lost but internal evidence makes it clear that he was an officer who served with the Royal Sussex throughout its stay in America. Regimental histories and army lists name only two men who fit this description: the commander of the 35th, Lieutenant Colonel Henry Fletcher, and Colin Campbell, who joined as an ensign in 1756. We feel that Fletcher was probably the author because the diary contains much information which might not have been available to a junior officer.
>
> The manuscript is primarily a military document but contains a number of comments on civilian affairs. The author noted in October 1757 that Nassau Hall at Princeton was almost finished. He found Philadelphia the most attractive American city, and of it he said, "the Markets are Extreamly well Provided & Cheap; in Short 'tis a most Flourishing Place." This diary is made particularly attractive by twenty-five watercolors, signed "W.B. Engineer," which include plans of fortifications, battle plans, maps, views, and tropical fish.[1]

This 1966 description of the document and its possible attribution to Lieutenant Colonel Henry Fletcher was all that was generally known about the diary when the editor began his investigations. This information provided the basis for cataloging the item with the library system and also when it was made widely available in digitized format on the Internet through the online Internet Archive.[2] The illustrations are also readily available on the John Carter Brown Library's website which contain its library of digitized maps and early American images.[3]

In England, the rich collections of the National Army Museum in London, the National Archives at Kew, and the archives of the Royal Sussex Regiment at the West Sussex Record Office in Chichester all provided general background that illuminated the published regimental histories in the collection of the Anne S.K. Brown Military Collection at Brown University. This general information provided few clues to who the author of the diary might be, but provided some context.

Arthur Chichester, 3rd Earl of Donegall, first raised the regiment in Belfast and was its first colonel from 1701 to 1706. Raised at Donegall's personal expense, it was initially known as the Earl of Donegall's Regiment of Foot or the Belfast regiment, one of the Protestant regiments formed to counter threats on Ireland from French forces under Louis XIV. At its formation, the regiment was given orange

1 John Carter Brown Library. *Annual Reports, 1901-1966*. Vol. 7, "Annual Report, July 1 1966," pp. 6-8.

2 See https://archive.org/details/sevenyearswarjou00flet/page/n2.

3 See https://www.brown.edu/academics/libraries/john-carter-brown/jcb-online/image-collections.

facings to its red uniforms, symbolising Lord Donegall's support for King William III. During the War of the Spanish Succession, the regiment was one of six designated for sea service. Donegall took his regiment to Spain, where the regiment was at Cadiz in 1702, Gibraltar in 1705, and the siege of Barcelona in 1706, where the Earl of Donegall was killed in action at Fort Montjuich. He was succeeded by Brigadier Richard Gorges between 1706 and 1717, when General Charles Otway took command of what then became known as Otway's Regiment. Otway remained colonel of the regiment for 47 years until August 1764.

At the outset of the French and Indian War, Otway's regiment was not well prepared for combat. Under the immediate command of Lieutenant Colonel George Munro, the regiment embarked in Ireland for service in North America in April 1756. In October 1756, not long after their arrival, Lord Loudon, commander-in-chief of the British Army in North America, reported to HRH William Augustus, Duke of Cumberland, Captain-General of the British Army, that the situation on the frontier in New York was bad. His main force was based at Fort Edward, where he had to choose between the Royal American Regiment and Otway's. He placed his lesser forces at Fort William Henry. Loudon wrote,

> Your Royal Highness will be surprised, I have chose to take the *Royal Americans,* rather than Lieutenant General *Otways*; this last are entirely Raw Officers and Soldiers, and everything new to them; the prest Men, I dare not trust so near the Enemy; I had Six of them deserted together, to go to the French; two of them, after losing themselves in the Woods, and being Starving with Hunger, Surrendered to some of the Parties above; those I tried and hanged directly; the other four were taken at *Wood-Creek,* by our Ranging Companies.[4]

In Cumberland's response to Loudon's report in December 1756, the duke noted: 'As to *Otway's* Regiment, I am not surprised at the scandalous Account you give me of them. They have never seen any manner of Service; & I am afraid, your Letter convinces me of what I feared before, that it was composed of a Set of ignorant, undisciplined Officers, you will never make a Regiment of it'.[5]

Six months later, in mid-1757, Fort William Henry, came under the command of Lieutenant Colonel Munro with Otway's Regiment and the Royal American Regiment along with provincial forces from New York and Massachusetts totalling 2,372 men. In August 1757, the French, with their Native American allies, under the Marquis de Montcalm advanced on Fort William Henry with an overwhelming force of an estimated 8,000. Monro hoped and requested reinforcements from Major General Daniel Webb in command at Fort Edward, but Webb declined to risk his soldiers in the face of such odds. After the French besieged Fort William Henry for a week, Munro had no option but to surrender on 9 August. The next day, British

---

4 Loudon to Cumberland, Albany, 3 Oct 1756, in Stanley Pargellis, (ed.), *Military Affairs in North America, 1748-1765: Selected Documents from the Cumberland Papers in Windsor Castle* (New York and London: D. Appleton-Century Company, Incorporated, 1936), p.239.

5 Cumberland to Loudon. Private. St James's 2 Dec. 1756, in Pargellis, (ed.), *Military Affairs*, p. 254.

forces were retreating along the road to Fort Edward, when the Native Americans attacked them in what became known as the massacre at Fort William Henry. Munro and his officers were taken to a French camp and held as prisoners until Fort William Henry had been destroyed.[6]

On might speculate that the regiment's general unpreparedness for combat and its accompanying professional embarrassments, along with the defeat at Port William Henry, may explain the absence in the surviving diary of the pages in Bamford's diary that dealt with this situation. The only remnant of the dairy for this period is Bamford's transcription of Major General Daniel Webb's letter to Colonel Munro, declining to send him reinforcements in Chapter 9: 'A few Notes relative to the forgoing Journal'.

During Otway's tenure as colonel, King George II issued a royal warrant in 1751 that formally stopped the practice of calling regiments by the name of their colonel, and replaced the name with the number of the regiment's seniority. Thus, Otway's Foot became the 35th Regiment, but the practice of using the colonel's name did not die out immediately, as Bamford's diary demonstrates. General Henry Fletcher succeeded Otway as the colonel of the 35th Foot in 1764 and maintained that post for 36 years, until March 1803. When George III connected the names of counties to regiments in 1782 as means of promoting recruitment and unit cohesion, the 35th Foot was associated with Dorsetshire from 1783 to 1805, when the 25th Foot relinquished its connection to Sussex and it was attached to the 35th Foot.[7]

Taking a different tack, a search for the mysterious 'W.B.' the artist who did the illustrations, eventually provided an answer through Dr John A. Houlding's invaluable database of Georgian Military Officers for the period 1714-1794. Dr Houlding was able to quickly ascertain from his database that there was only one officer in the 35th Regiment of Foot with the initials W.B. who had served over the entire period of the diary from 1757 to 1765: Lieutenant William Bamford. His information showed that William Bamford had been born in Ireland in 1728 and that he had been commissioned an ensign in the 35th Regiment of Foot in Ireland on 10 March 1742, New Style. He was promoted to second lieutenant of the 35th Foot on 26 February 1746, and then to lieutenant in the 35th Foot on 16 February 1756. Subsequently, he was promoted to captain-lieutenant in the 35th Foot on 25 December 1762, then to brevet captain in the 35th Foot on 25 May 1772, and finally to captain in the 40th Foot while in Ireland on 25 March 1775. In January 1779, the *London Gazette* announced that Captain Bamford of the 40th Foot had been appointed to the staff office in America of 'Town-Major of New York'. While his regiment was still serving in New York, Bamford retired from the British Army on 15 October 1778 at the age of fifty, with 36 years and seven months of commissioned service.

Moving to the next step in the research, a search for information about Bamford turned up a published diary for the year 1776 by Captain William Bamford of the

6 David R. Starbuck, *Massacre at Fort William Henry* (Hanover, NH: University Press of New England, 2002), pp.8-10.

7 West Sussex Record Office, Record of the Services of the Thirty-fifth Royal Sussex Regiment (Typescript), p.vi; Gerard Durani Martineau, *A History of the Royal Sussex Regiment: a History of the Old Belfast Regiment and the Regiment of Sussex, 1701-1953* (Chichester: Moore & Tillyer [1954]), passim.

40th Regiment of Foot. The *Maryland Historical Magazine* published the journal in 1932-33.[8] The anonymous introduction to that three-part publication indicated that the manuscript was still in private hands in the library of the American diplomat, the Hon. John Work Garrett (1872-1942), who was then serving as the U.S. Ambassador to Italy from 1929 to 1933. His collection of 30,000 rare books and manuscripts was housed in his home, Evergreen House, a Gilded Age estate in Baltimore, Maryland, that his grandfather, the president of the Baltimore and Ohio Railroad, had acquired in 1878. Garret's father, T. Harrison Garrett (1849-1888), had acquired the Bamford manuscript diary for 1776 several decades earlier. In 1952, the Garret family donated Evergreen House, with its library, to The Johns Hopkins University, where it remains to this day.

With the location of the original 1776 manuscript, it became possible to compare the handwriting in the two diaries. The Johns Hopkins Library system readily provided a digital copy of the full manuscript. A comparison of the two readily confirmed that the diaries were written by the same individual. Additionally, a memorial from Captain-Lieutenant William Bamford to General Gage requesting promotion to Captain in 1765 in the papers of General Thomas Gage at the William L. Clements Library added further insight into Bamford's experiences with the 35th Foot in Florida and provided another verification of the handwriting and correlated with the internal information in the 1757-1765 diary.

The 40th Foot was originally established by General Richard Philipps in 1717 as Philipp's Regiment of Foot at Annapolis Royal in Nova Scotia. It was made up of previously independent companies that had been serving in North America, It served entirely in North America and the West Indies from 1717 until 1767, when it was rotated to Ireland for the first time in its history. Ordered to prepare for deployment to North America in February 1775, the 40th Foot was part of the second Irish embarkation that experienced great delays in its departure due to civil unrest in Ireland.[9] After its arrival in North America, the 40th Foot soon came under the command of General Sir William Howe and participated in the siege of Boston. From his headquarters on the 'Heights of Charlestown' on 22 August 1775, Howe gave an order that 'Captn Bamford of the 40th Regiment is appointed an Assistant Engineer'.[10]

The anonymous contributor who wrote the introduction to the published 1776 diary had apparently done some research work on William Bamford's career in the War Office records in London—or at least in the published *Army Lists*—but provided no citations to sources.[11] He or she reported the additional information

8 Anon. "Bamford's Diary: The Revolutionary War Diary of a British Officer", *Maryland Historical Magazine*, vol. 27 (1932), pp. 240-59, 296-314; vol. 28 (1933), pp.9-26.

9 R.H. Raymond Smythies, *Historical Records of the 40th (2nd Somersetshire) Regiment* (Devonport: A.H. Swiss for the Subscribers, 1894), pp.1-7, 140-160; R.E Burns. "Ireland and British Military Preparations, 1775", *Cithara*, Vol.11 (1963), p.44.

10 Benjamin Franklin Stevens (ed.), *General Sir William Howe's Orderly Book 1775-1776. General Sir William Howe's Orderly Book at Charlestown, Boston and Halifax, June 17, 1775 to 1776 26 May* (London: B.F. Stevens, 1890; reprint, Port Washington, NY: Kennikat Press, 1970), p.74.

11 Anon., "Bamford's Diary", pp. 240-42.

that William Bamford was on recruiting duty in the Windsor district on recruiting duty in 1768 and was back home with the 35th Foot in Ireland in the early 1770s, perhaps dealing with the suppression of the various uprisings at that time. On 25 July 1774, Captain Bamford was present with his new regiment, the 40th Foot, when Major General Charles Moore, 6th Earl of Drogheda and Master-General of the Irish Ordnance, reviewed the regiment in Dublin.

The contributor to The *Maryland Historical Magazine* noted in 1932 that no other information on Bamford's family, birth, death, will, or later life had emerged. In 2019, despite the growth in genealogical interests and the accompanying wide availability of genealogical research materials, nothing more on these aspects of William Bamford's life have yet been found 87 years later. The 1776 diary provides one interesting clue to his possible place of death at the garrison town of Banagher, Ireland, with the undated inscription on the final page of the diary. A grandniece or grandnephew wrote 'This Book became my property after my dearly beloved Father obtained it through a friend at Bannagher after the Death of his uncle William Bamford JB[rd] '.

Taken together, these collected documents on the military career of William Bamford as a junior officer in the British Army during the third quarter of the 18th century provide an individual, eye witness views of some of the key military events of the French and Indian War over the span of years between 1757 to 1765 and in the 1776 campaign during the War for America. At the same time, the diaries provide insight and evidence for a range of broader historical trends and issues. One of these is certainly to underscore the interdependence of overseas military and naval operations in the growth of the British Empire in this period, not only for fighting battles, but also in sustaining military presence. The experience of the 35th Regiment in the French and Indian Wars is illustrative of a fundamental problem that the British Army faced in deploying forces into tropical climates. The shattered condition of the 35th on its return home in 1765 after a decade in North America and the West Indies illustrated the desperate need for the wider and more effective implementation of the Duke of Cumberland's 1749 concept for rotation of regiments.[12] The experience of the 35th Foot in West Florida in the conflict that arose there between the governor and the military commanders as to who was in charge of military direction was part of a much larger dispute in civil-military affairs in British North America. It was one that stretched back to the late 17th century with the royal governors in New England and the royal control of militias in the charter colonies.[13] A variant of that issue surfaced again in the context of the new colony of British West Florida.[14]

A notable and easily overlooked aspect of the diaries is Bamford's practice of loaning small sums of money to his fellow officers, soldiers, and others. It is not clear whether Bamford had any responsibilities for local regimental finance or whether he was privately profiting from his loans. There is one instance on board the troop

12 J.A. Houlding, *Fit For Service* (Oxford: Clarendon Press, 1981), pp.19-23; John Shy, *Toward Lexington Service* (Princeton: Princeton University Press, 1965), p.282.

13 Richard R. Johnson, *Adjustment to Empire: The New England Colonies 1675-1715* (Leicester: Leicester University Press, 1981), pp.235, 256, 262.

14 Shy, *Toward Lexington,* pp. 282-87; Cecil Johnson, *British West Florida, 1763-1783* (New Haven: Yale University Press, 1943), pp.53-56.

transport *Spy* on 15 June 1776, when records that he 'Paid for our Sea Store', and that money was due him from some of the captains for soldiers in their companies. Bamford's practices may provide an instance that illuminates regimental practices.[15]

Bamford's own experience of great British military success under Jeffrey Amherst and James Wolfe during the French and Indian War led him to reflect on the contrast in leadership and the lack of initiative that he saw in his commanders in 1776. In one frustrating moment in early November 1776, Bamford exclaimed, 'O thou Spirit of the Great Wolf the More I see, the more I think of thee, & the more I revere they most Sacred Memory'. Wondering about the motives of his superiors in command, Bamford used similar sentiments to those that the 20th century military historian, Piers Mackesy, later used when he asked: 'Was it negligence or design which caused the failure?'[16]

15 Alan J. Guy, *Oeconomy and Discipline: Officership and Administration in the British Army 1714-1763* (Manchester: Manchester University Press, 1985), pp.53-74.

16 Piers Mackesy, *The War for America, 1775-1783* (London: Longmans, 1964), p.99.

Book Organisation, Document Description, and Editorial Principles

To render the documents more readable and to provide a guide to the subject matter, the editor has divided the documents into three parts. Part 1 is William Bamford's 1757-1765 journal, owned by the John Carter Brown Library at Brown University in Providence, Rhode Island. Part II is Bamford's 1765 Memorial to General Gage, owned by the William L. Clements Library at the University of Michigan in Ann Arbor, Michigan, and Bamford's 1774 commission as a captain that is bound into the 1776 diary. Part III is Bamford's 1776 journal owned by the John Work Garrett Library (Evergreen Museum and Library) which is part of the Sheridan Libraries of The Johns Hopkins University, Baltimore Maryland. The editor has artificially subdivided each of the two diaries into chapters that focus on the military operations that those sections of the documents describe, placing the memorial and the commission between them in Part II to reflect the chronological position of those documents.

The editor has transcribed each document using the literal method, reproducing in type as closely as possible, Lieutenant Bamford's original writing style, preserving his capitalization, original spelling, and his use of a dash for punctuation. Bamford consistently used superscript letters and a full stop as abbreviations for ordinal numbers ("st.", "nd.", "rd.", "th."). Helion's house style prevents the replication of Bamford's usage of superscript with a full stop for ordinal numbers, but these are used in this transcription with Bamford's other uses of superscript letters. All ships' names are rendered in italics. Bamford sometimes used single, double or even triple dashes. The size of the dash also varies in the manuscript, but it is standardized here as a an en-dash. The number of dashes used has been preserved. In cases where a dash in place of a period or full stop is missing at the end of a sentence, the author did not use a capital letter to start a sentence and often, but not consistently, left a small gap or began the new sentence on a new line. Such gaps have been removed

In places where the author has insert missing words above a sentence, the editor has inserted them in the intended place. In cases where words or portions of words have been lost in the margins or though deterioration at the edges of the paper, the missing portions have been placed between square brackets to indicate an editorial insertion. The editor's interpretation of the meaning of misspelled words, unusual abbreviations, or phrases is found in the footnotes. Footnotes also provide information on the people mentioned or clarify and explain other references in the text. The editor has italicized all ships' names.

The 18th century spelling of words that appear to modern eyes as an 'f" without a crossbar, for example, as in 'distrefs' has been rendered here as 's'. In cases where the author has used a caret to indicate the placement of an added word, that word has been silently placed in its intended location. Bamford typically used a superscript abbreviation with a full stop directly below it. This has been rendered with the superscript letters, but with the full stop following and not superscript.

Bamford's journal from the French and Indian War at the John Carter Brown Library has 110 pages with 22 leaves with illustrations, plans and maps. It is a quarto volume 21 centimetres tall. In this journal, Bamford generally repeats the year and the month at the top of each manuscript page. These repetitions have been omitted. Throughout both documents, William Bamford has made notes in the margin, some of which are marked with a + for insertion. The editor has understood the author's intention was to indicate a general location for insertion, typically at the beginning of the sentence or at a key word, rather than an exact location. Thus, the editor has made the insertion where it makes the most sense in context. If Bamford's + mark was taken as exact, the insertion would often disrupt and confuse the sense of Bamford's original statement. These insertions are always placed between square brackets within in the main text. The footnotes are limited to providing the editor's explanatory notes.

The French and Indian War Journal is the only document that includes Bamford's original sketches and drawings. In the original document, these are not always located to the text to which they refer. In this edition, the editor has arbitrarily placed them closer to the relevant text of the journal.

The journal for 1776 is a very small booklet, apparently meant to be kept in a pocket. A Garret Library's special collections librarian described the volume as 'a wee little thing, measuring 12.5 cm by 9 cm by 1.5 cm, and somewhat tightly bound'. Unlike the 1757-1765 journal, which had all blank pages for Bamford to use, each page of the 1776 journal has a ruled red line around each page and designed so that, when opened, the double pages are meant to shown an entire week. The left-hand page has nine small rectangular compartments that stretch across the page, each ruled in red, for each day of the week. The right-hand page, also ruled in red around the edges is an otherwise empty large box for remarks.

A typical page of Bamford's 1776 journal is laid out as shown on the next page.

The top line on the far left indicates the place, 'Boston', while the remainder of the rectangular box states the span of the week. In the sample shown, 'February 4th to' is on the left page, with 'February 16th' on the right-hand page. The second line on the left hand page indicates the number of the week on the far left, in this case, '6th week' with the remainder of the rectangular box there is a heading: 'Memd^{s}.'. On the right-hand page, the corresponding rectangular box is a heading labelled 'Remarks &c^{a}.'. Inside the large box on the remainder of the right-hand page, Bamford typically, but not always, shows the date related to the remarks. With limited writing space available to him, Bamford often made multiple remarks found in various places on the page, each of which he dated.

For the purposes of this edition, the editor has not attempted to replicate fully the format of the manuscript pages. The place, span of the week, and the number of the week have been included, but the repetitious 'Memd^{s}.' and 'Remarks &c^{a}.'

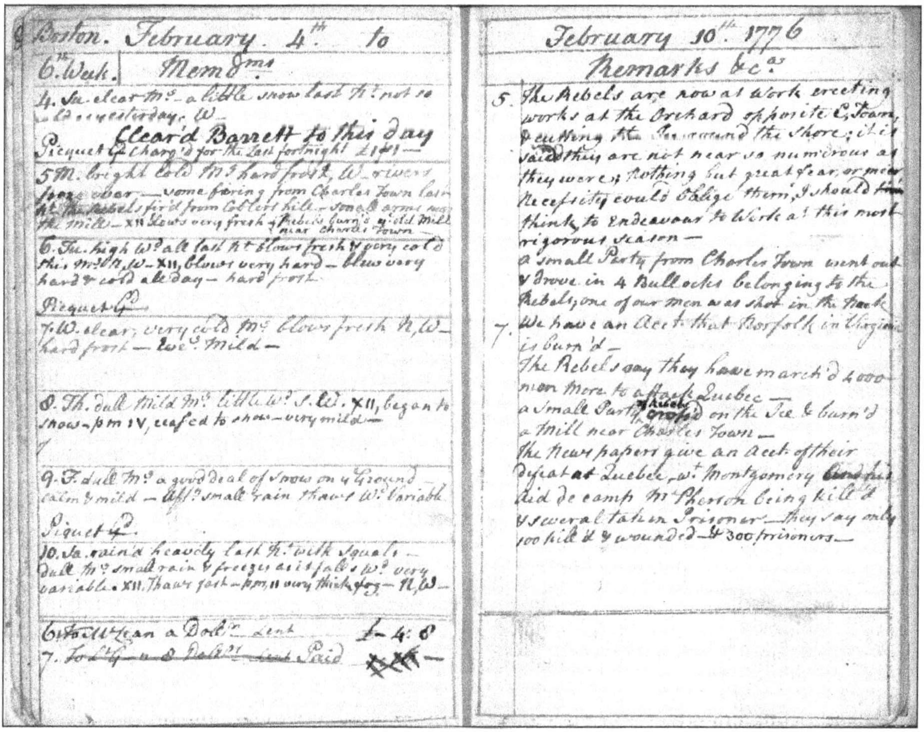

A Page from the 1776 Diary showing its organization and layout.

have been omitted and the two columns on facing pages have been put together into one chronologically dated entry, with the dated entries which had originally appeared on the 'Memd[s].' page placed first, with the directly related dated entries in the 'Remarks &c[a].' and other sections following and indented under it without square brackets. The numerical date of the additional entries have been omitted.

The very limited space for entries in the 1776 journal apparently led Bamford to abbreviate words much more frequently in this journal. The editor has not expanded these abbreviations, but left them as shown in the manuscript.

Part I:

Journal, 1757-1762

1

The Louisbourg Expedition, 1758

[The preceding eight pages on four folios are missing or reduced to fragments. The cohesive document begins with the following text.]

Oct— just [as][1] we left Albany, Col°. monro[2] was seized [with][3] an apoplectick Fit,[4] going down Stairs from Lord Loudon's[5] Levee, & died in a few days. We went down Hudson's River in Sloops, got as far as New-York in One Day. The Town of Albany is Pleasantly situated on Hudson's river, about 170 miles above New York, it's inhabited mostly by Dutch, not very hospitable, nor Extremely civil. from New York we crossed the river[6] to Elizabeth Town Point in the jerseys; from hence we had a Pleasant March by Land, quite through this Country to Philadelphia, about 100 Miles. Tis extremely Fertile, well Peopled, it has several very good towns at convenient Distances. at Prince town, about Mid-way between New York & Philadelphia, they are Greeting a colledge for the Education of young Gentleman. Tis almost finish'd, is a large well built Edifice.[7]

---

1 Page torn.

2 Lieutenant Colonel George Munro, sometimes, as here, spelled Monro (1700-1757) was born in Ireland, a younger son of George Munro (1660-1720, who had distinguished himself at the Battle of Dunkeld in 1689, during the Jacobite rising, and at the siege of Namur in 1695. He was the first of the Munros of Auchinbowie, a branch of the Scottish Highlands clan Munro. His son and namesake mentioned here was first commissioned as lieutenant of the 11th Foot, 19 August 1718. He retired onto British half pay, 17 March 1735/6; transferred from half pay as captain, 35th Foot in Ireland on 27 September 1737; promoted to major in the 35th Foot on 18 August 1747; to lieutenant colonel of the 35th Foot, on 4 January 1749/50. In 1757, he was in command at Fort William Henry at the southern end of Lake George, where he was forced to surrender to Montcalm in August 1757. By the terms of the surrender, the British garrison was allowed to withdraw to Fort Edward, but Native Americans allied with the French attacked the British soldiers en route, capturing and massacring a large number in one of the most notorious incidents of the war. He died 3 November 1757 at Albany, New York.

3 Page torn.

4 Apoplectic fit

5 John Campbell, 4th Earl of Loudon was born in Scotland in 1705. In 1755, he was sent as governor of Virginia and commander-in chief. Following the loss of Fort William Henry, he was relieved by his second-in-command, James Abercrombie and left North America in December 1757.

6 The Hudson River

7 The Presbyterian Synod established the College of New Jersey at Elizabeth, New Jersey, in 1746, as the fourth institution of higher education in the British North American colonies. It

March 22, 1758 about 10 o'clock this night, a small shock of an Earth-quake[8] was felt at Philadelphia, it did no Damage—

April. The beginning of this Month we reciev'd orders to be ready to Embark, & transport were taken up—

18th [April]. The 35th Regiment Embark'd[9] with the 2nd Battalion of the royal American Regiment,[10] which had March'd to Philadelphia for that Purpose—

Philadelphia is a large, thriving, Popular City, the strets broad & well laid out, running parallel with each other, by which means the whole town is divided into Squares, the Houses are good, mostly of brick, to make an Handsome appearance, here are some Publick buildings, the Stadt-house, Colledge,[11] Market house, & a

moved to Newark, New Jersey, in 1747. In 1753, private donors provided land at Princeton, New Jersey, where the college's first building, Nassau Hall, was begun in 1754 and completed in 1756. Upon the building's completion, the College moved from Newark to Princeton. In 1896, the institution was renamed Princeton University.

8 *The Pennsylvania Gazette*, 30 March 1758, p. 3, reported "On Wednesday, the 22nd Instant, between Ten and Eleven at Night, a small Shock of an Earthquake was felt here."

9 According to the list made by Transport Master, Captain David Pryce, RN, 138 men of the 35th embarked in the transport, *Concorde*, George Carr, master. The 217-ton vessel had a crew of 13 and carried 2 guns. Another 188 men of the 35th embarked in the 230-ton transport *Wade*, James Millar, master, with a crew of 19 and carrying 19 guns [?].

The Second Battalion of the Royal American Regiment (60th Regiment) embarked in seven transports: 176 men in the 252-ton transport *Dragon*, Francis Hammett, master, with a crew of 15 and carrying 1 gun. A second group of 173 additional men of the Second Battalion embarked in the 233-ton transport *Friendship*, Daniel Reese, master, with a crew of 13 and carrying 2 guns. A third group of 124 men of the Second Battalion, 60th Regiment embarked in the transport *Hilary*, Thomas Scraggs, master, with a crew of 10 and carrying no guns. A fourth group of 163 men embarked in the 208-ton transport *King of Prussia*, James Robinson, master, with a crew of 13 and carrying 8 guns. A fifth group of 160 men embarked in the 189-ton transport *Lydia*, William Camble, Master, with a crew of 11 and no guns. A sixth group of 127 men embarked in the transport *Moggy*, William Allison, master, with a crew of 19 and carrying 2 guns. A seventh group of 109 men embarked in the 180-ton transport *Nancy 2nd*, James Billings, master, with a crew of 11, carrying 4 guns. See the list from TNA, ADM 2 /2295 in Robert J. Andrews, *The Journals of Jeffrey Amherst* (East Lansing: Michigan State University, 2015), Vol.2, pp.385-389.

10 The Royal American Regiment, initially designated the 62nd Regiment of Foot, was first authorized by Parliament in late 1755 and raised in 1756. Designed for recruits from Germany or German colonists in the British colonies in North America, it soon became a multinational unit. Its first colonel in chief was Major General John Campbell, 4th Earl of Loudon. In 1757, the regiment was re-designated as the 60th Regiment of Foot. *The Pennsylvania Gazette*, 16 March 1758, p.2, announced 'His Majesty has been pleased to make the following Promotions in the Army serving in North-America, viz. Major-General James Abercromby, Commander in Chief and likewise Colonel in Chief of the Royal American Regiment, consisting of four Battalions of 1000 private men each….'

11 The Academy and College of Philadelphia, founded in 1749 by Benjamin Franklin and others. Upon receiving its collegiate charter in 1751 classes began. In 1791, it merged with a newer institution to become the University of Pennsylvania. The college was located in the disused Whitfield Meeting House that Edmund Wooley designed and built in 1740. At that time, it was the largest building in the colonies.

Very fine Hospital,[12] all Executed in a very good taste, Particularly the Latter; the Markets are Extremely well Provided & Cheap; in short it's a most Flourishing Place, Superior to New York in Every respect, it lies on a Point of Land made by the River Delaware & Schoolkill,[13] which joyn here and run to the sea; the Inhabitants are a mixture of all Country & all Religions, but the Prevailing Party are Quakers, tho' of late they left much of their influence. the Scotch Presbyterians are undermining them fast. This City carrys on a very Extensive trade. In the Country round about are numbers of Germans, who are Exceedingly industrious, supply the markets most abundantly with Vegetables of all kinds, Poultry, Eggs, butter, Cheese, all of these things they bring a great many Waggon Loads constantly to Market. at a Place call'd German Town,[14] about 7 Miles from Philadelphia, they carry on a remarkable manufactory for thread Stockings. Whilst one day here some of our Soldiers, who had been taken by the savages from Fort William Henry Joyn'd us, they were purchased from them by the Governour of Canada & sent to us—

1757 [1758][15] April—
April 22nd— Sail'd from Philadelphia down the River Delaware.

26th Pass'd the Capes Henlopen & May,[16] and steer'd for Halifax Nova Scotia, under convoy of the *Scarborough* Frigate[17] & *Beaver* Sloop.[18]

12 Dr Thomas Bond and Benjamin Franklin founded the Pennsylvania Hospital in 1751. Its first purpose-built building was erected in 1755 to designs of Samuel Rhoads

13 'Schoolkill' = Schuylkill River.

14 A group of Quakers and Mennonites from Krefeld, then under the rule of the Stadholder-King William III, founded Germantown, Pennsylvania, in 1683 as a place for them to practice their religion freely. Coincidently shortly after Bamford wrote this entry, Krefeld, which became a part of Prussia in 1702, was the scene of a battle that occurred on 28 June 1758 between the French and Prussian-Hanoverian armies.

15 Bamford errs here, as the year is 1758 as shown in the previous entries.

16 Cape Henlopen, Delaware, is on the southern side of the entrance from the Atlantic to Delaware Bay. Cape May, New Jersey, is on the northern side.

17 *Scarborough* was one the last pair of ships in the later *Gibraltar*-class of 20-gun frigates. Her gun deck was 107 feet, 8 inches long; keel 88 feet six inches; breadth 30 feet 4 inches, depth of hold 9 feet 8 inches; Tonnage 433 13/94 bm; draft 6 feet 3 inches forward, 13 feet 3 inches aft. Built by Hugh Blades at Hull, she had been ordered on 12 June 1755 and was named on 17 July 1755. Her keel was laid on 21 July 1755 and she was commissioned at Portsmouth in April 1756, under Captain Robert Routh (d. 1760). The frigate sailed for North America on 24 September 1757.

18 The 18-gun ship sloop *Beaver* was a captured French privateer that had been named *Le Trudaine*. Built at St. Malo in 1748, the 64-gun *Ipswich* captured her on 15 September 1756. Purchased by the Admiralty in April 1757, she was named in May 1757 and fitted as a sloop by Henry Bird, Jr., at Rotherhithe and then at Deptford Dockyard. Commissioned in May 1757 under Commander Edward Gascoigne for the Rochefort expedition and then sailed for Virginia in December 1757. She was surveyed in 1760 and sold out of service in 1761.

May 8th— Made the land of Nova Scotia, we had a Very hard Gale the whole Voyage, but always fair. This day we fell in with Admiral Boscawen[19] in the *Namure*,[20] & ten Sail of Men of War, with ye Transports & troops from England, design'd for the Seige of Louisbourg.

9th Came to an anchor in Halifax Harbour. The town is Pleasantly situated on the side of a steep Hill, the Streets are Irregular, the houses mostly built of Wood. here is a large Handsome Church all of wood,[21] where Service is perform'd after the Mannor of the Church of England, tho' all sects are Tolerated. On the top of the Hill, above the Town, is a signal house to give notice on the approach of shipping, by hoisting flags; from hence they can see a great way to Sea. To the Harbour are some batterys,[22] but ill Excecuted & of but little consequence the Chief Defence is George's Island,[23] it lies in the Middle of the Harbour & Entirely commands the entire [.] this might be made extreamly strong.

[17]58
May— The soil is good but not just clear'd from the Humps of the trees, & immediately about the town. particularly to the Water side 'tis Rocky; the Inhabitants as yet raises nothing for themselves, all their Provisions, grain, flour, are brought from other Parts of America. The Harbour is unexceptionally fine, & never freezes it produces the greatest Plenty of excellent Fish of many different kinds; the tide in this harbor does not rise high. The town & Country are capable of great improvements. The officers of the 35th Regiment soon after their arrival, gave in a Memorial

19 The Hon. Edward Boscawen (1711-1761) joined the Navy at the age of 12 and was commissioned a lieutenant in 1732, promoted to commander in 1737, to captain in 1742, rear admiral of the blue in 1747, rear admiral of the white in 1749, vice admiral of the blue in 1755, vice admiral of the white in 1756, vice admiral of the red in 1757, admiral of the blue in 1758. He served as Member of Parliament for Truro, 1742-1761, and as a Commissioner of the Admiralty, 1751-1761. See *Oxford Dictionary of National Biography* and *History of Parliament http://www.historyofparliamentonline.org/volume/1715-1754/member/boscawen-hon-edward-1711-61*

20 The second rate, 90-gun *Namur* was a modified *Neptune*-class warship built at Chatham Dockyard between 1750 and 1756. She was launched 3 March 1756 and commissioned under the command of Captain James Hobbs in May 1756. She sailed for North America on 23 February 1758 under the command of Matthew Buckle as Boscawen's flagship. Length of gun deck: 175 feet 0 inches; length of keel: 142 feet 2½ inches; breadth: 48 feet 6 inches; draught: 20 feet 6 inches; 1,779 30/64 tons bm.

21 The parish church of St Paul's Church, Halifax, was founded in 1749 and construction began in 1750. Built of wood, its ground plan was based on James Gibbs's brick Marylebone Chapel, now St Peter, Vere Street, London. St Paul's is the oldest building in Halifax and the oldest surviving Protestant Church in Canada.

22 This is apparently a reference to Fort George on Citadel Hill, built in 1749 under Lieutenant General Edward Cornwallis (1713-1776), who as Governor of Nova Scotia from 1749 to 1752, founded Halifax in 1749.

23 Named George Island in 1749, after King George II, the island's fort, for which construction began in 1750, was later named Fort Charlotte, after King George III's consort, Queen Charlotte of Mecklenburg-Strelitz, who married King George III in 1761.

to the Commander in Chief (Gen Lawrence)[24] signed by all [(Capt Collins[25] & Ens. Phillips[26] excepted immediately after this, the Capt was oblig'd to sell out the Lieut. retir'd of his own accord)][27] those who had been at Fort Wm. Henry & suppos'd to be under that Capitulation, requesting to be employ'd on the first-service, as the French had most notoriously broke the Capitulation, by Pludering & Murdering our People, & making Prisoners countrary to the articles, they thought themselves released from their Parole, & beg'd his Excellency would allow them to act with the Forces going against Louisbourg. Brigadier Wolf[28] stood their friend, their request was granted & they were accordingly order'd to sail with the rest of the troops, a small Detachment only was left behind.

May—
28th The whole Fleet being ready, the Signal was made, & we sailed out of the Harbour of Halifax, in all about 170 sail, Commanded by Admiral Boscawen, General Lawrence recommanded the Land forces, General Amherst,[29] who was to

24 Brigadier Charles Lawrence (1709-1760) was born in England and commissioned in England as ensign in the 11th Foot on 26 December 1726; promoted to lieutenant, 11th Foot, on 15 November 1740; to captain-lieutenant in England in the new-raising 56th (later 45th) Foot on 28 January 1740/41; captain of the 56th Foot, 19 April 1742; major, 56th Foot, 12 June 1747; to lieutenant colonel, 40th Foot, 1 June 1750; to colonel-commandant, Third Battalion of the 60th Foot, , 28 September 1757; appointed brigadier in America on 31 December 1757. He died on 19 October 1760 at Halifax, Nova Scotia.

25 Captain Thomas Collins: Commissioned a second lieutenant in Ireland in the 21st Foot on 22 April 1735; promoted to lieutenant in Colonel Henry de Grangues's new-raising 60th Foot, 21 January 1740/1; promoted to captain-lieutenant in 60th Foot, 29 October 1745; to captain in the 60th Foot, 24 July 1746; onto Irish half pay when the regiment disbanded, 2 December 1748; from half pay as captain, 35th Foot in Ireland, 12 March 54; resigned 14 April 1759; He died at Boston, Massachusetts, 22 May 1766.

26 Ensign William Frederick Phillips was commissioned an ensign in the 35th Foot in England, 16 February 1756. He was promoted to lieutenant of the 35th Foot, 16 May 1757 and resigned 15 December 1758.

27 Marginal note with asterisk marking insertion at this point.

28 James Wolfe (1727-1759) was born in England and commissioned a second lieutenant in Edward Wolfe's 1st Marines in Jamaica on 3 November 1741. He transferred to ensign, 12th Foot in England 27 March 1742 as the regiment was about to embark for Flanders. He was promoted to lieutenant 12th Foot, 14 July 1743 (and adjutant, 22 July 1743 to 23 June 1744); promoted to captain, 4th Foot, 23 June 1744; brigade-major in Flanders, 12 June 1745; promoted to major, 20th Foot on 5 May 1748/9; to lieutenant colonel, 20th Foot, 20 March 1749/50; to brevet colonel, 21 October 1757 (as 'Barrack Master General and Quarter Master General in Ireland', 21 March 1757, an appointment he accepted but never took up and resigned it on 26 January 58 [PRONI, T/470, f.600]); promoted to brigadier in America, 23 January 1758; to colonel, 67th Foot, when regimented from late second battalion of the 20th Foot, 21 April 1758; promoted to major general in America, 12 January 1759; killed in action on 13 September 1759.

29 Jeffery, 1st Baron Amherst (1717-1797) was commissioned an ensign in the 20th Foot in Ireland on 1 December 1731; promoted to cornet, 9th Dragoons in Ireland, 12 June 1733; to cornet, Ligonier's 8th Horse in Ireland, 19 July 1735; to lieutenant, 8th Horse, 19 July 1740; to captain, 8th Horse, 29 May 1745; to captain and lieutenant colonel, 1st Foot Guards, 25 December 1745; to colonel, 15th Foot, 22 May 56 until 7 November 1768; He was simultaneously colonel-in-chief, 60th Foot, 30 September 1758 to 21 September 1768, when he resigned briefly, then re-appointed 7 November 1768 to 3 September 1797; Promoted

command, not being arrived; we were joyn'd at the Mouth of the harbor by the 28th Regiment, who had winter'd at Fort Cumberland, [call'd by the French Beau se Jour][30] in the Bay of Fundy, & had come in small sloops & Schooners.

29th Met Admiral Rodney[31] in the *Dublin*[32] Man of War, from England. in her Genl. Amherst came—

June 1st Made the Island of Breton. Saw fires on the shore

2nd came to an Anchor in Gabarus Bay[33], about 5 miles S:W. of the Harbour of Louisbourg. [all of the fleet did not get in the 2d, they were coming in for 2 or 3 days after][34]

---

to major general in North America, 1 March 1758; to major general in the Army, 25 June 1759; to lieutenant general, 19 January 1761; to colonel, 3rd Foot, 7 November 1768 to 21 April 1779); also Lieutenant-General of the Ordnance and colonel-in-chief, Royal Artillery, 22 October 1772 to 1 January 1784; promoted to general, 19 March 1778; He was appointed commander in chief of the army in Great Britain in April 1778, for the war's duration, and again in January 1793, resigning in February 1795; appointed captain and colonel, 2nd Troop of Horse Grenadier Guards, 21 April 1779; to captain and colonel, 2nd Troop of Horse Guards, 20 March 1782; to colonel, 2nd Regiment of Life Guards, 25 June 1788 to 3 August 1797; promoted to field marshal, 30 July 1796; died 3 August 1797.

30 The words between brackets are in a note in the margin marked for insertion at this point. Fort Beauséjour was located on the Chignecto Isthmus connecting Nova Scotia with present day New Brunswick. French forces built the five-bastioned, star-shaped fortification in 1751-52. Following the British victory in the Battle of Fort Beauséjour between 3 and 16 June 1755, the British renamed it Fort Cumberland. In 1920, its location became a National Historic Site of Canada.

31 George Brydges Rodney (1718-1792) entered the Royal Navy as a King's Letter Boy in 1732. He was promoted to lieutenant on 15 February 1740 and to captain, on 9 February 1742. At the time of this diary entry, he was a captain in command of HMS *Dublin.* He was promoted to rear admiral of the blue on 19 May 1759, vice admiral of the blue on 21 October 1762, vice admiral of the white 18 October 1770, vice admiral of the red 24 October 1770, admiral of the white 29 January 1778. He served as Member of Parliament for Saltash, 1751-54; Okehampton, 1759-61; Penryn, 1761-68; Northampton, 1768-74; and Westminster, 1780-82. See David Spinney, *Rodney* (London: Allen & Unwin, 1969) and *History of Parliament* http://www.historyofparliamentonline.org/volume/1715-1754/member/rodney-george-brydges-1719-92.

32 The third rate, 74-gun *Dublin was* built at Deptford Dockyard, where her keel was laid on 18 November 1755 and she was launched on 6 May 1757. She commissioned in April 1757 with Captain George Rodney in command. She served in the Rochefort expedition and then in Hawke's fleet before sailing for North America on 16 March 1758. Rodney was in command, when *Dublin* returned to England on 14 September 1758. Length of gun deck: 165 feet 6 inches; length of keel: 134 feet 4 inches; breadth: 46 feet 9 inches; depth of hold: 19 feet 9 inches; 1,561 63/94 tons bm; draught 12 feet 8½ inches forward, 18 feet 7½ inches aft.

33 Gabarus Bay is three miles wide and four miles deep. It located on the southeastern coast of Cape Breton Island on the south side of Louisbourg. Its beaches provided landing places for British troops to attack the Fortress Louisbourg. The bay is exposed to southerly and easterly winds with the sea floor of slate, coarse sand and stones. Hugh Boscawen, *Capture of Louisbourg, 1758* (Norman: University of Oklahoma Press, 2011), pp.154, 159.

34 Note in the margin

3rd Some of our Frigates were towed as close to the shore as they could lye with safety, to fire upon the Enemy who were very hard at Work, & we could plainly observe that they had very strong Entrenchments all along the Shore, with several Batteries of Cannon & Emplacements at small Distances; they seem'd well prepared to receive us. more of the Transports arrive'd.

4th June A Very high Wind with thick Fog; the Wind blew Directly on shore, & this being a very wild Open Bay with bad anchorage, many of the ships were in in extreme danger of driving on shore, some parted their Cables & Work'd out to Sea; the *Trent* Frigate[35] had her Rudder beat off by the Rocks, minute Guns were fired for several hours, & most of the Fleet were in great distress & the Enemy Cannonaded & Bombarded us the whole time [they threw great number of red hot shot at us without effect].[36]

6th The Troops Got into the Boats, early this morning, in Order to Land, but by a report from some officers of the Man of War, who had gone to reconnoitre the shore, that the surf ran so high that the boats could not live near the shore, the troops were order'd back to their ships.

7th the following Disposition for landing, with the generals instructions to the Army was read on board each transport. Brg Whitmore[37] in a Boat with a White Flag, to rendevouz with his Division to the right. Brg Gen Lawrence in a Boat with a blue flag, with his division, in the Center. & Brigd. Wolf with a Red flag, with the 4 eldest comp[s] of Grenadiers, supported by the Light Infantry, Highland Battalion, & remaining 8 Companys of Greenadiers, to row towards the Fresh Water Cove[38] on the Left, and Endeavour to Land.

June 8th The surf being something Abated, the troops for the first landing were in their boats before day, & having all got to their Proper Stations, about 5 o'clock, the

35 The 6th rate, 28-gun frigate *Trent* was built at Woolwich Dockyard, where her keel was laid on 18 May 1757 and she was launched 29 July 1757. She was commissioned under Captain John Lindsay in September 1757 and sailed for North America on 23 February 1758. Length of gun deck: 118 feet 5½ inches; length of keel: 97 feet 5 inches; breadth: 33 feet 8 inches; draught 10 feet 6 inches; 587 30/94 tons bm.

36 The words between square brackets appear in the manuscript as a note in the margin.

37 Brigadier Edward Whitmore was born in Ireland in 1695, He was commissioned as ensign, 36th Foot, 30 March 1711; promoted to lieutenant, 36th Foot, 1 June 1723; to captain-lieutenant, 36th Foot, 1 May 1739; to captain, 36th Foot, 1 November 1739; to major 36th Foot, 2 July 1747; to lieutenant colonel, 36th Foot, 17 July 1747; to colonel, 22nd Foot, 11 July 1757; brigadier in North America, 30 December 1757; to major general, 19 February 1761; died 11 December 1761. The *Gentleman's Magazine* (February 1762), p.93, reported that 'he put into Plymouth by stress of weather on his voyage from Louisbourg to Boston, where, going upon deck between 11 and 12 o'clock at night, by some accident he tumbled overboard, and was unfortunately drowned'.

38 Fresh Water Cover was later known as Kennington Cove and earlier as Anse de la Cormorandière.

whole moved towards the shore, under the fire of the *Sutherland*,[39] *Kent*,[40] *Gramont*[41] & *Kennington*,[42] &c these ships had kept up an Heavy cannonade all the morning. The 28th Regim^t^. were sent in their small Craft towards the Light house, to draw the Enemy attention that way. The French were most advantageously Posted, the Bank[43] was very high & almost perpendicular, the Beach large broken Rocks, over which the sea drove with great fury; wherever there was the least probability of Landing, it was well secur'd with Cannon & entrenchments large trees were fell'd & laid on the Shore, with their Tops to the Water' Edge, that you were both oppos'd & Entangled by the Branches; their Works more defended, by 1500 Men from the Garrison of Louisbourg. Brigadier Wolf with the Grenadiers, rowed towards the fresh water Cove, (afterwards call'd Kennington Cove from the Frigate which lay before it to cover the Landing.) The enemy reserv'd their fire till over Boats got pretty near, & then pour'd in a general discharge from their trenches & Battery's it was impossible to advance against so heavy a fire, most of the Boats were oblig'd do draw back, & most of them got into a smaller Cove. [Lt Brown[44] of the 35th Reg^t^ with 21 men as light Infantry was the first who got on shore. the L^t^. Infantry of the 48th Reg^t^ was

39 The 4th rate, 60-gun HMS *Sutherland* was commanded by Captain John Rous, Royal Navy, from May 1758. The ship had been built at Rotherhithe by James Taylor. Her keel was laid on 1 July 1740 and she was launched on 14 October 1741. She was first commissioned at Deptford in October 1742 under Captain George Pocock. She had sailed from England as a convoy escort to Virginia on 6 November 1756 and served as flagship for Rear Admiral Sir Charles Hardy in June 1757. She was 132 feet long on the gun deck, length of keel 109 feet 10 1/8 inches, breadth 38 feet 8 inches, draught 15 feet nine inches, 873 51/94 tons bm.

40 The 64-gun HMS *Kent* was not present. She had been hulked in East Indies in 1757 and was abandoned in 1763. Bamford may possibly be referring to the 28-gun *Trent*, on which see note 35 above.

41 The 18-gun former French privateer *La Comtesse de Grammont* was built at Bayonne in 1756-57. The 18-gun sixth rate HMS *Tartar* took her as a prize on 29 October 1757. The Admiralty purchased and named her *Gramont* on 6 January 1758. Fitted out at Portsmouth, she commissioned in January 1758 under Commander John Stott and sailed for North America on 15 February 1758. After Commander Philip Aleck took command in August 1758, she sailed for Gibraltar with troops in July 1759. After service in the Mediterranean she was refitted and commissioned in 1762. On 24 February 1762, she sailed for Newfoundland, where at the French capture of St. John's, the French retook her while her British crew was ashore supporting the garrison of Fort William. Taken into French service under her original name, *La Comtesse de Grammont*, she served in de Ternay's division and returned to France. Retired at Martinique, she was broken up in 1766. Her gun deck was 98 feet 1 inch long, length of keel 80 feet 5 inches, depth of hold 27 feet 6½ inches, draught 8 feet 8 inches, 324 41/94 tons bm.

42 The sixth rate, 20-gun frigate HMS *Kennington* of the later *Gibraltar*-class was built by Henry Adams at Buckler's Hard, where she was launched 1 May 1755. Commissioned in March 1756, she sailed for North America under Captain Dudley Digges on 6 November 1756 and returned to England as a convoy escort in 1757. Under Captain Maximilian Jacobs, she sailed for North America on 23 February 1758. She sailed for Mediterranean under Captain Robert Baxter on 8 September 1759. She was broken up at Sheerness in 1774. Her gun deck was 107 feet 8 inches long, keel 88 feet ⅝ inches long, depth of hold 30 feet 6¾ inches, draught 9 feet 8 inches, 437 45/94 tons bm.

43 Cap du Rouge, the fifty-foot high eastern headland of the cove, had a short stretch of stony beach about twelve yards wide that was out of sight of the French position.

44 Lieutenant William Brown was born in Ireland in 1735. He received a commission as ensign in the 35th Foot on 16 February 1556, just as the regiment was leaving Ireland. He was

the 2d Boat[45] that landed].[46] a little to the right, where the men jump'd into the sea above their Waists, the Enemy being engag'd in the defense of the Large Cove, did not perceive our Men climbing the Rocks, till a few had got to the top, who bravely Maintain'd their ground, tho' oppos'd by numbers, & being timely supported [Col S Julien[47] commanded the lines.][48] from the boats, gain'd the Enemy & Flank who fearfull of having their retreat cut off from the Garrison, abandon'd their Works, & fled with the greatest precipitation towards the town, Our Men pursuing them to the Suburbs with Brig. Wolf at their head. in Landing, many of the boats were dashed to pieces, [one Boat with 18 Gren'ders. of Amherst regt. were overset and the men lost][49] some overset & the Men Drowned, the Surf ran so high; every one was oblig'd to jump into the Water, almost middle deep to get on shore. We took 20 pieces of Cannon, from 24 to 6 Pounders, 14 large swivels & 2 mortars, all the ammunition that was in their trenches, & a large Magazine of Fresh bread, Wine & Brandy; a seasonable supply. We had about 90 men and officers kill'd wounded & drowned. The Enemy lost about 80 kill'd & as many taken Prisoner after we had gain'd the shore everybody was supriz'd to see such strong works, given up for whore nature had not made the shore totally inaccessible, art has nearly complete it. Our army March'd to the Hills near the Town, from Whence they Cannonade us. This Night we lay on our Arms. The Enemy burn'd their suburbs, & some small vessels they had on the stocks.

9th [June] Marking out the several Encampments & securing the passes leading to the Town.

12th Brigadier Wolfe with four Companys of Grenadiers, & Detachments from the Battalions is in all 1200 men, March'd round the Harbour & took Post at the Light house, where he began to erect Batteries. The French had dismantled and abandon'd

promoted to lieutenant in the 35th Foot on 31 August 1758, and to captain on 3 February 1769. He died on 17 July 1775.

45 Commanded by Lieutenant Joseph Hopkins of Webb's 48th Regiment.

46 The phrase between square brackets is a note in the margin.

47 *Lieutenant Colonel* Jean Mascle de St. Juhlien, an officer off French regular troops, was born at Lunel, France, in 1693. He had joined the French Army's Artois Regiment as a second lieutenant in 1709, during the War of the Spanish Succession. He fought in a dozen sieges and numerous battles. Awarded the Croix de St Louis in 1737, he was wounded at Dettingen in 1743 and at Assiette in 1747. Promoted to *lieutenant colonel* on 19 February 1755, he was ordered to Louisbourg as senior officer in command of the second battalions of the Artois and Bourgogne Regiments at Louisburg. After the arrival of additional regular troops at Louisbourg in 1756-57, he became an increasingly difficult personality. Mathieu-Henri Marchant de La Houlière superseded him in command of the French regular troops leaving St. Juhlien command of only the Artois Regiment. At the time of the British landing on 8 June 1758, he commanded the battalion at Anse de la Cormorandière (Kennington Cove), where he had failed to post lookouts. After the surrender of Louisbourg, he and his battalion were made prisoners of war and sent to England. They were exchanged at Calais in December 1758. He died in 1759.

48 The phrase between square brackets is a note in the margin.

49 The phrase between square brackets is a note in the margin.

both the light house & Grand Battery. Gen. Wolf had also 3 Comp use of Rangers, & some light Infantry.

13th Began to throw up three Redoubts on the hills to the Westward of the Town, the Enemy threw some shot at us, but without doing any mischief.

14th A large Party from the Garrison, attack'd our advance'd picket, they lost a few men & were beat back. Lt. Allen[50] of the 35th Reg was Wounded in the Wrist, & one man kill'd. The Surf ran so high that it was with the utmost difficulty, we could get any thing on shore, even Provisions.

1758 June 15th we got 2 brass 6 pounders landed; they were Plac'd near the left of the Encampments.

19th This night bring us Wolfe open'd a Mortar Battery at the light house, to Play on the Island Battery & Shipping. 6 French, 2 Deckers & 4 Frigates in the Harbour.

20th A Battery of Cannon open'd at the light house against the Island & Ships. These Batteries have great Effect, & Oblige the French to draw their shipping under the batteries of the Town.

21st The French fir'd a great deal from the Town, Island & Shipping; to little Purpose. An advanced Redoubt begun near the road leading to Green Hill.

22nd A Block-house was set up set up on the left of the army by the road from Miray.

26th a Small Party of the Enemy, dress'd like our Rangers attempted to burn our Block house; some of them got into it with their Combustibles, but were oblig'd to run away without Effecting their Purpose. 200 marines were landed to keep the Post at Kennington Cove.

29th Last night the Enemy sank four of their ships at the Entrance of the harbor. 1 of two decks[51] & 3 frigates.[52]

---

50 Lieutenant Hon. Richard Allen was born in Ireland in 1734. He as commissioned an ensign in the 35th Foot in Ireland on 8 April 1755; promoted to lieutenant, in the 35th Foot, 14 April 1756; to captain in the 35th Foot on 5 October 1760; to major, 35th Foot, 25 December 1768; lieutenant colonel, 35th Foot, 25 December 1772; retired 5 March 1775.

51 The 56-gun *Appolon*, built at Rochefort in 1738-41. Earlier in 1758, the vessel had been converted to a *flûte*, a large store ship. Length of gun deck 132 feet 6 inches, length of keel 118 feet, breadth 36 feet 4 inches, draught 16 feet forward and 18feet aft. *En flûte*, she carried 8 officers and 167 men.

52 The three frigates were: (1) *Chèvre*, a 22-gun frigate, built at Rochefort in 1751 by Antoine Groignard. She had departed the Île d'Aix for North America on 9 March 1757 and had arrived *en flûte* with supplies for Louisbourg on 3 May 1758. Length of gun deck 107 feet, breadth 24 feet, depth of hold 12 feet; (2) *Fidèle*, a 30-gun frigate, built at Rochefort in 1747-48. Length of gun deck 119 feet, breadth 31 feet, depth of hold 17 feet 7 inches, draught 15¼ feet forward and 16¾ feet aft, 400 tons, and (3) the merchant ship *Ville de St Malo*, armed

30th the Marines at Kennington Cove were alarmed in the Night, Imagin'd they saw Indians & fired [the marines were deceived by fire flies].[53]

1758 July
for a long time. we were Employ'd in Landing Cannon, making Fascines,[54] roads, and Communications, -- erecting small redoubts in the rear of the Camp; & throwing up trenches before the Town. —

July 3rd The Enemy kept up a very heavy Cannonade, against our Works, which we had pushed very forward, & made a strong Lodgment on Green Hill.

9th About 12 o'clock this night, just as we had began a Battery on the right of our first parallel near the Sea Side, the Enemy made a Sally from black Point, & by the negligence of our out Parties; [the out Parties were provincial troops—the French told us they were asleep under their Blanketts & that they trod on them, but they did not rise up][55] whom they passed, got as far as our trenches, & fir'd on our work men. Before they were perceive; they were repulsed by some companys of Grenadiers. Captn. Lord Dondonald[56] was kill'd & about 30 men kill'd and missing; they had 1 Captn & 17 Men kill'd on the spot & a few taken Prisoners. The Party that made the sortie were upwards of 800 men & all in liquor. We were greatly embarras'd making a road across a bog to draw our Cannon over to green Hill[57] being greatly annoy'd by the *Arethusa*,[58] a French Frigate of 46 guns, that was haul'd close in there & scour'd

with 14 guns, built at St Malo in 1748. She had departed St Malo under the command of her master, Auguste César Le Gentil. The commandant of Louisbourg ordered the arrest of the ship in order to sink her. For a list of crew on board *Ville de St Malo*, see http://www.migrations.fr/lavilledestmalo_1758.htm

53 Note in margin.

54 Fascines are bundles of brushwood, eight to ten feet long, used for filling ditches, trenches or breaches in walls.

55 Marginal note.

56 William Cochrane, 7th Earl of Dundonald, was born at Paisley in Scotland in October 1729. At the beginning of the Jacobite Rebellion, he volunteered at the age of sixteen to serve Prince Charles Edward Stuart. After soldiers of the British Garrison nearly killed him when he demanded entry to the West Gate of Edinburgh, he apparently reconsidered and too no further action to support the rebellion. In 1750, he went to the Dutch Republic, where he served as a captain in the Scots-Dutch Brigade from 1750 to 1753. Returning to Paisley, he was involved in local affairs for several years. On 21 January 1756, he was commissioned a lieutenant in England in the new-raising 52nd (later 50th) Foot. He was promoted to captain-lieutenant in the first battalion of the 1st or Royal Regiment of Foot in Ireland on 2 February 1757. On the same day, he was also promoted to captain in the 17th Foot in Ireland. At the siege of Louisbourg, he was captain of a company of grenadiers. He was killed in action on 9 July 1758 in a surprise sortie by the French garrison on the night of 8-9 July during the siege of Louisbourg. He was buried where he died. Today, a stone to his memory stands between the ruined walls of Louisbourg and the Black Rock.

57 Green Hill was the starting point for the entrenchments.

58 The 36-gun French frigate *Aréthuse* was designed and built by Jean-Joseph Ginoux at Le Havre as the privateer *Pèlerine*. The French Navy purchased and commissioned her shortly after her launching in December 1757 and renamed her *Aréthuse* on 21 January 1758. She was 127 feet long on the gun deck with a keel 111 feet long, breadth 32 feet 4 inches, depth

all the plain, we were oblig'd to erect a very large Work, call'd an Epaulment,[59] to cover the Road to Green Hill, it consumed a prodigious number of Fascines, & took up much time.

15th – the *Arethusa* Frigate that gave us so much disturbance, escap'd out of the Harbour, about 10 o'clock this night & got off, tho' she was chas'd by most of S^r^. Charles Hardy's[60] Fleet, that day before the Harbour's Mouth to block it up. [Gen. Abercrombie's manifesto was published in our army declaring the capitulation of Fort Wm. Henry by the French Void; & requiring all officers & sold'rs included therein to act as if no such capitulation had been made.][61] a number of Canadians

---

of hold 10 feet, draft 14 feet, 540 tons displacement. The ship carried seven officers and 245 men with four 12-pounder and 28 8-pounder guns on the lower deck and 8 4-pounders on the quarterdeck. Under the command of *Commandant* Vauquelin, *Aréthuse* returned to France and then returned again to North America in 1759. On her return to France, HMS *Venus*, HMS *Thames*, and HMS *Chatham* attacked her eight leagues southwest of Audierne Bay on the coast of Brittany. After a two-and-a-half-hour battle on 18 May 1759, she surrendered. She was taken into the Royal Navy as HMS *Arethusa* and served until she wrecked on the island of Molène in the Ponant islands off the coast of Brittany 19 March 1779.

59 An epaulement is a parapet of earth that is nine to twelve feet high and twenty to thirty feet thick to protect fieldworks, trenches and other areas from flanking or enfilade fire.

60 At this point, Rear Admiral Sir Charles Hardy (c.1717-1780) was second in command to Admiral Edward Boscawen. Hardy was the second son of Vice Admiral Sir Charles Hardy (c.1688-1744). Born in Portsmouth, the younger Hardy joined the Navy in 1731 and was commissioned lieutenant on 26 March 1737. Much of his earlier career was spent in North American waters. In 1741-43, he served off South Carolina and Georgia, where he was promoted to commander on 9 June 1741, and to captain on 10 August 1741. With the outbreak of war with France in 1744, Hardy was appointed governor of Newfoundland. He was court martialed for failing to take up his post, but was acquitted by proving that he had fought unsuccessfully against contrary winds for 63 days to try to get to his appointed station. In 1755, he was knighted and appointed governor of New York just as preparations began for the French and Indian War and New York City became the central arsenal for British forces in North America. Promoted to rear admiral of the blue on 4 June 1756. In June 1757, Hardy returned to sea duty, first convoying troops to Halifax for an intended attack on Louisbourg. The presence at Louisbourg of the French squadron under Comte Dubois de la Motte forced cancellation of the 1757 expedition while Hardy remained in Halifax as second in command to Vice Admiral Francis Holborne. Promoted to rear admiral of the white, 5 February 1758 and to vice admiral of the blue on 14 February 1759, Hardy served in home waters as second in command to admirals Boscawen and Hawke, participating in Hawke's victory over the French at Quiberon Bay in November 1759. He was promoted to vice admiral of the white, 21 October 1762. Elected to Parliament, he represented Rochester from 1764 to 1768 and as Member for Plymouth, 1771 to 1780. In 1771, he was appointed Governor of Greenwich Hospital, where he was serving when promoted to admiral of the white on 29 January 1778. In 1779, when Admiral Augustus Keppel resigned the Channel Command and no active duty officer would agree to serve in his stead, the Admiralty brought the 62-year old Hardy back to his first sea duty assignment in 20 years. The French fleet retreated without a battle and did not attempt to land their embarked 40,000 troops. The following year on the 18 May 1780, the day that Hardy resumed command of the fleet, he died.

61 Marginal note.

from Miray[62] attack'd a Post we had at the head of the N.E. harbor,[63] [commanded by Capt Sutherland.[64] Lt Col S – t[65] was sent W^t^. a large party to drive these Canadians away. he return'd & reported to the Genl. that they were on th'other side of the water. The Genl. said he did not send him to bring intelligence but to drive them away. bid him go & Incamp on the highest hill & remain there till sent for—was not employed afterwards.][66] they came before it was day, but were soon Oblig'd to go back to Mon^s^. Boibere,[67] who had about 300 Canadians at the other side of the river opposite Miray, they were pursued, but not overtaken.

---

62 The Mira River on the coast of northeast Cape Breton.

63 Northeast Harbour is the northern end of the larger bay named Louisbourg Harbour.

64 Captain Patrick Sutherland joined the army in 1733 and accompanied Oglethorpe's 42nd Regiment of Foot to Georgia as a volunteer in 1739. He was commissioned adjutant in that regiment on 24 September 1740, retaining that post until 12 May 1741. He was commissioned an ensign on 25 December 1740 and lieutenant on 12 May 1741. He was promoted to captain on 30 July 1745 and served in Scotland where he raised a North Briton Company and served with it from September 1745 to September 1746. He returned to the 42nd Regiment as a captain on 24 April 1747 and served until the regiment was disbanded on 29 May 1749. He was on half pay until he purchased a captain's commission in the 45th Regiment of Foot on 24 February 1750. On 22 March 1761, he joined the 77th Regiment (First Highland Battalion) as a major. When that regiment was disbanded on 24 December 1763, he returned to half pay. In August 1763, General Amherst gave Sutherland permission to stay in Nova Scotia, where he died in 1766.

65 Lieutenant Colonel George Scott was commissioned an ensign in the 40th Regiment of Foot on 24 January 1741 and promoted to captain-lieutenant in the new raising 65th Regiment of Foot on 1 September 1745, serving as quartermaster until 11 October 1748. He was promoted to captain in the 65th Regiment on 13 April 1746, serving until the 65th was disbanded on 24 May 1749. He was on half pay until he became captain of the 40th Foot on 28 June 1751. He commanded Fort Lawrence on the Chignecto Peninsula in 1753 and in 1755 appointed lieutenant colonel of a Massachusetts regiment during Monckton's campaign in Acadia and participated in the capture of Fort Beauséjour and the deportation of Acadians. Scott is sometimes credited with being the first ashore in the landing at Louisbourg on 8 June 1758, where commanded light troops. He later joined Monckton for the expedition to the Saint John River in November 1758. On 30 December 1758, he was appointed major of a ranger unit, which Wolfe used to destroy buildings on the south shore of the St. Lawrence River during the 1759 Québec operation. He was promoted to major in the army on 28 December 1759 and to lieutenant colonel in the army on 11 July 1761. Scott served as commander of light infantry in the Martinique Expedition in January–February 1762 under Monckton and became governor of Grenada when it surrendered on 5 March 1762. In 1764, he became lieutenant governor of Dominica. He resigned his commission on 1 April 1767. He died in Dominica following a duel c.6 November 1767.

66 Marginal note.

67 *Capitaine* Charles Deschamps de Boishébert et de Raffetot (1727-1797), an officer in the French colonial regular troops. Born in Québec, he entered military service was listed among cadets as early as 1739 when he was 12 years old. He served in Acadia in 1745-47 where he was wounded at the Battle of Grand Pré on 11 February 1757. Promoted to *lieutenant* in 1748, he served in Detroit, when it was under danger from a Native American upraising. Returning to Acadia in 1749, Boishébert was ordered to deference the mouth of the Saint John River from the British and rebuilt Fort Menagouèche at present-day St John, New Brunswick. In 1751, he was honored by orders to carry official dispatches to Versailles. Returning to New France, he commanded an advance detachment sent to protect the Ohio Valley at Presqu'île (present day Erie, Pennsylvania) and Fort de la Rivière de la Boeuf (present day Waterford, Pennsylvania). In 1754, he returned to Québec and to Acadia, where he became commandant of Fort La Tour at the mouth of the Saint John River, but was forced to burn his fort to prevent its capture by the British. Promoted to *capitaine* on 17 March 1756. In a variety of actions,

the Suburbs had stood. Here he began batterys against the Town. by his battery at the light house, he dismantled the Island Battery. Oblig'd the Shipping to remove close under the Fortifications, & threw shot into the Town.

18th—the Enemy fired their small arms from the Covert way the whole night: Our Works being pushed pretty near.

21st A shot from the Battery on the left [these batteries were erected by Gen Wolf][68] struck one of the French Men of War[69] & blew up some loose Powder, which set her on fire; the Flames were communicated to two more,[70] & all three burn'd to the keels. [the men escaped in their boats to the town—][71]

22d Open'd two Batterys of Cannon on the Right, against the Town, one of six, the other of a Guns 24 Pounders, & a Battery of Seven mortars, of different bores, some of 13 inches. This day our shells set the Citadel Barracks on fire, it burn'd down with the Church & Steeple.

24th Early this morning the New barracks were set on fire by the shells, & burn'd with great fury, till the whole, a large building was entirely consumed. This Day Brig[dr]. Wolfe open'd a four Gun battery on the left. one for 5 Guns erecting.

25th—This Night [under the Command of the Leut[s]. Lafuroy[72] & Belyour[73]][74] 500 Seamen in boats rowed into the Harbour & attacked the *Prudent* of 74 Guns[75] and

Boishébert sought to protect Acadians from being deported by the British. In January 1757, he set up a refuge for Acadians on the Mirimichi River, which is located in east-central New Brunswick and drains into the Gulf of St. Lawrence. Ordered to help defend Louisbourg, he established a position at Mira and conducted guerrilla operations against the British with a small force of Native Americans and Acadians. After the fall of Louisburg, he commanded a group of Acadian volunteers in defending Québec in 1759. After the fall of Canada 1760, he returned to France, where he died in 1797, without further military service.

68 Note in margin marked for insertion here.

69 The 64-gun *Célèbre.*

70 The 74-gun *Entreprenant* and the 64-gun *Capricieux.*

71 Note added.

72 Captain John Lindsay, Royal Navy, commanding the frigate *Trent.* Lindsay was commissioned a lieutenant on 2 March 1756, promoted to commander on 4 April 1757, to captain 29 September 1757. Knighted in 1771, he served as a commissioner of the Admiralty 10 April to 31 December 1783. He was promoted to rear admiral of the red, 24 September 1787 and died 4 June 1788.

73 Captain George Balfour, Royal Navy, commanded the 8-gun fireship *Aetna.* Balfour had been commissioned a lieutenant on 5 July 1748, promoted to commander on 15 November 1756, to captain on 26 July 1758, and to superannuated rear admiral in 1787. He died 28 June 1794.

74 Note in margin marked for insertion here. One of Boscawen's early actions was to create an early form of a joint operational planning staff. Among the naval officers, Boscawen selected three junior commanding officers, including both Balfour and Lindsay, to assist with the organization and training for assault landings.

75 The 74-gun *Prudent* was built at Rochefort by Pierre Morineau between 1751 and 1754. Length 166 feet on the gun deck, breadth 45 feet, depth of hold 22 feet 3 inches, 1,500 tons, draught 20½ feet forward and 22½ aft.

the *Bienfaisant* of 64,[76] & after some resistance carry'd them both, the Tide being low the *Prudent* was aground with much Water in her hold, the town fired, round & Grape shot so Exceedingly hot on the ships, that our People were oblig'd to set the *Prudent* on fire, but towed the *Bienfaisant* into the N.E. Harbour. This was a very bold enterprize, 'twas much conducted, & bravely Executed. This day the Scaling ladders were carred into our trenches. A breach made near the West Gate.

26th The French hung out a flag to Capitulate. they could obtain no other terms but to surrender the Prisoners of War. Mons Drucour[77] was Governour of Louisbourg. and its dependencies

27th The West gate was taken Possession of by our Grenadiers. The French Troops laid down their arms on the Parade.

August 9th— the French Embark'd to be sent to England.

French troops at Louisbourg &c. taken at Louisbourg[78]

Regiments	N° of Men
Artois[79]	640.
Burgoine[80]	640.
Cambyse[81]	750.
Voluntier Estrangé[82]	750.
Marine, 24 Comp^{ys}[83]	960.
Seamen	2606
Inhabitants	4000

76 The 64-*Bienfaisant* was built at Brest by Mathurin-Louis Geoffrey between 1752 and 1754. Length of gun deck 150 feet, breadth 40 feet 8 inches, depth of hold 20 feet, 1,100 tons, draught 17 feet forward and 20 feet aft. Purchased by the Admiralty and fitted out at Portsmouth, she kept her name as HMS *Bienfaisant.* She remained in service until broken up at Plymouth in 1814.

77 Augustin de Boschenry de Drucour was born at Drucourt, in the present-day Département de Eure in Normandy, France in 1703. From a Norman aristocratic family without wealth, he joined the Navy at Toulon as a *cadet* in the gardes de la marine in 1719. He was regularly promoted and became *lieutenant* of the 'gardes du pavillon amiral' in 1743, and *capitaine de vaisseau* in 1751. In 1754, he was appointed governor of Île Royale (Cape Breton Island) for four years, departing as a prisoner of war after its surrender in August 1758. He was repatriated to France. He returned to service in the Navy in 1759, but soon retired to Le Havre, where he died in 1762. See John Fortier, "Boschenry de Drucour, Augustin de,," in *Dictionary of Canadian Biography*, vol. 3, University of Toronto/Université Laval, 2003–, accessed May 24, 2019, http://www.biographi.ca/en/bio/boschenry_de_drucour_augustin_de_3E.html.

78 The statistics here vary with French records. See H. Boscawen, *The Siege of Louisbourg,* p. 357.

79 Second Battalion, Artois Regiment, commanded by *Lieutenant Colonel* de St. Juhlien.

80 Second Battalion, Bourgogne Regiment, commanded by *Lieutenant Colonel* Marin de Bourzet.

81 Second Battalion, Cambis Regiment, commanded by *Colonel* de Villepreast.

82 Second Battalion, Volontaires Etrangers, commanded by *Lieutenant Colonel* d'Anthonay

83 Troupes de la Marine, 24 companies, commanded by the governor.

The regulars were reduc'd to	3031
Total Taken	9637

Total Regulars 3740. The regiment of Cambyse got into Louisbourg only the Night before we landed. having just come from France in some men of war that put in St. Ann's bay[84] in the Island, & landed this Regiment—

Ships	Guns
Le Prudent	74 Taken in the Harbour by our boats & burn'd
L' Entreprenant[85]	74 Burn'd by a Shot from our Batterys
Le Capriceux[86]	64 Set on fire by the *Entreprenant* & burn'd
Le Celebre[87]	*64 Do*
Le Bienfaisant	64 Taken by our boats in y^e^. harbor & towed off.
le Apollon	50 Sunk by the French at the Mouth of y^e^. Harbour
La Fidelle	36 D°
Diana[88]	36 Taken off the Harbour, by the *Boreas*[89]
La Chevre[90]	16 sunk at the Mouth of the Harbour
La Biche[91]	16 D°
L'Arethusa	36 Escaped out of the Harbour
L'Eccho[92]	20 Taken off the Harbour by the *Juno*[93]

84 Baie de Ste Anne or Port Dauphin, present-day Englishtown, Victoria County, Nova Scotia.

85 The 74-gun *Entreprenant* was built at Brest by Jacques-Luc de Coloumb between 1750 and 1752. Length of gun deck 160 feet, breadth 43 feet, depth of hold 20 feet 4 inches, draught 19 feet forward/20 feet 5 inches aft, 1,445 tons.

86 The 64-gun *Capricieux* was built at Rochefort by François-Guillaume Claitain-Deslauriers between 1752 and 1754. Length on gun deck 150 feet, breadth 40 feet 2 inches, depth of hold 19 feet 3 inches, 1,100 tons.

87 The 64-gun *Célèbre* was built at Brest by Pierre Salinac between 1755 and 1757. Length on gun deck 150 feet, breadth 40 feet 6 inches, 1,200 tons.

88 The 28-gun *Diane* was built at Toulon by François Coulomb, Jr., between 1743 and 1745. Length of gun deck 115 feet, breadth 30 feet 4 inches, depth of hold 13 feet 8 inches, draught 13¾ feet forward/ 15¼ aft, 436 tons.

89 The sixth rate, 28-gun frigate HMS *Boreas* was built at Woolwich by Israel Pownoll in 1757. Length of gun deck 118 feet 5½ inches, length of keel 97 feet 5 inches, breadth 33 feet 8 inches, depth of hold 10 feet 6 inches, 587 30/94 tons bm.

90 The *flûte Chèvre* was built at Rochefort by Antoine Groignard in 1751. Length of gun deck 107 feet, breadth 24 feet, depth of hold, 12 feet, 300 tons. She departed Île d'Aix to resupply Louisbourg on 9 March 1758 and arrived on 3 May 1758. One contemporary source lists the number of guns that she carried at Louisbourg as 16, another lists 22.

91 The 26-gun frigate *Biche* was built at St Malo in 1754. Length 108½ feet, breadth 27½ feet, 290 tons. She arrived at Louisbourg with *Chèvre* and, like her, was said to be carrying 16 guns and 150 men.

92 The 30-gun corvette *Écho* was built at Nantes. While under construction in December 1757 as the privateer *Maréchal de Richelieu*, the French Navy purchased the vessel and renamed her *l'Écho* on 21 January 1758, prior to her completion. After her capture by HMS *Juno* in 1758, the Admiralty purchased here and anglicized her name to *Echo*. She served in the Royal Navy, notably in North American and West Indian waters, until 1770. Length 113 feet, breadth 30 feet 6 inches. 400 tons.

93 The 32-gun *Richmond*-class frigate *Juno* was built at Rotherhithe by William Alexander in 1756-57. Commissioned in September 1757 under Captain John Vaughan, she sailed on 29

English Ships &c at the Reduction of Louisbourg

Ships	Comanders[94]	Guns
Namure	Ad^{l} Boscawen	90
Royal William[95]	S^{r}. Chas. Hardy	84
Princess Amelia[96]	Ph^{p} Durell[97]	80
Dublin	Ad^{l} Rodney	74
Terrible[98]	Capt. Collins[99]	74

January 1758 for Louisbourg on her first deployment. She remained in service until August 1778, when she was burnt at Newport, Rhode Island, to prevent capture. Length on gun deck 127 feet 10 inches, length of keel 107 feet ⅛ inch, breadth 34 feet 3 inches, 667 67/94 tons bm.

94 It appears as though the names of commanders were added later.

95 The 84-gun *Royal William* was originally built at Chatham in 1670 as the first-rate 100-gun *Prince*, then rebuilt and renamed *Royal William* in 1692. Rebuilt again in 1719, she was relaunched and laid up. She saw no service for 39 years. In 1756-57, she was cut down to her upper deck at Portsmouth and re-rated as a second-rate 84-gun ship. She was commissioned in April 1757 under Captain Wittewrong Taylor and served with the Channel Fleet and in the Rochefort expedition, before sailing to North America under Captain Thomas Evans on 5 February 1758. She served as the flagship for Rear Admiral Sir Charles Hardy from June through October 1758 at Louisbourg. She returned to Canada in 1759 to participate in the capture of Québec and returned home with the body of Wolfe. She remained in service until 1812 and was broken up in 1813. Length of gun deck 175 feet 4 inches, breadth 50 feet 3 inches, 1,918 22/94 tons bm, draught 14 feet 3½ inches forward/ 16 feet 4 inches aft.

96 The 80-gun *Princess Amelia* was built at Woolwich by five successive master shipwrights between 1751 and 1755. Originally named *Norfolk*, she was renamed in 1755. Commissioned in 1757, she served in the Rochefort expedition and in Hawke's fleet before sailing to North America on 23 February 1758 under the command of Captain John Bray and carrying the broad pennant of Captain Philip Durell and then served as Durell's flagship as a rear admiral during the Louisbourg operation. She remained in service until 1818, when she was sold. Length of gun deck 165 feet, breadth 47 feet 3 inches, 1, 579 39/94 tons, draught 12 feet 5 inches forward/17 feet 8 inches aft.

97 Philip Durell was born at St Helier, Jersey, in 1707, the son of the solicitor-general of Jersey. He joined the Navy in 1721, passed his lieutenant's examination in 1729 and was commissioned lieutenant in 1731. He was promoted to captain 6 February 1742, to rear admiral of the blue 8 July 1758, to rear admiral of the red 14 February 1759, and vice admiral of the blue 21 October 1762. He died 23 September 1762

98 The 74-gun *Terrible* was the former French *Le Terrible*, built at Toulon between 1736 and 1740 to the design of François Coulomb. She was taken as a prize by Admiral Hawke's squadron off Cape Finisterre on 14 October 1747 and purchased by the Navy Board. Length of gun deck 164 feet 3 inches, length of keel 133 feet 11 inches, breadth 47 feet 3 inches, depth of hold 20 feet 7½ inches, 1,590 28/94 tons bm.

99 Richard Collins passed his lieutenant's examination in 1725 and was commissioned a lieutenant in the Navy on 11 November 1729. He was promoted to commander on 27 July 1743, to captain 7 July 1744, and to superannuated rear admiral in 1762. He died in 1779.

Northumberland[100]	L^d^. Collvill[101]	74
Vanguard[102]	Swanton[103]	74
Orford[104]	Spry[105]	70

100 The 74-gun *Northumberland* was built at Plymouth by three consecutive master shipwrights—Thomas Fellowes, Benjamin Slade, and Thomas Slade—between 1744 and 1753. She first commissioned in January 1753 under Captain Lord Colville. She served as a guard ship in 1753-54 at Minorca and Plymouth, then was in North American waters in 1754 before serving with Osborne's, Hawke's, Boscawen's, and Knowles's fleets in 1756. She sailed again for North America on 22 April 1757. She remained in service until 1777, when she was renamed *Leviathan* and refitted as a 30-gun store ship. In 1779, she became a 50-gun Fourth Rate. She foundered in the North Atlantic on a return passage from Jamaica 27 February 1780. Length of gun deck 160 feet, length of keel 131 feet 4 inches, breadth 45 feet, depth of hold 19 feet 4 inches, 1,414 56/94 tons bm.

101 Alexander Colvill, 7th Baron Colvill of Culross, was born in February 1718 in Scotland and joined the Navy as a King's Letter Boy in 1732 and the following spring joined HMS *Lime*, in which he became a midshipman in 1735. In 1737-38 he served in the frigates *Phoenix* and *Rose*. He passed his lieutenant's examination in January 1739 and was commissioned lieutenant in August that year. On the death of his father, he succeeded to his title. He was promoted to commander on 5 March 1744, and to captain on 24 July 1744. When he took command of *Northumberland* in 1753, he began a nine-year association with the ship as captain and commodore. On Vice Admiral Francis Holbourne's departure from North America in November 1757, Colvill became commander-in-chief, North America, as a commodore until superseded in June 1758. At the end of the 1758 campaign, he returned to England, but returned in 1759. Following the surrender of Québec in 1759, Vice Admiral Charles Saunders left Colvill as commander in chief, North America, a post he held until 1762. In May 1760, Colvill's ability to get his ships in the St. Lawrence despite icy conditions, played a key role in the conquest of Canada. Returning to England, he was promoted to rear admiral of the white on 21 October 1762. After a brief six-months in the first half of 1763 as port admiral at Plymouth, Colvill was ordered back to North America to serve again as commander-in-chief at Halifax, a post he held until 1766, when he retired. He died 21 May 1770.

102 The 74-gun *Vanguard* was built by Philemon Ewer at East Cowes between 1745 and 1748. She served in the Eastern Atlantic, Channel, and Mediterranean until refitted during 1757. Recommissioned under Captain Robert Swanton, she sailed for North America on 8 April 1758. She remained in service until 1765 and was sold at Portsmouth in 1774. Length of gun deck 160 feet, length of keel 130 feet 9½ inches, breadth 45 feet 2 inches, depth of hold 19 feet 4 inches, 1,419 23/94 tons bm.

103 Robert Swanton was commissioned a lieutenant in the Royal Navy on 17 January 1735. He was promoted to captain on 27 August 1744, and to rear admiral of the red on 21 October 1762. He died on 1 August 1765.

104 The 70-gun *Orford* was built at Woolwich by successive master shipwrights John Holland and Thomas Fellowes between 1746 and 1749. Under Captain Richard Spry, she sailed for North America in 16 April 1758. She remained in service until 1782, and was sunk as a breakwater at Sheerness. Length of gun deck 160 feet 2 inches, length of keel 131 feet 4 inches, breadth 45 feet, depth of hold 19 feet 4 inches, 1,414 56/94 tons bm.

105 Richard Spry was born about 1715 and educated at Truro Grammar School in Cornwall. He entered the Navy as a volunteer in 1733, receiving his commission as lieutenant on 27 September 1740. He was promoted to commander on 21 September 1744. Following the sinking of his ship by the Spanish, he was taken prisoner. Released, he was promoted to captain on 23 September 1745. He was senior officer at Halifax in 1755, with the fleet blockading at Louisburg in 1756, and served in Holbourne's fleet in 1756. He commanded *Orford* at both Louisbourg in 1758 and Québec in 1759. He served as commodore and commander-in-chief, North American station in 1762-63. After serving in command of a

Burford[106]	Gambier[107]	70
Somerset[108]	Hughes[109]	70

yacht, he was appointed commodore and commander-in-chief, Mediterranean, 1766-69. Spry became rear admiral of the blue on 18 October 1770 and rear admiral of the white on 28 October 1770. He served as port admiral at Plymouth in 1770-71. He was knighted on 24 June 1773, shortly before his retirement. He was promoted to rear admiral of the red on 23 March 1775 and died 1 December 1775.

106 The 70-gun *Burford* was built at Chatham by Adam Hayes and John Lock between 1754 and 1757. She first commissioned in April 1757 and served at Rochefort and in Hawke's fleet. Under the command of Captain James Gambier between 1758 and 1763, she first sailed for North America on 23 February 1758, returning home after Louisbourg then sailing for the Leeward Islands in the same year and was present at the actions at Martinique and Guadeloupe before returning Home to join Hawke at Quiberon Bay. The ship remained in service until 1784 and was sold in 1785. Length of gun deck 162 feet 1 inch, length of keel 134 feet, breadth 44 feet 8½ inches, depth of hold 19 feet 8¾ inches, 1,424 39/94 tons bm.

107 Of Huguenot stock, James Gambier was born in 1723, joined the Navy about 1740, and was commissioned lieutenant on 6 March 1744. He was promoted to commander on 3 April 1746 and to captain on 5 December 1747. From 1770 to 1773, he was commodore and commander-in-chief, North American Station. Following this assignment, he served a commissioner of the victualling board for some months in 1773, before becoming commissioner of Portsmouth Dockyard, 1773-1778. He was promoted to rear admiral of the blue on 23 January 1778 and briefly served again as commander-in-chief, North American Station. He was promoted to rear admiral of the red on 23 March 1779, and to vice admiral of the blue on 26 September 1780. He served as commander-in-chief, Jamaica, in 1783-84, and was promoted to vice admiral of the red on 4 September 1787. He died 8 January 1789. He was the uncle of Admiral James Gambier, first Baron Gambier (1756-1833).

108 The 70-gun *Somerset* was built at Chatham by John Ward between 1746 and 1748. She served as a guard ship in 1748-50 and was then laid up at Sheerness. Recommissioned in 1753, she was with Boscawen's fleet in North America in 1755, served as flagship for Vice Admiral Henry Osborne, then served under Hawke, Boscawen, and Knowles in 1756. In 1757, she sailed to North America as reinforcement for Holbourne. Under the command of Captain Edward Hughes, 1758-1762, she was at Louisbourg and later served as flagship for Saunders at Québec in 1759. She joined Hawke after Quiberon Bay and sailed for the Mediterranean in 1760. She was paid off in 1763. Recommissioned in 1771 and under Hughes again until 1774, she returned to North America, where she remained until 1776. She sailed again for America in 1777 and was at Sandy Hook at the encounter with d'Estaing in August 1778. She was wrecked off Cape Cod on 2 November 1778. Length of gun deck 160 feet, length of keel 131 feet 4 inches, breadth 45 feet 4 inches, depth of hold 19 feet 4 inches, 1.435 62/94 tons bm.

109 Edward Hughes was born about 1720 and joined the Royal Navy on 4 January 1735. He was present at the attack on Portobello. After he was commissioned lieutenant on 25 August 1740, he served in the 1741 Cartagena expedition and was present at the Battle of Toulon in 1744. He promoted to captain on 6 February 1748. He was appointed commodore and commander-in-chief in the East Indies in September 1773 and remain in post until 1777. He was promoted to rear admiral of the blue on 23 January 1778 and, on 9 December 1778, Knight Companion of the Bath. Promoted to vice admiral of the blue on 26 September 1780, he returned to India as commander-in-chief in the East Indies, where he served until 1784. During this period, he fought the French naval commander Suffren in five battles. In retirement, he was promoted to vice admiral of the white on 24 September 1787, vice admiral of the red on 21 September 1790, and admiral of the blue on 1 February 1793. He died on 17 February 1794.

Lancaster[110]	Edgcomb[111]	70
Devonshire[112]	Gordon[113]	66

110 The 66-gun, third rate *Lancaster* was built at Woolwich by John Holland between 1744 and 1749. Captain George Edgcumbe took command in 1756 and commanded her at the Battle of Minorca in 1756, and with the Western Squadron in 1757. She departed for North America on 23 February 1758. She remained in service until 1763 and was broken up at Portsmouth in 1773. Length of gun deck 161 feet, length of keel 130 feet 10 inches, breadth 46 feet 11 inches, depth of hold 19 feet 4 inches, 1,477 85/95 tons bm.

111 The Honourable George Edgcumbe was the second son of Richard, First Baron Edgcumbe. Born in 1721, he passed his lieutenant's examination in the Royal Navy in 1739 and was commissioned on 5 October 1739. He was promoted to commander in 1742 and to captain on 19 August 1744. He was elected Member of Parliament for Fowey in 1746 and held the position until 1761. He was in the Mediterranean in command of the 50-gun *Deptford*, when the French invaded *Minorca* in 1756. Admiral John Byng ordered him to move to the command of *Lancaster* and in her participated in the Battle of Minorca. After his return from Louisbourg, he commanded the 74-gun *Hero* at the Battle of Quiberon Bay in 1759. He was raised to the peerage on the death of his elder brother in 1761, becoming 3rd Baron Edgcumbe. He was promoted to rear admiral of the blue on 21 October 1762 and served as commander-in-chief at Plymouth in 1766 to 1771. He was promoted to rear admiral of the red on 18 October 1770, to vice admiral of the blue on 24 October 1770, to vice admiral of the white on 25 June 1773, to vice admiral of the red on 5 February 1776. He was promoted to admiral of the blue on 29 January 1778. On 21 February 1781, he was made Viscount Mount Edgcumbe and Valletort. Promoted to admiral of the white on 8 April 1782, the Royal Society elected him a Fellow in 1784. In 1789, he was created Earl of Mount Edgcumbe. See *History of Parliament* http://www.historyofparliamentonline.org/volume/1715-1754/member/edgcumbe-hon-george-1720-95

112 The 66-gun third-rate *Devonshire* was originally built as an 80-gun ship at Woolwich by shipwrights John Hayward and John Holland between 1740 and 1745. After service with the western squadron and at Lorient in 1745-46, she was cut down to a 74-gun ship, and then to a 66-gun razée before being recommissioned in 1747. She saw action in the two Battles of Finisterre in 1747. Paid off in 1752, she was recommissioned in 1756. Captain William Gordon command her in 1757-59. She sailed for North America 28 January 1758. After Louisburg, she participated in the Québec operation in 1759, the Leeward Islands and Martinique in 1762, and Havana. Paid off in 1763, she was broken up at Portsmouth in 1772. Length of gun deck 161 feet 2 inches, length of keel 130 feet 4 inches, breadth 46 feet ¾ inch, depth of hold 19 feet 4 inches, 1,470 88/94 tons.

113 William Gordon was born about 1709, the son of a merchant in Elgin, Scotland. He joined the Royal Navy in 1726. He passed the examination for lieutenant on 23 March 1733 and was commissioned on 26 December 1735. He was promoted to commander on 22 May 1742 and to captain on 4 August 1744. He was placed on half-pay on 1 July 1760 to 5 August 1761. Returning to sea service, he served as commodore in 1762. Promoted to rear admiral of the white on 21 October 1762, he died 25 April 1768.

Bedford[114]	Fowke[115]	64
Captain[116]	Amherst[117]	64
Prince Frederick[118]	Mann[119]	64

114 The 64-gun, third-rate *Bedford* was originally built as a 70-gun ship at Portsmouth by Joseph Allin between 1737 and 1741. Commissioned in 1741, she participated in the Battle of Toulon in 1744 and was probably reduced to 64 guns while undergoing repair in 1749-50. Recommissioned in 1755, she served under Boscawen and Knowles in 1756. She sailed for North America on 15 April 1757, arriving on 9 July 1757. Returning to England, she sailed for Louisbourg on 23 February 1758. She returned to England and sailed again for the Québec operation in 1759. Returning to Hawke's fleet, she captured the 32-gun *Comète* in 1761 and convoyed ships to Portugal. Paid off in December 1762, she sold in 1787. Length of gun deck 150 feet 10½ inches, length of keel 121 feet 6 inches, breadth 43 feet 7½ inches, depth of hold 17 feet 10 inches, 1, 229 89/94 tons.

115 Thorpe Fowke passed the examination for lieutenant in the Royal Navy in 1714 and received his commission on 20 September 1730. He was promoted to captain on 24 May 1744 and became a superannuated rear admiral in 1759. He died on 14 March 1784.

116 The 64-gun *Captain* was originally built as a 70-gun ship at Woolwich by John Haywood between 1740 and 1743. Commissioned in 1743, she saw extensive service until put under repair in 1750-51, during which she was probably reduced to 64 guns. Recommissioned in 1753, she joined Hawke's fleet in 1755, then served in the Mediterranean and was at the Battle of Minorca on 20 May 1756. Captain John Amherst took command about September 1756 in the Mediterranean. She sailed for North America on 16 April 1757, where she took the 22-gun store ship *Le Foudroyant* in February 1758. After Louisbourg she participated in the Québec operation and returned home. After repairs in 1771, she was flagship of Rear Admiral John Montagu on the North American station in 1771-1774. In 1777, she was fitted as a 30-gun store ship and renamed *Buffalo.* Raised to a 50-gun, fourth-rate in 1778, she was flagship for Vice Admiral Matthew Buckle in 1778, was at the Battle of the Dogger Bank in 1781, and with Howe when he relieved Gibraltar in 1782. She was paid off and broken up at Woolwich in 1783. Length of gun deck 151 feet, length of keel 122 feet, breadth 43 feet 6½ inches, depth of hold 17 feet 9 inches, 1,230 28/94 tons.

117 John Amherst was a year younger than his brother Major General Jeffery Amherst. Born in January 1718, he joined the Royal Navy and passed his examination for lieutenant in 1736 and was commissioned lieutenant on 24 July 17 39. He was promoted to captain on 29 December 1744, then rear admiral of the blue in 1764, rear admiral of the white on 18 October 1770, vice admiral of the blue on 24 October 1770, vice admiral of the white on 5 February 1776, vice admiral of the red in 1777, and admiral of the blue on 29 January 1778. He died on 14 February 1778.

118 The 64-gun, third-rate *Prince Frederick* was originally built as a 70-gun ship at Deptford by Richard Stacey between 1736 and 1740. Commissioned in 1740, the ship saw extensive service, taking four privateers in 1745-46, and participating in the Battle of Finisterre on 3 May 1748. After undergoing a great repair in 1751-52, when she was likely reduced to 64 guns, she was recommissioned in April 1755. Captain Robert Man took command and sailed to North America on 29 January 1758. In August 1758, Captain Robert Routh succeeded Man. After Louisbourg, she participated in the Québec operation in 1759, and was with the western squadron in 1760, off Brest in 1761, and at the blockade of Basque Roads in 1762. Paid off in 1763, she was fitted as a lazarette at Chatham in 1764 and after being moved to Stangate Creek eventually sold in 1784. Length of gun deck 151 feet, length of keel 122 feet 2 inches, breadth 43 feet 5 inches, depth of hold 17 feet 9 inches, 1,224 64/94 tons bm.

119 Robert Man or Mann was commissioned lieutenant in the Royal Navy on 6 March 1747. He was promoted to commander on 10 November 1756, and to captain on 16 November 1757. He was killed while in command of HMS *Milford* while capturing the privateer *Gloire* on 7 March 1762. His son, Robert Mann (c.1748-1813), joined the Navy, became a lieutenant in 1768, and rose to be admiral of the red.

Pembroke[120]	Simco[121]	60
Kingston[122]	Parry[123]	60
York[124]	Pigott[125]	60

120 The 60-gun, fourth rate *Pembroke* was designed by Joseph Allin after the French prize *Monarch* and built by John Lock at Plymouth between 1753 and 1757. Commissioned in May 1757 under Captain John Simcoe with the future explorer James Cook as master, the ship served in Cornish's squadron in November and December 1757, then sailed for North America on 23 February 1758. After Simcoe's death on 14 May 1759, Captain John Wheelock took command at Québec. She spent the winter of 1759-60 in North America and was in the St. Lawrence in 1760. In 1761, she sailed for Jamaica and was at the blockade of Cape François, then at Havana in 1762, and the Leeward Islands in 1763. Paid off in 1764, she was reduced to 50 guns at Plymouth in 1766-68. Recommissioned in 1769, she served in the Mediterranean until paid off in 1772. In 1776, she was refitted at Chatham as a hospital ship for Halifax, Nova Scotia, where she was broken up in 1793. Length of gun deck 156 feet, length of keel 132 feet 6 inches, breadth 42 feet, depth of hold 18 feet, 1,247 52/94 tons bm.

121 John Simcoe was born the son of a clergyman in 1710 at Staindrop, County Durham, and commissioned a lieutenant in the Royal Navy on 7 August 1739. He was promoted to captain on 28 December 1743. Simcoe commanded the 90-gun, second rate *Saint George*, hosting the court martial of Admiral John Byng in December 1757-January 1758. Ordered to *Pembroke* in May 1758, Simcoe died of pneumonia on board *Pembroke* on 14 May 1758, off Anticosti Island at the mouth of the St. Lawrence River. His third and only surviving son, John Graves Simcoe (1752-1806) joined the Army, commanded the Queen's Rangers, served as lieutenant governor of Upper Canada, 1791-1797, and governor of St Domingo, 1797.

122 The 60-gun, fourth rate *Kingston* was built by Peirson Lock at Plymouth between 1737 and 1741.Commissioned in 1740, she had seen service in the Mediterranean and was at the Battle of Toulon in 1744, then in the Leeward Islands in 1745, at Louisbourg and in the St. Lawrence in 1746, before returning home for a middling repairs in 1750-51. Recommissioned in February 1755 under command of Captain William Parry, who retained command until 1761, she sailed for the Mediterranean in April 1756 and participated in the Battle of Minorca. *Kingston* sailed for North America on 16 Aril 1757. After the surrender of Louisbourg, she carried the French Regiment Bourgogne and Voluntières Étrangers back to Britain, was then in Hawke's fleet in 1759 and at the Battle of Quiberon Bay. She returned to North America in in 1760 before being paid off in 1761. She was sold to private investors in 1762, renamed *Lord Clive*, and used to attack the Spanish settlements at La Plata, where she was burned in 1763. Length of gun deck 144 feet, length of keel 116 feet 7 inches, breadth 41 feet 5 inches, depth of hold 16 feet 11 inches, 1,067 77/94 tons bm.

123 William Parry was born in 1705. He passed his examination for lieutenant in the Royal Navy on 23 July 1738. He was promoted to commander on 29 December 1743 and to captain on 2 October 1744. He was appointed rear admiral of the blue in 1763 and served as commander in chief of the Jamaica Station from 1763 to 1766. He became rear admiral of the red on 18 October 1770 and to vice admiral of the blue on 24 October 1770. He served as commander in chief of the Leeward Islands Station from 1772 to 1775. He was promoted to vice admiral of the white on 31 March 1775, to vice admiral of the red on 5 February 1776, and to admiral of the blue on 29 January 1778. He died on 29 April 1779.

124 The 60-gun *York* was built at Plymouth by Thomas Slade and John Lock between 1751 and 1755. First commissioned in 1755 under Captain Hugh Pigot, she served with Boscawen's and Knowles's fleets as well as the Western Squadron in 1756-57. She sailed for North America 30 January 1758. She served in the fleet until 1771 and was broken up at Plymouth in 1772. Length of gun deck 150 feet 2 inches, length of keel 123 feet ½ inch, breadth 42 feet 10½ inches, depth of hold 18 feet 6 inches, 1,203 10/94 tons bm.

125 Hugh Pigot or Piggot was born about 1721 and joined the Navy as an able seaman and captain's servant in 1735. He was appointed midshipman in 1739 and passed his lieutenant's examination in 1741. He was commissioned a lieutenant on 9 February 1742 and then

Prince of Orange[126]	Ferguson[127]	60
Defiance[128]	Beard[129]	60
Nottingham[130]	Marshall[131]	60

promoted to captain on 22 April 1746. Following his command of York at Louisbourg, he commanded *Royal William* at Québec in 1759. He was elected Member of Parliament for Penryn from 1768 to 1774 and appointed colonel of the Royal Marines in 1770. He was promoted to rear admiral of the white, 31 March 1776 and to vice admiral of the white on 29 January 1778. In 1778, he succeeded his brother as Member of Parliament for Bridgenorth, maintaining that seat until 1784. He was promoted to vice admiral of the red on 26 September 1780. The Rockingham ministry appointed him a commissioner of the Admiralty from 1 April 1782 to 31 December 1783, during which time he was promoted to admiral of the blue on 24 April 1782 and appointed to succeed Sir George Rodney in command of the Leeward Islands station. After the signing of the peace in 1783, he returned to England and retired from the Navy. He was promoted to admiral of the white on 24 September 1787 and died on 15 December 1791. See *History of Parliament* http://www.historyofparliamentonline.org/volume/1754-1790/member/pigot-hugh-1722-92

126 The 60-gun *Prince of Orange* was built at Deptford as a third-rate 70-gun ship by Richard Stacey between 1731 and 1734. Originally named *Bredah*, her name was changed while she was under construction on 5 September 1733. During a middling repair in 1747-48 after going ashore during a hurricane in the West Indies, she was reduced from a 70-gun third rate to a 60-gun fourth rate. After another middling repair at Chatham, she was recommissioned in March 1757 under Captain John Fergusson. She sailed for North America on 23 March 1758. Captain Samuel Wallis took command in September 1758. She was at Québec in 1759 and spent the winter of 1759-60 in North America. She was in the Belleisle operation and served with the Western Squadron in 1760 and 1762-63. She was paid off in March 1763. She was fitted as a sheer hulk at Sheerness in 1771-72 and finally sold in 1815.

127 John Ferguson (also Fergussonne or Fergussone) was a trusted friend of Boscawen, who assigned him as shore officer during the landing at Louisbourg in 1758. Ferguson was commissioned as a lieutenant on 2 October 1739, promoted to commander on 12 November 1745, and to captain on 6 October 1746. He died 12 June 1767.

128 The 60-gun *Defiance* was built at Deptford by Thomas West between 1743 and 1745. She sailed for North America under Captain Baird 2 May 1757. In 1759, she participated in the Battle of Quiberon Bay and the blockade of Basque Roads in 1759. She was in Jamaica 1760-62 and then took part in the Havana operation in 1762. She was paid off in 1763 and finally sold in 1766. Length of gun deck 147 feet 4½ inches, length of keel 119 feet 5¼ inches, breadth 42 feet 3½ inches, depth of hold 18 feet 1¼ inches, 1,136 29/94 tons.

129 Patrick Baird was commissioned a lieutenant in the Royal Navy on 29 November 1738. He was promoted to commander on 12 July 1745, and to captain on 27 May 1747. He died in 1761.

130 The 60-gun *Nottingham* was built at Sheerness by three successive master shipwrights between 1740 and 1745. After active service between 1745 and 1748, she underwent repair at Portsmouth in 1750. She was recommissioned about December 1754 under Captain Samuel Marshall and sailed for North America on 22 April 1755. She returned to England and sailed again on 15 April 1756 for America, where she remained until 1758. After Louisbourg, she was with Hawke's fleet, then with Barrington in 1759. She served in the Channel and the Downs in 1760-61, before sailing for the West Indies in 1761. In 1762, she was at Jamaica, Cape François, and Havana. She was paid off in 1763 and sunk as a breakwater at Sheerness in 1773. Length of gun deck 144 feet, length of keel 116 feet 7 inches, breadth 41 feet 8 inches, depth of hold 16 feet ii inches, 1,076 57/94 tons bm.

131 Samuel Marshall passed his lieutenant's examination in the Royal Navy in 1731 and was commissioned lieutenant on 26 August 1731. He was promoted to commander on 12 September 1743, and to captain on 17 July 1747. He died on 17 April 1768.

Centurion[132]	Mantel[133]	54
Sutherland	Rouse[134]	50

Frigates

Diana	36
Boreas	36
Shannon[135]	36
Juno	32
Trent	28
Gramont	24
Portmahon[136]	22

132 The 54-gun *Centurion* was originally built as a 60-gun, fourth rate at Portsmouth by Joseph Allin between 1729 and 1733. She was Anson's flagship on his voyage around the world in 1739-1744 and had captured the Spanish Manila galleon *Nuestra Señora de Covadonga* in 1743. Completely worn-out on her return, she was given a Middling repair at Portsmouth in 1744-46 and reduced to 50-guns. After active service between 1746 and 1752, she was repaired at Chatham in 1752-53 and recommissioned in October 1754 under Captain William Mantell to be flagship for Commodore Augustus Keppel, who had commanded her in 1748-52. She made voyages to Virginia in 1754 and Nova Scotia in 1756 before sailing for North America on 16 April 1757. After Louisbourg, she was at Québec in 1759. In 1760, she was at Jamaica and served as flagship for Commodore Sir James Douglas. In 1762, she was present during the Havana operation before being paid off. Recommissioned in 1763, she served in the Mediterranean until 1766. She was broken up at Chatham in 1769. Length of gun deck 144 feet 1 inch, length of keel 117 feet 5 inches, breadth 40 feet 1½ inch, depth of hold 16 feet 5 inches, 1,005 34/94 tons bm.

133 William Mantell passed his examination for lieutenant in the Royal Navy in 1737 and was commissioned lieutenant on 12 May 1740. He was promoted to commander on 1 March 1749, and to captain on 8 June 1749. Superannuated in 1762, he died on 13 December 1765.

134 John Rous was born in Charlestown, Massachusetts, on 21 May 1702. He was briefly master's mate in the 50-gun *Ruby* in 1740. He commanded the Massachusetts armed snow *Shirley*, capturing numerous French privateers in 1744. With *Shirley* during the 1745 siege of Louisbourg, he was second in command of the New England vessels. Rear Admiral Sir Peter Warren gave him a commission as third lieutenant in the 60-gun French prize *Vigilan*t on 22 June 1745. Sent to England with news of the capitulation of Louisbourg, the Admiralty purchased the 10-14 gun *Shirley*, placing Rous in command and returning him to Cape Breton. He was promoted to post-captain on 24 September 1745. When *Shirley* was paid off after being damaged in a hurricane in 1747, he was sent to England to consult on plans for the settlement at Chebucto (Halifax). He convoyed the first settlers to Halifax and served as senior naval officer at Nova Scotia, 1749-55. He participated in the sieges of Beauséjour in 1755 in command of the 24-gun *Success*. He commanded *Sutherland* at Louisbourg in 1758 and at Québec in 1759. Rous died on 3 April 1760 at Portsmouth, England.

135 The 28-gun frigate *Shannon* was built at Deptford by Adams Hayes in 1757. Commissioned in August 1757 under Captain Archibald Clevland, she cruised in the Western Approaches and took a French privateer. Under Captain Charles Medows, she sailed for North America on 23 February 1758. After Louisbourg, she continues in service until 1765, when she was broken up at Portsmouth. Length of keel 118 feet 6 inches, length of keel 97 feet 5½ inches, breadth 33 feet 8 inches, depth of hold 10 feet 6 inches, 587 53/94 tons bm.

136 The 22-gun, sixth rate *Port Mahon* was built at Deptford in 1739-1740. Commissioned in July 1741, she took a number of privateers before 1748. After repairs in 1752, she was recommissioned and in 1753 served in Newfoundland and New England waters. In 1754, she was in Virginia. Returning to Home Waters, she sailed for North America under Captain Samuel Wallis on 23 April 1757. Under the temporary command of Lieutenant John

Nightingale[137.]	22
Kennington	20
Scarborough	20
Squirrel[130]	20
Hynd[139]	20
Sloops	
Beaver	16
Hunter[140]	14

Ferguson in 1758, Wallis resumed command in August before Louisbourg. In 1759, she was in Jamaica and participated in the Havana operation from June to August 1762. Paid off in 1763, she was sold at Portsmouth in the same year. Length of gun deck 106 feet 4 inches, length of keel 87 feet 5¼ inches, breadth 30 feet 8 inches, depth of hold 9 feet 4 inches, 437 34/94 tons bm.

137 The 22-gun *Nightingale* was built on speculation by Henry Bird at Globe Stairs, Rotherhithe in 1746. Purchased by the Navy on 16 June 1746 while still on the stocks, she was named on 2 October 1746 and completed to naval specifications. Commissioned in 1746, the ship was on the Flemish coast in 1747, in the Mediterranean in 1749 and 1752. After a middling repair at Deptford, she was recommissioned in 1754 and sailed for Virginia in 1755. Under Captain James Campbell from 1756 to 1761, she was based at New York in 1756-59. After participating in operations in the St. Lawrence River in 1759, she returned to England. She sailed again for North America on 25 April 1760 and served in the Leeward Islands in 1761 and at Martinique in 1762. Paid off in 1763, she was used as a receiving ship for pressed men, then a hospital for new recruits before finally being sunk as a breakwater at Harwich in 1783. Length of gun deck 113 feet 3 inches, length of keel 94 feet 5 inches, breadth 32 feet 2¾ inches, depth of hold 11 feet 1 inch, 521 62/94 tons bm, draught 8 feet forward / 11 feet aft.

138 The 20-gun, sixth rate *Squirrel* was built at Woolwich by Edward Allin in 1755. Commissioned in October 1755, she captured a privateer in 1756 while under the command of Captain Hyde Parker. In December 1757, Captain John Wheelock took command and remained in command until 1759, although Commander George Hamilton commandeered her in the period between June and September 1758. She sailed for North America on 15 January 1758. After Louisbourg, she participated in the Québec operation and then served in the Mediterranean in 1760, returned to North America and went back again to the Mediterranean in 1762. She remained in service until 1782, when she was sold. Length of gun deck 107 feet 3 inches, length of keel 89 feet 5¼ inches, breadth 29 feet 1½ inches, depth of hold 9 feet 2 inches, 403 52/94 tons bm, draught 7 feet 3 inches forward / 10 feet 4 inches aft.

139 The 20- to 24-gun, sixth rate *Hind* was built at Chichester by Chitty & Vernon between 1747 and 1749, then completed at Portsmouth between 1749 and 1752. Commissioned in 1752, by 1758 she was under Captain Robert Bond and sailed for North America on 25 January 1758. After Louisbourg, she was at Québec in 1759. She remained in service until 1783. She was sold in 1784. Length of gun deck 112 feet 10 inches, length of keel 91 feet 10¾ inches, breadth 32 feet 3¾ inches, depth of hold 11 feet, 510 34/94 tons.

140 The two-masted, 10-gun snow *Hunter* was built at Rotherhithe by Stanton & Wells in 1755-56. Based on a design by Thomas Slade, *Hunter* had a narrower stern and longer keel than her sister ship *Viper*. Commissioned in 1756, she saw her first service with the Iceland Fishery. Under Commander John Laforey, she sailed for North America on 16 April 1757. Commander William Adams took command in August 1758. In January 1759, she sailed from the Bahamas, but returned north to be at Québec in 1759. She remained in service and returned to North America in 1775, where she was taken by American privateers, then retaken by HMS *Greyhound*. She was placed out of commission in 1779 and used as a prison ship at New York until sold in 1780. Length of gun deck 88 feet 8 inches, length of keel 75

Hawke[141] 14

Fireships
Etna[142]
Lightning[143]
Tyloe[144]

July---Regiments &c at the Reduction of Louisbourg[145]
1st St. Clair's 2d Batallion 1st Brigade W
15th Amhersts 2d Brigade L
17th Forbes's 3d Brigade W
22d Whitmore's 1st Brigade L
28th Bragg's 2d Brigade
35th Otway's 3d Brigade L

---

feet 11⅜ inches, breadth 24 feet 3 inches, depth of hold 7 feet, 237 53/94 tons bm, draught 6 feet 6 inches forward / 8 feet 5 inches aft.

141 The two-masted ketch *Hawke* was designed by Joseph Allin in 1755, built by Robert Batson at Limehouse in 1755, and completed at Deptford in 1756. Commissioned in April 1756, she sailed for North America on 16 April 1757. Commander Robert Hathorn took command in January 1758. In November 1759, she was taken by the French privateer *Duc de Choiseul* off Cape Clear. She named changed to *La Duchesse de Grammont,* she operated out of St Malo until 4 February 1760, when HMS *Juno* retook her. Recommissioned under her original name, she remained in service until 1780. She was sold at Portsmouth on 13 August 1781. Length of gun deck 88 feet, length of keel 72 feet 1½ inches, breadth 24 feet, depth of hold 10 feet 7½ inches, 220 86/94 tons. She carried 80 men and was armed with 8-3 pounders and 10-½ pounder swivel guns.

142 The fireship *Etna* was built in 1750 as a merchant vessel named *Charlotte.* Purchased from M. Hutchinson on 10 November 1756. She was fitted by Wells at Deptford as a 16-gun sloop and renamed in 1756. Commissioned in 1756, she served in the Downs. In January 1758, she was refitted as a fireship. In August 1758, Commander Richard Bickerton was in command. In 1759, she was in the Mediterranean and served in the Belle Isle operation in 1761. Paid off in 1762, she was sold at Portsmouth in 1763. Length of gun deck 98 feet, length of keel 79 feet 9¼ inches, breadth 27 feet 4 inches, depth of hold 11 feet 8½ inches, 317 1/94 tons bm.

143 The fireship *Lightning* was originally built as the 14-gun sloop *Viper* at Poole by Tito Durell in 1745-46. Commissioned in 1746, she took four privateers and participated in the raid at Sediere Bay before being paid off in 1753. Converted to a fireship at Plymouth and renamed *Lightning* in 1755. At Louisbourg, she was commanded by Commander William Goostrey. After returning to England, she was a receiving ship for new men. She was sold in 1762. Length of gun deck 91 feet, length of keel 74 feet 9 inches, breadth 26 feet 1 inch, depth of hold 12 feet 1 inch, 270 48/94 tons bm. As a fireship she was manned by 45 men and carried eight 4-pounders and six ½ pounder swivel guns.

144 The armed sloop *Tyloe* was hired by the Admiralty Board in January 1758. Commander David Pryce commanded her, while also serving as agent for transports. She sailed from Portsmouth on 24 January 1758, armed with 6 guns and a crew of 30 men, as one of the escorts for a convoy transports for New York in company with *Hind* and *Hunter.* After reaching New York, she sailed with the convoy of troops from New York on 6 May and reached Halifax on 19 May. *Tyloe* sailed with the main fleet and 143 troop ships from Halifax for Louisburg on 28 May. She departed from Louisbourg for Boston on 30 August with a convoy of 36 transports.

145 It is unclear what Bamford meant to signify by the annotations W and L next to the majority of battalions in this list.

40th Hopson's 1st Brigade L
45th Warburtons 2d Brigade L
47th Lascelles 3d Brigade W
48th Webb's W 1st Brigadc
58th Anstruther's W 2d Brigade
60th Monkton's 2d Bat. 3d Brigade R.A
60th Lawrences 3d D°. 1st Brigade
78th Frazer's Highlanders 2d Brigade

Artillery
Marines
Rangers
in all about 12,000 men

The town of Louisbourg makes a pretty good appreance here are several good houses & some publick buildings it is remarkably strong to the Sea, & well Fortified to the land side: 'tis an irregular modern fortification, without a good Ditch, covert Way & an Extraodinary fine glacis; the houses were in a very shatter'd condition & most of their artillery Disabled. The Harbour is not very good, the Wind has great Effect, the land lying low & a very heavy Sea rolls in: the Entrance is defended, by the Island battery mounting 48 Pieces of heavy Cannon 48 Pounders, with Mortars; the Batterys at the Lighthouse & grand Battery, with several very strong Batterys from the town.

A list of the Kill'd & Wounded in the English Army at the Siege of Louisbourg

----------	Captains	Lieut^s	Ensigns	Serjeants	Corporals	Private	Drum^rs
Kill'd	2	8	2	3	7	146	----
Wounded	3	16	3	4	3	317	2

Kill'd
Royal L^t. Fenton[146]—L^t. Howe[147]

146 James Fenton was born in Ireland and joined the army at an unknown date and place. He was commissioned as a lieutenant in Scotland on 23 April 1746 in the second battalion of the 1st or Royal Regiment of Foot. In 1748, he transferred the same commission to first battalion of the 1st Foot; on 16 February 1756, he became lieutenant in the second battalion of the 1st Foot. He died on 15 June 1758 of wounds suffered during siege of Louisbourg.

147 Josiah Howe was commissioned 2nd lieutenant in the 7th Marines on 31 October 1747. When the regiment was disbanded on 3 November 1748, he went on British half pay. He returned to active service from half pay on 15 September 1754 as a lieutenant in Pepperrell's new-raising 51st Foot. He became Lieutenant in the 2/1st Foot, 26 December 1756. He was killed in action on 18 July 1758 in the trenches during the siege of Louisbourg.

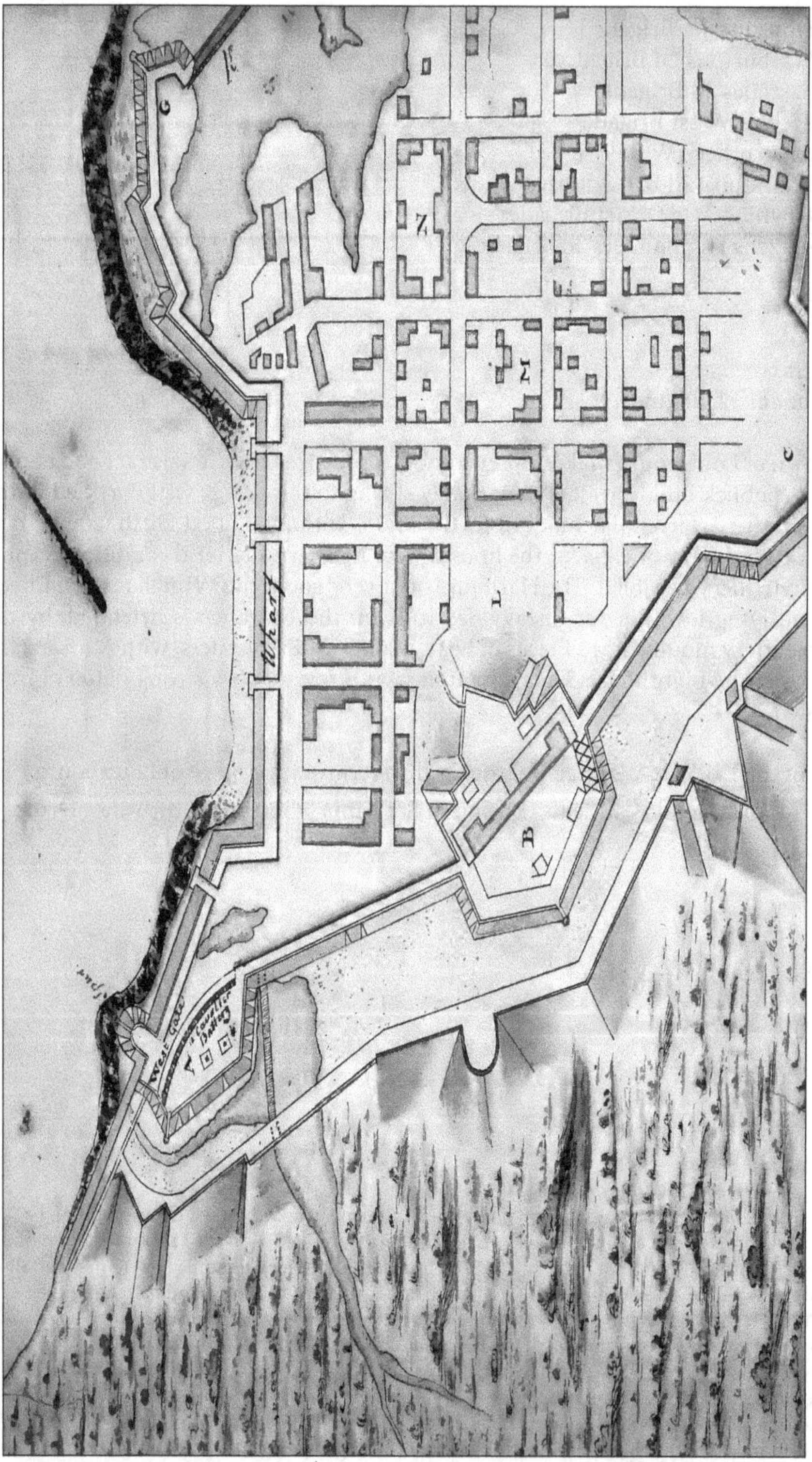

'Fragment of plan of Louisbourg, Nova Scotia, Canada'.

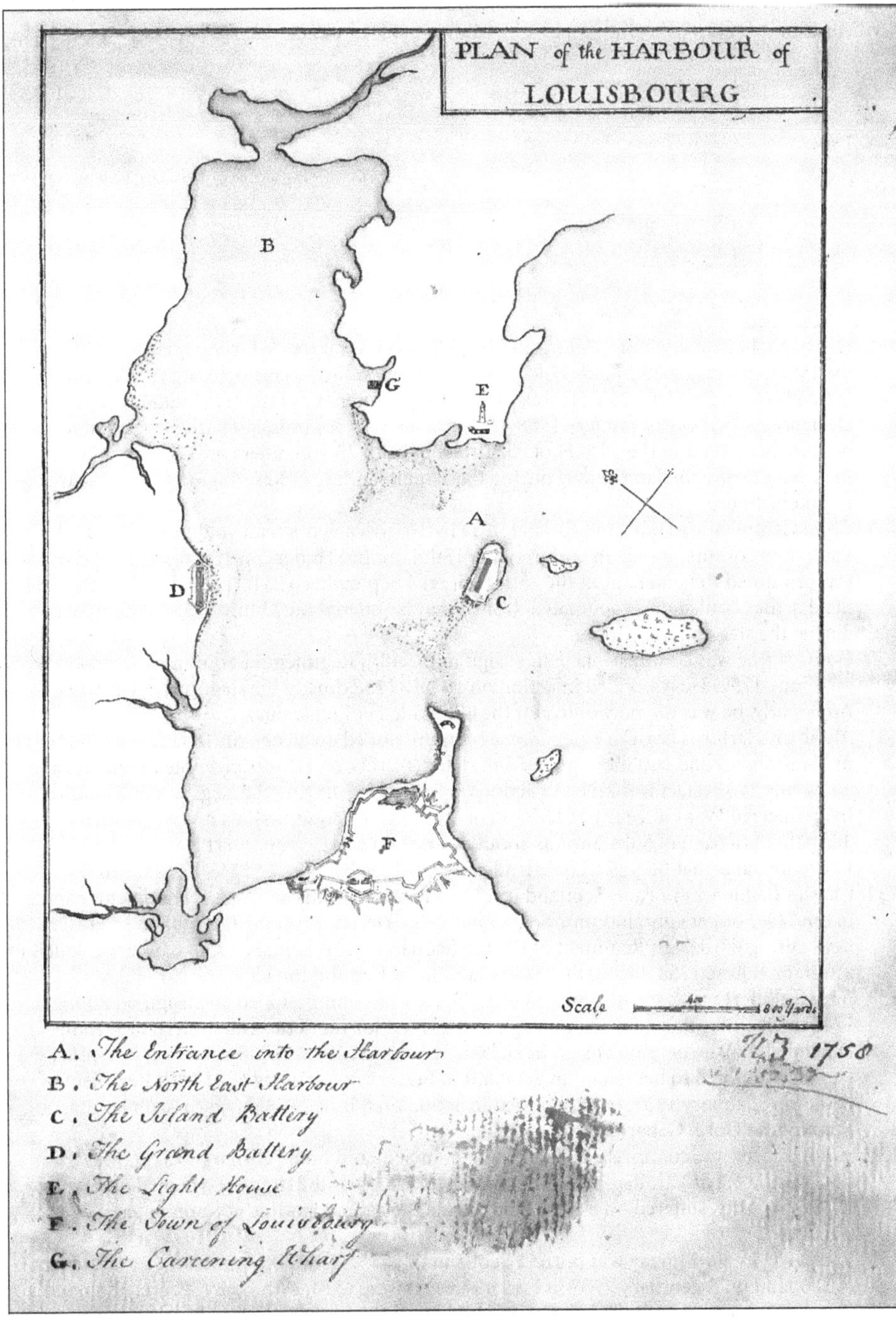

'Plan of the harbour of Louisbourg'.

G^{l}. Amherst's—L^{t}. Nicholson[148]—L^{t}. Campbell[149]
G^{l}. Forbes—Capt. Earl of Dondonald
G^{l}. Webb's—En^{n}. Godfrey Roe[150]
Col^{o} Monckton's—L^{t}. Hart[151]
Col^{o} Frazer's—Capt. Baylie[152]—L^{t}. Cuthbert[153]—L^{t}. Frazer[154]—L^{t}. Murray[155]

148 Henry Nicholson was born in England in 1725. He was appointed troop quartermaster of the 1st Dragoons on 25 March 1744. He was commissioned a cornet in the 1st Dragoons in Scotland on 20 May 1752. He was promoted to lieutenant in the 1st Dragoons on 25 December 1755. On 11 January 1758, he exchanged his commission with J. Freemantle to become lieutenant in the 15th Foot. He drowned with 25 grenadiers on 8 June 1758 when their boat overturned in the surf during the assault landing at Kennington Cove, Gabarus Bay, Louisbourg.

149 Colin Campbell was born in Scotland in 1716. He was a gentleman volunteer with the 15th Foot, then commissioned an ensign in the 15th Foot in Flanders on 15 August 1545. He was promoted to lieutenant in the 15th Foot on 4 September 1754. He died on 26 July 1758, the day that Louisbourg capitulated, from wounds suffered on 23 July 1758 in the trenches during the siege of Louisbourg.

150 Godfrey Roe was commissioned an ensign in the 48th Regiment of Foot in Nova Scotia on 6 June 1757. He was killed in action on 19 July 1758 during the siege of Louisbourg. Apparently, he was the only officer of the 48th killed at Louisbourg.

151 Abraham Hart was born in 1732, He was commissioned an ensign on 16 January 1756 in the new-raising second battalion of the 62nd (later 60th) Foot. He was promoted to lieutenant on 24 July 1757. Hart was killed in action on 8 July 1758 during the siege of Louisbourg. In an internal War Office list of 1755-56 of aspirants for commissions it was recorded that 'his father is a Man of Substance. Is about 24 yrs. Old and is very Smart & has had good Education', and that he was recommended by Lord Digby (BL, Add.MS 73,594, f.102).

152 Charles Baillie was born in Scotland in 1725. He was commissioned as second lieutenant in the 21st Foot at Gibraltar on 2 September 1756. He was promoted to captain in Fraser's new-raising 63rd/78th Regiment of Foot in Scotland on 10 January 1757. Baillie was killed in action on 8 June 1758 during the assault landing at Kennington Cove, Gabarus Bay.

153 John Cuthbert was born in Scotland in 1729. He was commissioned an ensign on 2 June 1747 in Drumlanrig's new raising Regiment of Foot for the Scots-Dutch Brigade. From Dutch half pay he became ensign in Halkett's Foot in Scots-Dutch Brigade, on 25 April 1756. He was promoted to lieutenant in Scotland in Fraser's new-raising 63rd/78th Regiment of Foot on 18 January 1757. Cuthbert died in action on 8 June 1758 during assault landing at Kennington Cove, Gabarus Bay.

154 Simon Fraser was commissioned a lieutenant in Scotland on 8 February 1757 in Fraser's new-raising 63rd/78th Regiment of Foot (Second Highland Battalion). He died on 18 June 1758 of wounds suffered on 8 June 1758 during the assault landing at Kennington Cove, Gabarus Bay.

155 John MacGregor Murray was born in Scotland in 1735. He was commissioned a lieutenant in Scotland on 6 February 1757 in Fraser's new-raising 63rd/78th Foot (Second Highland Battalion). Murray was killed in action on 21 July 1758 in the trenches during the siege of Louisbourg.

Capt Rogers's Rangers[156]—En^{n}. Francis Caruthers[157]

Wounded
Col Bastide[158] Chief Engineer

156 Rangers were troops skilled in North American frontier conditions and used for scouting. Major Robert Rogers organized independent companies between 1756 and 1761, mainly for the Lake Champlain corridor. When Brigadier Charles Lawrence went to Boston in March 1758, he recruited several independent ranger companies. Since Robert Rogers had engaged some of his men for the Crown Point expedition, his brother Captain James Rogers took command of the unit bound for Halifax and Louisbourg. See Boscawen, *Louisbourg*, pp.119, 138, 166, 349. For a note on Rogers' career, see, Chapter 5, Note 18.

157 Francis Carruthers was listed as a 'Voluntier' from the 44th Regiment in Roger's Cadet Company of 1757. He was commissioned ensign in the Rangers on 30 March 1758. He was killed on 8 June 1758 during the landing Kennington Cove, Gabarus Bay.

158 John Henry Bastide born at The Hague in 1700 and naturalized in England in 1713. He was commissioned an ensign as a minor in the Colonel John Hill's 11th Regiment of Foot on 23 August 1711. He was promoted to lieutenant in Montagu's 11th Regiment of Foot on 25 February 1718. He was promoted to captain at Louisbourg in Shirley's new-raising 65th Regiment of Foot on 1 August 1745. He resigned his commission in the 65th Foot on 24 May 1749. He was serving simultaneously in the Corps of Engineers, with a warrant as a sub-engineer from 14 February 1733, serving in Scotland, Guernsey, and Jersey. He was appointed engineer extraordinary on 11 August 1741 and in this capacity was chief engineer at Annapolis Royal and dealing with the defences of Nova Scotia and New England. Appointed engineer-in-ordinary on 8 March 1744, he was a Louisbourg in 1745 with Sir William Pepperell. After the French surrendered Louisbourg to the British in 1745, he made improvements to the fortifications. After the return of Louisbourg to the French in 1749, Bastide served at Annapolis Royal until 1751, when he returned to England. In 1754, he was assigned to Minorca and was there when the French captured the island. He was appointed director of engineers on 2 February 1748·(a commission re-dated to 14 May 1757 when the Corps of Engineers regimented and he was additionally made lieutenant-colonel. He was promoted to chief director of engineers and brevet colonel in America in 9 January 1758. In 1758, he was appointed chief engineer under Amherst for the Louisbourg expedition. He was promoted to major general on 21 February 1761 and assigned to the construction of fortifications at Halifax. Returning to England in 1762, he was promoted to lieutenant general on 30 April 1770. He died on 4 December 1770.

Royal____ L^{t}. Fitzsimond[159]__ L^{t}. Baylie[160]__L^{t}. Ash[161]__En^{n}. Waterson[162]___

159 Francis Fitzsimmons was born in Ireland in 1724. A manuscript Army List in TNA, War Office 64/9 lists him as 'of H.Gds', thus he was a superannuated Private Gentleman of the 3rd or 4th Troop of Horse Guards, disbanded in December 1746. He was commissioned an ensign in Pepperrell's 66th Regiment of Foot at Louisbourg on 15 August 1747. When the regiment was disbanded, he entered British half pay on 15 May 1749. From half pay, he was promoted to lieutenant in Shirley's new-raising 50th Regiment of Foot on 16 August 1754, He became lieutenant in the second battalion of the 1st Regiment of Foot on 27 December 1756. He transferred as a lieutenant to the first battalion of the 1st Foot on 25 January 1765. He was promoted to captain-lieutenant in the first battalion, 1st Foot on 26 December 1767. He was promoted to brevet captain on 25 May 1772 and retired 29 March 1774.

160 Alexander Baillie was commissioned in Ireland as an ensign in the first battalion of the 1st Regiment of Foot on 9 April 1756. In an internal War Office list of aspirants 1755-56 for commissions n 1755-56, it was recorded of Baillie, whose 'father was a Lieut. and Killed at Dettengen (sic)', was recommended by Lord Forbes (BL Add.MS 73,594, f.138). He was promoted to lieutenant in the second battalion of the 1st Foot on 2 February 1757. He was promoted to captain in the second battalion of the 1st Foot on 30 November 1761 in the place of Captain Benjamin Gordon. He went onto British half pay on 4 February 1767. He resigned his half pay in 1774 when he was appointed fort major at Fort George in Ardersier, northeast of Inverness, Scotland. He transferred from Fort George to be a captain in Lord Strathaven's Corps in Great Britain on 2 April 1783. He entered onto British half pay when Strathaven's Corps disbanded on 5 April 1783. From half pay as a captain, he became captain of the late Captain Robert McCrea's Guernsey Invalid Company on 12 March 1789. He then became captain in one of fourteen new British invalid companies on 20 October 1790. From that date. The company was reduced, but Baillie remained on full pay. In 1793, he became captain of his own new-raising Jersey Invalid Company. He was promoted to brevet colonel on 1 March 1794. His name last appears in the *Army List* in 1814.

161 Dudley Ashe was born in Ireland in 1730. He was commissioned in Ireland as ensign in the second battalion of the 1st Regiment of Foot on 16 February 1756. He was promoted to lieutenant in the second battalion of the 1st Foot on 22 November 1756. After being wounded at Louisburg, he served in the West Indies and was killed in action on 23 July 1762 at Havana during the siege of the Morro Castle.

162 Henry Waterson was commissioned in Ireland as an ensign in the second battalion of the 1st Regiment of Foot on 22 November 1756. Two years after he was wounded at Louisbourg, he was promoted to lieutenant in the second battalion of the 1st Foot on 18 September 1760. He died on 11 March 1763.

G^{l}. Amherst__ L^{t}. Hamilton[163]__L^{t}. Makins[164]__ Ens^{n}. Moneypenny[165]
G^{l}. Forbes—Capt Rycaut[166]__ L^{t}. F^{s} Tew[167]

---

163 Henry Hamilton was born in Dublin, Ireland in 1735. He was a younger son of Henry Hamilton, Member of Parliament for Donegal and collector of the port of Cork. The younger Henry Hamilton was commissioned as an ensign in the 15th Regiment of Foot on 4 September 1754 in Ireland. He was promoted to lieutenant in the 15th Foot on 2 September 1756. He was wounded at Louisbourg, he was wounded again at Québec on 28 April 1760 and taken prisoner. He was repatriated on 28 April 1762 and took part in the West Indies campaign. He was promoted to captain-lieutenant in the 15th Foot on 28 July 1762, and then to captain in the same regiment on 30 October 1762. In 1766, he was posted to Trois-Rivières in Québec province and, soon after, assigned command of Crown Point. In 1767, he was appointed brigade major to Brigadier Guy Carleton at Québec. He returned to Britain in 1768 when the 15th Foot returned. He retired from the Army on 7 July 1775, but returned to Canada. Going initially to Montréal, he became lieutenant governor of Detroit in 1775. When the settlers at Fort Vincennes declared an interest in joining Virginia during the war for American Independence, Hamilton took possession of the fort on 18 December 1778. On 23 February 1779, Hamilton surrendered to George Rogers Clark and was taken as a prisoner of war to Virginia. Accused of encouraging the native tribes to scalp patriot Americans, he was treated harshly and imprisoned at Williamsburg for eighteen months until exchanged in March 1781. In 1782, he returned as lieutenant governor of Québec. He reigned this office in 1785, returned to England, and then became governor of Bermuda, 1787-1794. He then became governor of Dominica in 1794-95. He died at Antigua on 29 September 1796.

164 Francis Mukins was born in Ireland in 1732. He was commissioned as an ensign in the 15th Regiment of Foot on 20 June 1753 in Ireland. He was promoted to lieutenant in the 15th Foot on 30 March 1756, serving as adjutant from 29 August 1756 to 31 August 1762. He was promoted to captain-lieutenant in the 15th Foot on 6 May 1762, and then to captain on 28 July 1762. He transferred onto British half pay on 27 May 1768. His name last appears in the *Army List* for 1800.

165 Joseph Moneypenny was commissioned an Ensign in the 15th Regiment of Foot on 6 October 1757 in England. He was promoted to lieutenant in the 15th Foot on 29 April 1760. He died of disease in Cuba on 13 November 1762.

166 Paul Rycaut was commissioned a lieutenant in the 49th Regiment of Foot in Jamaica on 13 February 1750. He transferred onto British half pay on 2 July 1753. From half pay, he promoted to lieutenant in the 17th Regiment of Foot in Ireland on 28 August 1753. He was promoted to captain-lieutenant in the 17th Foot on 2 February 1757, then to captain on 10 July 1758, and to brevet major on 13 October 1762. He died in 1768.

167 Francis Tew was born in Ireland in 1737. He was commissioned as an ensign in the 17th Regiment of Foot in Ireland on 27 April 1756. He was promoted to lieutenant in the 17th Foot on 2 February 1757. He was wounded and taken prisoner at Louisbourg on 11 July 1758. Released, he returned to serve in his regiment. He was promoted to captain-lieutenant of the colonel's company of the 17th Foot on 6 August 1770. Promoted to captain, on 14 November 1771, he was killed in action on 16 July 1779 in defence of the garrison of Stony Point, New York.

G^{l}. Whitmore's—L^{t}. Butler[168]__ L^{t}. Jermyn[169]__ L^{t}. Hamilton[170]
G^{l}. Braggs---- Capt. Browne[171]
G^{l}. Otway's--- L^{t}. Allen[172]__ L^{t}. Brown[173]__ L^{t}. Cockburn[174]__ Ens^{n}. Armstrong[175]

---

168 Piers Butler was born in Ireland and commissioned as an ensign the 35th Regiment of Foot in Ireland on 11 May 1748. He was reduced onto Irish half pay on 23 November 1748. From half pay, he was promoted to lieutenant in the 22nd Foot in Ireland on 16 February 1756. He was promoted to captain-lieutenant in the 22nd Foot on 26 May 1760; to captain on 12 November 1761. He transferred onto British half pay on 9 May 1764, where he remained. He last appeared in the *Army List* in 1808.

169 John Jermyn was commissioned an ensign in the 48th Regiment of Foot in the Middle Colonies on 1 July 1755. He was promoted to lieutenant in the 22nd Regiment of Foot on 4 May 1757. He was killed in action on 27 January 1762 at the Morne Grenier in Martinique.

170 William Hamilton was commissioned an ensign in the 22nd Regiment of Foot in Ireland on 16 February 1756. He was promoted to lieutenant in the 22nd Foot on 17 May 1757. Although wounded at Louisbourg he recovered sufficiently to serve in the West Indies. He died at sea on board the transport *Elizabeth* on 15 November 1762 en route from Havana to New York.

171 Hon. Arthur Browne was the second son of John Browne (ca. 1709-1776), 1st Earl of Altamont. Arthur Browne was born in Ireland 14 March 1732. His first recorded commission is an untraced captaincy of 6 March 1747. He became town major of Galway on 25 March 1748. He transferred onto Irish half pay on 16 December 1752. From half pay, he became captain in the 28th Regiment of Foot in Ireland on 10 December 1755. He was promoted to major in the 28th Foot on 16 December 1763, to lieutenant colonel on 17 June 1767. He resigned 8 September 1775. He sat in the Irish House of Commons as Member for Gowran from 1769 to 1776, and as Member for Mayo from 1776 to 1779. He died in July 1779.

172 Hon. Richard Allen was born in Ireland 1734. He was commissioned an ensign in the 35th Regiment of Foot in Ireland on 8 April 1755. He was promoted to lieutenant in the 35th Regiment of Foot on 14 April 1756. He was promoted to captain in the 35th Foot on 5 October 1760, to major on 25 December 1768, to lieutenant colonel on 25 December 1772. He retired 5 March 1775. It is uncertain if he was from the family of the viscounts Allen of County Kildare.

173 Thomas Brown was born in Ireland and commissioned an ensign in the 35th Regiment of Foot in Ireland on 2 May 1751. He was promoted to lieutenant in the 35th Foot on 16 February 1756. At Louisbourg, he was promoted to acting captain during the siege. He may have been the Lieut. Brown, who was one of the three officers who successfully landed their boats in the initial landing on 8 June 1758. On this issue, see Andrews, (ed.), *Journals*, Vol.2, p. 43, and Boscawen, *Louisbourg*, pp.389-90, note 35. Thomas Brown is not listed with the 35th Foot in the *Army List* for 1760. Later, he was promoted to captain in the 83rd Regiment of Foot in Ireland on 17 June 1761. When the regiment disbanded, he went onto Irish half pay on 6 June 1763. From half pay he became captain on the 13th Dragoons in Ireland on 2 June 1770. He retired 14 March 1772.

174 James Cockburne was born in Ireland in 1729. He was a gentleman volunteer on Braddock's expedition in 1755 and was made an ensign in the 44th Regiment of Foot on 26 June 1755. He was promoted to lieutenant in the 35th Foot on 26 November 1756, and served as adjutant from 25 March 1757 to 27 March 1772. On his promotion to lieutenant in the 35th Foot, Lord Loudoun described him as 'a very good Officer Putt in to Improve the Regt fitt for an Adjutant' (Pargellis, (ed.), *Military Affairs*, p.281). He was promoted to captain in the 35th Foot on 13 April 1767, to major on 13 January 1776, to lieutenant colonel on 30 October 1776. He was cashiered 3 June 1783. For the situation in the regiment in 1783, see Mark F. Odintz, "Charles Heathcote and the 35th Regiment" *Journal of the Society for Army Historical Research* 65, no. 263 (1987), pp.183-84.

175 Thomas Armstrong was born in Ireland. He served as a private in the 6th Dragoons and was commissioned ensign in the 35th Foot in England 9 April 1756. He resigned on 6 April

G^{l}. Hopson's--- L^{t}. Lilley[176]
G^{l}. Webb's----L^{t}. Hopkins[177]
Col^{o}. Anstruthers---Capt Smith[178]

1770, when he was appointed fort major at Dartmouth. He transferred from Dartmouth as a lieutenant to an Irish invalid company in 23 January 1779. He was reduced onto Irish half pay from 24 June 1783. His name last appears in the half pay list in 1791.

176 Moses Lilly was commissioned an ensign in the 40th Regiment of Foot in Nova Scotia on 26 June 1755. He was promoted to lieutenant in the 40th Foot on 18 March 1758. He was promoted to captain in in England in his own new-raising Senegal Independent Company on 1 March 1760. He died on 17 January 1762 in the Senegal.

177 Joseph Hopkins was the son of Benjamin Hopkins of Kent County, Maryland, but later claimed to have been born in New York. He may have served in the Maryland Militia in 1748. He was commissioned as paymaster general of Maryland troops in 1754 and was a gentleman volunteer on Braddock's expedition in 1755. He was commissioned an ensign in the 48th Regiment of Foot on 3 July 1755. He was promoted to lieutenant in the 48th Foot on 6 June 1757. He resigned his commission on 8 March 1759 and may possibly have joined Robert's Rangers as a sergeant and led the raid on Île aux Noix in September 1759. He returned to the British Army on 8 May 1762 as a captain with permission to raise his own company of rangers, 'The Queen's Royal North American Rangers or Hopkins's Rangers'. He went onto British half pay when the company disbanded on 24 December 1763. He resigned his half pay in 1766. He joined French forces in Canada and became a general in French colonial service. For further details, see Andrews (ed.), *Journals*, Vol.2, pp.171-72.

178 Edward Smith was born in 1735). He was commissioned a cornet in the 3rd Horse in Ireland on 9 February 1751. He was promoted to lieutenant in the 3rd Horse on 14 July 1756. An internal War Office list from 1755-56 of officers seeking promotion recorded of Smith that he 'Would quit the Horse for the sake of Rank in the Foot as the more Active part of Service. Was Aid de Camp to Ld. Rothes' (BL Add. MS 73,594, f.120). He did leave the cavalry for the infantry with his promotion to captain-lieutenant in the 58th Regiment of Foot in Ireland on 17 December 1757. He was promoted to captain in the 58th Foot on 26 January 1758, then promoted to captain in the 7th Dragoons in England as it was embarking for Germany on 1 May 1760. He was then promoted to major in the second battalion of the 60th Foot on 14 October 1761. He was reduced onto British half pay when the 3rd and 4th battalions of the 60th were disbanded on 24 August 1763. From half pay, he was promoted to lieutenant colonel in the 6th Foot in England on 24 October 1770. He then became lieutenant colonel in the 4th Horse in Ireland on 29 June 1771. On 12 December 1777, he became lieutenant and lieutenant colonel in the 2nd Troop of Horse Grenadier Guards on 12 December 1777. He was promoted to brevet colonel on 19 February 1779, then to major general on 20 November 1782. He became colonel of the 43rd Regiment of Foot on 26 April 1792 and held that post until his death. He was promoted to lieutenant general on 3 May 1796 and to general on 1 January 1801. He died 5 January 1809.

Col°. Frazer's---Capt McDonald[179]__ L^t. Campbell[180]__ L^t. McDonald[181]
___kill'd____ ____Wounded_____
Artillery – 1 Gunner- 3 Matrosses[182]_____ 1 Corp^l. 1 Gunner- 3 Matrosses

179 There were four captains 'McDonald' in Fraser's 63rd/78th Regiment of Foot. Making the following from a reasoned conjecture, this may be Donald McDonald, who was commissioned captain in the 63rd/78th Foot (Second Highland Battalion), on 12 January 1757, after having served in the French Army at Culloden in 1746 and elsewhere. After being wounded at Louisbourg, he distinguished himself the following year at Québec, where he led rescue parties from the Beauport beach after the abortive attack on 31 July 1759. He is credited with capturing *Capitaine* Louis Du Pont Duchambon de Vergor, who commanded the key sentry post on the cliff above the Anse au Foulon that protected the road that James Wolfe's troops was taking to the Plains of Abraham. In 24 April 1760, he was given command of his own company of men, who he had selected. He commanded this company in the second Battle of Québec on 28 April 1760, when he was killed in action.

180 Not identified among the five lieutenants 'McDonald' in Fraser's 63rd/78th Regiment of Foot.

181 There were four three lieutenants 'Campbell' in Fraser's 63rd/78th Regiment of Foot, making the following identification a reasoned conjecture. This one may be John McDonald, born in Scotland in 1727. He was commissioned a lieutenant in the new raising 63rd/78th Foot (Second Highland Battalion) on 23 June 1757. After being wounded at Louisbourg, he was mistakenly reportedly killed at Québec in April 1760, and survived the action at Îsle Royale. He exchanged as a lieutenant into Amherst's 15th Regiment of Foot on 14 August 1763 and served from that time as regimental quartermaster until 1775. He was promoted to captain in the 1st Battalion of the 71st Foot on 17 August 1776. He was reduced onto British half pay when his unit was disbanded on 4 June 1784. From half pay on 3 January 1787, he became captain of what had been Graham's Berwick Invalid Company. When the invalid companies were disbanded, he continued in the 'List of Officers of the Late Independent Companies of Invalids receiving full Pay' until his last appearance in the *Army List* in 1807.

182 Matrosses is the plural of matross, a junior or apprentice soldier in the artillery who ranked below a gunner. His role was assist the gunners by carrying ammunition as well as loading, firing, and sponging the guns. When marching, matrosses were beside the guns to guard them.

2

St. John River Campaign, July 1758–21 May 1759

July 1758--- All along this Coast, which is excessively rocky are great Plenty of Fish, & lobsters in shoals. at first it was Imagin'd we should have reduc'd Louisbourg time enough to have proceeded up the river St Laurence against Quebec, as the French had drawn away the greatest part of their forces, to Ticonderoga[1] to oppose General Abercrombie,[2] [Gen[l]. Abercrombie had 16,000 men][3] who was advancing into their country with a Numerous army. but he had the misfortune to miscarry, having met with a most severe repulse near Ticonderoga from Gen[l]. Moncalm[4] with 3,000 men

1 Fort Ticonderoga, a star-shaped fort originally built by the French in 1755-57 at the narrows near the southern end of Lake Champlain in New York. The fort was strategically placed to control the portage between Lake Champlain and Lake George, a key point on the water route connecting the St. Lawrence and the Hudson River valleys.

2 James Abercromby was born in Banffshire, Scotland, in 1706 and was commissioned a second lieutenant in the 15th Regiment of Foot on 27 August 1717, when he was 11 years old. His first serving position was as an ensign in the 17th Foot on 13 August 1725. He was promoted to captain in the first battalion or the 1st or Royal Regiment of Foot on 18 June 1736. He became major in the first battalion of the Royal Regiment on 22 June 1742 and was promoted to lieutenant colonel on 1 July 1742. On 16 June 1746, he was promoted to colonel. He served as quartermaster general for the 1746 expedition to Lorient, France. On 18 December 1755, he was appointed colonel to the raising 52nd (later 50th) Regiment of Foot. Following Lord Loudon's appointment as commander in chief, North America, in 1756, Abercromby became his deputy with the rank of major general. On Loudon's recall, Abercrombie became on 27 December 1757 commander in chief in North America and colonel in chief of the four battalions of the 60th or Royal American Regiment. After the French defeated him, at Fort Carillon (Ticonderoga) on 8 July 1758, he was recalled and replaced by Major General Jeffrey Amherst on 30 September 1758. Returning to England, Abercromby was promoted to lieutenant general on 31 March 1758 and to general on 25 May 1772. He became Member of Parliament for Banffshire in 1734 and in 1770, deputy governor of Stirling Castle. He died in 1781.

3 Note in margin marked for insertion here.

4 Louis-Joseph de Montcalm-Gozon, Marquis de Saint-Véran (called de Montcalm), seigneur de Saint-Veran, Candiac, Tournemine, Vestric, Saint-Julien, Arpaon, and baron de Gabriac was born in 1712 in the château at Candiac. At the age of nine, he received a commission as *ensigne* in the Régiment d' Hainaut on 16 August 1721. He purchased a commission as *capitaine* in the same regiment in 1729. His first active service was in the War of the Polish Succession (1733-35), when he served in the Rhineland. At the beginning of the War of the Austrian Succession (1740-1748), he was aide-de-camp to a general and then purchased a commission as *colonel* in the Régiment d'Auxerrois on 6 March 1743. While serving in Italy,

who was strongly entrench'd in well defended lines. [this affair was sadly bungled. The Genl, was ill advis'd had he not retreated but remain'd on the Ground after his repulse, the French were preparing, & determined to Abandon the Fort but he went away—precipitately][5] General Abercrombie retreated to the ground where Fort Willm Henry had stood & Entrench'd __on that part. where the breast work of Logs was was made by the troops in 1757—: he there began a Fort. the affairs of Louisbourg had taken up too much time, & the season being far advanc'd any further Attempts that way were laid aside, & the works of the Town being repair'd, the Regiments were Order'd to their different destinations; the 35th Reg^{t} & 2d Batallion Royal Americans were Order'd to the bay of Fundy under Col^{o}. Monckton.[6]
Aug 30th: the 35th. & 2d Batt^{n}. R^{l} Americans, Embark'd & saild for Hallifax

---

he was made a chevalier of the Order of Saint-Louis. He was wounded and taken prisoner at the Battle of Piacenza in June 1748. After he was paroled, he was promoted to *brigadier* on 20 March 1747. On 11 March 1756, he was promoted to *maréchel de camp* and placed in command of the land troops in Canada. He left France for North America on 14 March 1756 and opened his first offensive in August, capturing Fort Oswego on Lake Ontario. In 1757, he successfully attacked Fort William Henry at the head of Lake George. Following his defence of Fort Carillon (Ticonderoga) in 1758, he and the Governor of General of Canada and New France, Pierre de Rigaud de Vaudreuil, Marquis de Vaudreuil, had developed serious differences over military strategy. James Wolfe defeated Montcalm on the Plains of Abraham, where Montcalm died the next day of his wounds on 14 September 1759.

5 The comment between brackets is a note in the margin marked for insertion here.

6 The Honourable Robert Monckton was born in Yorkshire in 1726, the second son of John Monckton (1695-1751), 1st Viscount Galway (of the Fourth Creation). Robert Monkton was commissioned an ensign in the 3rd Foot Guards on 23 April 1741 and served in Flanders. He was present at the battles of Dettingen and Fontenoy. He was promoted to captain in the 34th Regiment of Foot on 17 June 1744 and in 1745, became aide de camp to the Earl of Dunmore, who had been colonel of the 3rd Foot Guards, when Monckton had entered service. In 1752, he was ordered to Nova Scotia and became a member of the Halifax Council, quelling an insurrection at Luneburg in a notably humane manner. He became lieutenant governor of Annapolis Royal on 21 August 1754. He commanded the force that conducted the 12-day siege that subdued Fort Beauséjour on 16 June 1755. He participated in the deportation of Acadians from the Chignecto Peninsula. In December 1755, he became lieutenant governor of Nova Scotia. While in Nova Scotia, he was appointed colonel commandant of the 2nd Battalion of the 60th Royal American regiment on 20 December 1757. While the Governor, Charles Lawrence, went to Louisbourg, Monckton stayed at Halifax. Following the expedition to the St. John's River in 1758, he was promoted to brigadier general on 9 September 1758. In May 1759, Amherst ordered Monckton to New York to command the Southern District in May 1759, but Prime Minister Pitt assigned him as second in command to Wolfe for the expedition to Québec. Seriously wounded in the lung on the Plains of Abraham, Monckton was unable to take up Wolfe's command due to his own wounds. While recovering, Monckton was made colonel of the 17th Regiment of Foot on 24 October 1759. In 1760, he took command of the Southern District and was promoted to major general on 20 February 1761. A month later on 20 March 1761, he became governor of New York and nominally held that post until 14 June 1765, although in absentia much of the time. He commanded the expedition to Martinique in 1761-62 and left for England on 28 June 1763 and did not return to New York. He became governor of Berwick-upon-Tweed on 14 June 1765, serving until 1778. He was promoted to lieutenant general on 30 April 1770. He served briefly in 1774 as Member of Parliament for Pontefract, a seat his father and grandfather had held. In 1778, he was appointed Governor of Portsmouth and was elected Member of Parliament for Portsmouth, holding both positions until his death in 1782. See *Oxford Dictionary of National Biography* and *Dictionary of Canadian Biography.*

Sept 5th. Anchor'd in Hallifax harbor, a detachment of the two Regiments that had been left here when we went for Louisbourg now Joyn'd us.

11th. Sail'd for the River St John in the Bay of Fundy.

18th. Game to an anchor near Partridge Island off the Mouth of the Harbour.

19th. Sail'd into the Basin.

20th. Landed near the remains of the Fort, built here by the French in 1750, which they demolish'd & abandon'd in 1755 in the appearance of a few arm'd vessels, under Capt Rouse, who had been with Col°. Monckton at the Reduction of the French fort at the Head of the Bay, call'd Beau-se-jour, now Fort Cumberland.

24th Began to build a Fort & make barracks for Winter Quarters: We had brought artificers tools & materials with us; the Soldiers made fascines & rais'd the Work on y^{e}. Bank which the French had not leveled;

Octr 30th The Fort being pretty far advanc'd, Col°. Monckton with about 400 Men from the Regiments & three Companys of Rangers, embark'd on board some sloops & schooners & went up the River St John's; it was imagin'd there might be settlements of the French on the Banks, which would be troublesome to use in Winter. An arm'd schooner [*Ulysses*][7] was lost in passing the Falls; these falls are about two miles above the fort, they form an Elbow, run with great rapidity, are very dangerous, full of Rocks & not to be passed except at Full Tide, then large vessels may go with safety & The River is of Considerable Breadth & Extreamly beautifull, appearing in several places like a large Lake, with many Islands & small rivers Emptying themselves into it; it has a diversity of Windings, but its Course in general is nearly North by West from the Fort; we found but one small Village call'd Grimross,[8] & a few stragling houses; these we destroy'd, with some Cattle, Gardens & fields of Indian corn, the Inhabitatns had fled into the woods with their Effects upon our first Landing at the Fort. We went up the River about 40 Miles.

7 Name in the margin and marked to be inserted. No information has been found on this vessel.

8 Now Gagetown, New Brunswick.

Novr. 12th. Col Monckton with the Troops return'd to the Fort, which was now nearly Campleted & Call'd Fort Frederick [under Maj^{r}. Morris[9] of 35th Reg^{t}.][10] A detachment from the five Regiments,[11] had landed at Cape Sable[12] to destroy some Settlements which the Enemy had there, they surpriz'd about 50 People with their Priest as they were Celebrating Mass in a Chapple, there were here a good Number of Inhabitants; who were a Terror to our back settlers in Nova Scotia: the detachm^{t}. destroy'd, all the Houses, Corn, Gardens &c. that they could find[13] & joyn'd us at Fort Frederick.

21st. Seven Companys of the 35th Regim^{t}, the Royal American Batt^{n} & 2 Comp^{ys}. of New England Rangers, Embark'd & sail'd for their Winter Quarters, the Roy^{l}. Americans & Rangers to Boston. five Comp^{ys} of the 35th to Anāpolis Royal, & 2 to Pisquid[14] in the Bay of Fundy. 3 Comp^{ys} of the 35th one Comp of Rangers Capt

---

9 Roger Morris was born in 1727 in Yorkshire. After serving as a volunteer, he was commissioned a second lieutenant in the 21st Regiment of Foot in 1 May 1745. He was promoted to captain in the 59th (later 48th) Foot on 13 September 1745. The regiment went to North America with Braddock in 1755. Morris was appointed major of brigade on 8 March 1757. In January 1758, he married Mary Philipse of the wealthy family of Yonkers, New York. Before her marriage, George Washington had once had a romantic dalliance with her. In February 1758, Morris was commissioned major in the 35th Foot, serving at Louisbourg and at Québec, where he served as second in command to Colonel Ralph Burton. Morris commanded a wing of Murray's army in the second Battle of Québec on 28 April 1760. He was promoted to lieutenant colonel in the 47th Foot on 19 May 1760, which he retained until he resigned in 1764. Morris settled in New York and built a country house on 135 acres of farm land called Mount Morris on the second highest point on Manhattan, stretching across the island from the Hudson to the Harlem River in present-day Harlem. The property was confiscated during the American Revolution. In September 1776, General Washington made his headquarters in the house, which survives today as the oldest house on Manhattan. It is a museum now known as the Morris-Jumel Mansion. In 1776, Morris returned to England, where he died in 1794.

10 The words between brackets are a comment in the margin marked for insertion here.

11 Lieutenant Colonel Henry Fletcher of the 35th Foot led this detachment.

12 Cape Sable is an island at the southern tip of Nova Scotia.

13 The detachment seized one hundred Acadians along with their priest, Père Jean Baptiste de Gray. About 130 Acadians and seven Mi'kmaq escaped. The Acadians were taken as prisoners to George Island in Halifax Harbour. For details, see John Grenier, *Far Reaches of Empire* (Norman: University of Oklahoma Press, 2008), p.108.

14 Pisiguit, sometimes alternatively spelled as Pisiquit, Pigiguit, Pisiquid, Pisiguid, is a region of western Nova Scotia of the former Acadian settlements along the Pisiguit River.

McCurdy's[15][L^{t}. Hazen[16] Ens^{n}. Butler[17]][18] were left to Garrison Fort Frederick. We had Plac'd two strong Block-houses on the Eminences near the Fort. These serv'd the Rangers as barracks. The fort is a square with 4 Bastions, built upon the bank of the Old French Fort, at the Entrance of the River St Johns, on West side of the Bay Fundy part of the Rampart, & the parapet entirely is rais'd with Fascines, after the Manner of a battery, with stiff Clay well ram'd between, about 10 feet thick, a strong Ravelin Covers the Gate, the Whole is stoutly Stockaded insde the Parapet, & well Friesed along the Cordon; we have 18 pieces of Cannon Mounted, from 12 to 24 Pounders: tis a most Excellent defense against Musketry.

15 John McCurdy was the son of James McCurdy of New Hampshire. He was one of the first 24 men that Robert Rogers recruited in New Hampshire to form Rogers' Rangers in 1755. He first served as a sergeant. On 24 July 1756, he was commissioned a second lieutenant in Rogers' company. He was promoted to first lieutenant on 24 February 1757. Nearly a year later on 14 January 1758, he was placed in command of one of the six companies destined for the Louisbourg campaign. After serving at Louisbourg, Amherst assigned him to Monckton for the St. John River Campaign. He was killed near Fort Frederick on 30 January 1759, when on woodcutting duty with his company, after a tree fell on him.

16 Moses Hazen was born in 1733 in Haverhill, Massachusetts. As a young man, he was apprenticed to a tanner. His first military service came in 1755, when he served in Nova Scotia as lieutenant under Major General John Winslow in Shirley's Massachusetts Regiment. In early 1765, he enlisted in Colonel Richard Saltonstall's Regiment to serve at Fort George. Commissioned as a lieutenant in the company commanded by his uncle Edmond Mooers, he served at Fort Edward and then Fort William Henry. In 1758, Robert Rogers offered him a commission as second lieutenant in Roberts' Rangers, but he declines on the grounds that he was already a lieutenant. On 7 April 1758, he accepted appointment as a first lieutenant in Captain John McCurdy's company of Roberts' Rangers and accompanied them to Louisbourg. On McCurdy's accidental death in January 1759, he succeeded him as captain in command of the company. He led the company in its attacks on Sainte Anne (Fredericton) and Grimross. He and his company served under Wolfe at Québec in 1759. Remaining there, he was wounded in 1760 and was convalescing while his company went on to Montréal. He accompanied Rogers' Rangers in taking Detroit. On the disbandment of his company on 24 March 1761, he had already purchased a commission as lieutenant in the 44th Regiment of Foot on 21 February 1761. When the regiment was reduced in 1763, he went onto half pay and settled at Iberville on the Richelieu, River, where he and his partner, Lieutenant Colonel Gabriel Christie, invested in land. At the outbreak of the American Revolution, he sided with the patriots and assisted the American attack on Québec in 1775. In 1776, he was commissioned as a colonel in the Continental Army and placed in command of the 2nd Canadian Regiment, also called Congress' Own or Hazen's Regiment, made up of soldiers raised locally in Québec. Hazen commanded it a number of actions—including Brandywine, Germantown, and Yorktown—becoming a brevet brigadier general in the Continental Army. He retired from service in 1783 and died at Troy, New York, in 1803.

17 John Butler of Boston, Massachusetts, joined Captain John McCurdy's company of Rogers' Rangers sometime after April 1758. Within a year, he was promoted to second lieutenant in Moses Hazen's company. A year later in 1760, he had become first lieutenant. As an officer in Hazen's company, he accompanied his unit to Detroit in September – November 1760. Rogers ordered Butler, who spoke French, to receive the capitulations of the French garrisons at Fort Ouiatenon (three miles southwest of present-day West Lafayette, Indiana) and Fort St. Philippe or Fort des Miamis (modem-day Fort Wayne, Indiana). Leaving these posts in October 1761, his unit was disbanded in New Yok on 24 January 1762. He is not to be confused with John Butler (1728-1796), who commanded Butler's Rangers in the American Revolution.

18 The names between brackets are a note in margin marked for insertion here.

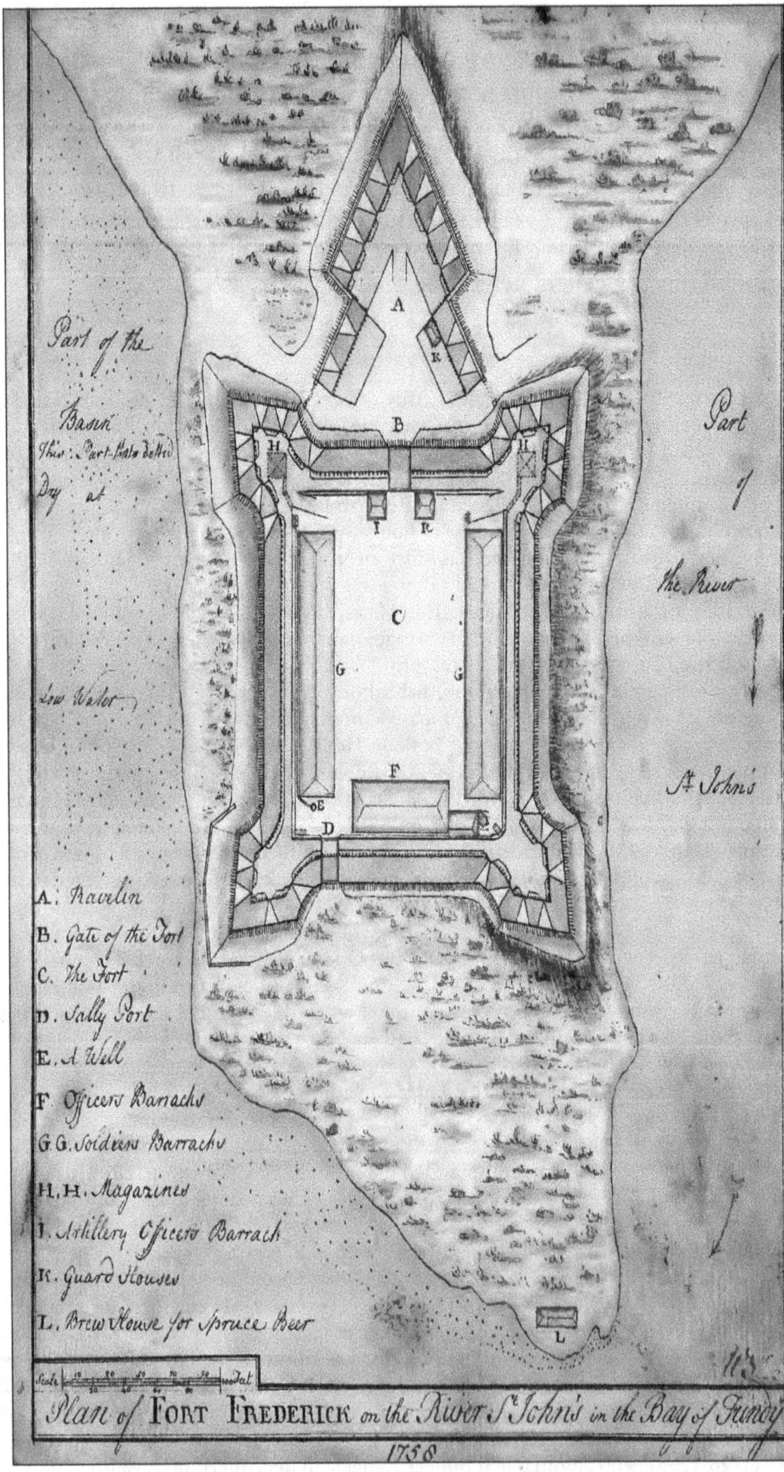

'Plan of Fort Frederick on the river St. John's in the Bay of Fundy' (dated 1758).

This Fort is Seperated from all our other Posts in the Bay of Fundy & if attack'd in Winter could not Expect to be succour'd, every port besides this, being Froze up, & no comeing here only by Water: we were therefor under the Necessity of keeping reconnoit'ring Partys constantly up the River, which was froze up to within about 5 Miles of the Fort. —(it Seldom freezes lower Down) these partys never got any intelligence, or made the least discovery, & we suspected the Enemy might assemble at S^t^. Anns[19] [a little Village on the side of the River St John's],[20] if they had any design, or making an attempt on us. the Winter was excessively severe, very hard Frost & deep snow.

1759
Feb 12th. L^t^. Hazzen of the Rangers with 21 men went up the River on the Ice with a design to go to St. Anne's to discover whether the Enemy were assembling or making any Preparations to disturb us. Capt McCurdy was kill'd by the fall of a tree, going on the same journey some little time before.

March 6th Lt. Hazzen return'd having been up as far as St Ann's, a very pretty French Settlement of about 140 houses, he did not find any inhabitants, & the Houses he burn'd; on his return through the woods, he chanc'd to fall in with one poor family, 6 he made Prisoners & after the Cruel custom of the Savages, whom the Americans Copy, scalped 2 Women & 2 Children. The Oldest Prisoner was a man of some Consequence & had a Commission as Major of Militia;[21] he gave us the Following account of the River St Johns; 'tis a Branch of the River S^t^. Laurence runs about 150 French leagues[22] through Accadia & emptys itself into the Bay of Fundy at this fort;[23] during the Summer it is navigable for sloops or schooners upwards of 10 French leagues,[24] but while the floods came down in Spring they may go farther. Bark Canoes or light boats may go entirely to Quebec. about 70 Leagues above this Fort, is a Prodigious Rock over which the Water falls 200 feet Perpendicular,[25]

19 Pointe-Sainte-Anne (later often anglicized to 'Ste. Anne's Point') was settled on the south side of the St Johns River in 1732 by Acadians who had fled Nova Scotia. It is present-day Fredericton, New Brunswick. This settlement was located on the opposite bank, about one mile upriver from the previous settlement at Fort Nashwaak, built in 1692 and captured by the English in 1695, abandoned in 1700.

20 The words between brackets are a note in margin marked for insert here.

21 Not identified.

22 A French league or *lieue* had several definitions at different periods. In France, there were different lengths for leagues for maritime, astronomical, and for roads. Taking the 1675 definition for roads established in Paris, it was 12,000 French *pied* or about 3.898 km or 2.422 miles, making the river about 363 miles long (584 kilometres). A slightly different modern definition is used in present-day Québec.

23 This informant either misinformed or was being misleading. The Saint John River is 418-miles long (673 kilometers). It rises in northern Maine flows north into Canada, and then runs south creating the western border of modern-day New Brunswick, emptying into the Atlantic Ocean in the Bay of Fundy.

24 The manuscript seems to show the number 11 written over to make 10. The number 50 is written in the margin on the same line of text, but it is not clear what its reference might be.

25 Grand Falls, or as originally named in 1686 Grand Sault St-Jean-Baptiste, where the water drops 75 feet (23 meters) into a gorge.

in an entire sheet across the River. A little below this they are oblig'd to Land, & bring both goods & boats on shore, & carry them near 9 leagues before they can launch them again, but from hence they meet with no interruption to Quebec, this is the Only Carrying Place on the River & they have made a very fine Road for the Convenience of Carriage. The French setled on this river about 70 years ago: when we arriv'd upwards of 90 familys liv'd on the banks, the back parts being uninhabited; when they first settled this River, there were about 300 Indians liv'd here, but by Wars & diseases lately introduce'd amongst them, they are diminished to less than half that number. When first we landed here, all the savages with most of the Inhabitants fled to Canada, a few only remaining, whom the suddenness of the Winter, & Domestick affairs prevented, & even those abandon'd their houses near the river, & made themselves little huts back in the Woods, to wait till the River should open, when they might go to Quebec. The only trade of these People was fur, & sometimes a little Indian Corn which they Carry'd to Louisbourg & Exchang'd for Wine, Brandy, tools and Woolen Cloath, or such Necessarys as they Wanted; the course of this River is Nearly S. & by E. thus far the french Man's account.

April 5th a Comet[26] was seen at Fort Frederick, it rose about 3 o'clock in the Morning, nearly E.S.E of the Fort it's course S.S.W it was seen only 5 or 6 Mornings, it's motion amazingly rapid.

22d. A man belonging to the Rangers, was taken away within a mile & half of the Fort, by a small Party of Acadians,[27] they were pursued but got off in their boat

Here we pass'd a very disagreable Winter, shut up in a Fort in the Midst of a Desart, totally secluded from all communication with our other Settlements in the Bay; Our Provision only salt beef, Pork & Pease; at one time we had only 5 days Provision for the Garrison, in store, but a small Vessel going to Fort Cumberland with Provisions, was fortunately drove in here, out of Which we got a supply. The Harbour forms a Basin,[28] extremely good, well secur'd from Winds, & tho' the River is very every year froze over, (seldom nearer than about 5 Miles of the Fort) yet the Ice is broke so small in Passing the Falls, that large flakes are rarely seen in the Basin to be any way hurtful to shiping. in spring & all Summer the Harbour is well stock'd with Excellent fish of Many Different kinds. here the tide rises 38 feet Perpendicular. The Soil of this Country seems to be very fine & if cultivated Capable of Producing every thing natural to the Climate. All about this bay we found as we thought, .Some very rich Oar, but when put into the fire Vanish'd in a sinking fume.

May 6th. Transports with Provincial Forces on Board, arriv'd here to relieve us.

8th. We Embark'd & sail'd about 12 o'Clock this Night, for Anāpolis Royal.

26 This was Halley's Comet, first observed in December 1758. It reached its perihelion nearest to earth on 13 March 1759. In 1759, the French astronomer Nicolas-Louis de Lecaille named it in honour of the English astronomer Edmond Halley (1656-1742), who had predicted the comet's periodicity and its reappearance in 1758-59.

27 Arcadians

28 Today, known as Grand Bay.

9th. at 7 o'Clock this Morning we anchor'd near the Town of Annapolis, it appears better at Distance than near hand, it lyes directly across the Bay about 12 leagues from S^{t}. John's. [Annapolis Royal was taken from the French in 1710—Here is a very pritty fort well constructed with Timber, with ravelins before the Curtains, but is much commanded by the rising grounds near it—& now in bad repair—][29] The Fort has been strong, but is now much out of Repair. Not long since this part of the Country, was well inhabited by French, who when it was ceded to the English, were allow'd to keep their Posessions, & were not to joyn, either French, or English in any future disputes, & were call'd Neutrals; but upon the Breaking out of the Present Troubles in America, they assisted the French as much as they were able, in giving them Intelligence, & frequently Joyning Partys of them from Cape Sable, & other parts of Acadia, who fell upon our back Setters, & either murder'd, or drove, them from their Lands; for these & other acts of infidelity they were dispossess'd, Many of them were seiz'd & sent to Boston, New York, Philadelphia &c^{a}. where they were well maintain'd at the Expense of our Colonies: at Present there is not above 30 of these familys, living here, & those of the better kind. from hence there is but little Trade. the two Companys of the 35th. Regim^{t}. Who had winter'd at Pisguid Joyn'd us here.

17th the 5 Comp^{ys} at Annapolis being Embark'd the Whole sail'd down the River[30] to the Basin.[31] a pleasant Passage of about 3 hours. [some small Vessels with part of the 43d Reg^{t}. came in here from Fort Cumberland where they had Winter'd—][32] The entrance into this Basin from the Bay of Fundy is through a Narrow Gut,[33] between two Excessive high hills, which with the amazing large rocks at bottom, over which the Sea rolls to a prodigious height, makes rather a dreadful than Pleasing appearance; however this Basin, a very fine Extensive piece of Water, soon opens to View the Prospect up the river is really delightfull.

21st. Sail'd from the Basin for Louisbourg.

29 The information between brackets is a note in the margin with no indication of placement.
30 The Annapolis River.
31 Annapolis Basin.
32 The words between brackets are in a note in the margin with no indication of placement.
33 The entrance into the Basin from the Bay of Fundy

3

Québec, 31 May 1759–24 November 1759

[May] 31st. Anchor'd in Louisbourg harbor: here the Fleet and army intended for the Siege of Quebec rendezvous'd.

June 4th. Many of the Men of War with most of the transports sail'd out of the Harbour, a very thick fog coming suddenly on, prevented the rest. it continued all the Next Day. & is very frequent in these Parts.

June 6th. The Weather being clear, the remaining Part of the Ships sail'd out of the Harbour; the Fleet under Admiral Saunders;[1] the army under Gen. Wolf.

The Fleet as Follows

Ships	Guns
Neptune	90
Royal William	84
Princess Amelia	80
Dublin	74

1 Charles Saunders was born about 1715. He passed his lieutenant's examination in the Royal Navy in 1734 and was commissioned a lieutenant on 8 November 1734. He served as first lieutenant in HMS *Centurion* during Anson's circumnavigation of the globe in 1740-44, rising to captain during the voyage, commanded the *Tryal Prize*, and later brought home Anson's dispatches. He was promoted to commander on 19 February 1743, and to captain on 26 September 1744. Place on half pay in in 1749, he was elected Member of Parliament for Plymouth on 1750, serving until 1754. He then served as Member for Hedon, holding that position until 1775. He served as treasurer of Greenwich Hospital from 1754 to 1756, and then comptroller of the Navy for a year in 1755 -56. On 4 June 1756, he was promoted to rear admiral of the blue and to rear admiral of the white in 1758. On 9 January 1759, he was appointed as commander of the fleet designed to attack Québec, with Rear Admirals Charles Holmes and Philip Durrell as his subordinate flag officers. On 14 February 1759, he was promoted to rear admiral of the red. After his return from Canada, he was appointed lieutenant general of Marines and Knight of the Bath on 16 May 1761. He was promoted to vice admiral of the white on 21 October 1766. He served as an Admiralty commissioner from 31 July 1765 to 11 December 1766. For the period 15 September to 11 December 1766, he served as First Lord of the Admiralty, resigning over a dispute with Prime Minister Pitt. Saunders was promoted to admiral of the blue on 18 October 1770. On 7 December 1775, he died and was subsequently buried in Westminster Abbey. See *Oxford Dictionary of National Biography* and *History of Parliament http://www.historyofparliamentonline.org/volume/1715-1754/member/saunders-charles-1713-75*

Vanguard	74
Terrible	74
Sterling Castle[2]	64
Shrewsbury[3]	74
Orford	70
Somerset	70
Devonshire	66
Bedford	64
Prince Frederick	64
Captain	64
Alcide[4]	64
Trident[5]	64

2 The 70-gun, third rate *Stirling Castle* was built by John Ward at Chatham between 1740 and 1742. Commissioned in May 1742, she served in the Mediterranean from 1742 to 1747 and was present in the Battle of Toulon on 11 February 1744. After a great repair at Chatham between March 1748 and August 1749, during which she was reduced to 60 guns, she was recommissioned in July 1755. After a voyage to New York and the West Indies, she carried the broad pennant of Samuel Cornish in the Channel in 1757 and was with Anson's fleet in 1758. Under Captain Michael Everett, she sailed to North America on 16 February 1759. After Québec, she returned to the Nore in 1760, then sailed for the Leeward Islands 9 September 1760. In North American waters in early 1761, she returned to the Leeward Islands in June 1761. During 1762, she was at Martinique in January-February, at Jamaica in April, and in the Havana operations between 6 June and 13 August. On Admiral Pocock's orders, she was stripped and scuttled on 14 August in the upper reaches of Havana harbor as unserviceable. Length of gun deck 151 feet, length of keel 121 feet 9 inches, breadth 43 feet 6 inches, depth of hold 17 feet 9 inches, 1,225 40/94 tons bm.

3 The 74-gun, third rate *Shrewsbury* was built by Wells & Co., at Deptford between 1756 and 1758. Commissioned in March 1758 under Captain Hugh Palliser, she was in Anson's fleet in 1758 when she participated in the capture of the French frigate *La Calypso.* She sailed for North America on 16 February 1759. After operations at Québec in 1759, he returned to England and sailed for the Mediterranean on 5 June 1760. She was refitted and paid off in 1763. After repairs at intervals in 1765, 1773, and 1777, she was recommissioned in 1777. She participated in the relief of Gibraltar in 1780 and was in the West Indies in 1780-81. Assigned to Hood's squadron in North America, she participated in the Battle of the Chesapeake Capes in 1781, then returned to the West Indies. In April 1782, Rodney declared her unfit. She was condemned and scuttled at Jamaica on 12 June 1783. Length of gun deck 166 feet 1 inch, length of keel 135 feet 2½ inches, breadth 47 feet 1 inch, depth of keel 19 feet 9 inches, 1,594 31/94 tons bm.

4 The 64-gun *Alcide* was designed by Blaise Olivier and built as *l'Alcide* at the French naval dockyard in Brest between 1742 and 1744. Taken by two ships of Boscawen's squadron, *Dunkirk* and *Torbay,* on 8 June 1755, she was eventually brought to Portsmouth, where she was purchased and refitted in 1757. Commissioned in April 1757 under Captain James Douglas, who remained in command until 1761. After Québec, she was at Martinique and Havana, where she coordinated the landing boats for the assault on Morro Castle on 30 July 1762. She was surveyed in 1764, but not repaired for service. She was sold at Portsmouth on 27 May 1762. Length of gun deck 159 feet, length of keel 128 feet 4¼ inches, breadth 44 feet 10¼ inches, depth of hold 1,373 75/94 toms bm.

5 The 64-gun *Trident* was designed by Pierre Blaise Coulomb and built as *le Trident* at the French naval dockyard in Toulon between 1740 and 1744. Hawke's squadron took her off Cape Finisterre on 14 October 1747 brought her to Portsmouth, where she was purchased and repaired. She was not commissioned until May 1755. In 1756, she was in the

Medway[6]	64
Prince of Orange. . .	60
Pembroke	60
Centurion	54
Sutherland	50
Frigates	
Europa[7]	40
Diana	36
Trent	28
Richmond	32
Lowestoff[8]	22
Scarborough	20
Squirrel	20
Hynd	20
Sea Horse[9]	20

Mediterranean and present at the Battle of Minorca and later took two privateers. In 1757, she was in the Leeward Islands and returned home to sail for North America on 14 February 1759 under Captain Julian Legge, who remained in command until 1761. After arriving at Québec as a convoy escort on 12 August, she remained there for the winter of 1759-60. In 1761, she was in the Belleisle operation and at Basque Roads in 1762. She was sold at Chatham on 15 March 1763. Length of gun deck 151 feet 6 inches, length of keel 123 feet 7 inches, breadth 43 feet 9 inches, depth of hold 19 feet 8 inches, 1,258 21/94 tons bm.

6 The 64-gun *Medway* was built by the successive shipwrights John Holland, Thomas Fellowes, and Thomas Slade at Deptford between 1751 and 1755. Commissioned in 1755, she served in Hawke's fleet and the Western Squadron in 1756. In 1757 under Captain Charles Proby, she took several prizes and was with Hawke's fleet at Basque Roads. During 1758, she was with Hawke and the spring, and Anson in the summer. She sailed for North America on 16 February 1759. In 1760, Captain John Tinker took command and sailed to the East Indies, returning him in 1765. Paid off, she was repaired and eventually recommissioned in 1774. She saw service in the American war until laid up in 1783. In 1789 she became a receiving ship. Renamed *Arundel* in 1802, she was broken up at Plymouth in 1811. Length of gun deck 149 feet 4 inches, length of keel 123 feet ½ inch, breadth 42 feet 10¾ inches, depth of hold 18 feet 6 inches, 1,204 24/94 tons bm, draught 10 feet forward and 16 feet 3 inches aft.

7 This name appears to be an error on Bamford's part. There was no 40-gun frigate *Europa* in the Royal Navy at this time. It may be written in error for *Eurus*, listed below.

8 The 28-gun sixth-rate frigate *Lowestoffe* was built at Limehouse Hole by John Greaves in 1756. Commissioned in May 1756, she served in the Western Squadron and in Cornish's squadron in in 1756. She took seven privateers in 1756-58. In October 1758, Captain Joseph Deane took command, she sailed for North America on 8 February 1759. She took the privateer *Le Chevalier de Barran* on 26 March 1760 and participated in the destruction of the 36-gun *La Pomone* and the 32-gun *Atalanta* in the St. Lawrence on 16 May 1760. She wrecked on Pointe-aux-Trembles on 19 May 1760, while participating in raising the siege of Québec. Length of gun deck 118 feet 3 inches, length of keel 97 feet 7 ⅜ inches, breadth 33 feet 10 inches, depth of hold 10 feet 4 inches, 594 33/94 tons bm.

9 The 20-gun, sixth rate *Sea Horse* was designed by Acworth and built by John Barnard at Harwich in 1748 and completed at Chatham in 1749. Commissioned in November 1748 under Captain Samuel Barrington, she served in the Mediterranean until 1752, when she returned to the Channel. She sailed for North America under Captain Hugh Palliser in January 1755 and returned home to sail for Newfoundland in 1756. In 1757, she saw action in the North Sea. Under Captain James Smith, she sailed for North America on 14 February

Lizard[10]	20
Race Horse[11]	20
Echo	20
Eurus[12]	20

Sloops
Porcupine[13]

1759. In the operations at Québec, she operated on the St. Lawrence *above* Québec and participated in the landing at Anse au Foulon on 13 September 1759. Length of gun deck 112 feet, length of keel 92 feet 6 inches, breadth 32 feet, depth of hold 10 feet, 503 78/94 tons bm.

10 The 28-gun, sixth rate *Lizard* was built by Henry Bird at Globe Stairs, Rotherhithe, completed at Deptford between 1756 and 1757. Commissioned in March 1757, she took a privateer and was with Cornish's squadron in 1757. In 1758, she was with Anson's fleet and joined in taking two prizes, Captain James Doake took command in October 1758 and sailed for North America on 18 February 1759. After the 1759 Québec operation, she returned to England and sailed again for North America on 29 February 1760. In North American waters in 1760, she was in the Leeward Islands from June 1762, then at Martinique, and at Havana from 6 June to 13 August 1762. Paid off in June 1763, she underwent repairs in 1769 and recommissioned in 1770. She served in the American War and remained in active service until 1794. She served as a hospital ship from 1797 and was eventually sold on 22 September 1828.

11 The bomb vessel *Racehorse* was a French merchantman named *Marquis de Vaudreuil* built about 1754 at Nantes. It is not clear whether or not the vessel was a prize. She was purchased on 28 April 1757 and fitted out as an 18-gun ship sloop at Rotherhithe by John Randall and completed at Deptford in 1757. Commissioned in June 1757, she took a privateer in the North Sea in March 1758. Between April and May 1758, she was refitted as Chatham as a fireship to carry 45 men, 8 6-pounders and 8 swivel guns. In September through November 1758, she was refitted as a bomb vessel to carry 70-men, 1 13-inch mortar and 1 10-inch mortar, 8 6-pounders and 12 swivels. Recommissioned in September 1758 under Commander Francis Richards, she sailed for North America on 16 February 1759 and spent the winter of 1759-80 at Québec, where she was reportedly under Commander Richard Turner and Lieutenant George Miller. By May 1760, she had been refitted as a 16-gun 'frigate' and escorted a convoy to Newfoundland. Paid off in 1763, she was put back into service from 1771 to 1773. Refitted in 1773 at Deptford with a double hull, she sailed for the Arctic under Commander Constantine Phipps. Paid off in 1773, she was recommissioned, reclassed as a bomb, and renamed *Thunder* in 1775. Recommissioned she sailed to North America in in 1776 and served at Charleston and Sandy Hook until taken by d'Estaing's squadron on 14 August 1778. Length of gun deck 96 feet 7 inches, length of keel 77 feet 1¼ inches, breadth 30 feet 8 inches, depth of hold 13 feet 4 inches, 385 66/94 tons bm.

12 The 24-gun *Eurus* was built as the French privateer *le Dragon* at Bayonne in 1756. Taken as a prize on 4 December 1757 by the frigate *Coventry*, in company with *America* and *Brilliant*, she was purchased on 5 June 1758 and fitted out at Plymouth in January and February 1759. Commissioned in October 1758 under Captain Joseph Deane, Captain John Elphinston took command in February 1759. She sailed for North America on 16 February 1759, participated in the Québec operations, returned to England and again to North America, where she spent the winter of 1759-60 in the St. Lawrence. From March 1760, she was under the command of Nathanial Bateman and wrecked in the St. Lawrence River on 20 June 1760. Length of gun deck 121 feet 9½ inches, length of keel 101 feet 6 inches, breadth 31 feet 10 inches, depth of hold 10 feet 6 inches, 546 72/94 tons bm.

13 The sloop *Porcupine* was built by Taylor & Randall at Rotherhithe in 1746. Purchased while under construction, she was commissioned in September 1746 under Commander August Hervey. She was in the Channel and the West Indies and took three prizes in 1747,

Hunter
Zephyr[14]
Scorpion[15]

Bombs
Baltimore[16]
Pellican[17]

---

remaining in the Leeward Islands in 1748. Returning to England in 1749, she underwent repairs in 1749. Recommissioned in 1750, she served on the west coast of Scotland and in the Channel. Under Commander George Hamilton, she sailed for North America on 22 September 1758. In 1759, Commander John Jervis briefly commanded her from circa May to September 1759, when Commander John McCartney took command. From 1761, Commander James Harwood had command and participated in the Havana operation 6 June to 13 August 1762. She was paid off in March 1763 and sold at Deptford. Length of gun deck 94 feet 4 1¼ inches, length of keel 76 feet 4⅞ inches, breadth 27 feet 9⅝ inches, depth of hold 12 feet ¾ inch, 313 75/94 tons bm.

14 The 12-gun sloop *Zephyr* was built as the merchant vessel, *Martin*. Under Commander William Greenwood, she arrived at Québec as a convoy escort on 12 August 1759. She had a complement of 80-100 men and carried 12 4-pounder guns. Stacey, *Quebec*, p.233; not in Winfield, *British Warships*.

15 The sloop *Scorpion* was built by James Wyatt and John Major at Buckler's Hard in 1745-46. Completed at Portsmouth, she was commissioned in June 1746. In 1749, she was in Scotland and in 175051 at North Carolina. Paid off in 1752, she had a middling repair at Deptford in 1754-55 and was recommissioned in 1755. She was assigned to the Shetland fishery service in 1755 and then served in the Downs in 1756-57, where she took two privateers. Under Commander John Cleland, she sailed for North America on 16 February 1759. Commander John Jervis took command in May 1759. By August 1759, Commander Thomas Hallum was in command. In 1761, she took the 10-gun privateer *Boscawen* off St Malo. In 1762, while cruising in home waters under Commander John Henshaw she wrecked in a storm with the loss of all hands on the Isle of Man on 23 August 1762. Length of gun deck 91 feet 2 inches, length of keel, 74 feet 11 inches, breadth 26 feet 4 inches, depth of hold 12 feet, 276 31/94 tons bm.

16 The 14-gun sloop *Baltimore* was built by Thomas West at Deptford in 1742-43. She was rigged as a snow and had a 'pink' stern. Commissioned in 1742, she took a privateer off Oporto in 1744. She cruised off Cape Clear in 1745 and served briefly under the command of Commander Richard Howe. In 1746, she engaged a privateer off western Scotland. Refitted at Plymouth in 1747-48, she cruised off the coast of southern Ireland and was paid off in 1750. After refitting at Woolwich, she was recommissioned in 1753 and served in the waters of North Carolina in 1754 and 1756, then in 1757 on the Halifax station. In 1758, she was refitted, then recommissioned as a bomb ketch in September 1758. Under Commander Robert Carpenter, she sailed for North America on 16 February 1759. Following the operations at Québec, she was refitted as a sloop at Portsmouth and recommissioned in January 1760. In 1762 at Sheerness, she was refitted again as a bomb. After cruising in July 1762, she was surveyed and sold. Length of gun deck 89 feet, length of keel 73 feet 10 inches, breadth 25 feet 3¼ inches, 250 76/94 tons bm.

17 The 16-gun sloop *Pelican* was originally built as the merchant ship *St George* at Shoreham in 1754. She was purchased on 28 April 1757 and fitted as a sloop, initially by Stanton at Rotherhithe and completed at Deptford on 23 July 1757. Commissioned in May 1757, *Pelican* participated in the Rochefort expedition. In September and October 1758, she was converted to a bomb vessel at Sheerness, carrying 60 men, one 13-inch mortar, 8 4-pounders, and 12 swivels. Recommissioned in September 1758 under Commander Edward Mountford, she sailed for North America on 16 February 1759. After Québec, she returned to Portsmouth in

Fire Ships
Cormorant[18]
Strombolo[19]
Vesuvius[20]
Rodney[21] Cutter

The Army consisted of the Following Regiments
15th. Amherst's
20th. Bragg's
35th. Otway's
43d. Kennedy's
47th. Lascelle's
48th. Webb's

June 1760, where she was refitted as a sloop during June and July 1760. In October 1762, she was fitted again as a bomb vessel at Portsmouth. She was sold at Deptford on 3 May 1763. Length of gun deck 86 feet 10½ inches, length of keel 71 feet 7½ inches, breadth 24 feet 9½ inches, depth of hold 11 feet 1 inch, 234 15/94 tons bm.

18 The 18-gun, ship-sloop *Cormorant* was built as the French merchant vessel *Le Machault* at Nantes. She was captured as a prize in April 1757. The Royal Navy purchased her on 28 April 1757. John Randall refitted her as a 'frigate' at Rotherhithe between 22 April and 6 June 1757, with the conversion work being completed at Deptford on 22 July 1757. She was commissioned in May 1757 and served in the Rochefort expedition in September. Returning to Portsmouth, she was converted to a fireship, carrying 45 men, 8 6-pounder cannon, and 8 swivel guns. Recommissioned in May 1758 under Commander Patrick Mouat, she was with Anson's squadron off St Malo on 6 May 1758. She sailed for North America on 2 February 1759, After Québec, she returned to England in 1760. Remaining in commission until 1761 with Mouat in command, she was sold at Woolwich on 23 December 1762. Length of gun deck 100 feet 8 inches, length of keel 81 feet 3⅝ inches, breadth 30 feet 7 inches, depth of hold 13 feet 6 inches, 404 47/94 tons bm.

19 The fireship *Strombolo* was built as a merchant vessel named *Owner's Goodwill.* The Navy purchased her from John Randall on 31 December 1756 and renamed her on 17 March 1757. Randall refitted her at Rotherhithe and Deptford as a fireship between January and May 1757. Commissioned in March 1757 under Commander James Smith, she was with Anson's fleet in 1758. Under Commander Thomas Smith from October 1758, she sailed for North America on 16 February 1759. After Québec, she was refitted at Plymouth between December 1759 and November 1761. Paid off in 1763, she was sold at Deptford for April 1768. Length of gun deck 92 feet 10 inches, length of keel 74 feet 2¾ inches, breadth 26 feet 1 inch, depth of hold 11 feet 4 inches, 268 59/94 tons bm.

20 The fireship *Vesuvius* was built as the merchant vessel *King of Portugal.* The Navy renamed here on 15 November 1756 and purchased her on 17 November. She was fitted out as a 14-gun sloop by Wells at Deptford between 11 November 1756 and 6 April 1757. Commissioned in November 1756, she cruised in 1757 and was with Anson's fleet in 1758. Fitted out as a fireship at Sheerness in April and May 1759, she sailed for North America on 16 February 1759 under Commander James Chads. After the Québec operation, she returned to England in 1760 and served in the Belle Isle operations during April to June 1761. She was sold at Deptford on 3 May 1763. Length of gun deck 91 feet 6 inches, length of keel 72 feet 3¼ inches, breadth 27 feet 10½ inches, depth of hold 12 feet, 298 65/94 tons bm.

21 The cutter *Rodney* was purchased in 1759 and used only in that year. Commanded by Commander Philip Percival and carrying 4 4-pounder guns, she was sent from Québec to Louisbourg with dispatches in late August 1759. Stacey, *Quebec*, p. 234; not listed in Winfield, *British Warships.*

58th. Armstruther's
60th. Monckton's. 2d. B^{n}. R.A.
60th Lawrence's. 3d. Batt^{n}. R.A.
78th Frazer's. Highlanders
22d } One company of Grenadiers
40th } from each of these Regim^{ts}.
45th } the rest of the Batt^{ns}. at Louisbourg.
Six Companys Royal Artillery
Six Companys New England Rangers
Not 8,000 Men in all —

The Whole Fleet about 200 Sail steer'd for the River St Laurence.

10th. Anchor'd at the Isle of St Barnaby[22] in the River S^{t}. Laurence.

19th. Sail'd higher up the River, several settlements of the French pleasantly situated on each side.

24th. Anchor'd at the Isle of Coudre.[23] here Commodore Durell[24] Lay, who had been sent up Early in the Spring with some ships of War to prevent any French ships from passing with supplys to Quebec; however some Frigates & Merchant Men with stores &c^{a}. had got up before him.

25th. Sail'd for the Isle of Orleans.[25]

June 27th. Anchor'd in the South Channel of the River, between the South Shore & the Island of

Orelans & Immediately began to land on the Island, near the Church of St. Laurent[26] without opposition before the army was all Landed, a violent Storm arose, which detain'd many of the troops on board, drove some of the Transports on Shore, Stove a Number of our flat bottom'd boats to pieces, & damag'd many more.

28th. The Storm continued till this Evening. [Sr Hovenden walker in an attempt against Quebec in 1711[27] mis-carried, many of his transports were cast away & about

22 Île Saint-Barnabé is located off the southern bank of the St. Lawrence River, off the present-day city of Rimouski, Québec. It is approximately 196 miles from the city of Québec.

23 Île-aux-Coudres is about 65 miles from the city of Québec.

24 Philip Durell had been a commodore at Louisbourg, but in February had been promoted to rear admiral of the red.

25 Île d'Orléans is located about 3 miles from the city of Québec. It is 21 miles long and 5 miles wide at its widest point.

26 Church of St. Laurent (Our Lady of Fatima Parish)

27 For details of the expedition under Rear Admiral Sir Hovenden Walker (c.1655-56 – c.1725-28), see Gerald S. Graham (ed.), *The Walker Expedition*. Publications of the Navy Records Society, Vol. 94. (London: Navy Records Society, 1953).

900 men Lost—the French built a chapel[28] in memory of ye defeat & dedicated is to St Victoire][29] about 12 o'clock this Night the Enemy sent down from Quebec. 7 large ships, fitted up as fire ships, to destroy our Fleet, as they lay very thick in that narrow Chanel, & the tide runs down at the rate of 7 miles an hour. This was a favorite Scheme of the French & was thought could not fail either to burn our whole fleet, or at least such a part of it as would disable us from prosecuting our purpose, & oblige us to retire they had therefor fitted out these ships at a very great Expense, & gave the Management of them to Chosen Officers; we were apprehensive of something of this nature, & our commanders had Provided against it a Frigate was advance'd aHead of the Fleet each night as soon as it was dark, that the Enemy might not Observe it; [a French frigate was sent down to cover the fire ships but as soon as our advanc'd Frigate fir'd on her, she tack'd about & want back again.][30] the Boats were kept Mann'd & well provided with Iron Chains, hooks & Instruments, either for Pulling the Vessells to pieces in the Water, or towing them on shore. the Night was Dark, but the Frigate a head observ'd some Vessels moving down & fir'd upon them, the Enemy supposing our Whole Fleet had advanc'd set fire to their ships. Our boats quickly got along side of them, tow'd some on shore before they reach'd our ships & some they Towed Flaming through the Fleet without Injuring even a boat, such Vigilance & good Conduct had been shown that this scheme, so much depended on by the Enemy, was render'd ineffectual. The burning ships with all their sails in flames coming through the Fleet made a grand, but Awful Appearance. The Enemy had a guard Patroling along the South Shore to pick up our People who might Escape from the Ships when fir'd, so little did they doubt their success.

29th. This night Brigad^r^. Monckton with 4 Regim^ts^. & a Party of light Infantry, cross'd the River to the South Shore, & took Post at Point Levi,[31] obliging some french Troops & Irregulars that were there, to retire after a Slight Opposition: we were much surpriz'd, that they should so easily give up this important Post, from whence we can destroy the Town, & they have now upwards of 20,000 Men in the Field.

30th. Col° Carlton,[32] with the rest of the army, who were encamp'd near the Church of S^t^. Laurent on the Isle of Orleans, march'd to the West Point of the Island & Encamp'd.

---

28 This is a reference to L'église Notre-Dame-des-Victoires de Québec, located on the Place Royale in Old Québec in the lower area of the city. Construction on the church, originally named for the infant Jesus, was begun in 1685. In 1690, following the failure of Phipps Expedition, the church was renamed Notre-Dame-de-la-Victoire. In 1771, following the failure of the Walker expedition, the church was renamed Notre-Dame-des-Victoires. The building was destroyed during the British bombardment on 9 August 1759 and rebuilt in 1762-66.

29 The words between brackets are a note in the margin with no indication for their placement.

30 The statement between square brackets is written in the margin with no clear indication of its placement.

31 Pointe-Lévy, now part of the new city of Lévis, Québec.

32 Guy Carleton was born in 1724 in Ireland. He was commissioned ensign in the 25th Regiment of Foot on 22 May 1742 and promoted to lieutenant in 1745. On 22 July 1751, he transferred

From hence we had a fine view of the Falls of the River Montmorency,[33] & the French Encampments reaching from Hence, through the Village of Beauport to the River S^{t}. Charles close to Quebec about 9 miles. we could see they were strongly Entrench'd, entirely along the Top of a very high bank over the River, had many batterys of Cannon & Mortars along the shore, with a great Number of Floating Batterys.

July 7th. Brigadier Townsend[34] with 3 Regim^{ts}. 4 Comp^{ys} of Grenadiers, & the light Infantry under Col^{o}. How,[35] cross'd the North Channel about 12 oClock this Night

to the 1st Regiment of Foot Guards as a lieutenant. On 18 June 1757, he was promoted to captain-lieutenant and lieutenant colonel in the army while serving as aide-de-camp to the Duke of Cumberland. He was appointed lieutenant colonel of the 72nd Regiment on 24 August 1758 and promoted to colonel in America on 30 December 1758. Wolfe appointed him quartermaster general and engineer for the Québec campaign in 1759, He was wounded in the head during the battle on 13 September 1759, while commanding the second battalion of the 60th Regiment. He returned to England in October 1759 and served in the Belle-Île expedition, where he was wounded again. He served as quartermaster general at Havana under Albemarle in 1762, where he was again wounded. Promoted to colonel on 19 February 1762, he was colonel of the 93rd Foot until it disbanded in 1763. While commanding at Québec he was promoted to brigadier in America on 3 October 1766. He was appointed governor of Québec on 12 April 1768 and colonel of the 47th Regiment of Foot. On 2 April 1772, he was promoted to major general. Later, he was an author of the Québec Act of 1774. Promoted to lieutenant general on 29 August 1777, he served as commander in chief, North America in 1782-83, 1786-1794, serving also as governor of Upper and Lower Canada. Knighted in 1776, he was created Baron Dorchester in 1786 and promoted to general in 1783. He died in 1808.

33 An 84-meter (276 feet) high waterfall.

34 The Hon. George Townshend was born in 1724, the eldest son of Charles, 3rd Viscount Townshend. His godfather was King George I. Educated until the age of 18 at St. John's College, Cambridge, he left to become a volunteer in the army attached to Lord Dunmore's staff. He was present at the battles of Dettingen in 1743 and Fontenoy in 1745. On 29 May 1745 he was commissioned a captain in Bligh's 20th Regiment of Foot and was present at the Battle of Culloden in 1746. Appointed aide-de-camp to the Duke of Cumberland, he was at the Battle of Laffeldt in 1747. Elected a Member of Parliament for Norfolk in 1747, he obtained a captaincy in the 1st Foot Guards that gave him the rank of lieutenant colonel in the Army. After falling out with Cumberland in 1748, he resigned his commission in 1750. After Cumberland was forced out of office as commander-in-chief, Townshend returned to the army with a commission as colonel on 6 May 1758. He requested assignment to a command fighting the French and was appointed brigadier general in America on 27 December 1758. He became colonel, 64th Regiment of Foot, on 9 June 1759. At Québec on 13 September 1759, after Wolfe was killed and Monckton wounded, Townshend was in command of British forces and accepted the surrender of Québec on 18 September. He became colonel, 28th Regiment of Foot, on 24 October 1759. Townshend was promoted to major general on 6 March 1761, then served locally in Portugal as a lieutenant general in 1762 before becoming Lieutenant General of the Ordnance on 14 March 1763. While holding that office he succeeded his father as 4th Viscount Townshend on 12 March 1764. He served as Lord Lieutenant of Ireland from 14 October 1767 until 30 November 1772, when he became Master General of the Ordnance and retained that post until 1783. He was promoted to lieutenant general on 30 April 1770, to general on 3 December 1783, and to field marshal on 30 July 1796. He was created 1st Marquis of Townshend on 31 October 1787 and appointed lord lieutenant of Norfolk in 1792. He died on 14 September 1807. See *Dictionary of National Biography* and *History of Parliament* http://www.historyofparliamentonline.org/volume/1754-1790/member/townshend-hon-george-1724-1807

35 The Hon. William Howe was born in England in 1729, the third surviving son of Emanuel Scrope Howe, second Viscount Howe, and the brother of the Hon. George Augustus Howe. William Howe was commissioned a cornet in the Duke of Cumberland's 15th Dragoons on

& Encamp'd close to the Falls of the Montmorency, that small River only separating over army from the French; the Porcupine sloop & Boscawen arm'd vessel,[36] were plac'd in the Channel the day before to cover the landing.

8th. Early this Morning Capt. Dante's[37] Comp^y^. of Rangers were Attack'd in the Woods by a large body of Canadians and Indians, they were soon drove by our Troops who lay nearest, but the Rangers suffer'd so much, that they did not act afterwards during the Campaign, having above 30 Men kill'd & Wounded; some Indians were found kill'd after the Skirmish.

9th. The Rest of the Troops from Orleans pass'd to the Camp at Montmorency, leaving a body to Guard the Point, where we had Erected a strong Redoubt & Battery, with Hospitals for our sick. Our situation was now a little Delicate, our whole force in this Encampment did not exceed 4000 men, we were unacquainted with the Country, & within two hours March of an enemy of above 20,000 Men, it was probable to Imagine that now was the time for the French to make a Push, when they saw our Army was divided & our Camp not Fortify'd, & they well acquainted with our Numbers. Yet they remain'd quiet & suffer'd us to strengthen ourselves in such a manner, that we very soon despis'd their Whole force. Our army at Point Levi was very diligent erecting Redoubts to secure their Camp, & Batterys to fire on the Town.

Jul 12th. the French sent over from Quebec about 1600 Men to Destroy our Batteries at Point Levi, they Landed a few miles above the Point in two Divisions a little before day, & took different roads; when they met; by some Misconduct they fir'd on one

---

18 September 1746. He was promoted to lieutenant in the 15th Dragoons on 21 September 1747. He went onto half pay when the regiment disbanded on 3 February 1749. From half pay he was promoted to captain-lieutenant in the 20th Foot on 2 January 1750. He was promoted to captain in the 20th Foot on 1 June 1750 and then to major in Anstruther's new-raising 60th Foot on 4 January 1756. This regiment was re-numbered as the 58th in 1757. He was subsequently promoted to lieutenant colonel in the 58th Foot on 17 December 1757, then to brevet colonel in America on 27 January 1758. At Quebec he commanded the 58th Foot and was assigned command of the Light Infantry. He became brevet colonel in the Army on 19 February 1762. He took command as colonel of the 46th Foot on 21 November 1764 and, in 1768, became governor of the Isle of Wight. He was promoted to major general on 25 May 1772. Appointed colonel of the 23rd Foot and Knight of the Bath on 11 May 1775, he was sent to North America, despite his opposition to the war and doubt as to the abilities of General Thomas Gage. Howe commanded the right of the line at the Battle of Bunker Hill. He was promoted to lieutenant general in America on 1 September 1775 and succeeded Gage as commander in chief, North America, on 10 October 1775. He was promoted to general in America on 1 January 1776. He was promoted to lieutenant general in the Army on 29 August 1777, then became colonel of the 19th Light Dragoons on 21 April 1786. He was promoted to general on 12 October 1793 and simultaneously served as Lieutenant General of the Ordnance and colonel-en-second of the Royal Artillery from 1 January 1784 until he resigned those posts in 1803. He died in 1814.

36 The 47-ton armed auxiliary ship *Boscawen* was hired in 1759 until February 1760. She carried 6 3-pounder guns and was commanded by Commander Charles Douglas, Royal Navy.

37 Not identified.

another, this Mistake was soon rectify'd, & they march'd on till their Van perceive'd a small Friezed Redoubt we had thrown up, on a Rising Ground to the left of the Batterys, this they did not Expect nor did they think Proper to attack it, but march'd back got into their Boats & went to Quebec, almost before our camp was alarm'd.][38]

13th. A Battery erected by the Enemy to enfilade our camp camp was destroy'd this night by our howbitzers at Mountmorencie.][39]

18th. The Squirrel man of War, two arm'd Vessels & two large Ships call'd Catts, pass'd the Batterys of the Town in the Night & sail'd up the river. The Diana Frigate was to have gone up but ran aground on the Rocks near Point Levi; she was got off the next day, without much damage [The Enemy's Floating Batteries came down & fir'd briskly on her but were Beat away, by a few field pieces down down to the water side which play'd on them][40]

19th. Gen[l] Prideaux kill'd by one of our own Shells in the Trenches before Niagara.[41]

22d. The Army under Gen. Amherst debark'd at the second narrows near the Saw Mill under Ticonderoga where Colonel L[d]. How was kill'd the year before.[42]

38 Bamford mistakenly entered this entry for 12 July 1759 in the manuscript at 12 August 1759. At the latter point in his diary he wrote in the margin alongside this entry 'This affair happen'd the 12th of July —by mistake was inserted here'. At the entry for 12 July, he placed a marginal entry that read: 'The enemy crosse'd the River St. Lawrence with 1600 men to attack the batteries but soon return'ed—as mention'd by mistake the 12th. of August—'.

39 The entry for 13 July 1759 is written in the margin.

40 The words between brackets are inserted in the line at the end of the paragraph.

41 John Prideaux was born in 1718, the second son of Sir John Prideaux (1695–1766), 6th Baronet. Commissioned an ensign in the 3rd Regiment of Foot Guards on 17 July 1739. When his elder brother, Saunderson Prideaux, was killed at Cartagena in December 1739, John became heir to the baronetcy. His son, John Wilmot, eventually succeeded as 7th baronet in 1766. John Prideaux was adjutant of his regiment at Dettingen in 1743. He was promoted to lieutenant in the 3rd Foot Guards and captain in the Army on 1 May 1745. He was promoted to captain in the 3rd Guards and lieutenant colonel in the Army on 24 February 1748. He became second major and brevet colonel on 2 May 1758. Following Lord Howe's death at Ticonderoga, Prideaux became colonel of the 55th Regiment of Foot on 20 October 1758. On 5 May 1759, Amherst was advised that Prideaux had been promoted to brigadier general. On 19 July 1759, while commanding the siege at Fort Niagara, he accidently steeped in front of one of his own mortars, just as it was fired. He was struck in the head and decapitated.

42 George Augustus Howe was born in 1725, the second, but eldest surviving, son of Emanuel Scrope Howe, 2nd Viscount Howe in the Irish peerage. George Augustus succeeded to his father's title on 29 March 1735. He was commissioned an ensign in the 1st Regiment of Guards and a lieutenant in the Army on 9 March 1745. He was promoted to lieutenant of the 1st Guards and captain in the Army on 9 May 1746. As an Irish peer, he was technically a commoner in England and became Member of Parliament for Nottingham in 1747 and retained the seat until his death. He was appointed aide-de-camp to the Duke of Cumberland for the 1747 campaign in Flanders. Promoted to captain in the 1st Foot Guards, this promotion made him a lieutenant colonel in the Army. On 25 February 1757, he became colonel commandant of the 3rd Battalion of the 60th Royal American Regiment. He was made brigadier general in America on 29 December 1757. Lord Loudon gave him a major

23d. The Enemy abandon'd their Entrenchments near Ticonderoga the Grend^{rs}. took Possession.

24th. Gen Johnson[43] defeated the French army going to reinforce the Garrison.

25th. Niagra surrender'd

25th. Colonel Townsend kill'd by a cannon ball in the Trenches before Ticonderoga.

26th. The French abandon'd the Fort at Ticonderoga this night—blew their magazine up & then set the Wooden Works of the Place on fire. at Ticonderoga Our Loss was 1 L^{t}. 15 priv^{te}. kill'd, 50 Wound^{d}. The above news was brought by 2 New England Rangers][44]

---

role in planning the 1758 campaign against Carillon in which he became a revolutionary tactician in adapting to conditions in North America. While at the head of an advance party of the Army, he was killed in an accidental encounter with French troops on 6 July 1758. His body was taken for burial at St. Peter's Church, Albany, New York. The original 1715 church building was replaced in 1808 and, again, in 1876, but his grave remains in the present church. See *Oxford Dictionary of National Biography and History of Parliament* http://www.historyofparliamentonline.org/volume/1715-1754/member/howe-george-augustus-1724-58

43 William Johnson was born in County Meath, Ireland, in about 1715. His mother was a sister of Admiral Sir Peter Warren (1703-1752). Johnson came to New York's Mohawk River Valley in 1737 to oversee one of Warren's properties. In 1739, he built the first of two home near Amsterdam, New York, called 'Mount Johnson'. Here, he developed a key trading post in the area between Albany, New York City, and Oswego. By the mid-1740s, he had developed close ties with the Native American alliance, the Six Nations, and particularly with the Mohawks. Governor George Clinton appointed him 'Colonel of the Warriors of the Six Nations' in 1746. Involved in local political and governmental affairs, Johnson was also appointed colonel of the 14 militia companies on the New York frontier in February, 1748. In May, he was also made colonel of the militia companies in the city and county of Albany. In 1750, he became member of New York's provincial council. By 1751, the subject arose of whether to have provincial or royal control of Native American affairs. At the 1754 Albany conference, Johnson had discussed the Native American views. The recommendations of the Congress were ignored in London to have the governor of New York be appointed commander-in-chief of provincial forces and that a unified policy in regard to Native Americans be administered by a superintendent of Indian affairs. On 15 April 1755, Major-General Edward Braddock gave Johnson the King's commission as 'Colonel of the Six United Nations of Indians and their Confederates in the Northern Parts of North America and Sole Agent and Superintendent of the said Indians'. With the agreement of the governors of the American colonies, Braddock agreed to the suggestion of Massachusetts Governor William Shirley to promote him to major general to command the expedition against French forces at Crown Point. Johnson had limited success at Lake George, but many considered him the victor. As a result, the king appointed Johnson 1st Baronet of New York and rewarded him with £5,000, while at the same time making his commission as 'colonel &c' a royal commission. In 1759, he was the senior surviving officer at Detroit and accepted the French surrender. He commanded the Native American forces in Amherst's 1760 campaign. He died in 1774.

44 The notes for 19 through 25 July are written in the margin and are all pieces of news from other places. They have been placed in chronological order here, but in the original document they appear in the following order: 19, 24, 25, 22, 23, 25, and 26 July, apparently based on when Bamford received the information.

26th. The 35th Regim^t. & some light Infantry being out with General Wolfe to reconnoitre a ford, about 2 miles up the River Montmorency, Were fire'd on by some savages; soon after the French sent up a large body of men to dispute the Passage, they supposing we had an Intent to cross here; these attack'd us with great Violence, & a sharp skirmish ensued, which lasted some time, this happening as they could wish, in a thick Wood, made them more bold & confident of success, however they were drove in the greatest disorder, we pursued them to the River side & kill'd several of them in the Water, tho' they fir'd smartly on us from a strong Entrenchment They had on the Opposite Bank. of the 35th. Regiment Capt Fletcher[45] & Lt Hamilton[46] were kill'd L^t. Field[47] wounded. Capt Mitchelson[48] of the Light Infantry Wounded. about 50 Men kill'd & Wounded; the Enemy lost someMen, & a few Indians—

28th. This Night the enemy sent down a Very long Raft of fire, compos'd of several large stages Chain'd together, it streach'd a great way across the River; many of our ships had mov'd up opposite the Point of Orleans.[49] The Fire Raft caught one of our Transports, but was soon Towed off without doing any mischief. [Our Sailors Ludicrously asked each other if ever they had Hell in tow before; alluding to the amazing body of fire on the raft when they were towing it away.][50]

31st. We made an attempt on the Enemys lines near Beauport [The attack at Beauport was not a plan of Genl Wolf's but by an order from the King—],[51] the Centurion lay in the north channel, & two arm'd Catts [Large flat bottom'd ships][52] were run on shore

45 George Fletcher was commissioned an ensign in the 35th Regiment of Foot on 6 June 1741. He was promoted to second lieutenant on 15 May 1742, to lieutenant on 29 October 1745, and to captain on 8 April 1755. He was killed on 26 July, although the commission books record his day of death as 27 July 1759.

46 William Hamilton had served in army of the Dutch Republic before he was commissioned as a lieutenant in the 35th Regiment of Foot on 15 April 1756. He was appointed quartermaster of the 35th Regiment on 24 February 1757. The date of his death is recorded in Army records as 25 July 1759.

47 James Field was born in England in 1743. He was commissioned ensign in the 48th Regiment of Foot (with Braddock's column) on 28 June 1755. He was promoted to lieutenant in the 35th Foot on 29 November 1756, to captain in the new-raising 108th Foot in Scotland on 20 October 1761. This regiment was raised for rank and sent to Ireland in spring 1762, where it remained until disbanded. Field wen onto Irish half pay when the regiment disbanded on 31 March 1763. He transferred from half pay as captain in the 44th Foot in Ireland on 30 June 1766. He was promoted to brevet major on 29 August 1777 in a general promotion; and retired on 31 January 1778.

48 James Mitchelson was born in Scotland in 1728). He was commissioned an ensign in the 28th Regiment of Foot in Flanders on 12 April 1744 (OS). He was subsequently promoted to lieutenant in the 28th Foot on 29 May 1745 and served as adjutant from 22 January 1755 to 9 April 1756. He was promoted to captain in the 28th Foot on 11 December 1755 and retired 23 June 1769. He died 5 August 1769 (*Gentleman's Magazine*, August 1769).

49 The tip of Île d'Orléans. The island is 21 miles long and its western end is located about 3 miles from Québec.

50 The sentence between brackets is a comment in the margin.

51 The words between brackets are in a note in the margin with no indication for their placement.

52 The words between brackets are an explanatory note in the margin.

near the Places Design'd to be attack'd. The Army from Point Levi was in Boats, & the Troops from the Montmorrency were in Motion crossing below the Falls to sustain the assault, the Grenadiers were to begin the Attack, who as soon as they were out of their boats, rush'd forward without Order or Regularity, nor did they wait for the troops that were to support them, they soon possess'd themselves of an Advanc'd redoubt and two Batterys, these lay close under the enemy, who were most strongly Entrench'd on a very high & steep Precipice, from whence they Pour'd on incessant fire on the Grenadiers, then—in some confusion in & about the Redoubts, many of them were kill'd & a great number wounded, & were oblig'd to retire to the other troops, now drawn up in Excellent Order on the Beach, whose Appearance deterr'd the French from following the check they had given the Grenadiers; [the Troops from the Camp at the Montmorency waded the River both going to the attack and returning, the Stream was very strong, & up to the Men's Middle. We were oblig'd to hold fast by each other to prevent being carried away.][53] An exceeding heavy shower of Rain falling at this time render'd their Entrenchments inaccesable The General seeing it impracticable to attack the upper Works, & the tide flowing in fast, which would prevent the return of the Troops to the Montmorency, thought Proper to Order a Retreat, this was perform'd with as much coolness & in as much form as troops would pass at Review, tho under the fire of three Batterys of Cannon & Mortars, which Play'd on them all the while. When the attempt was given Over & the troops drawn away the two Catts were burn'd. We had 11 officers kill'd, 46 wounded; 9 sergiants kill'd 26 wounded; 160 Men kill'd 580 Wounded, Drum^{rs}. included. We came back to our former Encampment.

Aug 1st. a scouting party of ours from Ticonderoga came in trade a report to the Genl. that the Enemy had abandon'd Crown Point.[54]

Aug 4th General Amhurst took Posession of the Fort, situated as the Head of Lake Champlain.

Aug 6th. Brigadier Murray with 1200 men, went up the River above the Town, in order to destroy some magazines. which the enemy had in the Country.

11th. a large body of Canadians & Savages fell upon a Party of our soldiers, making Fascines on the Montmorency side, the light Infantry push'd into the Woods after them, & put them to flight, however, they kill'd & wounded us a good many men & our loss Exceeded theirs greatly. the Batterys at Point Levi have good Effect, the Lower town is almost destroy'd & the Upper has been frequently in Flames. From our Camp at the Mountmorrency we insult the French Camp, throwing a shot into it constantly from our Morning & Evening Gun—

53 The words between brackets are a note in the margin with no indication of placement.

54 The entries for 1 and 4 August are written in the margin.

[12th. last night an Indian was taken alive by two of our centries. the Gen[l]. gave the Centries 5 Gui[nes] on 21st the Above Pris[r]. got into the sea from on board & Escap'd—It was the Admiral's ship][55]

Aug[st]. 25th. Brigadier Murray[56] return'd having Landed on the Quebec side of the River near De Chambaud[57] after two unsuccessful attempts; he burn'd a Large Magazine, with some Provisions, Baggage, a Quantity of Ammunition, Spare Arms, Stores & the Cloathing of the Whole French Army.

[26. a Serj[t]. of the 35th. Reg[t]. deserted to the Enemy he cross'd below the Falls, in the Middle of the day. Several shot fir'd at him both from Cannon & small arms—][58]

27th. Part of our army at the Montmorencie embark'd on board boats & joyn'd those at Point Levi.

---

55 This entry is written in the margin. It is not clear to which admiral's flagship Bamford refers. Vice Admiral Saunders's flagship was the 90-gun HMS *Neptune*; Rear Admiral Durrell flew his flag in the 80-gun HMS *Princess Amelia*; Rear Admiral Charles Holmes flew his flag in the 74-gun HMS *Dublin*.

56 James Murray was born at Ballencrieff House, Scotland, in 1722, the fifth son and 14th child of Alexander Murray (1677–1736), 4th Baron Elibank. James Murray became a cadet in Colyear's Regiment in the Scots Brigade of the Army of the Dutch Republic on 6 December 1736. He was commissioned second lieutenant in the new rising 4th Marine Regiment on 2 February 1740. He was promoted by a free death vacancy to lieutenant on 10 April 1741. He exchanged this commission, with a purchase, to become captain-lieutenant in the 15th Regiment of Foot on 5 November 1741. Subsequently, he was promoted through a free death vacancy to captain on 21 November 1741. When Murray became brigade major, he was promoted in the Army to major on 26 August 1746. He then purchased a major's commission in the 15th Regiment following the retirement of another officer on 15 April 1749. He was promoted to lieutenant colonel in the regiment on 5 January 1751. Murray was promoted to colonel in America on 7 January 1758 and on for the duration of Wolfe's expedition to Canada, he was made brigadier general in America. At the end of the expedition, he reverted back to colonel in America, but his substantive rank in the Army changed to colonel when he became colonel commandant of the second battalion of the 60th Royal American Regiment on 24 October 1759. As the surviving senior officer, Murray commanded British troops at Québec after September 1759. With the conquest of Canada, Murray governed at Québec one of the three jurisdictions of Canada. He nominally retained the post of governor until 12 April 1768, although he was recalled to England in 1766 to answer charges that were later dismissed. He was promoted to major general on 10 July 1762 and when the second battalion of the Royal American regiment was reduced, he became colonel commandant of the first battalion. He became colonel of the 13th Regiment of Foot on 16 December 1767 and was promoted to lieutenant general on 25 May 1772. He became lieutenant governor of Fort St. Philip at Minorca in 1775 and was named governor of Minorca in 1779. He defended the island against Franco-Spanish forces in 1781-82, but eventually capitulated. He was promoted to general on 19 February 1783 and became colonel of the 21st Regiment of Royal North British Fusiliers and governor of Hull on 5 June 1779. He died on 18 June 1794.

57 Deschambault, located on the north bank of the St. Lawrence River, is about 44 miles upstream and west of Québec. In recent times, this village combined with another and is currently known as Deschambault-Grondines.

58 The entry for 26 August is written in the margin.

Septr 3rd. The Last of Our Army at the Montmorency embark'd on board the Flat Boats, pass'd to Point Levi, & encamp'd there. at the same time this body was Getting into the boats, Brigadier Monckton Corps had got into boats & rowed towards the river St. Charles as if they intended to land there, by this the Enemy's attention was divided, & tho Gen Wolfe had only 1000 men, he perform'd a rest retreat without the loss of a single man, from an army above ten times his number, who lay within a few hundred yards of him, & dare not Venture to give him any Disturbance, except from their batterys. Whilst we lay encamp'd here, the General us'd many strategens & insults, to draw the French from behind their lines, & provoke them to action, but in Vain, they always remain'd quiet spectators of his Operations.

[4th. An Express was brought from Gen. Amherst by 2 Officers of Rangers & 4 private men they came from Crown Point in 27 days—whilst we lay in the Camp at Mountmorency we had frequent scrimishes with the Enemy who often disturb'd our Wood Cutters and fascine makers but they were always beat off.][59]

[5th. a small Schooner pass'd the Town about 3'oclock this afternoon, the Enemy fir'd a number of shot It was to no purpose—Schooner nam'd Terror of France.[60]]

5th a Body of 4500 men, were detach'd from the army, and march'd up the river on the South side about 9 miles above Point Levi, where they Embark'd on board the ships that had pass'd the Town, some time before; we frequently sail'd up the River & fell down again to amuse the Enemy, a large body of whom always attended us on the North shore throwing up works whenever we anchor'd.

[Sir Hovenden Walker miscarried in an Attempt against Quebec in Aug 1711—Many of his Transports being cast away & near 900 men lost—

At a meeting of the Gen[l]. officers w. Gen[l]. Wolf on consulting about this attack, they all disagreed with the Gen[l]. & protested against the action, Gen[l]. Monckton said he must agree w[t]. the Gen[ls], but whateer Gen[l]. Wolf pleas'd to order he would forward in & give it every assistance in his power.][61]

12th — The following Orders were given out

The Enemys force is now divided, great scarcity of Provisions in their Camp, & universal discontent amongst the Canadians, the Second Officer in Command is gone to Montreal or S[t] John's which gives reason to think that Gen[l]. Amherst is advancing into the Colonie, a Vigorous blow, struck by the army at this juncture may determine the Fate of Canada, Our Troops below are in readiness to

59 The entries between brackets for 4 and 5 September are notes in the margin.

60 Probably a British colonial vessel or privateer; there was no British or French warship of this name.

61 The two separate undated comments between brackets appear in the margin alongside the following entry for 12 September.

Joyn us, all the light Artillery & tools are Embark'd at Point Levi & the Troops will Land where the French seem least to Expect it.

The first body that gets on shore is to March directly to the Enemy & drive them from any little Posts they may Occupy; the Officers must be careful that the Succeeding Bodies do not by any Mistake fire up on those that go before them.

The Battalions must form on the Upper Ground with Expedition & be ready to charge whatever presents itself.

When the artillery & troops are landed, a Corps be left to secure the Landing Place, whilst the rest march on & endeavor to bring the French & Canadian to a Battle.

The officers & Men will remember what their Country Expects from them, & What a destermined body of soldiers innur'd to War are Capable of doing against five Weak french Battalions mingled with a disorderly Peasantry.

The Soldiers must be Obedient & attentive to their officers & resolute in the Execution of their Duty.

In consequence of the above order as many men as the F[l]att boats would carry were Embark'd in them at Night, from on board the Ships, & silently fell down the River with the Stream.

13th. before day break the Light Infantry under Col°. How had landed, the boats fell down a little lower than was intended, whereby the Men had a very Steep Precipice to climb, however they made no difficulties but pull'd themselves up by the stumps & twiggs that grow on the side of the Hill; a Captain's Party ported on the Top oppos'd them, these they soon routed taking the Captain, who was wounded, & most of the men Prisoners, & having dispen'd some Canadians, secur'd the road for the troops to March up, which they did as fast as they were disembark'd, the ships were the remaining part of the troops, came down & anchor'd near the Landing. Place, the boats brought the Men on shore with all expedition they form'd on the Hill as soon as they got up; the Forces from Point Levi were brought over & joyn'd the Rest; We landed at a Place call'd Fouloon cove,[62] about 3 Miles above Quebec. The Genl. observing the French Moving from their Camp at Beauport, & crossing the River S^t^. Charles, immediately form'd his line of Battle on the heights of Abraham, about 2 miles from Quebec; here we lay on our Arms, & were very much annoy'd by some Canadians, who from behind the Hills, & from a thicket on our Left, kept up a very galling fire, killing & wounding many Officers & Men.

About 9 o'clock the French Army had drawn up under the Walls of the Town, and advanc'd towards us, briskly & in good Order we stood to receive them; they began their fire at a distance, we reserv'd ours, & as they came nearer fir'd on them by Divisions, this did execution & seem'd to check them a little, however they stilladvanc'd pretty quick. we encreased our fire without altering our position, and when they were within less than an hundred yards, gave them a full fire, fix'd our bayonets, & under cover of the smoak the Whole line charg'd, when they perceived us, they immediately turn'd their backs & fled in great disorder, we follow'd them

62 L'Anse au Foulon, later sometimes called Wolfe's Cove, is located about one and a half miles west of the modern city of Québec.

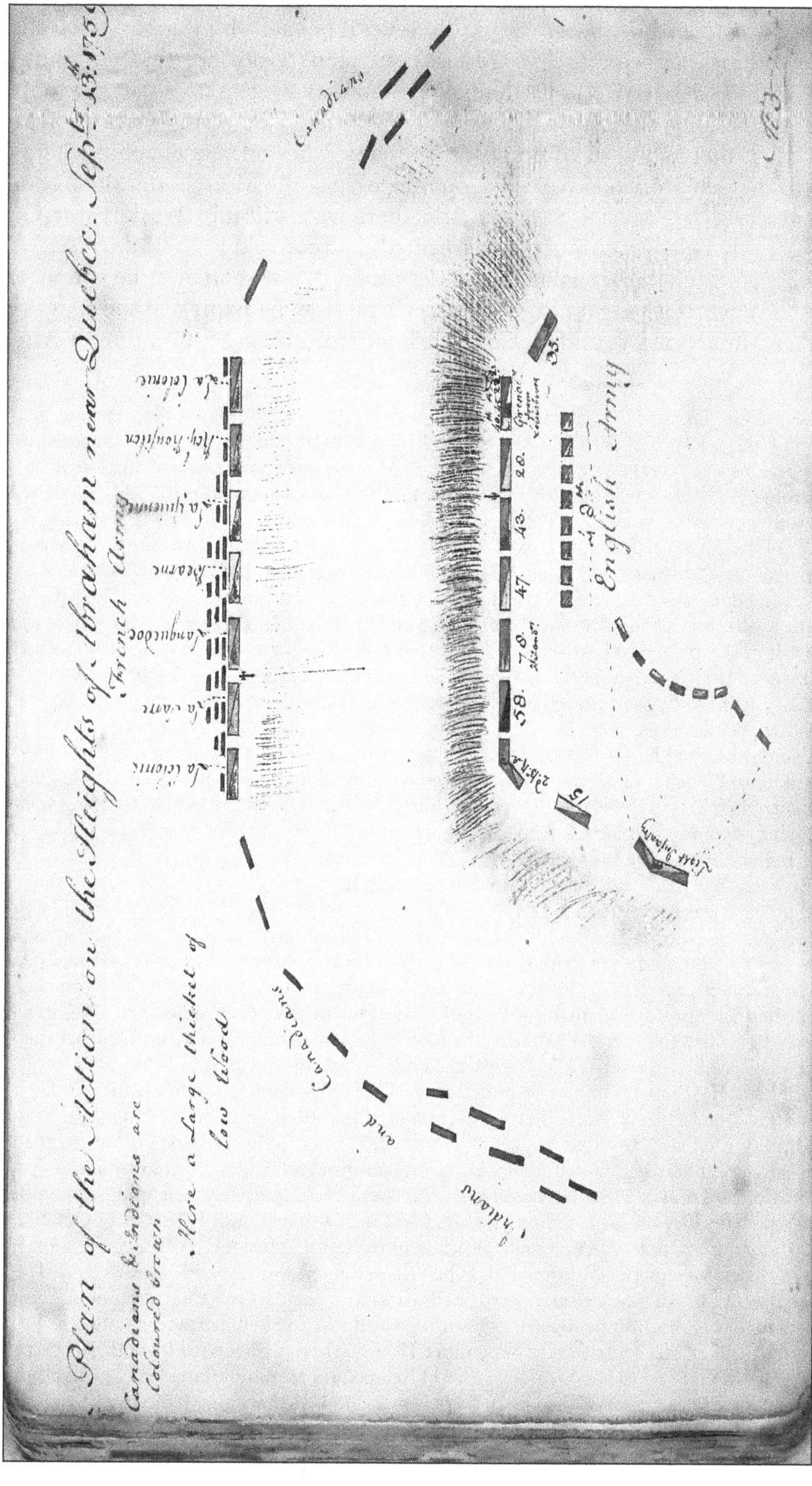

'Plan of the action on the heights of Abraham near Quebec. Sept. 13', 1759.

near the Walls, & some of our shot kill'd several people who were on the walls to see the action. they were in the greatest confusion, & did not think of Shutting their Gates till above two hours after the affair was over; nor did anyone appear on the Walls, long after the gates were shut. On the side of the French, General Moncalm & the second in command with many other officers & about 1500 men were kill'd. [Gen[l]. Montcalm Died about one o'clock the Morn[g]. after the Action—M[r]. Senesergue[63] —M[r]. De S[t]. Ours Brigadiers were kill'd.][64] We lost our Good General, truly belov'd, & Sincerely lamented, he receive'd a Wound in the Wrist very early & only wrap'd his handkerchief round it, but soon after he got another in the Body, which Oblig'd him to be carry'd away, & he Expir'd at the water side; Brigadier Monckton Wounded, Col[o]. Carlton, Major Barré,[65] Capt Smyth Aid De

63 Étienne-Guillaume de Senezergues de la Rodde was born in 1709 at Aurillac, France, the son of the governor of Aurillac. At the age of 14 in 1723, he entered his father's regiment, la Sarre, as a supernumerary *lieutenant* on half pay and was commissioned an *ensigne* on 1 October 1726. He was promoted to *lieutenant* in 1727 and, to *capitaine* in 1734. He served in Italy during the War of the Polish Succession and in both Germany and Italy during the War of the Austrian Succession. By 1747, when his *lieutenant-colonel* was unable to serve, Senezergues commanded the second battalion of his regiment. In 1756, now promoted to *lieutenant-colonel* he volunteered to go to Canada with part of his regiment. He sailed with his battalion from Brest on 3 April 1756 and arrived at Québec on 13 May, where the battalion was posted to Fort Frontenac at present-day Kingston, Ontario. He distinguished himself at the capture of Fort Oswego and at Fort William Henry. In 1757, he was second in command to Lévis in the expedition to relieve Fort Carillon (Ticonderoga). For his distinguished service in action, he was promoted to brigadier on 10 February 1759. At the battle on the Plains of Abraham, Montcalm ordered Senezergues to hold the Beauport flank until British intentions were clear, then to proceed in a forced march to the Heights. On arriving, Senezergues was ordered to charge the enemy's left line and in so doing was mortally wounded, dying the next day, 14 September 1759, on board a British warship. *Dictionary of Canadian Biography*

64 The words between brackets are a note in the margin.

65 Isaac Barré was born in Ireland in 1726, the son of a French Huguenot refugee from La Rochelle. He entered Trinity College, Dublin, in 1740 and graduated in 1745. Commissioned a second lieutenant in the 32nd Regiment of Foot on 12 February 1747, his rank was later changed to ensign in 1752. He was promoted to lieutenant on 1 October 1752. It has been reported but not documented that he took part in the Rochefort expedition in 1757 and served as a lieutenant under Wolfe in the 67th Regiment. At Louisbourg and Québec, he served as Wolfe's major of brigade with the rank of captain in America. In the action on the Plains of Abraham, he was wounded in the face and is depicted in Benjamin West's painting 'The Death of Wolfe'. Barré was promoted to captain in in the 28th Regiment on 27 February 1760 and served as brigade major under Amherst. On Amherst's recommendation, he was appointed Deputy Adjutant General in America and lieutenant colonel in the Army on 29 January 1761. He was elected Member of Parliament for Chepping Wycombe, Buckinghamshire, in 1761 and retained that seat until the seat until 1774. On 17 October 1761, he was appointed lieutenant colonel commandant to raise the 106th Regiment of Foot (Black Musquetteers) in Ireland. When the regiment was disbanded on 28 April 1763, Barré went on half pay. Through Lord Shelburne's influence, he was then appointed Adjutant General of the Army and Governor of Stirling Castle. With Shelburne's resignation as First Lord of Trade and Plantations in September 1763, Barré was dismissed from these offices. He subsequently served as Vice Treasurer of Ireland and Member of the Privy Council from 1766 to 1768. He resigned from the Army in 1774. He became Member of Parliament for Calne in Wiltshire from 1774 to 1790, and became a noted opponent of Parliamentary taxation on Americans. In Parliamentary debate, he is said to have coined the term 'Sons

Camp to Gen[l]. Wolfe,[66] & Capt Spittle[67] Major of Brigade Wounded, 1 Capt kill'd 12 Wounded, 6 Lieuts kill'd 26 Wounded; 1 Ens[n]. killed, 10 Wounded about 50 men kill'd; 540 Wounded & Missing. [650 kill'd, wound'd & missing including all ranks][68] the French had 9000 [9580 by the French returns][69] men in the field besides Savages, and a great number of the militia of Quebec who arm'd themselves & joy'nd their Canadians. Each army had only one piece of Cannon.

[thus soley & alone in opinion, he plan'd & put in execution that scheme, which will ever denominate him the Conqueror of Canada.][70]

Very soon after the action, a Large body appear'd in our Rear, these were the Forces that watch'd us up the River, under the Command of Mons. Bougainville.[71] [See a

of Liberty' to characterize Americans who opposed the Stamp Act. He became Treasurer of the Navy in 1782, Paymaster General of the Forces in 1782-83, and Clerk of the Pells from 1784-1802. He, along with John Wilkes, is commemorated in the name of Wilkes-Barre, Pennsylvania. See *History of Parliament* http://www.historyofparliamentonline.org/volume/1754-1790/member/barreacute-isaac-1726-1802

66 Hervey Smythe was born in Ampton, England, in 1734, the son of Sir Robert Smythe, Bart. His maternal grandfather was John Hervey, 1st Earl of Bristol. He served as a page of honour to King George II before being commissioned a cornet in the Blues at the age of 19 on 27 August 1753. He was promoted to captain in the 15th Regiment of Foot on 8 November 1756 and participated in the Louisbourg expedition, where he came to the attention of James Wolfe. On 4 May1759, Wolfe appointed Smythe one of aides-de-camp for the Québec campaign. He participated in the attack on Montmorency Falls and was severely wounded on the Plains of Abraham, where Wolfe was killed. Wolfe left him and several others 100 guineas each for swords and rings of remembrance. Due to his wounds, he returned to England shortly after the battle and brought with him sketches that he had done. Smythe became noted as one of the first military artists to depict Canadian scenes. His sketch of the attack on Québec was engraved and published about 1760 in London in addition to 'Six Elegant Views of the most remarkable places in the River and Gulph of St. Lawrence'. Smythe returned to military service as was promoted to captain in the 2nd Dragoon Guards on 13 January 1760, to brevet lieutenant colonel on 26 November 1762, and to captain and lieutenant colonel in the 3rd Foot Guards on 26 October 1763. He retired on 12 May 1769. It is said that Benjamin West included his portrait in his painting of 'The Death of General Wolfe' in 1770-71, depicting him in the center of the painting holding his right arm. Smythe succeeded his father as baronet in 1783 and died in 1811, having never fully recovered from his wounds.

67 John Spital was commissioned an ensign in the 58th Regiment of Foot on 8 February 1743. He was promoted to lieutenant on 8 March 1748. The 58th regiment was renumbered in 1749, while Spital was serving in it and when it became the 47th Foot. He was promoted to captain-lieutenant in the 47th Foot on 2 July 1753, to captain on 24 November 1755, to major on 1 March 1760, and to lieutenant colonel of the 47th Foot on 15 June 1764. He died on 4 March 1765 at Cork, Ireland.

68 The information between brackets is Bamford's updated casualty statistics written in the margin.

69 The information between brackets is Bamford's updated casualty statistics written in the margin.

70 The words between brackets are a reference to Wolfe in the margin with no indication for their placement.

71 Louis-Antoine de Bougainville was born in 1729 in Paris, where his father was a notary at Châtelet and a member of the King's Council. He received a classical education and excelled in mathematics, he joined the Mousquetaires Noirs in 1750. He became adjutant in the

Remark at the later end of the book][72] Brig^r Townsend, who now Commanded us, sent two Regiments with two pieces of Cannon against them; They did not chuse to try the event of Scuffle, but made off. Lay on the field of battle this Night.

14th. Encamp'd on the Place of Action, began to build Redoubts to secure our Camp, & Throw up some Works towards the Town, the Enemy threw shot and shells from the Ramparts into the Camp.

Sept 17th. The French sent out from Quebec to desire terms of Capitulation; several well drest People came out & told us they were Starving in town.

18th. Terms [They were allow'd the Honours of war][73] being agreed on Monsr Ramsay,[74] the Lieut: Governour, Deliver'd up the Town. The Inhabitants had no

---

Régiment de Picardie in 1753. *Lieutenant Général* François de Chevert appointed his as his aide-de camp in 1754. In 1755, he served as secretary to *Maréchal* de Lévis-Mirepoix on a diplomatic mission to London and, in the same yea, published his *Traité de calcul integral.* On completion of his assignment in London, he was promoted to lieutenant in the Régiment d'Apchon. On 8 January 1756, the Royal Society of London elected him Fellow, recognizing his work on integral calculus. Promoted to *capitaine* on 27 February 1757. He sailed for Canada, where the Marquis de Montcalm selected him as his aide-de-camp. He was with Montcalm at Oswego in August 1756 and was wounded at Fort Carillon in July 1758. He returned to France in September 1758 with Montcalm's reports and was prompted to *colonel* and appointed Chevalier de Saint-Louis on 28 March 1759. He sailed for Canada, arriving on 10 May. He took command of French troops located between Québec and Montréal. Unaware of Wolfe's landing on 13 September, he was not able to supply troops to counter that attack. In March 1760, he was ordered to command on the Île aux Noix. When attacked by Haviland on 17 August 1760, he abandoned the position. After the Seven Years War, he returned to France. At his own expense, he attempted to colonize the Falkland Islands in 1763, but abandoned the project. He obtained an appointment in the French Navy in command of the frigate *La Boudeuse* and the transport *L'Etoile* and sailed on a voyage of discovery in 1766-69. He published an account of his voyage and saw much active service in command of a frigate during the War of the American Revolution between 1779 and 1782 and was promoted to *chef d'escadre*. He reentered the army and became *maréchel de camp*. After the end of the American War, he returned to Paris and was promoted to *vice-amiral* in 1791. He escaped the Paris massacres of the French Revolution and retired to his estate in Normandy where he devoted himself to science. Napoleon appointed him a senator, count of the Empire, and a member of the Légion d'Honneur. He died 1811. The largest island of the Solomon Group in the Pacific Ocean is named after Bougainville as is the strait separating it from Choiseul Island. His name was given to the plant Bougainvillea.

72 The comment between brackets is a note in the margin that appears, by the placement of an "x" in front of Townshend's name to apply to him rather than to Bougainville, whose name is on the previous line. See note dated 13 September 1759 on p.156.

73 The words between brackets are a note in the margin.

74 Jean-Baptiste-Nicolas-Roc de Ramezay was born in 1708 at Montreal, where he spent his childhood in the Château de Ramezay (now a museum in Montreal). In 1720, he was commissioned an *ensigne* in the Compagnie franche de la Marine. He was promoted to *lieutenant* on 23 April 1726. For the next twenty years, he served mainly in the west, ranging from Fort Niagara, Chaquemegon on Lake Superior to Fort La Tourette on Lake Nipigon at the mouth of the Onaman River. On 20 March 1734, he was promoted to *capitaine* and in 1736 commanded an expedition to Acadia. He was appointed Chevalier de Saint-Louis on 15 February 1748. On 1 May 1749, he was appointed major of Québec and in 1758 was

provisions for some Days, but as they were served with it from our stores. Monsr. Vaudruiel[75] the Governour Genl. of Canada went off with the remains of the French army, towards Montreal—

[26th. the French troops to the number of 600 embark'd for France.][76]

Oct 10th. The Admiral & Fleet in the Baison weighed anchor & sail'd for Coudre. Saluting the Garrison with 21 Guns—2 Sloops of War. the Race Horse 20 & Porupine 18 Guns to winter at Quebec Captaims Miller & McCartney—

26th Gen Moncton sail'd down the river.

Nov 24th this night the French ships passed the Town & sail'd down the river except one which ran aground above the town- their number 6 or 7. Capt Millar with about 40 of his Men going on board the French ship which ran aground & striking a light it catch'd some loose powder which communicated with the Amunition & blew up the Vessel, kill'd most of the men & wounded the Capt so dreadfully that he died soon after.[77]

---

promoted to *lieutenant-colonel* while serving as the King's Lieutenant at Québec. Following Montcalm's defeat on the Plains of Abraham, Ramezay was left in charge at Québec. As instructed by Vaudreuil, he surrendered the city on 18 September 1759. He embarked for France on 22 September and sailed in October. His wife sold the family property and joined him in 1763 in Blaye on the Gironde River in southwestern France, where he died in 1777.

75 Pierre de Rigaud de Vaudreuil de Cavignal, marquis de Vaudreuil de Cavignal, was born at Québec in 1698, the son of Philippe de Rigaud, Marquis de Vaudreuil, governor-general of New France 1703-1725. In 1708, Pierre de Rigàud de Vaudreuil was commissioned *ensigne* in the Compagnies Franches de la Marine. On 5 July 1711, he was promoted to *lieutenant* and in the same year also was entered as a midshipman in the French Navy. In 1713, his father sent him to France as his personal messenger. He returned to Canada in 1715 promoted to *capitaine.* He was promoted to major in 1726. Through family influence, he became governor of Trois-Rivières from 1733 to 1743, and then governor of Louisiana, serving from 1 July 1741 to 8 May 1753. He returned to France, where on 1 January 1755, he was appointed governor-general of New France. He served as the last French governor–general of New France, 1755-1760. He died in Paris in 1778.

76 A note in the margin

77 George Miller was commissioned on 1 March 1758 as a lieutenant in the Royal Navy. On 24 November 1759, he was in command of HM frigate *Seahorse.* He died of his wounds on 29 November and his lieutenant died on 1 December 1759.

4

The Reduction of Canada, November 1759–September 1760

[This Winter a subscription was made for the starving Canadians; by the Officers Sold to English merchants in Quebec, by which much money was gather'd & reliev'd the poor Wretches. This their own Clergy confest would not have been done had it been our Case.][1]

Upon our taking Posession of Quebec, we found every thing in the greatest disorder, the Upper Town very much shatter'd & the lower Town quite demolish'd; [torn page; word missing] Effect had our batterys at the Point Levi.

We Immediately began to repair the Houses to quarter our troops; the Winter set in Early & very severe, which caus'd our Soldiers to suffer many but unavoidable hardships, such as Cold & bad Lodging; cutting & drawing home the firing for themselves & the officers, in the extremity of the Weather; frequent Fatigues & watchings hard duty & much Affliction from the Scurvy, occasion'd by living entirely on salt Provisions, nor could the Officers procure fresh for themselves at all times. Some officers, & a great number of Men died, or were disabled during the Course of this Winter, which was more severe than commonly happens here—

Upon the Frost setting in, the People of this Country kill all the Meat they propose using for the Winter it freezes & is preserv'd fresh, the Enemy knowing this, & suspecting we might be supply'd, sent down partys on the South side the river to secure all the provisions they could find; as we were ignorant of their intent, at first we did not mind them, tho' we could see them every day going backward & forward on the opposite side the Water, but when we were told who they were about, our light Infantry were sent over [the] River on the Ice, & presently dislodg'd them & made a few prisoners, however we had the Mortification to find they had carry'd off all the French Provisions to Jacques' Cartier,[2] where their army had taken Post & strongly fortify'd, this lyes on the Quebec side about 30 miles up the River, by which they prevented any provisions being brought into the Garrison from that side, & the Inhabitants on the South side being Now plunder'd by them, made our distresses in

1 This entry is an undated note in the margin.

2 The Jacques-Cartier River flows into the St. Lawrence River about 25 miles west of the city of Québec. The mouth of the river is the sire of the early 20th century industrial town, Donnacona. Before the town was founded the place was known as Pointe-aux-Écureuils.

that point very great. Some time after this they went down a Large force, to Establish a post at Point Levi and bombard the town.

[Feb 1760. The River St. Lawrence froze across.]

[Feb^{ry} from the 12th to 28th][3]
we march'd over the river on the Ice, drawing two pieces of Cannon 6 Pounds with us, [4 Regiments with Lt infantry march'd crossed the River on the Ice & drag'd 4 Six Pounders with them. 2 more were left on the ice ready if wanted. The Enemy had near 1000 Men they lost about 60 Men—][4] soon oblig'd them to relinquish that scheme, & make the best of their way back, we took a few prisoners to prevent any more disturbances from the Quarter, we built block houses on the Eminences opposite the Town; we likewise erected a chain of Block houses on the Back of the Town towards the Heights of Abraham at our proper distances from the Wall.

During the Winter the French army at Jacques Cartier, were Victual'd & prepar'd to come down two different times, to attempt an escalade on the back of the town; [the Enemy rais'd Ladders against a Church to practice their Men to Mount and many accidents happening they [illegible] the Enterprize][5] but by our intelligence & good precautions, which their Friends in town punctually acquinted them with, they found they could not surprize us & we should be ready to receive them, therefor they thought it must adviseable to postpone their visit 'till the weather would permit them to keep the Field as lying out a few nights in that inclement season, must inevitably have destroy'd a great part of their Army. Thus we pass'd the Winter in continual Alarms, & suffer'd more hardships than perhaps any Troops were war before expos'd to.

[March a strong Post of the Enemy's was attack'd by our Lt Infantry & carry'd the Place was call'd Calvaire near St Augustina.[6] The Enemy had about 20 Kill'd & Wounded—This Winter we had plenty of very good fish call'd frost fish. Quebec is upwards of 300 miles N.W. of Boston.][7]

April. Quebec is divided into two Towns, the Upper & the lower, the communication is up a Steep high rock, to be render'd inaccessible; the Lower town is next the Harbour, & here reside chiefly the Merchants & traders with their stores, & here in general were the best Houses. The Upper town is on an excessive high Rock hanging over the Lower, & so defended with Batterys, that no ships can lye before it, being above the reach of their Guns; the Rock in most places is cut down perpendicular. in the Upper Town the Gentry live, & all the Publick Buildings are here. To the Field it is weak, as you may see the foot of the Wall from the Heights at 600 or 700 yards distance, & in some places it is low, it has a very indifferent ditch which adds but

3 The words between brackets are two separate notes in the margin.
4 The words between brackets are a note in the margin.
5 The lines between brackets are a note in the margin.
6 Now known as Saint-Augustin-de-Desmaures.
7 The words between brackets are notes in the margin.

little to its strength. the town in general must have look'd well before we demolish'd it.

[April the River open'd & the Ice broke about the middle of this Month. Drink made Like Spruce Beer from the Hemlock tree found to recover our Scorbutic Men very fast.][8]

[21st. A small Schooner was fitted out & the command given to L^t^ fortye[9] of the 35th. She sail'd down the River to hasten up our Fleet if she could meet it—]

[The Canadians brought in some good brown Sugar drawn from a Tree not unlike the Maple.][10]

April 27th. Very early this Morning a French man was taken up floating on a Cake of Ice passing the town [a sergeant of the French Artilery he had pass'd the town on the ice and the tide of flood had brought him back again],[11] he inform'd us that the French army, above 12,000 men were coming down to beseige us, that he was in a batteau[12] with some cannon, & was overset by the Ice in ye Violent Storm which happend yesterday Evening—that the Regular troops were in the Frigates & Vessels that lay up the River all Winter, the Canadians & Indians came past in Canoes & part by land, were now within about 9 miles from us; their Cannon &c. stores were most in their ships. The Regim. were immediately Order'd out to oppose their Landing, but they were before hand with us, & had already Landed at Carouge;[13] however we prevented them from cutting off our out posts at St Foix [14] & Loretto, as they intended.

---

8 The three entries between brackets are notes in the margin.

9 Thomas Fortye was commissioned as ensign in Shirley's new-raising in New England 50th Regiment of Foot on, 17 December 1754. He was promoted to lieutenant in the 50th Foot on 25 November 1755. When the regiment was disbanded on 7 March 1757, he went onto British half pay. From half pay, be became lieutenant in the 35th Foot, 8 March 1757. He exchanged onto British half pay on 19 March 1764. From half pay he became lieutenant in the 75th Foot on 23 July 1778, returning to half pay after 14.1 years of service when the regiment disbanded on 10 May 1783. His name was removed from the half pay list in 1783.

10 The three entries between brackets are notes in the margin.

11 The words between brackets are an explanatory note in the margin.

12 A batteau (alternatively spelled bateau) is a generic term for a type of vessel used extensively in the 17th and 18th century fur trade in Canada to carry cargo in shallow rivers and inland waterways. It was a shallow-draft, flat-bottomed, double-ended vessel, ranging in length from 24 to 50 feet (7.3 to 15.2 meters) with a breadth of 5 to 8 feet (1.5 to 2.4 meters), had a draught of about 1 foot and carried a cargo up to one to ten tons. Depending on conditions, batteaux could alternatively be propelled by a pole, oars, or a small sail, but most commonly used oars.

13 Cape Rouge, or Carouge, is located on the north bank of the St. Lawrence River about nine miles upstream from Québec. From this place on 13 September 1759, as Hervey Smythe depicted it in a popular engraving, about 1,500 British embarked to go down the river with the current to the landing place for the Plains of Abraham.

14 Sainte-Foy was a small settlement of Christian Native Americans, traders, and merchants that had been established in 1669. On 28 April 1760, a major battle occurred here,

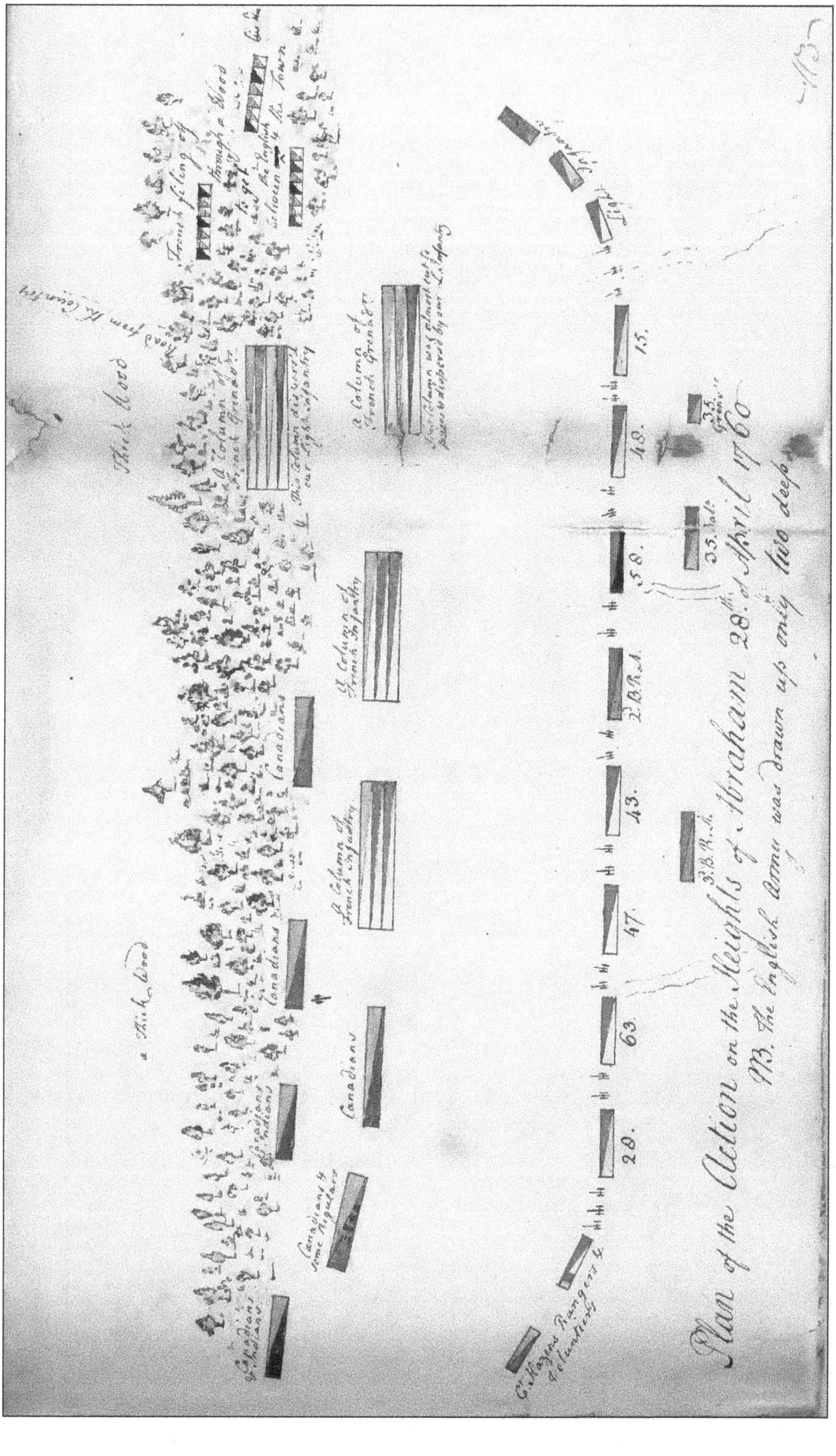

'Plan of the action on the heights of Abraham 28th of April 1760'.

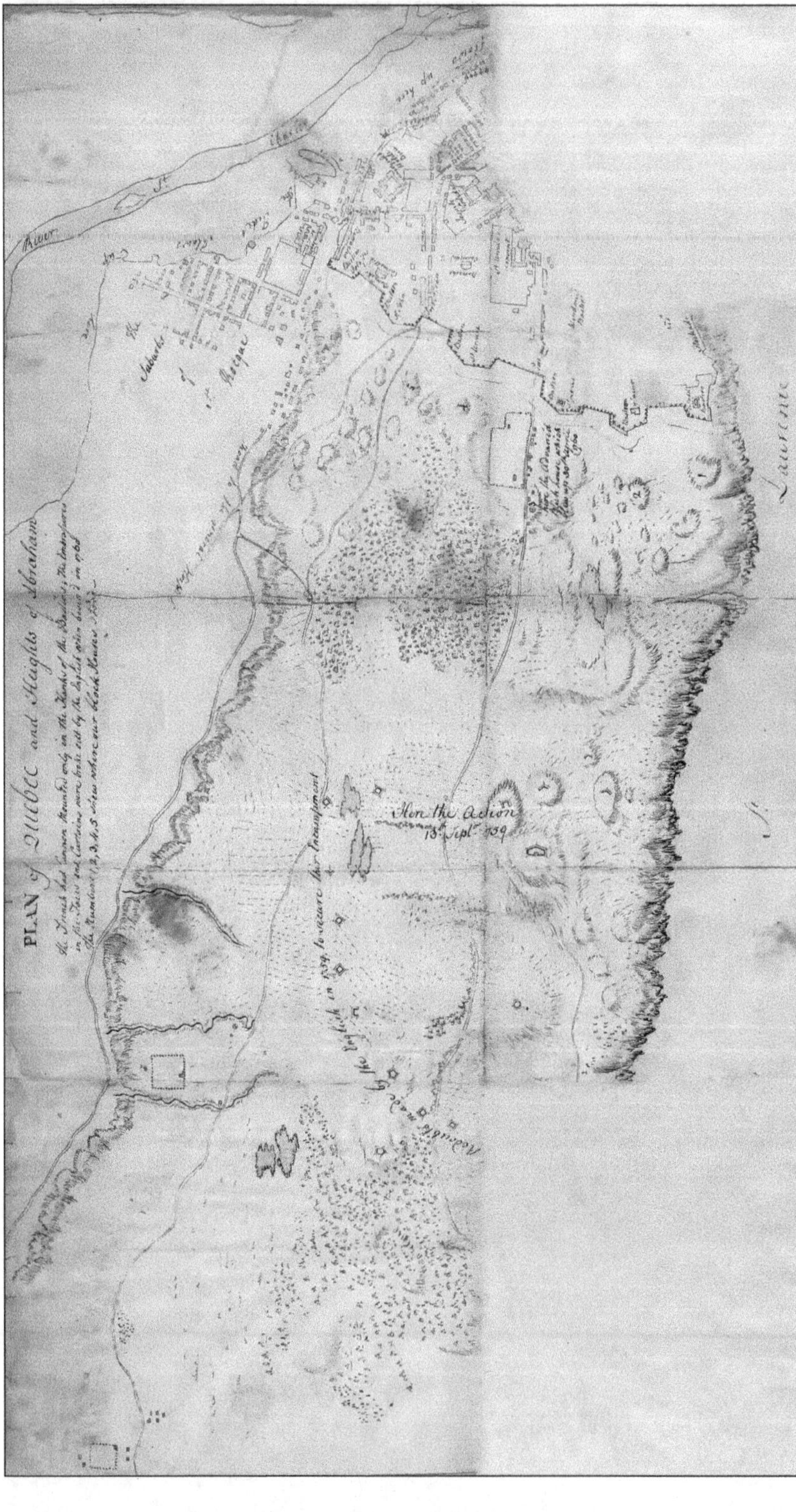

'Plan of Québec and heights of Abraham, 1760'.

28th. Our Whole army consisiting of 3100 Men march'd out of the Garrison, carrying spades & pick axes with them in Order, to throw up lines on the Heights. [our Artillery were 2 twelve & 16 six pound^rs^. with 2 Howitzers. These lines were laid out by the Chief Eng^r^. 2 days before][15] to keep the Enemy as far from the town as possible. Genl. Murray, seeing the French Army Assembling in some hurry & confusion, & our army being drawn up in good order, each battalion having two peices of Cannon, thought this a favourable opportunity to endeavor to route them; we March'd towards, them in the same order. we were drawn up, but to Extend our line as far as possible to prevent our being flank'd, we were oblig'd to make only two ranks; we beat them out of some redoubts, & from several Eminences they had Occupied in our Front, a heavy Column of French Grenadiers oppos'd our light Infantry who were advanc'd on our Right, the French Grenadiers were drove & almost cut to pieces by the light Infantry who pursued them quite into the front of our Army, but having broke in the Pursuit, were easily Routed by a second Column, sent to sustain the first, & our L^t^. Infantry being strech'd far along the Front, prevented our Right Wing from firing. Most of the officers of the Light Infrantry were kill'd or wounded & the men were not brought up again during the Action. The Grenadiers of the 35th were sent up to Support the light Infantry, [These Grenadiers took a small Mill from the French Column & maintained it. See a note on this at the latter end of the book][16] they pass'd the French column, but suffer'd exceedingly, 16 men only, of that Comp^y^ returning [they were 60 marching out]:[17] we follow'd the retreating Enemy close to a Wood, where the Fugitives had rally'd, & their Savages had gather'd, from hence they fir'd furiously on us, killing our men very fast, & being cover'd by the Trees we could see but few of them, [we were oblig'd to leave our Cannon sticking in the snow][18] Our cannon were of no service to us, as we could not draw them through the soft ground & gullies of Snow, near three feet deep. The Enemy now began to file off through the Skirts of the Wood, to get between us & the Town, the General Observing this, & having Lost above a third of his Army, Order'd a Retreat, the Enemy did not pursue us Closely, nor did we retire in very good order. they had suffer'd much, & some of our Army drawing up near our advanc'd Block-house, put an entire stop to them. [This Action Lasted near two hours very obstinately disputed. the French say they lost 2000 Men][19] we lost 1100 Men & several of our best officers; had a great many wounded & return'd to Town in a poor condition. The Odds were too great 3100 against 14000 men; [the French returns made 18000 men.][20] however we were determin'd to keep them out of the Town as long as possible, & without loss of time, set to Work to put the almost naked Fortification into some posture of Defence.

---

as described in the next entry. The formerly separate, modern city of Sainte-Foy was amalgamated into Québec City in 2002.

15 The words between brackets are a note in the margin.

16 The words between brackets are a note in the margin. See Bamford's additional note on this incident dated 28 April 1760 in Chapter 9, p.157.

17 The words between brackets are a note in the margin.

18 The words between brackets are a note in the margin.

19 The words between brackets are a note in the margin.

20 The words between brackets are a note in the margin.

29th. Last Night the Enemy open'd trenches about 600 yards from the Walls, they were hard at Work prolonging & strengthening them, & we were busy within filling up the Empty Parapet,[21] breaking out Embrasures[22] in the Curtains[23] & faces[24] of these Bastions.[25] Drawing the Cannon from the lower town & face towards the sea, & mounting them where they were now more necessary. The general had caus'd a large Quanity of Fascines, pickets & stockades to be made in Winter [these fascines the Canadians were oblig'd to make in the winter & bring them in—],[26] with these we fac'd the Cheeks of our Embrasures & friesed[27] the lower parts of the Walls, & they were of the greatest service to us, preventing the stones from flying about & killing our men & securing us against an Escalade.[28] We wanted much the Direction of our Chief Engineer Major Mackellar,[29] he was shot in the body the day of the action & lay dangerously ill.

---

21 A parapet is a protective breastwork on the forward side of a trench, battery, bastion, or curtain wall. Boscawen, *Louisbourg,* p.417

22 Embrasures are the gaps in a parapet through which cannons fire. Boscawen, *Louisbourg,* p.414.

23 A curtain is a wall that joins two bastions or other fortification and is sometimes backed by gun platforms or ramparts. Boscawen, *Louisbourg,* p.413.

24 Faces are the outer wall of a bastion facing the glacis, usually without embrasures. The faces meet at an obtuse angle. Boscawen, *Louisbourg,* p.414.

25 A bastion is a permanent defensive work of fortification comprising two faces 300-500 feet long at an angle greater than 60 degrees to each other. Boscawen, *Louisbourg,* pp. 411-12.

26 The words between brackets are a note in the margin marked for insertion here.

27 'To fraise' is to create a defensive barrier by driving pointed stakes into the ramparts of a fortification in a horizontal or inclined position.

28 'To escalade' is to scale the walls of a fortification.

29 Patrick Mackellar or McKellar was born in Argyllshire, Scotland, in 1717 and entered the Ordnance service in 1735 as a clerk at the Royal Arsenal at Woolwich. In 1739, he was made Clerk of the Works and assigned to Minorca. He was granted a warrant as practitioner engineer on 7 December 1742. He was promoted to engineer extraordinary on 8 March 1744 and commissioned an ensign in Wyngard's 4th Regiment of Marines on 1 December 1745. He was promoted to engineer in ordinary on 31 July 1751. Recalled to England in 1754, he was assigned as engineer to Major General Braddock in North America. He took part in the expedition to Fort Duquesne in 1755 and was wounded at the Battle of Monongahela. In 1756, while acting engineer at Fort Oswego, he was captured by the French and taken as a prisoner of war to Québec. He was exchanged in 1757 and returned to England, having become engineer in ordinary and captain of Foot. On 4 January 1758, he was appointed subdirector of engineers and major of Foot and made deputy chief engineer to Colonel John Henry Bastide for the Louisbourg expedition. When Bastide was wounded. McKellar succeeded him as acting chief engineer. In 1759, he was appointed Wolfe's chief engineer and was wounded at on 31 July 1759 at Montmorency Falls, but was with Wolfe in scaling the cliffs to the Plains of Abraham in September. While directing the artillery at the Battle of Sainte-Foy on 28 April 1760, he was wounded, but continued to supervise the defence of Québec during his period of recovery. In November, he became chief engineer at Halifax and served in that capacity until being selected as Monckton's chief engineer for the expedition to Martinique in 1761. He continued in post in 1762 under the Earl of Albemarle at Havana, where he was wounded. He was promoted to lieutenant colonel in the army on 3 January 1762, and then to director of engineers and lieutenant colonel of foot on 2 February 1775. He was promoted to chief engineer and colonel of foot on 29 August 1777. He died at Minorca in 1778.

[30th. Our Large Advanc'd Block house blew up by a spark which fell on the moving magazine there were not any lives lost tho the men & officers were much burn'd][30]

[May 3d. The Fortify'd House was set on Fire by a [ball] from one of our Guns & most part of the Town in that Quarter was burn'd down by this Accident.]

[5th. A moving Magazine on Cape Diamond Bastion[31] was blown up by a spark reaching it, several men were scorch'd but none kill'd.]

May 9th. the *Lowestoff* Frigate, Captⁿ Dean[32] came up to the town; being the first Vessel since the fleet went away. this gave the Garrison great spirits, convincing us that there was not a French Fleet in the River, which the French positively asserted. The Frigates & ships which brought down their Army lay at Fouloon Cove.

10th. The Enemy Open'd two batterys against us, one of 6, the other of 4 guns, from 12 to 24 Pounders, & threw shells from two Mortars of 10 & 13 inches—

11th. They open'd another Battery of 3 Guns, fired extremely brisk from all their Artillery, we preserv'd a great superiority of Fire, as by this time we had got 40 peices of heavy Cannon, to bear on their Works, wherewith we ply'd them most Effectually. Having compleated what we intended on the Ramparts, we began to erect two Cavalier Batterys[33] on the highest ground within the Walls, & to make Redans[34] on the outside to cover the gates.

12th. Directed over fire chiefly against the Enemy, Six Gun Battery, which we silenced till Evening, they afterwards fir'd from three smaller guns only, in that Battery.

13th. Disabled some of the Enemys guns in the other Batterys, as we Observ'd they lessen'd their fire & closed their Embrasures, they threw several Carcasses[35] towards our Provision store.

---

30 The entries between brackets for 30 April, 3 May, and 5 May 1760 are written in the margin.

31 A bastion located at Cap Diamant, the location of the city of Québec. The cape is formed by the bend in the St. Lawrence River at the promontory of Québec.

32 Joseph Deane passed his examination for lieutenant in the Royal Navy in the Royal Navy in 1753 and was commissioned a lieutenant on 29 April 1755. He commanded the sloop *Mohawk*, based at Oswego on Lake Ontario, in 1756 and was taken as a prisoner of war at Oswego on 14 August 1756. Repatriated, he was promoted to commander on 23 April 1758, he commissioned the 24-gun *Eurus*. He was promoted captain on 17 October 1758, and took command of *Lowestoffe*.

33 A 'cavalier battery' is a raised battery within a bastion that enables the artillery to fire over the heads of those on the ramparts below. Boscawen, *Louisbourg, 1758*, p. 413.

34 A 'redan'is a field work placed to defend important terrain or outer works. Boscawen, *Louisbourg, 1758*, p. 418.

35 A 'carcass' is a mortar shell containing incendiary material.

14th. The fire from the Enemy very slack, ours encrease, having brought more Cannon against them. Our artillery exceedingly well serv'd, beating down their Works very fast. They have made no material impression on the Walls.

15th. about 9 o'clock this Night his Majestys ship the *Vanguard* 70 Guns, Commodore Swanton, & the *Diana* Frigate, capt. Schomberg,[36] came up to the Town. The Enemy beat to arms in their Camp we did the same in Town.

16th. Early this Morning our two Frigates [the *Loestoff* & *Diana*][37] sail'd up above the town to attack the 4 French Frigates at the Foulon. The French got all their ships under way in the greatest hurry & made off. It was an Agreeable prospect to us, to see our two Frigates drive a fleet before them, & in sight of an Hostile Army. Three of the French Frigates were forc'd a shore & destroy'd, the other escap'd to Montreal [the French Vessel their escap'd was the *Marie*].[38] The *Vanguard* follow'd the Frigates above the Foulon.

17th. Some time last night the French rais'd the Siege [the French had 150 officers kill'd in the action & siege—by their own Confession][39] leaving their tents standing, all their Artillery, and Stores, Numbers of arms, baggage, & a Quanity of Merchandize of Various kinds; the Merchants from Montreal crowding to the Camp with their goods. as they thought having gain'd the Action, they were certain of taking the town in a few days; they went off so precipitantly, that they forgot even their Church Plate, which fell a prey to some of our Light Infantry, who thought it no sacriledge, to secure it, and apply it to their own Use. We pursued some Miles, took several Waggons, with Wounded Men & some baggage, but could not come

36 Alexander Schomberg was born in London in 1720, the son of a successful German-Jewish medical doctor from Württemberg who had immigrated to England. Alexander Schomberg attended St Paul's School. He renounced the Jewish faith and converted to Anglicanism, allowing him to enter the Navy in November 1743. He became midshipman, served in the West Indies, passed his examination, and was promoted to lieutenant on 12 December 1747. In July 1751, his ship was paid off and he was placed on half pay. From half pay he returned to active service in 1755-56. After another brief period on half pay in 1756, he returned to duty and was promoted to captain and took command of the new 32-gun frigate *Richmond* on 5 April 1757 and transferred to the command of the 32-gun frigate *Diana*. He played a distinguished role at Louisbourg, taking Boscawen in to reconnoiter the landing and then led a landing party. At Québec in 1759 and 1760, he helped repulse the French attempt to regain the city. Ordered to return to England with dispatches in 1760, he took command of the 64-gun *Essex* and participated in the Belle Îsle expedition in 1764. He commanded the 64-gun *Prudent* during the Falkland Islands crisis of 1770, then in 1771 took command of the Lord Lieutenant of Ireland's yacht, holding that assignment until his death in 1804. In 1777, he was knighted for his long service and in 1789, published *A Sea Manual recommended to the Young Officers of the Royal Navy as a Companion to the Signal-book.*

37 The words between brackets are an explanatory note in the margin.

38 The words between brackets are an explanatory note in the margin. The 200-ton *Marie* was built at Brest in 1751-1752. She is reported to have had 12 guns. In May 1760, the vessel grounded in the St. Lawrence, but was refloated. She was at Montréal at the capitulation of that city. British forces left the vessel to the French to repatriate civilians to France. She was last reported to be in the Vilaine River in February 1762. Her dimensions are not known.

39 The words between brackets are an explanatory note in the margin

up with the Body; we only took care of the Baggage, the Wounded we let proceed. The Enemy's Loss was considerable, they confess that the action & siege cost them above 3000 Men, & a great number of Officers, that each night they were oblig'd to pay their Canadians half a Dollar a man, before they would go to work in the Trenches, our artillery did them so much Mischief, they kill'd us every few Men in the siege, nor did they do much damage to the Walls, tho' an Opinion prevail'd amongst them, that firing our own Cannon from the Ramparts, would tumble the Walls down. The Lowestoff going up the river to Cannonade the French army in their retreat, unlucklily struck upon an hidden Rock & sunk, all the People & many things were saved. This is a most afflicting stroke to the French, as all their hopes for restoring their affairs in Canada, depended on the retaking Quebec, so on the contrary by obliging them to raise the Siege, the Canadians & Indians have forsaken them, they have ruin'd their army, lost all their stores & Expended the Amunition which they may Want for the Defence of the upper parts of their Country; & their Miscarriage here, in all probability will greatly contribute to render the Conquest of the other parts less difficult.

18th. Lord Colvil with the Fleet from Hallifax Arriv'd.

[June 21st Gen Amhersts army Embarkd for Oswigo].[40]

[June 29th a sergeant of the Highlanders was kill'd by Lightning & 2 men were much hurt].[41]

[This summer we were well supply'd with Salmon & other fish][42]

July 13th. Gen[l.] Murray with about 2100 Men embark'd in Sloops & schooners, & next day sail'd up the River for Montreal, to cooperate with Gen. Amherst towards the reduction of Canada. Two Regiments from Louisbourg, the 22d. & 40th. joyn'd them in the River, they landed on several Islands in their progress up: this Army had the Honour of being attended by the Whole French Army All The Way. As the Passage is extreamly Difficult, the little fleet was oblig'd to Anchor every Night, the French Marching as they sail'd, & when they Anchor'd, constantly encamped on the North Shore opposite to them. The Navigation was conducted by Capt[n] Deane, with the *Diana* Frigate, for which he has great Merit. Numbers of the Country people came in to Gen[l]. Murray, & laid down their Arms, & several small Villages surrendered to him. [Aug 10th & 11th. This army sail'd from Oswego in Batteaus][43] The Army Under Gen[l]. Amherst came by the way of the Lakes [this Army sail'd from Crown Point 11th August][44] reduc'd fort Levi [August 25th Fort Levi capitulated 'tis

40 The entry for 21 June is a note in the margin.
41 The entry for 29 June is a note in the margin.
42 The undated entry between brackets is a note in the margin.
43 The entry for 10 & 11 August is a note in the margin
44 The words between square brackets are an explanatory note in the margin.

situated most advantageously on Isle Royal.][45] & some other Posts; Col Haviland[46] with an army had come by Lake Champlain, to Reduce Isle Aux Noix,[47] which lies in the Lake about 6 Leagues from S^t^. John's,[48] this Island the French had fortify'd & had a large body of Men here to prevent our Boats from passing to St. John's with our Army, as they Expected Our greatest forces Would come this Way. after some batteries had been rais'd against the Island, the French stole away from it; Genl. Amherst reduc'd the Fort at La Galette[49] & some other posts on his Way, & the three armys without the Knowledge of each other, accidentally landed on the Island of Montreal and much about the same time. General Murray as soon as he landed proceeded to attack the Town, he had just prepar'd to storm a Redoubt that led to one of the Gates, whilst the body of the Army march'd forwards, drawing two shott 24 Pounders with them. but he was stop'd by a French officer with a flag whom the Governour General had sent out to acquaint him they were then capitulating with Genl. Amherst, having sent to treat with him immediately on his landing. During these operations against Montreal, a part of the army left behind at Quebec, who were not recover'd when Genl. Murray sail'd, embark'd on board small Vessels & went up the River to reduce the strong Post at Jacques Cartier; we had near 1200 men under the Command of Col^o^. Frazer[50]—landed about 2 miles above the Fort

45 The words between brackets are a note in the margin.

46 William Haviland was born in Ireland in 1718, the son of Captain Peter Haviland of Colonel Handaysd's 31st Regiment of Foot. He served as a 'voluntier' in Handaysde's Regiment for seven years. On 26 December 1739, he was commissioned a lieutenant in Spotswood's 43rd Regiment of Foot. On 25 July 1742, he purchased a company in the 27th Inniskilling Regiment of Foot, serving as aide de camp to Colonel William Blakeney during the siege of Stirling Castle by the Jacobite Army in 1745. He was promoted to major on 24 May 1751, then to lieutenant colonel in the 27th Foot on 16 December 1752, commanding the regiment in the field. He brought the 27th Foot to America for Lord Loudon's planned attack on Louisbourg and when that expedition did not materialize, the regiment stayed in New York. In the winter of 1757-58, Haviland commanded Fort Edward located at the Great Carrying Place, the portage around the falls on the Hudson River. Contemptuous of colonials, he was not popular with provincial militia. Promoted to colonel in America on 9 January 1758, Amherst placed him in command of the forces around Lake Champlain in 1760. On 9 December 1760, Haviland became colonel-commandant of the 3rd Battalion of the 60th Regiment of Foot. He acted as brigadier in Monckton's expedition to Martinique and at Havana in 1762. Promoted to major general on 10 July 1762, he went on half-pay when his regiment was disbanded on 24 August 1763. From half-pay, he was appointed colonel of the 45th Foot on 1 June 1767. He was promoted to lieutenant general in on 25 May 1772 and to general on 19 February 1783. He died on 16 September 1784. See also, *Oxford Dictionary of National Biography* and *Dictionary of Canadian Biography*. http://www.biographi.ca/en/bio/haviland_william_4E.html

47 Îsle aux Noix is an island in the Richelieu River. The French constructed a fort there in 1759 to hinder British passage from the South toward Montréal.

48 Known to the English as Fort St John's, Saint-Jean-sur-Richelieu is situated further north than Île aux Noix. It is approximately 25 miles (40 km) southeast of Montréal on the west bank of the Richelieu River at the head of navigation for Lake Champlain.

49 The Fort de La Présentation, also known as Fort La Galette, was built by the French in 1749 at the confluence of Oswegatchie River with the St. Lawrence River at what is now Ogdensburg, New York.

50 The Hon. Simon Fraser, or Fraser, Master of Lovat, was born in 1726, the eldest son of Simon Fraser, 11th Baron Lovat (ca. 1660-1748). Educated at the University of St. Andrews between

& March'd directly towards it, we reciev'd some Cannon shot on the road, from a few guns they had planted in Different Places, a messenger with a flag met us on the road to desire a truce for two days, till word could be received concerning the fate of Montreal, but this Was rejected, and an immediate surrender of the Place demanded, & this in turn was refus'd—we March'd on, drawing two field Pieces & an Howitzer with us; the Commandant, the Marquis d'Albergotti,[51] had collected the Militia of the Country into the Fort, as he had but few regular troops; we Carry'd with us seven Cohorn Mortars [52] & upon throwing a few shells into the place, all the Militia ran out the back way, & it was surrender'd.

[August] 17th. the French brig *Ottawa*[53] taken by 5 Row gallies each carrying some Guns.

1743 and 1745, his father placed the younger Simon as colonel of a Jacobite regiment that he had raised during the rebellion. After Culloden, the elder Lovat was executed and the lordship of Lovat attainted. The younger Simon was continuing his studies at the University of Glasgow, when he was pardoned for his Jacobite activities in 1745-46. He was called to the bar in Scotland and continued his legal studies in England at the Middle Temple and was made a barrister in 1756. In 1756, he raised two battalions of Highlanders and was commissioned lieutenant colonel commandant of the 2nd Highland Battalion (63rd Foot, renumbered on 5 January 1757 as the 78th). He was promoted to colonel in America on 22 January 1758. Wounded at Montmorency on 31 July 1759 and at Québec on 28 April 1760, he was given leave to return to England in October 1760. From 1761 to 1782, he was Member of Parliament for Inverness-shire. He was promoted to brigadier general in 1762 and served in Portugal during the Spanish invasion. Promoted to major general on 25 May 1772 and became colonel of the 71st Regiment of Foot on 25 October 1775, but did not serve with Fraser's Highlanders during the American War. Promoted to lieutenant general on 29 August 1777, he died in London 8 February 1782. See also *Oxford Dictionary of National Biography* and History of Parliament http://www.historyofparliamentonline.org/volume/1754-1790/member/fraser-simon-1726-82

51 The commander of Fort Jacques-Cartier, François-Marie-Lucien, marquis d' Albergati-Vezza, was born at Notre-Dame-del-Maratelle, Bologna, Italy. He was a *colonel* and chevalier de l'ordre royal et militaire de Saint-Louis. He arrived in Canada between 1755 and 1757, when he married Charlotte-Marie-Anne-Joseph Aubert de la Chesnaye d'Aubert-Gayon (1737-1801) at Québec on 18 January 1757. He died in France between 1772 and 1788.

52 A cohorn or coehorn mortar was a lightweight mortar designed by Menno, Marquis de Coehorn (1640-1704), a Dutch engineer who was the counterpart of the French fortification expert Sébastien Le Prestre de Vauban, comte de Vauban. The mortar could be carried by 2-4 men.

53 The 10-gun schooner-rigged corvette *Outaouaise* was one of three vessels that the French built on Lake Ontario after the fall of Fort Frontenac to try to re-establish French control of the lake. She was built at Pointe au Baril on the St. Lawrence River (near present-day Maitland, Ontario) in 1758-59. After capture, she was rigged as a brig and renamed HMS *Williamson*. She was sunk in the attack on Fort Lévis and then raised. Due in part to unrepaired battle damage, she sprang a leak and was run ashore near Niagara on 22 October 1760 and could not be salvaged. Approximate dimensions: Length 84 feet, breadth 22 feet, depth of hold 9 feet 2 inches, 160 tons.

They were command'd by Col Williamson.[54] the French Brig mounted one 18 pounder seven 12 poundrs. two 8 poundrs. was 150 tons had 100 men on board.][55]

[Sept 4th Genl. Amherst's army pass'd. these Rapids Cotau de Lac,[56] Halteur de Cedres, Buisson & Trautet de cascade, a most dangerous passage—he lost 46 Batteaus, 17 Whale Boats, 1 Row Galley, & 84 men were drowned—][57]

[Sept 6th—Gen Amhurst army landed on the Isle of Montreal][58]

[Sept 7th. General Murray's army landed on the Island of Montreal.][59]

[8th Brigadier Haviland's army landed on Montreal Isle.][60]

9th. We march'd into it [Fort Jacques-Cartier] the same day we landed, found but 3 officers & 25 Soldiers. The Situation of this Place is extremely strong, & if properly defended, would cost much trouble & many lives to reduce it. The Marquis said he had the Honour of surrendering the last place in all Canada—Montreal surrender'd the day before.

Septr 8th. The Town of Montreal with all Canada was surrender'd to his Britanick Majesty. The Articles are very Numerous. Montreal lyes on the River St Laurence, in the Island of Montreal, above Quebec to the Southward about 60 leagues [180 miles];[61] its situation is very pleasant, & the town looks well, the Fortifications are very poor not calculated for a Defence against Cannon. This place was a great Mart, where the Indians bought in their Furrs.

---

54 George Williamson was born about 1704. He entered the Royal Artillery as a cadet on 1 February 1722 and was commissioned a lieutenant fire worker five years later on 1 November 1727. He was promoted to second lieutenant on 1 October 1731, to first lieutenant on 1 December 1737, and to captain on 1 July 1740. He served on Minorca from 1731 to 1746, and then fought in the campaigns in Flanders from 1746 to 1748. He was promoted to major on 22 June 1747, with the rank being confirmed on 8 March 1751, and he was subsequently promoted to lieutenant colonel on 3 February 1757. After volunteering to serve in North America, he was placed in charge of the artillery for the unsuccessful 1757 expedition to Louisbourg, but got no further than Halifax. He returned to Albany, New York, preparing the artillery for the 1758 Louisbourg expedition. On 25 January 1758, he was promoted to colonel in America to command the artillery at Louisbourg under Amherst. Williamson commanded the troops who raised the Union Flag over Louisbourg when the French surrendered. In 1759, Wolfe selected him to command the artillery at Québec. On 18 September, Williamson again raised the Union Flag at the French surrender of Québec. On 29 November 1759, he was appointed colonel commandant, then promoted to major general on 10 August 1762, and to lieutenant-general on 25 March 1772. He died on 10 November 1781.

55 The entry for 17 August is a note in the margin.

56 Coteau-du-Lac

57 The entry for 4 September 1760 is a note in the margin.

58 The entry for 6 September 1760 is a note in the margin.

59 The entry for 7 September 1760 is a note in the margin.

60 The entry for 8 September 1760 is a note in the margin.

61 The distance is given in a note in the margin.

5

From Québec to Crown Point, Albany, and Staten Island, 10 September 1760–8 August 1761

After the Reduction of Canada, a part of the Army return'd to Quebec, the rest were quarter'd in Villages between that & Montreal. This Winter we pass'd with more ease & satisfaction than we had done the Proceeding one, we had no Enemy to alarm us, the Necessities of life were tolerably Plenty, & we suffer'd no hardships. The Summers in Canada are extreamly Pleasant & tho' the Ground is bound up in Frost seven Months of the year, yet the soil is so good that Immediately after it's released from it frozen fetters, it produces Vegetables of all sorts in great abundance, the Vegatation being surprisingly Quick. The Hares & foxes of this Country in Winter, change their colour from brown or Red to almost white.

1761
June 1st. An order came from Genl. Amherst for several of the Regiments to march for Crown Point, from Quebec.

6th. The 15th. Regiment March'd

8th. The 35th Regiment March'd to St Augustine 15 Miles. part of the 28th Reg^{t}. were Canton'd here.

9th. To Jacques Cartier, 15 miles. Thus far the Cantonements of the 28th. Reach'd.

10th. March'd to De Chambaud, 15 miles, part of the 43rd. Regim^{t}. were Canton'd here.

11th. Halted at de Chambaud.

June 12th. March'd to S^{t}. Ann's,[1] 16 Miles, part of the 48th. Reg^{t}. here.

1 Sainte-Anne-de-Beaupré located on the north bank of the St. Lawrence River about 22 miles (35 km) northeast of Québec City.

13th. To Champlain, 14 miles, part of the 48th. Reg^{t}. here.

14th. To Trois Riviers,[2] 14 miles. Part of the 48th. Reg^{t}. here. This is a very pretty compact Town, in a pleasant Situation, on the Banks of the River S$^{t.}$ Lawrence; nearly central between Quebec & Montreal. Here Col^{o}. Burton[3] resided as Governer.

15th. Halted

16th. March'd to Maschiesch,[4] 17 miles. part of the 48th. Reg^{t}.

17th. March'd to Maskingongie,[5] 15 Miles, this was the last of the Cartonements of the 48th. Regiment. [very large fish are caught here called Maskinongie[6] not unlike a pike very good tho][7]

18th. March'd to Bertie,[8] 6 miles, here part of the 46th. were. Thus far we March'd on the North Banks of the River St Laurence. All those Villages we pass'd through, are most Charmingly situated in well chosen fertile spots, on the North Banks of the River, the houses are but very indifferent, tho built of Stone, all in a stragling manner and four or five hundred yards Distance between many of them.

19th Cross'd the River in large boats to Sorrel[9] on the South Side, about 4 Miles Over. Cantonement of the 44th Rg^{t}. Our Baggage was brought in sloops from Quebec, up

---

2 Trois-Rivières, where the Saint-Maurice River has three channels, around two islands, at the point of confluence with the Saint-Lawrence River.

3 Ralph Burton was likely born at Hall Bank, Cottingham, near Hull, Yorkshire. He was commissioned a second lieutenant in the 32nd Regiment of Foot on 15 June 1742 and then sub-lieutenant in the 2nd Troop of Horse Grenadier Guards on 11 April 1745. He was promoted to lieutenant and captain in the 2nd Troop of Horse Grenadier Guards on 26 May 1747, and then to major in the 2nd Troop of Horse Grenadier Guards on 26 May 1747. He exchanged his position as major in the 2nd Troop of Horse Grenadier Guards to become lieutenant colonel of the 48th Foot on 15 October 1754. In 1755, he was in America with Braddock and led the vanguard in the engagement on 9 July 1755, when he was wounded. Promoted to colonel in America on 10 January 1758, he commanded the 3rd Brigade at Louisbourg and commanded the 48th Foot at Québec in 1759. Under Murray, he commanded the right wing at Québec on 28 April 1760. His performance of duty at Québec was controversial and some blamed him for causing the British retreat within the city walls. He participated in the expedition to Montréal and was made colonel of a newly formed 95th Regiment of Foot on 10 December 1760. In 1762, he commanded a contingent at Havana as either a colonel or brigadier general. He was promoted to major general on 10 July 1762. When the 95th was disbanded on 11 March 1763, he was placed on half pay. He became colonel of the 3rd Foot on 22 February 1764 and died in 1768.

4 Machiche, now known as Yamachiche.

5 Maskinongé

6 A large North American fresh water pike called maskinonge or muskellunge (*Esox masquinongy*). It has dark markings and may weigh over 60 pounds (27 kilograms).

7 The statement between brackets is a note in the margin next to the entry for 17 June 1761.

8 Berthier, now Berthierville.

9 Sorel, now Sorel-Tracy, on the south bank of the St. Lawrence River at the confluence of the Richelieu River and the St. Lawrence River, marks the geographical end of the Lake

the River St Laurence into the Lake St Peters,[10] within about 3 Miles of this Place, but the sloops could go no farther with us, as we were to go up the River Sorrel;[11] we were therefore Employ'd the 3 following days in removing our baggage into batteaus (flat bottomed boats that will carry from 14 to 20 Men). We had about 50 for our Reg^t.; the Soldiers row these boats except upon Particular Occasions.

22d. Our Soldiers made 150 Oars this night by moon light. The Oars of the Batteaus being lost—

23d. Set off in Our Batteaus & rowed to the Parish of St Antoine, 18 miles against the Stream.

24th. Rowed to the Parish of St Charles,[12] 21 Miles.

25th. Rowed to Fort Chamblé,[13] [blank] Miles, built by the French in 1711, & abandon'd by them in 1760, on the approach of the English Army under Col^o Haviland; The Walls are strong & high a square of 4 Bastions, The Dwellings are built schedwise[14] all round inside, & not to be seen from without; it mounts several small cannon, Patterara's,[15] & Swivels,[16] all under Cover, a great advantage in this Country;—the River washes the Walls on one side, & to the Land it is surrounded with very strong stockades 'tis a most noble defense against Indians, or any Body of men with small arms only. here part of the 44th. Regim^t. was quarter'd.

26th. Went by land to St Teresa,[17] 7 Miles, [here the French had a small stockaded Fort, which was surpriz'd & burn'd & the People made Prisoners by Major Rogers[18]

Champlain valley.

10 Lac Saint-Pierre is a widening of the St. Lawrence River between Sorel-Tracy and Trois-Rivières. The Lake marks the beginning of the St. Lawrence estuary.

11 The Richelieu River.

12 Saint-Charles-sur-Richelieu

13 Fort Chambly.

14 The meaning of 'schedwise' – presumably shedwise – is unclear, but likely is meant to describe simple 'lean-to' structures that were common in frontier America. In this case, they may have shared one wall with the inside of the bastion and have a roof that leaned against the bastion wall.

15 Pateraro, a type of swivel gun.

16 A swivel gun is a small, hand-aimed cannon mounted on a swiveling bracket. It fired round shot. They were commonly used to clear the area in front of a fort, or, at sea, to repel boarders.

17 Fort Sainte Thérèse

18 Robert Rogers was born in 1731 in Methuen, Massachusetts. Sometime before 1738, the family moved to New Hampshire. He became a militiaman by the age of 14. Between 1743 and 1755, he become well acquainted with Native Americans, frontier life, and both British and French settlements, providing him the basis for his skills as a scout and ranger. In 1755, he recruited 24 men for a Massachusetts regiment in New Hampshire, which later was brought under the control of the provincial New Hampshire authorities. On 24 April, be became captain of Company 1 of the New Hampshire Regiment. Deployed to the upper Hudson River, they came under the command of Sir William Johnson. During the winter of 1755-56, he led scouting expeditions into Canada. In the spring of 1756, Governor Shirley of

with a Party of Rangers—].[19] Very few inhabitants. From Chamblé to this place our batteaus were oblig'd to be drag'd up the River by the soldiers, the Men frequently wading to their Necks, & with much difficulty & great Labour got them up, the stream is so very rapid; our Baggage was carry'd on Waggons & Carts; this they call a Carrying Place, where you are forc'd to unload your boat & carry your goods, & sometimes your boats too by Land. No troops here & only two or 3 distant houses.

27th. March'd to S[t] Johns,[20] 9 Miles, no habituations on the road, nor Troops quarter'd here. This was a Place of Consequence, lying on a Deep Navigable River, which runs directly into Lake Champlain, about 16 miles from hence. here the French had a Strong Fort[21] & large Stores, this was the Port for their Arm'd Vessels & other Craft, by which they were Masters of the Lake, supported Crown Point and Ticonderoga & made incursions into our Colonies. They burn'd & abandon'd it in 1760. Since we left Sorrel we have met with no Villages, only here & there a single house at 5 or 6 Miles distance. We Encamp'd here two Days. inconceiveable numbers of Muskitos.

30th. Embark'd on board Briggs, Schooners & Sloops; these had been arm'd Vessels belonging to the French. we saild for Crown Point.

July 4th. Arriv'd at Crown Point, near 50 leagues leagues from S[t] John's, directly through Lake Champlain, a very pleasant navigation & seldom attended with any trouble, we pass'd by Isle aux Noix which was attack'd by an army under Col[o]. Haviland in 1760 [Isle aux Noix lies between 5 & 6 leagues from S[t] John's on ye Lake Champlain. The French stole away from it when Col[o]. Haviland's Army appear'd before it & began to raise Bat[ys].][22] the Situation is extremely strong & the French had fortify'd it with a triple row of Entrenchments well Friezed & mounted with many Cannon. The Island is surrounded, except in one small Place with an impassable Morass, the Whole is but a few Acres, it lyes on the lake Champlain between five & Six leagues from S[t]. Johns, 'tis a great pass.

Massachusetts ordered Roberts to raise a company of Rangers. On 6 April 1758, Abercromby promoted Rogers to major and appointed him to command all companies of Rangers. In November 1758, Amherst confirmed Abercromby's action and raised the number of Ranger companies to twelve. With the fall of Canada, Rogers was ordered to accept the French surrenders at Detroit and Michilimackinac. On 25 October 1760, Amherst gave him a commission as captain in an independent company in South Carolina. He returned to New York in 1763 and took command of an independent New York company, which went to the relief of Detroit. With the end of the war, he went to England, where he published accounts of activities to supplement his half pay. In October 1765, he was commissioned commandant at Michilimackinac. Accused of treason, he was tried and found innocent, but treated as unreliable. He returned to England to the to regain favour and income, but failed. He was imprisoned for debt in 1769, 1771, and 1772. Released from prison in 1774, he returned to America. With the outbreak of the American Revolution, Roberts was commissioned to raise a battalion of loyalists rangers, but was not successful as a regimental commander. In 1784, he returned to England, where he died in 1795.

19 The words between brackets are a note in the margin.

20 Saint-Jean-sur-Richelieu

21 Fort Saint-Jean

22 The words between square brackets are a note in the margin.

The following Regiments were encamped at Crown Point when we [35th. Reg^{t}.][23] Arriv'd. 15th. Amherst's . — . 27th. Blackeney's five Comp^{ys}. 40th. Armigers . — . 42d. Royal Highlanders, 2 Battalions, & about 2000 Provincials, under their Genl. Lyman.[24]

July 8th. The 28th Reg^{t}. arriv'd, they cross'd the Lake in Sloops & batteau's, as did the rest of the Regiments that came—after us from Canada, all pursuing the same route. every Regiment whilst they remain'd here work'd at the New Fort,[25] it stands on a rising ground about 250 yards from the Old French Fort,[26] demolish'd & abandon'd by them when Genl. Amherst was marching into this country, & he took prosession of it July 4th 1759. This is a pentagon, capable of containing a great Number of Men, & if ever finish'd properly will be strong, but must cost much labour, Expence & time; the Ditch is cut out of the solid Rock; the Plan was laid by Col^{o}. Eyres.[27] Three large Strong Casmated Redoubts are built on Eminences near the Fort.

---

23 The information between square brackets is a note in the margin.

24 Phineas Lyman was born about 1716 in Durham, Connecticut. Initially, he worked as a weaver, then attended Yale College, where he studied law. From 1742 to 1756, he practiced law and served in the militia. For Johnson's 1755 campaign on Lake George, he was commissioned major general and commander in chief of Connecticut's forces. In 1755, he built a fort at the southern end of the 'Great Carrying Place', the portage between the Hudson River and Lake George, initially called Fort Lyman, Sir William Johnson renamed it in 1756 as Fort Edward in honour of Prince Edward, Duke of York and Albany. Lyman commanded a regiment in both the 1758 and 1759 campaigns around Lake Champlain. In 1762, he commanded a range of Provincial troops at Havana. Between 1763 and 1771, he was in England procuring land grants for veterans, including himself, of the French and Indian War. By the end of 1773, he had established himself at Natchez, on the Mississippi River. He died in 1774.

25 Fort Crown Point

26 Fort Saint-Frédéric

27 William Eyre became a cadet in the Royal Regiment of Artillery on 1 October 1742. He was appointed practitioner engineer on 12 March 1744 and on 26 March 1744, second lieutenant in the 8th Regiment of Marines. During 1744, he served as 5th practitioner engineer. He was promoted to lieutenant fireworker for a brief time, probably while serving as captain-lieutenant in the Duke of Montagu's Ordnance Regiment of Foot during the Jacobite Rebellion. When that regiment was disbanded on 2 August 1747, Eyre was placed on half pay. From half pay, he was appointed on 3 February 1747 as engineer in ordinary in Flanders. Eleven months later on 2 January 1748, he was appointed to the lower grade of sub-engineer. Well before it became common for engineers to have dual ranks, he was also appointed on 25 December 1747 captain in the 55th (later 44th) Regiment of Foot and engineer extraordinary on 2 August 1751. Eyre was posted to North America to serve with the 44th Regiment under Braddock, but was assigned instead to New York, where he served in Sir William Johnson's expedition to Fort Saint-Frédéric. Eyre designed and built Fort William Henry and Fort Edward. He was promoted to major in the 44th Foot on 7 January 1756. When the engineers were commissioned on 14 May 1757, he was made engineer extraordinary and captain-lieutenant of foot. In the absence of his senior officers, Eyre commanded the 44th Foot at Carillon in 1758 and was wounded. Promoted to lieutenant colonel on 17 July 1758, he commanded the 55th Foot in 1759. In this capacity, he began to rebuild Fort Ticonderoga after the French had destroyed portions of it. On 29 October 1759, Amherst assigned him to command his old regiment, the 44th Foot, at Niagara. In 1760, he and his regiment accompanied Amherst on the St. Lawrence. Given leave to return home on leave, he drowned off the coast of England in December 1764.

19th. The 40th. Regim & 1st. Batt^{n}. of Roy^{l}. Highlanders, march'd from hence [from Crown Point][28] for Ticonderoga—

22d. The 2d. Batt^{n}. of the Roy^{l}. Highlanders march'd.

24th. The 15th Regiment march'd.

27th. The 35 Reg^{t}. March'd, to Ticonderoga 18 Miles; we pass'd by the Saw Mills, near Which Lord How was kill'd soon after landing [8th July 1750];[29] & Genl. Abercrombie with Sixteen thousand men was defeated July 8th. 1758 [a most pusillanimous Action],[30] in attempting to force the French lines, defended by Genl. Moncalm with 3000 Men. Genl. Abercrombie with the remains of his Army, repass'd Lake George to the Ground where Fort W^{m}. Henry had stood there he Encamp'd, & Order'd the Army to Intrench themselves. ['tis about 2 miles from the Saw Mills to the Landing place the Entrance into Lake George][31]

28th. Embark'd in Batteaus & rowed towards Fort George; at Night we put in at Sabbath day Point. here a large detachment of the Jersey Provincial Reg^{t}. under their Col^{o}. (Parker)[32] was cut off in July 1757 being met by the Van of Genl. Moncalm's Army, going to besiege Fort Willm. Henry.

29th. Arriv'd at Fort George, about 40 Miles from Ticonderoga, quite the length of Lake George. This Fort is on a rising ground four or five hundred yards from the Place Fort Willm. Henry Stood, taken & demolish'd by the French in Augst. 1757; this is built of Stone, was intended for a large Pentagon, as yet one Bastion only is finish'd. it was begun by Genl. Abercrombie after he had retreated to This ground from Ticonderoga. Col^{o}. Eyres was the Projector—

30th. March'd to Fort Edward, 14 miles. This Fort is a pretty large oblong square of four Bastions irregular, 'tis built of Wood, has 37 Peices of heavy Cannon besides

28 The words between brackets are an explanatory note in the margin marked for insertion.
29 The date within square brackets is a note in the margin marked for placement here.
30 The words between brackets are a note in the margin with no indication of placement.
31 The words between square brackets are a note in the margin.
32 John Parker entered the Royal Navy as an able seaman on 1 July 1746 and served in the 50-gun, fourth rate *Chester* in Boscawen's squadron. On 1 July 1749, he was appointed midshipman and remained in that position until July 1750, when he left the Navy to immigrate to America. He was commissioned a captain in the First New Jersey Regiment (the Jersey Blues) on 23 April 1755. In 1756-57, he served as colonel. While at Fort William Henry, he led a scouting expedition down Lake George during which he and his men were ambushed near Sabbath Day Point. He escaped, but 24 boats and 250 of his 300 men were lost. On 30 December 1756, he was commissioned lieutenant in the 3rd Battalion of the 60th Royal American Regiment. Gage selected him and he was commissioned on 25 December 1757 as captain-lieutenant in the 80th Light Armed Foot. He was promoted to captain in the 4th Battalion of the 60th, but then transferred as to the 17th Foot on 17 September 1760. He was killed in action in the West Indies, probably during the Martinique operation, on 7 March 1762.

Mortars Mounted; but like most of our Forts in this part of the World, greatly commanded by the Hills near it. This Lyes close on Hudson's River.

31st. March'd to Saratoga, 14 miles; remarkable for the lines thrown up here by the 44th. & 48th. Reg^{t}. in 1755

Augst. 1st. Halted here

2d. March'd to the Half Moon,[33] 28 Miles: pass'd by Still Water,[34] about Mid Way. the half Moon was so Call'd because the Course of the River runs in that shape at this Place. & Still Water on account of the slowness of the Steam.

3d. March'd to the half way house, 6 Miles

4th. March'd to Albany, 6 Miles, & Immediately without stopping Embark'd on board sloops, prepar'd to receive us, & sail'd down Hudson River for New York. all these Places from Fort Edward lye on Hudson's river, the Inhabitants are but few. [a very fatiguing March of more than 630 miles][35]

8th. Pass'd New York & landed at Staten Island, about 6 Miles below New York & 170 from Albany. We ecamp'd on Statten Island with the Reg^{ts}. that had march'd before us from Crown Point. & the other Reg^{ts}, follow'd in succession. We had 11 Reg^{ts}. Encamp'd here

15th. Amherst's . — 17th Monckton's . — 27th. Blackeney's . — 28th. Townsend's . — 35th. Otway's . — 40th. Amiger's . — 42d. Royal Highlanders, two Battalions, — 43d. Talbot's — 48th. Webb's— 60th. Haviland's, 4th. Batt^{n}. Roy^{l}. Americans

Whilst we remain'd Encamp'd here we were constantly Exercis'd & every Regiment in turn Reviewed by Genl. Amherst.

---

33 The area that includes the 'sprouts of the Mohawk River', the multiple mouths of the Mohawk River as it enters the Hudson River, creating a number of islands. In 1788, a town in this general area was named Halfmoon, New York.

34 Stillwater, New York.

35 A note in the margin next to the entry for 4 August 1761. It is unclear what the reference is to 630 miles, but it is roughly comparable to the 537 miles on modern roads between Québec and Staten Island.

6

Martinique, 8 November 1761–7 May 1762

Novr. 8th. The Regim[ts]. began to Embark for an Expedition against Martinico.

11th. The Embarkation was finish'd & the Fleet Sail'd down to Sandy hook, About 25 miles below NYork.

19th. Sail'd out of the Hook under Convoy of the *Devonshire* 66 Guns, the *Alcide* 60 Guns, *Norwich* 50 Guns,[1] & *Penzance* 40 Guns.[2] Gen[l]. Monckton Commanded the Troops. Steered for the Islands of Barbadoes.

1 The 50-gun, fourth rate *Norwich* was built at Blackwall by Philip Perry between 1743 and 1745, and completed at Woolwich. Commissioned in 1745, she was in the Downs during the autumn and winter of 1745. She sailed for North America in 1746, carrying the broad pendant of Charles Knowles. She was at Louisbourg in 1746, then in the West Indies during the winter of 1746-47, returning to Louisbourg in 1748. Returning to England she was given a middling repair at Chatham and recommissioned in 1754. She sailed with Braddock in February 1754 and served with Keppel's squadron in 1755, then with Boscawen's squadron at Halifax, and with Spry in North America in 1756, taking the French 50-gun *L'Arc-en-Ciel* in 1756. She convoyed mast ships in 1758 and was with Rodney's squadron in the Channel. In 1760, she sailed under the command of Captain William McCleverty for New York on 6 May 1760 she sailed for the Leeward Islands in December 1761. She was at Martinique 7 January to 10 February 1762 and then with Rodney's squadron at St Lucia 24-25 March 1762. Paid off in September 1762, she was sold at Chatham in 1768. Length of gun deck 140 feet 2½ inches, length of keel 114 feet 1 inch, breadth 40 feet 5½ inches, depth of hold 17 feet 2½ inches, 993 28/94 tons bm.

2 The 44-gun, fifth rate *Penzance* was built at Chichester by Chitty & Vernon between 1746 and 1748, and completed at Portsmouth. Commissioned in 1747, she served in North American waters in 1748 and was surveyed in 1749. She recommissioned in 1752 under the broad pendant of Captain Charles Saunders. She served in Newfoundland waters in successive years between 1752 and 1755, refitted in 1757-58, she sailed with a Baltic convoy in 1758, then cruised in home waters. She sailed for North America on 11 March 1760 and was in the advance on Montreal. Under Captain John Boyd, she served in North American waters in and the Leeward Islands in 1761. She was at Martinique from 7 January to 10 February 1762, at St Lucia 24-25 February 1762. In March 1762, she participated in the Havana operation from 6 June to 13 August 1762. She was sold at Plymouth in 1766. Length of gun deck 134 feet 9 inches, length of keel 109 feet 4 inches, breadth 37 feet 7½ inches, depth of 15 feet 10½ inches, 823 26/94 tons bm.

24th. Spoke with the Packet from England, were told Mr Pitt[3] had resigne'd. In our Passage we had one very heavy Squall of Wind, most of the ships suffer'd in their Masts, yards, or Sails, but none Materially—

Dec[r]. 23d. Made the Island of Barbadoes.

24th Anchor'd in Carlisle bay. five Batt[ns]. from Bellisle 61st Grey's—69th Colvill's, 76th. Ruffanes, 2 Batt[ns]. 90th Morgans had got in 10 days before us. with the foll[g]. Ships of War.

Under Admiral Rodney

Ships	Guns
Foudroyant[4]	80
Dublin	74
Temeraire[5]	74
Culloden[6]	74

3 William Pitt, the elder, resigned on 5 October 1761 as Secretary of the State for the Southern Department and as Leader of the House of Commons.

4 The 80-gun, third rate *Foudroyant* was built at Toulon to the design of François Coulomb as the French warship *Le Foudroyant* between 1748 and 1751. The 64-gun HMS *Monmouth*, with *Hampton Court* and *Swiftsure*, took *Le Foudroyant* in a hard-fought action in the Mediterranean on 28 Februay 1758. The Admiralty purchased the prize and refitted the vessel at Portsmouth in 1759. Commissioned in 1759, she served as Vice Admiral Sir Thomas Hardy's flagship with Hawke's fleet. In 1760, under Captain Robert Duff, she sailed for the Leeward Islands, then returned to Portsmouth for a refit in 1761, she sailed again to the West Indies. She served in the Martinique operation in 1762. Later in 1762, under Captain Molyneux Shuldham, she was Rodney's flagship in the Leeward Islands. Paid off in 1763, she was recommissioned in August 1775 under Captain John Jervis, who held command until 1782. She was at the first Battle of Ushant in 1778 and the Relief of Gibraltar. Jervis was knighted after the ship took the French 74-gun *Le Pégase*. The ship was broken up at Plymouth in 1787. Length of gun deck 180 feet 5 inches, length of keel 147 feet 3 inches, breadth 50 feet 3 inches, depth of hold 23 feet, 1,977 69/94 tons bm.

5 The 74-gun third rate *Temeraire* was built as the French *Le Téméraire* at Toulon between 1748 and 1750. Taken as a prize by Boscawen at the Battle of Lagos on 18 August 1759, the Admiralty purchased here and fitted her out at Portsmouth in 1760-61. Commissioned in 1760 under Captain Matthew Burton, she served with Hawke's fleet, then participated in the Belleisle operation from 6 April to 8 June 1761, before sailing for the Leeward Islands on 16 October 1761. After serving at Martinique in 1762, she sailed for Jamaica, blockaded Cape François, and was in the Havana operation 6 June to 13 August 1762. Returning home in 1763, she was paid off and repaired. She recommissioned in 1764 as a guard ship at Plymouth. In 1769, she was refitted for carrying troops. Paid off in 1771, she served an un-commissioned guard ship at Plymouth in 1771-1774, then in 1784 a floating battery. She was sold at Plymouth in 1784. Length of gun deck 169 feet 2 inches, length of keel 137 feet 2 ⅜ inches, breadth 48 feet ¾ inch, depth of hold 20 feet 9½ inches, 1,685 80/94 tons bm.

6 The 74-gun, third rate *Culloden* was designed by Acworth and built at Deptford by John Holland between 1745 and 1747. Named after the recent victory on 16 April 1746 over Jacobite forces, she was the first 74 to be built in over 75 years and the smallest of the century. Five feet shorter than those that followed, she became noted for her poor sailing qualities. Commissioned in 1747, she served with Warren fleet, then became a guard ship until 1754, refitted for Channel service, she joined Hawke's fleet in 1755, and she was with Byng in the Mediterranean in 1756, participated in the Battle of Minorca on 20 May 1756,

Dragon[7]	74
Vanguard	74
Temple[8]	70
Marlborough[9]	68
Stirling Castle	64
Raisonable[10]	64

---

the Battle of Lagos in 1759. Under Captain John Barker, she sailed for the Leeward Islands on 7 September 1760. She served with Hawke's fleet, participated at Martinique in 1762, then at Jamaica and in the Havana operation in 1762. Returning home, she was paid off in 1763 and sold in 1770. Length of gun deck 161 feet, length of keel 130 feet 10 inches, breadth 46 feet, depth of hold 19 feet 4 inches, 1,472 54/94 tons bm.

7 The 74-gun, *Bellona* class, third-rate *Dragon* was built at Deptford by Adam Hayes between 1758 and 1760. Commissioned in 1760, she served in the western Squadron and participated in the Belleisle operation in 1761. Under Captain John Lendrick, she sailed for the Leeward Islands on 30 October 1761. In 1762, under the Hon. Augustus Hervey, she participated in the operations at Martinique, St Lucia, Jamaica, the blockade of Cape François and the Havana Operation. Paid off in 1763, she was recommissioned as a guard ship, serving in that role until 1769, when she was refitted to carry troops. Paid off in 1770, she served as a receiving ship at Portsmouth in 1780. Paid off in 1783, she was sold in 1784. Length of gun deck 168 feet, length of keel 137 feet 11 inches, breadth 46 feet 11 inches, depth of hold 19 feet 9 inches, 1,614 73/94 tons bm, draught 12 feet 7 inches forward / 17 feet 11 inches aft.

8 The 68-gun, third rate *Temple* was built by Hugh Blaydes at Hull between 1756 and 1759. Commissioned in 1759, she was present in the Battle of Quiberon Bay 20 November 1759 and then in the blockade force at Basque Roads. She sailed for the Leeward Islands under Captain Lucius O'Brien on 26 March 1760 and, with *Griffin*, retook the 12-gun *Virgin* off Grenada on 10 August 1760. She served in the Leeward Islands in 1761-62. Under Captain Julien Legge, she was at Jamaica in April 1762 and in the Havana operation June-August 1762. Under Captain Thomas Collingwood, she sailed for home in October 1762, foundering during the voyage off Cape Clear on 18 December 1762. Length of gun deck 159 feet 11 inches, length of keel 131 feet 11 inches, breadth 45 feet 1½ inches, depth of hold 19 feet 4 inches, 1,428 76/94 tons bm

9 The 68-gun *Marlborough* was built as a 90-gun second rate at Chatham with three gun decks between 1725 and 1732. She was not completed until 1741, when she was first commissioned. She served in the Mediterranean in 1741 and was present in the Battle of Toulon on 14 February 1744, losing 25 killed, including the captain, and 25 wounded. At Portsmouth between 1753 and 1757, she was reduced to an 80-gun third rate, recommissioned in 1756, she served as flagship in 1756 and 1757. In 1760, she was cut down at Portsmouth to a two-deck 68-gun ship. Recommissioned in 1760, she served as flagship for Rear Admiral George Rodney and sailed for the Leeward Islands under the temporary command of Captain Molyneux Shuldham. After Martinique and Havana, she sailed for home under Captain Thomas Burnett. She founded in the Atlantic due to leaks on 29 November 1762; all hands were taken off by *Antelope*. Length of gun deck 164 feet, length of keel 132 feet 5 inches, breadth 47 feet 2 inches, depth of hold 18 feet 10 inches, 1,566 89/94 tons bm.

10 The 64-gun, third rate *Raisonnable* was built as the French *Le Raisonnable* at Rochefort to a design by Pierre Morineau between 1754 and 1757. Taken as a prize on 29 May 1758 by *Achilles* and *Dorsetshire*, the Admiralty purchased her and refitted her at Portsmouth. Commissioned under Captain John Montagu, she sailed on 18 April 1759 for the Leeward Islands. From 1760, Captain Molyneux Shuldham commanded herShe participated in the attack on Martinique in 1762, where she grounded on a reef and was wrecked on 7 January 1762. Length of gun deck 159 feet 2 inches, length of keel 129 feet 7 inches, breadth 43 feet 10½ inches, depth of hold 19 feet 6¾ inches, 1,326 84/93 tons bm

Modeste[11]	64
Nottingham	60
Falkland[12]	50
Sutherland	50
Frigates	
Repulse[13]	32
Crescent[14]	2

11 The 64-gun, third rate *Modeste* was built as the French *La Modeste* at Toulon to a design by Noël Pomet between 1758 and 1759. Taken as a prize by Boscawen's squadron at Lagos on 18 August 1759, the Admiralty purchased and fitted her out at Portsmouth. Commissioned in 1760, she sailed to the Mediterranean and took the 32-gun *La Bouffonne* off Cadiz in 1761. Under Captain Robert Walsingham, she sailed for the Leeward Islands on 18 October 1761. She participated in the Martinique operation and remained in the Leeward Islands afterwards under Captain John Hollwall. Paid off in 1764, she underwent repair and was recommissioned in 1771 as a guard ship at Jamaica, then served as a receiving ship in Portsmouth. She was broken up at Portsmouth in 1800. Length of gun deck 158 feet 6 inches, length of keel 139 feet, breadth 44 feet 5¾ inches, depth of hold 19 feet 8 inches, 1, 357 47/94 tons bm.

12 The 50-gun, fourth rate *Falkland* was built at Bursledon by Philemon Ewer between 1743 and 1744 and completed at Portsmouth in 1744. Commissioned in 1744, *Falkland* participated in the Battle of Finisterre on 3 May 1745 and took five privateers during the War of 1739-48. Placed on ordinary in 1748, she was recommissioned in October 1755 under Captain Francis William Drake, who remained in command into 1762. She sailed to America on 30 June 1757 with the Highland Regiments (Montgomery's First Highland 62nd/63rd/77th Regiment or Fraser's Second Highland 63rd/64th/78th Regiment) and was in the West Indies in 1758. In 1759, she sailed to meet East India ships, served with Hawke's fleet and participated in the Battle of Quiberon Bay on 20 November, after which she served in the blockade of Lorient. She sailed to North America with Swanton's squadron for the Leeward Islands in June 1761 and participated in the Martinique operation. In 1762 under Captain William Tucker, she was with Rodney's squadron in the Leeward Islands, then returned to England in 1783. She was given to the agent victualler at Chatham in 1768. Length of gun deck 140 feet 2¾ inches, length of keel 113 feet 6¼ inches, breadth 40 feet 2 inches, depth of hold 17 feet 3¼ inches, 974 19/94 tons bm

13 The 32-gun, fifth rate frigate *Repulse* was built as the French *La Bellone* to a design by François-Guillaume Clairin-Deslauriers at Rochefort between 1755 and 1758. Taken in the Soundings by the 32-gun *Vestal* on 21 February 1759, the Admiralty purchased her. She was refitted at Portsmouth and commissioned in August 1758 under Captain John Carter Allen. She sailed on 10 March 1760 with Byron's squadron for Louisbourg, where she took the 20-gun *Le Chevalier de Bavro,* and participate in the destruction of the 32-gun *Le Machault* and *La Bienfaisant,* and the 16-gun *Le Marquis de Marloze* in Chaleur Bay on 8 July 1761. In June 1761, she sailed for the Leeward Islands and participated in operation at Martinique. From November 1761, Captain Peregrine Bertie was in command, followed by Captain Sir Alexander Holburne in February 1763. *Repulse* remained in the Leeward Islands until she returned home and was paid off in 1763. Recommissioned in December 1775, she sailed for North America in May 1776 and was presumably lost with all hands in a tropical storm off Bermuda in December 1776. Length of gun deck 122 feet 7 inches, length of keel 104 feet ½ inch, breadth 34 feet 11½ inches, depth of hold 10 feet 10½ inches, 676 67/94 tons bm

14 The 32-gun, fifth rate frigate *Crescent* was built at Bordeaux as the French privateer *Le Rostan* and requisitioned by the French Navy in October 1757. She was taken as a prize by the 74-gun, third rates, *Torbay* and *Chichester* on 3 February 1758. Purchased by the Admiralty and named *Crescent* in 1758, she was fitted out at Portsmouth. Commissioned in October 1758

Stag[15]	32
Acteon[16]	28
Lizard	28
Levant[17]	28
Echo	24
Greyhound[18]	24

under Captain Thomas Collingwood, she sailed for the Leeward Islands on 23 April 1759. In 1759, she took as prizes the French 26-gun warships *Le Berkeley* and *L'Hermione*In 1760, she took two privateers, *Le Saint-Antoine* and *Le Saint-Michel*, and, in 1761, *Le Colibri*. After participating in the Martinique operation, she served in Rodney's squadron. From May 1762, she was under the command of Captain Robert Brice. She returned home and after repairs at Sheerness in 1763-63 and 1770-71, she was recommissioned for the Falkland Islands dispute. She sailed for the Leeward Islands in 1771 and returned in 1774, when she was paid off. She was sold at Woolwich in 1777. Length of gun deck 130 feet 5 inches, length of keel 107 feet 5½ inches, breadth 35 feet 9 inches, depth of hold 11 feet 2 inches, 732 8/94 tons bm.

15 The 32-gun, *Niger* class, fifth rate frigate *Stag* was designed by Thomas Slade and built at Rotherhithe by Thomas Stanton & Co. in 1757 and completed at Deptford in 1758. She was commissioned under Captain Henry Angel. She served off Dunkirk in 1759, with Hawke's fleet in 1760, and in the Mediterranean in 1761 before sailing as an escort with a troop convoy to the West Indies on 17 October 1761. She was at Martinique from 1 January to 10 February 1762. Then, under Captain William Bayne, she was with Rodney's fleet and at Jamaica in 1763. Paid off in 1764, she was recommissioned in 1769 and served in the East Indies. Paid off in 1772, she was reduced to a 28-gun sixth rate, then recommissioned in 1777 and served in home waters. She was reestablished as a 32-gun fifth rate in 1779 and took a number of vessels before being paid off and broken up at Deptford in 1783. Length of gun deck 125 feet, length of keel 103 feet 4 inches, breadth 35 feet 2 inches, depth of hold 12 feet, 679 67/94 tons bm.

16 The 28-gun, sixth rate frigate *Actaeon* was built at Chatham by John Lock in 1757. Commissioned in 1757, she served in Anson's fleet and took a prize in 1758. In 1759, she as with Hawke's fleet and then with Rodney's squadron in the Channel in 1760, taking two prizes. She was in both the Belleisle and Île d'Aix operations in 1761 before sailing for the Leeward Islands under Captain John Ourry on 16 October1761. She took a privateer, and participated in the Martinique operation, after which she remained with Rodney's squadron and took a Spanish ship in 1762. Paid off in 1763, she recommissioned in 1763 and sailed again for the Leeward Islands in 1765-66. Paid off in 1766, she was sold at Deptford. Length of gun deck 118 feet 2¾ inches, length of keel 97 feet 3 inches, breadth 33 feet 7½ inches, depth of hold 10 feet 6 inches, 584 81/94 tons bm.

17 The 28-gun, Coventry class, sixth rate frigate *Levant* was built at Buckler's Hard by Henry Adams in 1756 and completed at Portsmouth in 1757. Commissioned in 1758 under Captain William Tucker, she sailed for the Leeward Islands on 23 July 1759 and took three privateers in 1760, three more in 1761, and another in 1761. After she participated in the Martinique operation, Captain John Laforey commanded her in the Leeward Islands. Paid off in 1763, she was recommissioned in 1766 and sailed for Jamaica. Paid off in 1770, she underwent a great repair at Deptford. She was recommissioned in 1771 and sailed for the Mediterranean in 1772 and 1774. She took a privateer in 1777 and another in 1779. She was broken up ay Deptford in 1780. Length of gun deck 118 feet 5 inches, length of keel 97 feet 3⅝ inches, breadth 33 feet 11 inches, depth of hold 10 feet 6 inches, 595 34/94 tons bm.

18 The 20-gun, sixth rate frigate *Greyhound* was built at Limehouse by Thomas Snelgrove in 1741 and completed at Deptford. Commissioned in 1741, she took a privateer off Lisbon in 1743, served off the African coast in 1743, she served in Scottish waters in 1745, and she sailed for North America in December 1761 under the command of Captain Thomas Francis. She was in the Leeward Islands in December 1761 and in the Martinique operation in 1762. After the death of Francis, Captain Patrick Drummond took command in October

Rose[19]	20
Virgin[20]	20
Woolwich[21]	
Guardalupe[22]	
Barbadoes[23]	

1762, when she served with Rodney's squadron. Returning to England, she was paid off in March 1763. Recommissioned under Drummond, she sailed to the Leeward Islands 15 October 1763. She was resheathed at Antigua in 1765 and 1767. Paid off in 1768, she was sold. Length of gun deck 108 feet 1 inch, length of keel 88 feet 3⅜ inches, breadth 30 feet 11¾ inches, depth of hold 10 feet 1½ inches, 450 64/94 tons bm.

19 The 20-gun, sixth rate, *Seaforth* class frigate *Rose* was built at Hull by Hugh Blaydes in 1756-57. Commissioned in 1757, she served in Howe's squadron and participated in the St Malo, Cherbourg, and St Cast operations in 1758. In 1760, she was in Rodney's squadron and sailed for the Leeward Islands. Under Captain John N.P. Knott, she took a privateer in 1761, participated in the operations at Martinique and Havana in 1762. Paid off in 1764, she underwent a large repair at Sheerness and was recommissioned in 1768. She sailed for Newfoundland under Captain James Wallace in 1772 and was in Rhode Island and New York waters until 1776, when she returned home. In 1778, she was with Parker's squadron at Savannah in December 1778. There, she was sunk as a block ship to prevent the approach of the French 18 August 1779. Length of gun deck 108 feet 11½ inches, length of keel 90 feet 10¼ inches, breadth 30 feet 6 inches, depth of hold 9 feet 7 inches, 449 52/94 tons bm.

20 The 12-gun sloop *Virgin* was a French vessel, *La Vierge,* taken as a prize in 1760 and purchased by the Admiralty. Renamed Virgin, she was commissioned under Commander Edward St Loe. While escorting a convoy in the West Indies, three French privateers boarded her, killed 6 men, including the captain, and took her as a prize on 17 May 1760. While serving as a French privateer, *Temple*, with *Griffin*, retook her in September 1760. In September 1761, Commander Charles Buckner took command and she participated in the Martinique operation. From October 1762, Commander Richard Bligh commanded her. She was sold at Antigua in 1764.

21 The 44-gun, fifth rate frigate *Woolwich* was built at Buckler's Hard by John Darley and completed by Moody Janverin between 1746 and 1749. Commissioned in 1755 under Captain Peter Parker, she sailed for the Leeward Islands in December 1756. She participated in the operations at Martinique and Guadeloupe in 1759. Under Captain William Bayne, she sailed for Africa and the Leeward Islands on 30 October 1760 and participated in the Martinique operation in 1762, taking the privateer *La Dame Auguste* on 7 February 1762. After serving with Rodney's squadron she was paid off and sold in December 1762. Length of gun deck 133 feet 4 inches, length of keel 108 feet 6 inches, breadth 37 feet 9¾ inches, depth of hold 16 feet ½ inch, 825 16/94 tons bm

22 A Sloop on the Leeward Islands Station, commanded by Commander Robert Brice until June 1762, then by Lieutenant James Dalrymple. Mentioned in David Syrett (ed.), *Siege of Havana*. Publications of the Navy Record Society, Vol. 114 (London: Navy Records Society, 1970), p.70n; David Syrett (ed.), *Rodney Papers: Selections from the Papers of Admiral Lord Rodney,* volume 1, 1742-1763. Publications of the Navy Record Society, Vol. 148 (London: Ashgate for the Navy Records Society, 2005), pp.442, 457. The 28-gun, *Coventry* class, sixth rate frigate *Guadeloupe was* not commissioned until 1764.

23 The 14-gun *Barbadoes* was a British merchant ship that was purchased on 25 November 1757 at Antigua. She was commissioned in January 1758 for service in the Leeward Islands, where she remained. She took a privateer in 1758. Under the command of Commander Stair Douglas, she participated in the Martinique and Havana operations in 1762, after which she sailed for Plymouth. In 1763, she was surveyed and sold at Deptford. Length of gun deck 80 feet, length of keel 52 feet 10 inches, breadth 21 feet 6 inches, 129 85/94 tons bm

Antigua[24]

Bombs
Grenada[25] 10
Basilisk[26] 10
Thunder[27] 10

Jan 5th. The Fleet sail'd from Barbadoes—it is an exceeding pleasant Island, rising from the water with a gradual Assent towards the center, interspersed with Plantations of Cocoa & other Exotics, the whole has the Appearance of a Beautiful

---

24 The 14-gun *Antigua* was a British privateer purchased at Antigua in 1757 for service in the Leeward Islands, where she remained. From August 1761, Commander John Nott commanded her, when she participated in the Martinique and Havana operations. She was sold at Antigua on 13 August 1763. Length of gun deck 71 feet 6 inches, length of keel 53 feet, breadth 23 feet 7½ inches, depth of hold 10 feet 6 inches, 157 32/94 tons bm.

25 The bomb vessel *Granado* was built at Harwich by John Barnard between 1741 and 1742, and completed as a 10-gun sloop at Harwich Dockyard in 1742. First commissioned as a sloop in 1741, she served in the North Sea and Channel in 1742-43, then escorted a convoy to Lisbon in 1744. Laid up in 1748, she was recommissioned as a sloop in 1755 and then refitted as a bomb vessel at Harwich in 1756. Under Commander John Fortescue, she sailed for North America in June 1757. In 1758, she participated in operations at St Malo, Cherbourg, and St Cast. She sailed for the Leeward Islands on 12 November 1758, participating in the Martinique and Guadeloupe operations in 1759. In 1760, she was fitted as a sloop and operated in in the Downs and off Le Havre. From July to September 1761, she was refitted as a bomb at Portsmouth and sailed for the Leeward Islands under Commander James Hawker on 30 October 1761. She participated in the Martinique operation and, in March 1762, Commander Stair Douglas took command. She was in Jamaica in April and in the operations at Havana, where Commander Thomas took command in July. Paid off in June 1763, she was sold at Portsmouth on 30 August 1763. Length of gun deck 91 feet 1 inch, length of keel 74 feet 1½ inches, breadth 26 feet 2 inches, depth of hold 11 feet 3 inches, 269 90/94 tons bm.

26 The bomb vessel *Basilisk* was an *Infernal* class bomb vessel built to a design by Thomas Slade by William Wells & Co. at Deptford between 1758 and 1759 and completed at Deptford Dockyard in 1759. Commissioned in 1759, she participated in the bombardment of Le Havre in March 1759. In 1760, she was fitted as a sloop and operated in the ChannelIn 1761, she was refitted as a bomb and recommissioned under Commander Robert Brice. She sailed for the Leeward Islands and participated in the Martinique operation in January-February 1762, in the St Lucia operation in March 1762, and, under Commander William Lowfield from May 1762 in the Havana operation from June to August 1762. On 29 October 1762, the 26-gun French privateer from Bayonne, *L'Audacieuse* took *Basilisk* as a prize, killing 9 members of the ship's company including Lowfield, and wounding 6 others. Length of gun deck 91 feet 7 inches, length of keel 74 feet 4 ⅜ inches, breadth 28 feet 1 inch, depth of hold 12 feet 1½ inches, 311 90/94 tons bm.

27 The bomb vessel *Thunder* was an *Infernal* class bomb vessel built to a design by Thomas Slade by Thomas Henniker at Chatham between 1758 and 1759 and completed at Chatham Dockyard in 1759. Commissioned in 1759, she served in Duff Squadron and was at Quiberon Bay in November 1759. She was fitted as a sloop 1760. In the first half of 1761 she was fitted as a bomb at Portsmouth, she sailed under Commander Philip Boteler for the Leeward Islands on 18 October 1761. She participated in the Martinique operation in January and February 1762, and from March 1762, under Commander, she participated in the Havana operation. Paid off in 1763, she was sold in 1774. Length of gun deck 91 feet 6 inches, length of keel 74 feet 1¾ inches, breadth 27 feet 8¼ inches, depth of hold 12 feet 1 inch, 302 32/94 tons bm.

Garden. it was a very fine & uncommon sight to us, to see the ground wear so glorious a Verdure, & fruit ripening on the Trees at Christmas. We having just come from a country cover'd with snow.

6th. Made the Island of Martinico.

7th. anchor'd in the Cul de sac Marin,[28] [St. Anne's Bay][29] a large Bay to the Eastward of Fort Royal;[30] the Raisonable man of War, ran aground near this bay & was lost. [64 Guns commanded by Capt Shuldam. This is the second ship he lost].[31]

8th. at Night the Flat bottom'd boats were sent up to the head of this Bay, that by rowing along the shore, and firing their swivels, they might alarm the Enemy, and discover their strength. in one of the Boats, were 30 Marines, [They were order'd not to Land][32] who landed near a Battery & overset two Six pounders. a Midshipman was kill'd & 2 or 3 Sailors were Wounded.

9th. The second Brigade under Brigadier Ruffane[33] landed on the South side of this Bay, the Enemy abandon'd three Batterys of two Guns each & fled. The Rangers in Scouring the Country took an Officer of Militia Prisr. who was Excessively frightened, supposing the Rangers to be Indians, being drest & painted as such.

28 Cul de Sac du Marin is a deep bay on the southwest coast, near the southern tip, of Martinique. The village of Sainte Anne is located on the south shore of the Bay.

29 The place name in brackets is a note in the margin.

30 Cul de Sac du Marin is located about 16 miles (24 km) to the south east of Fort-Royal, the main city on Martinique, which was renamed in the nineteenth century as Fort-de-France.

31 The words within brackets are a comment in the margin. While in command of the 60-gun *Warwick* in 1756, a French 74 with two others had captured *Warwick* near Martinique. Shuldham and his crew were prisoners of war in France for two years. After their release in 1758, a court martial cleared Shuldham of blame.

32 The words within brackets are a note in the margin marked for placement here.

33 William Rufane was born in 1703 and commissioned an ensign in Howard's 24th Regiment of Foot on 29 May 1722. He was promoted to lieutenant in the 24th Foot on 17 April 1724, to captain on 27 September 1737, to major on 29 April 1741, and lieutenant colonel on 27 February 1751. He was made colonel of the 76th Regiment of Foot on 16 January 1761. When the 76th Foot was disbanded on 1 December 1763, he went on half pay. He was promoted to major general on 10 July 1762 and became colonel of the 6th Foot on 14 June 1765. He was promoted to lieutenant general on 25 May 1772.

10th. The 1st. and 3rd. Brigades, under the Brigadiers Haviland & Grant,[34] sail'd to the Great Cove d'Arlet[35] & landed with part of the light Infantry under Lt. Colo. Scott, who were sent to take post opposite the Isle Ramiers (Pidgeon Island),[36] the Brigades march'd to the same post, taking with them 4 Royal Mortars,[37] shell, & Ammunition.

11th. The Enemy threw some Shot & shells at us from the Island. some popping between our light Infantry & the Enemy. a battery was intended for the Mortars on the Point of the Hill nearest the Island. but upon a second Examination, it was thought more prudent to desist,—as the Island was found to be of no consequence, lying at too great a Distance from the opposite Shore to give the Ships any

34 James Grant was born in 1720, the second son of Lieutenant Colonel William Grant of Ballindalloch, Banffshire, Scotland. He was educated under the care of a kinsman, Patrick Grant, Lord Elchies, at the University of Edinburgh, where, on Elchies' advice, he read law from 1736 to 1740. More interested in a military career, he obtained a commission as ensign in his brother's regiment, the Royal or 1st Regiment of Foot under Hon. James St. Clair. He was promoted to lieutenant on 2 April 1744 and, then, to captain on 24 October 1744. Grant was present at the Battle of Fontenoy in 1745 and at Culloden in 1746. Thereafter, he served in Flanders. St Clair appointed him one of his aides de camp for a projected expedition to Canada, but when that expedition did not materialize, he served in that capacity in the Lorient operation and then on St Clair's diplomatic mission to Vienna and Turin in 1748. After the end of the war, Grant continued as St Clair's aide-de-camp until 1752, when St Clair ordered him to become a traveling tutor to St. Clair's grand-nephew, William, 17th Earl of Sutherland. Recalled to his regiment in the spring of 1755, St Clair helped obtain for him a promotion to major on 5 January 1757 in the Hon. Archibald Montgomerie's 62nd (later 77th) Highland Regiment and went with the regiment to South Carolina. In Forbes's expedition to Fort Duquesne on 14 September 1758, the French captured Grant and held him as a prisoner in Montréal until November 1759, when he was exchanged. Grant's 77th Foot was the major component in the expedition against the Cherokees in South Carolina for which Amherst appointed Grant lieutenant colonel on 8 March 1760. On 26 July 1760, Grant was made lieutenant colonel of the 40th Foot and colonel in America on 25 February 1762. In this period he is often confused with his cousin, lieutenant colonel Francis Grant with the 42nd Foot and 90th Foot. James Grant served in both the Martinique and Havana operations in 1762, during which James Grant was instrumental in obtaining slaves from Martinique to fight at Havana (Syrett, *Havana*, p.137). Returning to London in 1763, he was appointed governor of East Florida in 1764, retaining that post until 1773, but leaving Florida for health reasons in 1771. In 1773, he was elected Member of Parliament for Tains (northern) Burghs, retaining the seat until 1780. He was appointed colonel of the 55th Foot on 25 December 1755 and returned to America as brigadier general under Sir William Howe He was present at the Battles of Long Island, Brandywine, and Germantown. Promoted to major general on 29 August 1777, he commanded successfully the expedition to St Lucia in 1778 and returned to Britain in 1779 and promoted to lieutenant general on 20 November 1782. He was elected Member of Parliament for Sutherland in 1787 and retained the seat until the age of 86 in 1802. He was colonel of the 11th Foot from 9 November 1796, was promoted to general on 3 May 1796, and served as governor of Stirling Castle from 1790 to 1806. He died in 1806. *History of Parliament, 1754-1790* http://www.historyofparliamentonline.org/volume/1754-1790/member/grant-james-1720-1806

35 Grande Anse d'Arlet is the largest and most northerly of the three coves on the peninsula on the southwest coast of Martinique. It is located between Cul de Sac du Marin in the south and Fort-Royal Bay in the north.

36 L'îlet à Ramiers.

37 A type of small mortar.

Disturbance in going towards Fort Royal, & the Troops were order'd to March back. A number of boats from Fort Royal were discover'd landing Men on this side. Just as we began our March at 11 oClock at night, our light Infantry were attack'd by 150 Grenadiers, follow'd by a number of Militia and Negroes, the Grenadiers behaved tolerably well & advanc'd, our light Infantry reserv'd their fire till the Enemy were within 40 yards, & then gave them the fire of two or 3 plattoons, which put the Whole to the Route a Lieut of the Enemy was kill'd & four grenadiers taken Pris^{rs}., many were Wounded as were heard by their groans, & several must have been kill'd, we did not Loose a man.— went from hence to the Landing Place, about 6 miles, the most rugged Mountainous Way that can possibly be conceived. The Troops that had landed at Cul de sac Marin not finding fresh water Embark'd this day & Joyn'd those at d'Arlet.

12th. The two Brigades that had landed at Ance d'Arlet reimbark'd

16th. The Whole sail'd from d'Arlet for Port Royal, the Enemy had a Chain of Batterys along the shore from Cas des Navires to port Royal, the Ships of War that were sent against them, ran close to the Shore, & after a good deal of firing, silenc'd them; the Army landed without opposition at Cas Navires, to the Westward of Fort Royal, & march'd towards Point Negro, lay on our Arms this Night. here part of the Army Encamp'd, the rest were posted to the Left. from hence we had a View of many Redoubts & Entrenchment thrown up by the Enemy on the road Leading to Fort Royal; a Very deep Valley lying between us & their Nearest Works, two batterys were order'd to be Erected to facilitate our passage over it, & check the Enemys fire from the Redoubts, as they had large Cannon in all their Works.

20th. a Sergeant & Six men of the Working Party kill'd. Battery's near finish'd.

21st. Open'd two Batterys, one of five the other of four 24 Pounders, with three 8 inch mortars.

24th. The following Disposition being made, we attack'd the Enemys Works. the Second Brigade to make their push near the sea side & to joyn the Grenadiers as soon as they Ascend the hill; the Grenadiers supported by the 4th. Brigade to lead the attack on the left of the 2d. Brigade; the 5th. Brigade to attack on the left of the Grenadiers; the Rangers with a body of Light Infantry, supported by a Battalion of the Royal Highlanders to attack on the left of the 5th Brigade to these were afterwards added the 27th, 28th & 69 Reg^{ts}. The 1st. & 3d. Brigades with a body of Light Infantry, were to March to the Left, to attempt a passage over the Mountains & gullies, in Order to fall upon the right Flank & rear of the Enemy; they began their March before day, but found that Way impassable, & were Oblig'd to return & follow the Rest. Our Grenadiers made their attack with Spirit & success, pushed the Enemy from Redoubt to Redoubt, & from one Entrenchment to another, till at last we drove them into the Town, & took Post on Morne Tortensan which lies directly above the Town & overlooks the Fort at about 1200 Yards distance. [we drove the French out of 22 Redoubts & strong breast works extending above 2

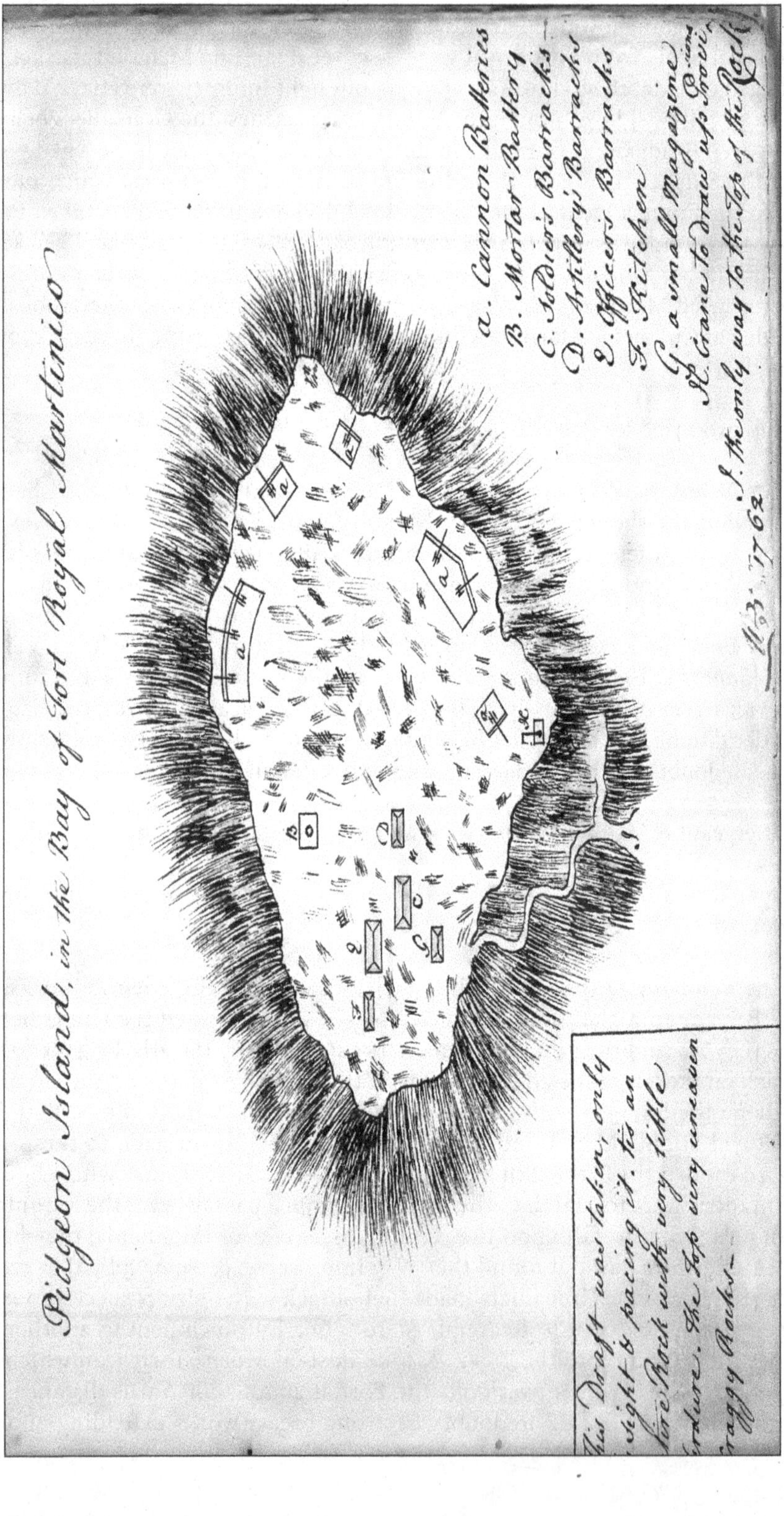

'Pidgeon island in the bay of Fort Royal Martinico' [1762].

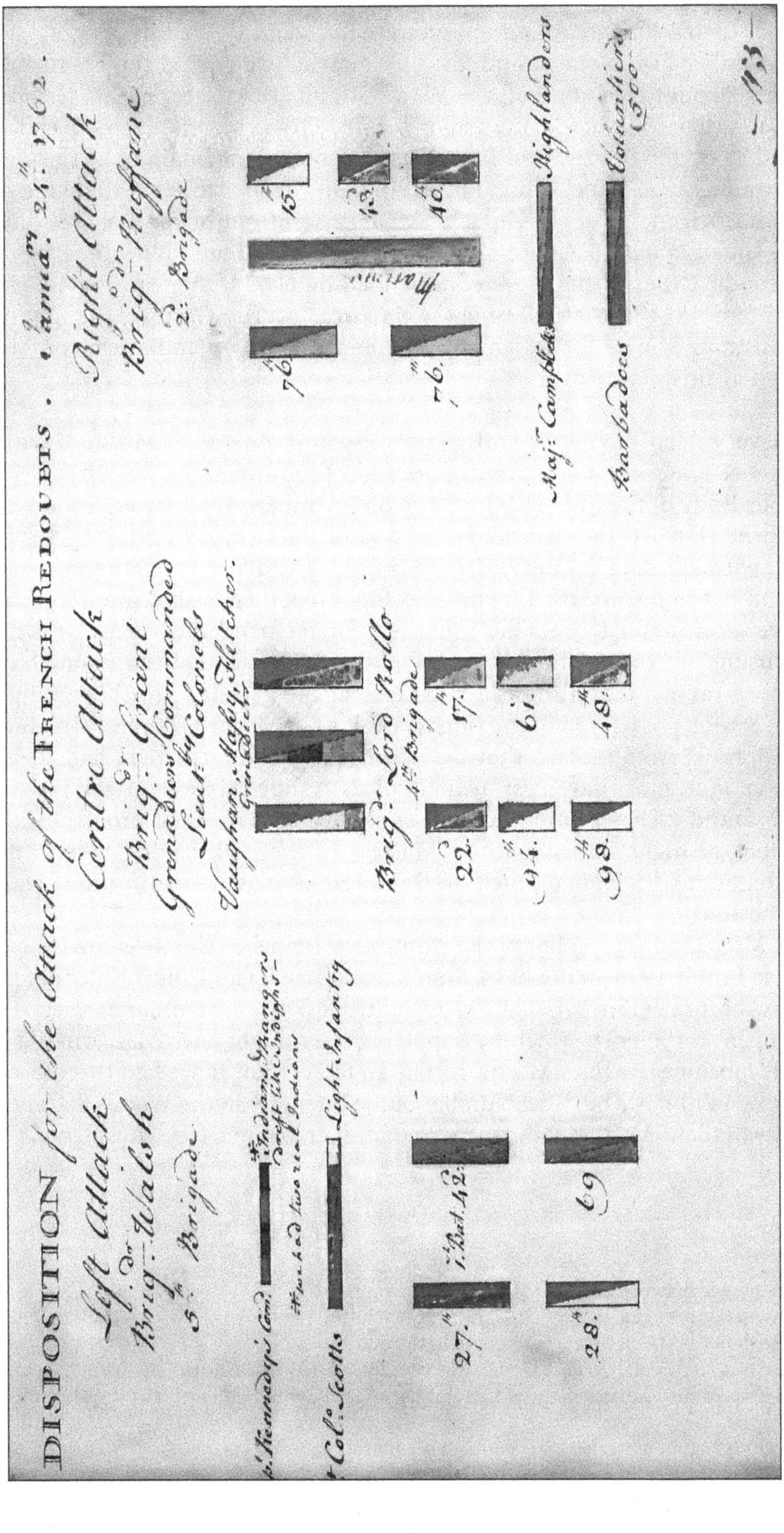

'Disposition for the attack of the French redoubts. January 24th. 1762'.

miles. 7 of their Works had Cannon mounted in them][38] We kill'd a great Many made a number of Prisoners, and lost but few, tho' we push'd the Enemy above two Miles, strongly Fortify'd all the Way, both by art & Nature. This service fell Chiefly on a few Men, upon the Grenadiers of Otway's 35th. 48th—Webb's the Highlanders & those of the 4th. Regim^t.., with some light Infantry, as the Nature of the Ground on our Side, would not admit many Troops to act at the same time. The second Brigade by some Unlucky Mistake went out of the Road & did not come up time Enough to assist the Grenadiers. [they did not follow the Party that way to conduct them. They were commanded by Genl Ruffane][39] The 1st. & 3d. Brigades took Post to the Left of the Army near Morne Garnier, the Rest were encamp'd along Morne Tortensan down to point Negro. Began Batterys on Morne Tortensan against Fort Royal.

27th. [A very deep Ravine or Gully lay between our army & Morne Garnier][40] between 4 & 5 oClock in the Afternoon, the left of our Army was attack'd by a Numerous Body of the Enemy, who came down unperceived through the Bushes from Morne Garnier; the Attack appear' formidable, as they were very Strong & came on with seeming resolution; upon our advanc'd Sentrys being fir'd at, the men stood to their arms, the first body that got together, rush'd into the Bushes, they were soon Supported, & after some very Smart firing, the Enemy were drove in Confusion, we seized the Glorious Opportunity, pursued the Enemy across a very deep ravine, mounting the Hill close at their heels against a number of Cannon, & took possession of the Important Post of Morne Garnier.[41] The Enemy flying before us from a Place they deem'd impregnable, & which, had they not thus led us to it, must have cost us many lives & much time to attack regularly; [here we found plenty of ammunition & about 900 barrels of provisions.][42] by nine oclock at night we were entire Masters of the Hill, having taken a large Strong Redoubt with a good Ditch, well Friezed, & mounted with nine pieces of heavy Cannon.

[Genl. Monckton was on board the Admiral's Ship when the welcome News was brought to him.][43] in the redoubt we found a few French Grenadiers which we made Prisoners.—Morne Garnier is an Extream Strong Post, & commands every thing near it, open to the Fort, which by Supplying they might have Maintain'd a long time, it is much nearer than Morne Tortensan to Fort Royal. we had two officers & 80 or 90 men kill'd. we buried a Number of the Enemy & in the Woods & Canes we find many of their Dead or dying men, so that their loss much be considerable.

---

38 The sentence between brackets is a note in the margin.
39 The sentence between brackets is a note in the margin.
40 The sentence between brackets is a note in the margin.
41 In reaction to this attack, Fort Desaix was later built on Morne Garnier between 1768 and 1772, to prevent a future enemy attack and use of artillery to bombard Fort Royal from above.
42 The words between brackets are a note in the margin.
43 The words between brackets are a note in the margin.

Six Plans depicting part of the works out of which the French were driven by the English, under the command of Genl. Monckton, at Martinico, January 24th. 1762.

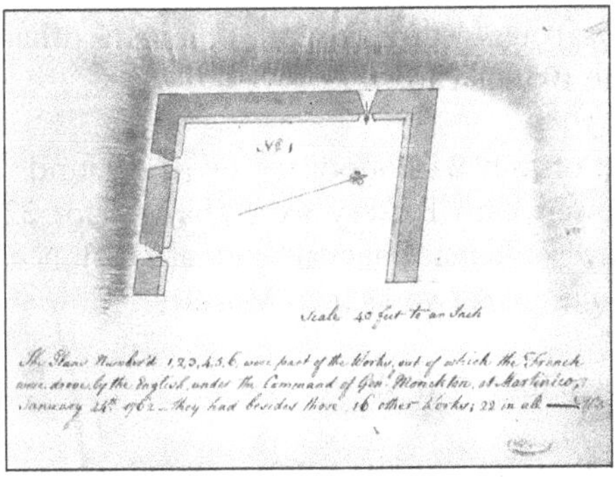

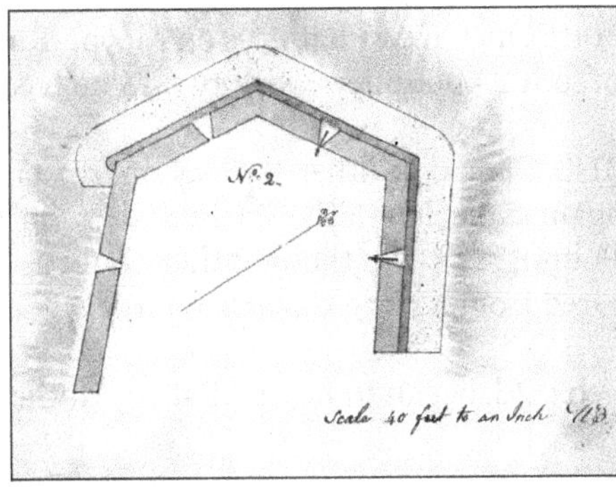

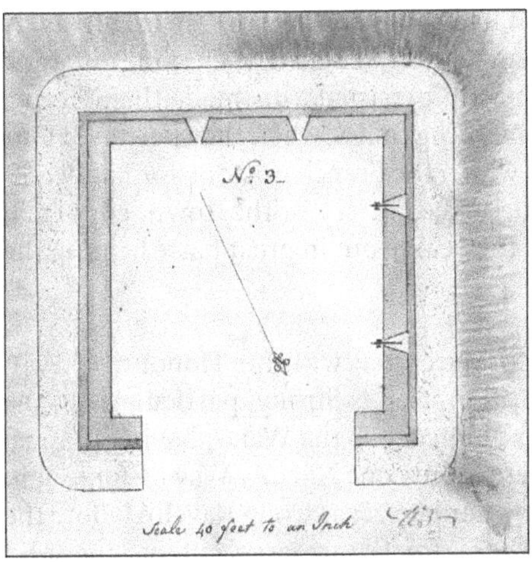

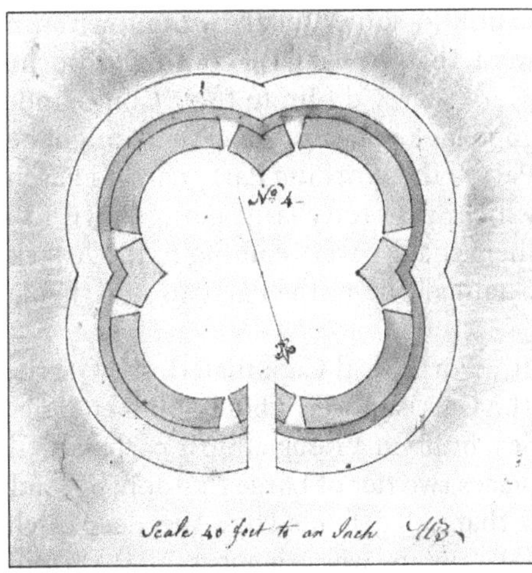

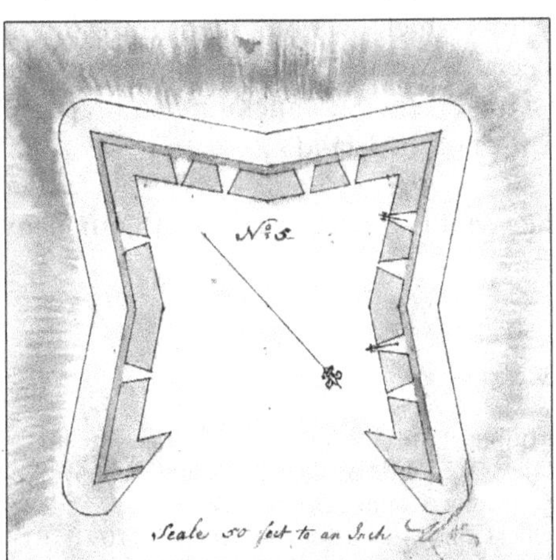

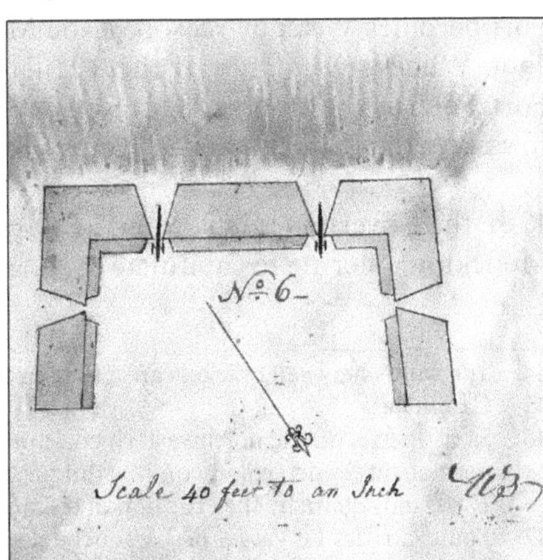

28th. Turn'd the Cannon & Mortars we Took on Morne Garnier against Fort Royal; the Enemy went off in such an Hurry that they either forgot or had not time to spike them.

30th. Open'd two Batterys on Morne Tortensan against the Fort one of ten, the other of four 24 pounders, with two 13 inch & one 10 inch Mortar.

31st. Open'd another Battery on Tortensan of four 24 Pound^rs^. & two 12 Pound^rs^. against the Fort. The 24 Pounders on the ten Gun Battery were chang'd for 32 Pound^rs^. as it was thought they could not have sufficient Effect at so great a distance. Fired from Morne Garnier with seven 32 pound^rs^. & two 13 inch Mortars.

Feb^ry^. 2d. began to Erect a Battery in the Town for small Mortars

3rd. This night the French beat the Chamade to Capitulate for fort Royal. a drole Circumstance having happen'd late in the Evening, an English Soldier who had got drunk in some Cellar in the town at night, stagger'd to the Fort, swearing as he went, that we were just coming to Storm them with 14,000 men, they came out, took him & carry'd him to their Commander, he still persisted, this made them keep a good look out, supposing there might be something in it & when they perceiv'd Our Party [The Working Party carry'd Fascines which the French mistook for Ladders][44] which was pretty large going down to work at the battery in the Town, confirm'd them that we were coming to the Attack, & they came out in great haste beating the Chamade, up to the Party to stop them.

4th. Fort Royal Capitulated, the Garrison to March out with the Honours of War. The Garrison were about 800 men. Fort Royal in itself is Strong, particularly to the Sea, built on a Rock almost perpendicular, & high above the Water; having in most places two tier of Large Cannon; by land there is only one Narrow Way to come at it, & that well defended by a Wet deep ditch, two flankers, & a strong Ravelin before the Curtain, the whole is substantial Masonry; the Casmets[45] are large, cut into the Solid Rock, capable of Containing many Men, & to be Enlarg'd to any Size; however the Fort becomes Weak by reason of the Many hills which overlook it within Cannon shot. Whoever is master of these Hills especially Morne Garnier Commands the Fort. Soon as the affairs of Fort Royal were settled General Monckton had Prepared to sail for the Reduction of S^t^. Pieres[46] & the Rest of the Island.

12th. the Governour Genl. Monsr. La Touche[47] sent two deputies to treat with Genl. Monckton, offering to capitulate

44 The words between brackets are a note in the margin.
45 Casemates
46 Saint-Pierre, on the northwestern coast of Martinique. The city, founded in 1635 as the first permanent French colony on Martinique, was destroyed, first by the Great Hurricane of 1780, and, again, by the eruption of the nearby volcano Mount Pelée in 1905.
47 Louis-Charles Le Vassor de La Touche de Tréville, Comte de La Touche-Tréville (1709-1781) had been governor of Martinique since 1760. Born in Martinique, his family had settled

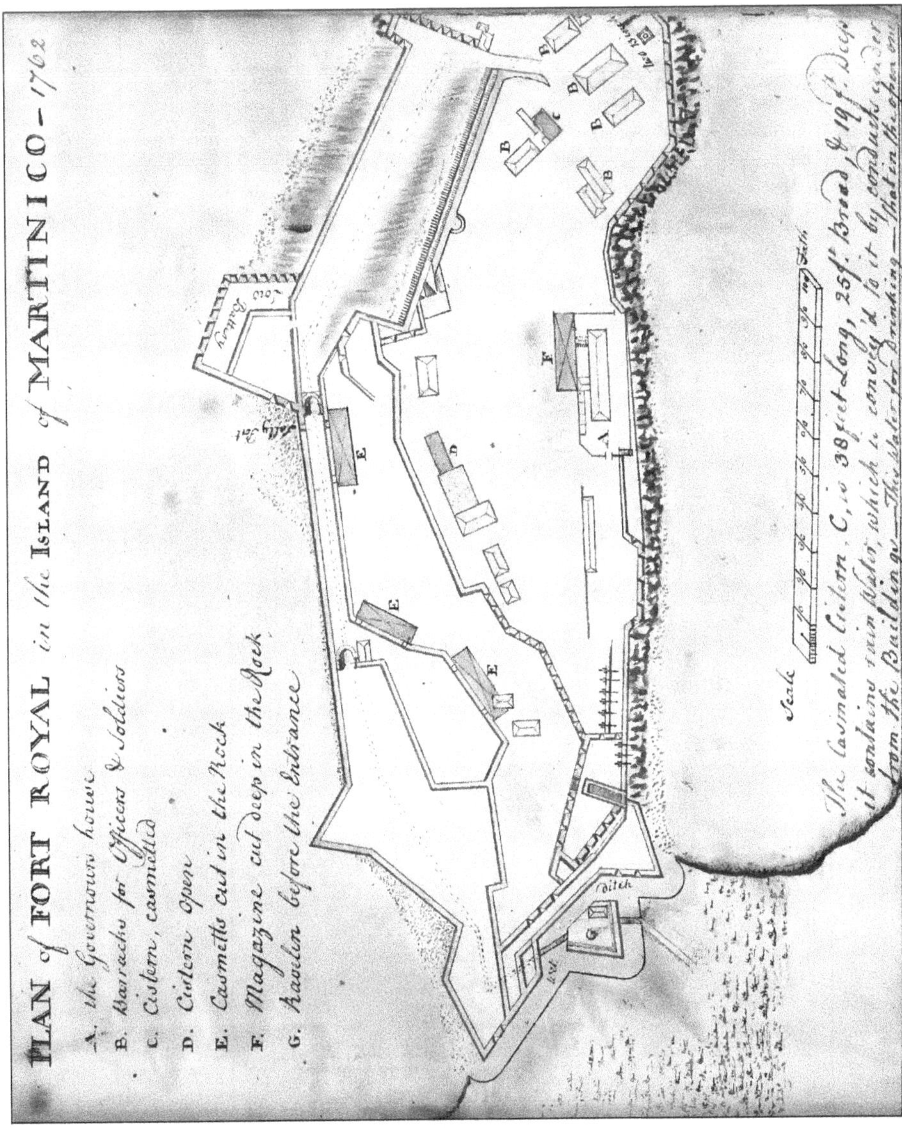

'Plan of Fort Royal in the island of Martinico, 1762'.

'View of Fort Royal in Martinico from the esplanade 1762'.

13th. for the Whole island: they went to St Pieres with the

14th. Gen$^{l's}$. answer, & next day retun'd with the Capitulation sign'd, it contain's 39 Articles. Thus was the conquest of this Important Island, completed in a short time, without any Material Lost, tho' look'd upon as a very Dangerous & Doubtful Enterprize; which, considering the Extream Natural Strength of the Country, with whatever additions the French could Devise, may be look'd upon as an Extroadinary conquest in so short a time. [Five Sail of Men of War from France with Troops on board to reinforce the Garrison Arriv'd off the Port of La Trinité[48] they sent a boat on shore but learning from a peasant in Fields that the Island was in our prosession sail'd away and Escap'd our Fleet tho' pursued][49]

General Hopson[50] landed here with an army Jan^{ry} 15th. 1759 to reduce the Island, he landed at Point Negro but saw so many difficulties in the Country to encounter but no Men to oppose him that he reinbark'd his troops the 17th at Night, left the Island & sail'd for Gaudaloupe. [surrender'd May 1st. 1759 to Genl. Barrington & Comodore Moore— Mons. Nadau Dutriel[51] was governour, & was banish'd to Martinico for giving up the Island—][52]

March 4th. The Isle of Grenada & it's dependencies, surrender'd to Brigd^{r}. Walsh[53] who sail'd there with the 5th. Brigade & L^{t}. Col^{o}. Scott's Corps of light Infantry.

---

in Martinique in the mid-17th century and had been ennobled in 1706. He had joined the French Navy and risen to become *capitaine de vaisseau*. His eldest son became a famous naval officer, *Vice Amiral* Louis René de La Touche Tréville, Comte de La Touche-Tréville (1745-1804).

48 La Trinité is located on the long, narrow eastward extending peninsula on the northeast coast of Martinique.

49 The section of the entry between brackets is a note in the margin that continues the entry.

50 Major General Peregrine Thomas Hopson (1696-1759). For modern studies of this operation, see Marshall Smelser, *The Campaign for the Sugar Islands 1759: A Study in Amphibious Warfare* (Chapel Hill: University of North Carolina Press, 1955); Frank McLynn, *1759: The Year Britain Became Master of the World* (London: Pimlico, 2005); Daniel Baugh, *The Global Seven Years War, 1754-1763* (London: Pearson, 2011), pp. 377-385.

51 Charles François Emmanuel Nadeau du Treil (1703-1786) was governor of Guadeloupe from 1757 to 1759.

52 The words between brackets are a note in the margin, marked for placement here.

53 Hunt Walsh was born in Ireland in 1721 to a family that had owned lands at Ballykilcavan, County Laois, in Ireland since the 1630s. He was commissioned an ensign in the 28th Regiment of Foot on 7 June 1741. He was promoted to lieutenant on 12 April 1744, to captain on 13 October 1744, to major on 28 August 1753, and to lieutenant colonel on 2 February 1757. He served with his regiment at Louisbourg and at Québec. While still a lieutenant colonel in the 28th Foot, he was promoted to colonel in America on 24 January 1758 and then colonel in the Army on 29 November 1762. After accepting the surrender of Grenada he participated in the Havana operation in 1762. He was appointed colonel of the 56th Foot on 22 May 1766, a post he held for the remainder of his life. He was promoted to major general on 25 May 1772, to lieutenant general 29 August 177, and to general 12 October 1795. From 1764 to 1776, he was Member of the Irish Parliament for Maryborough. He died in 1795

April 25th. Admiral Pocock[54] and the Earl of Albemarle,[55] with the Fleet & Forces from England, Arriv'd at Martinico & Our Troops were Embark'd for another Expedition. Here the Declaration of war against Spain was read with the Usual Solemnity. Since the reduction of Fort Royal we were Employ'd in repairing the Works, & fitting up the Barracks, which were much more damaged than we Expected to have found them; for the Walls in some places were considerably injur'd, Many of the Cannon disabled & the Barracks almost tore to peices, such effect had our Shot tho' at so great a distance. A General Court Martial, was here held on Major Kilberry Campbell,[56] who commanded a corps of Highlanders the 100 Reg^{t}. for killing a

54 George Pocock was born in England the son of Royal Navy chaplain. He entered the Royal Navy in 1718 and was commissioned a lieutenant on 7 December 1726. He was promoted to commander on 26 February 1734 and to captain on 1 August 1738. After serving in command of a ship in the East Indies, he was promoted to rear admiral of the white on 6 Jane 1755, to rear admiral of the red on 4 June 1756, and vice admiral of the white in February 1757. He succeeded Vice Admiral Charles Watson as commander-in-chief of the East Indies Station following Watson's death in August 1757. Promoted to vice admiral of the red on 5 February 1758, he continued to hold that command until 1760, fighting a number of actions against the French squadron under the Comte d'Aché. He returned him in 1760 and was elected Member of Parliament for Plymouth, holding that seat until 1768, and made Knight of the Bath on 23 March 1761. On 16 February 1762, the Admiralty selected Pocock to command the secret expedition to Havana. Following the Havana operation, he was promoted to admiral of the blue. Superannuated on 11 September 1766, he died on 3 April 1792. For more detail, see *Oxford Dictionary of National Biography* and the *History of Parliament, 1754-1790 http://www.historyofparliamentonline.org/volume/1754-1790/member/pocock-george-1706-92*

55 George Keppel, Viscount Bury, then 3rd Earl of Albemarle, was born in 1723, the eldest son of William Keppel, 2nd Earl of Albemarle. Educated at Westminster School from 1732 to 1740, he was commissioned an ensign in the 2nd Foot Guards in 1738 and promoted to captain-lieutenant in the 1st Dragoon Guards in 1741, to captain-lieutenant in the 2nd Foot Guards in 1743, to captain and lieutenant colonel in 1745, a brevet colonel in 1746. He was considered to be the chief favorite of the duke of Cumberland, who he served as aide-de-camp at the battles of Dettingen in 1743, Fontenoy in 1745, and Culloden in 1746. Cumberland sent him to report the news of Culloden to King George II, who rewarded him with a £1,000 and made him his own aide-de-camp. He served as Lord of the bedchamber to the Duke of Cumberland from 1746 to 1765 and equerry to the princess of Wales in 1751. He was elected Member of Parliament for Chichester in 1746, holding that seat until he succeeded his father as Earl of Albemarle on 22 December 1754. He became colonel of the 20th Foot in 1749, then colonel of the 3rd Dragoons from 1755 to his death. He was promoted to major general in 1756 and to lieutenant general in 1759. He became a Privy Councilor in January 1761 and governor of Jersey in 1761, holding that post for the remainder of his life. After serving as commander–in-chief for the Havana operation in 1762, he returned to England. He was made Knight of the Garter on 26 December 1765, He promoted to general and died in 1772. For more detail, see *Oxford Dictionary of National Biography* and the *History of Parliament, 1754-1790 http://www.historyofparliamentonline.org/volume/1715-1754/member/keppel-george-1724-72*

56 Colin Campbell of Kilberry was born in 1728, probably at Kilberry, Argyll, where the family had been landowners since the early 17th century. He was commissioned a lieutenant in Scotland in Lord Loudoun's new-raising 64th Foot on 8 June 1745. He went onto British half pay when regiment disbanded on 4 January 1749. He exchanged from half pay to lieutenant in the 42nd Foot in Ireland on 9 February 1751. He was promoted to captain in the second battalion of the 1st Foot in Ireland on 27 April 1756 through a free augmentation vacancy. He was made captain in the new-raising second battalion of the 4th Foot in England on 27

Captain [McCard][57] of his Corps. the Affair appear'd very black against him, & it was thought he would be found Guilty.[58] [Major Campbell afterwards escap'd from Martinico & fled to England where he had the assurance to Accuse Genl. Monckton of Malpractices, who demanded a Genl. Court Martial which acquitted him most honourably.][59] The island of Martinico makes a very rugged appearance, with hill above hill, yet the soil is Exceeding rich & fertile. The Sensitive Plant grows spontaneous in almost every field here.

August 1756 through a free augmentation vacancy. He became captain in the 38th Foot in the Leeward Islands on 20 August 1759 through a free death vacancy. He was appointed major-commandant of his own new-raising 100th Foot in Scotland on 4 April 1761. A General Court martial was held at Fort Royal on 6 April 1762. He was cashiered from the service on 20 August 1762 after 15.1 years of service. His charges against Major General Monckton were heard in a general court martial at the Horse Guards in April 1764. The family of the murdered captain brought a legal action of assythment against Campbell and won £200 in damages. (Assythment in Scots law dated from the 14th century, when a person who had killed another as a result of a criminal act might be required to pay a reasonable sum to the deceased's kin, to buy off criminal penalties. Over time, it included the principle of compensation for loss wrongfully or negligently caused, which did not require a crime to have been committed. Assythment was formally abolished in 1976). Later in life, Campbell became a well-known dandy in Edinburgh and at Buxton, the spa town in Derbyshire. He died in 1798. For further details, see *Oxford Dictionary of National Biography*.

57 Bamford has written the name 'McCard' in the margin marked for insertion here. A student of Scots anthroponomy has suggested to the editor that the surname was most likely McHarg, although contemporary accounts of the murder spell the name McKaarg and War Office clerks used other variants such as MacHarg or McHargg. John McHarg was born in Scotland in 1738. He was commissioned an ensign in England the new-raising second battalion of the 19th Regiment of Foot on 8 December 1756. He was promoted to lieutenant on 8 October 1757 by a free augmentation vacancy. He remained with the battalion when it was regimented in 1758 as the 66th Foot. He was promoted to captain in his own new-raising Independent Company in Scotland on 28 October 1760 and remained in the same commission when the Company amalgamated with others in Scotland on 5 July 1761, as Major-Commandant Colin Campbell's 100th Foot. He was murdered on 6 May 1762, having served 5.4 years.

58 To clarify, the General Court Martial in London acquitted Monckton. For the contemporary literature on this topic, see Colin Campbell, *Proceedings of a General Court Martial, Held at Fort Royal, in the Island of Martinico, on the 6th, and Continued by Adjournments to the 14th of April, 1762, upon the Tryal of Major Commandant Colin Campbell* (London: Printed for J. Walter at Homer's Head, Charing-Cross, 1763); Colin Campbell, *The Case of Colin Campbell, Esq. Late Major Commandant of His Majesty's Hundredth Regiment* (London, 1763); Robert Monckton, *Proceedings of a General Court Martial, Held at the Judge Advocate's Office, in the Horse Guards, On Saturday the 14th, and Continued by Adjournment to Wednesday the 18th April 1764; for the Trial of a Charge Preferred By Colin Campbell, Esq.; against the Honourable Major General Monckton* (London: Printed for James Robson, Bookseller to the Princess Dowager of Wales, in New Bond-Street, 1764). An academic assessment may be found in A.N. Gilbert, 'Law and Honour among Eighteenth Century British Army Officers', *Historical Journal*, vol. 19 (1976), pp. 75-85.

59 The information between brackets is found in a note in the margin.

7

Havana, 6 May 1762–9 July 1763

May 6th. The Fleet with the army sail'd from Port Royal; the Following Battalions were left in the islands; 61st. Grey's. 69th. Colvill's. 76th. Rufanes two batt^{ns}. 100th. Campbell's Highlan^{drs}.—The Fleet steer'd towards the Windward Passage,[1] we cruis'd about 10 days off Cape of S^{t}. Nicola[2] till Joyn'd by the Fleet from Jamaica, then the Destination was made Publick, & we steered for the Havanna Through the Old Streights of Bahama.[3] [a very difficult & dangerous Passage but not the smallest accident happen'd. great care was taken][4]

June 6th. Part of the Fleet with the troops on board anchor'd opposite a small Castle to the Eastward of the Havanna, call'd the Baccarans,[5] the rest of the fleet carrying the Provisions & Stores sail'd with the admiral to the West of the Town towards Chorera River.

7th. The Baccarans castle being silenc'd by two Frigates, the Army Landed on the Island of Cuba without opposition between the Baccarans & Coxemar Castle, the latter was silenc'd by the *Dragon* [Capt Harvey][6] of 74 Guns & a Frigate, the men

1 The Windward Passage is a 50-mile wide strait between the eastern end of Cuba, and the northwestern point of the island of Hispaniola (Haiti).
2 Cape St Nicolas is a cape at the northwestern tip of Haiti. The place was named by Columbus, who landed here on St Nicholas Day, 6 December 1492. A strategic position that came to be seen by some as 'the Gibraltar of the Caribbean', the French began to build a town and fortified position here in 1764, naming it Môle-Saint-Nicolas.
3 The Old Bahama Channel or *Canal Viejo de Bahama* is approximately 100 miles (161 km) long and 15 miles (24 km) wide. The Channel divides the Great Bahama Bank from Cuba. The northern side, near the Bahamas, is filled with low lying islands, called cays, and shallow sandbanks, making a treacherous passage.
4 The words between brackets are a note in the margin.
5 The battery at the mouth of the Bacuranao River was located about six miles east-southeast of El Morro.
6 The Hon. Augustus John Hervey, later the 3rd Earl of Bristol, was born in 1724, the second son of John, Lord Hervey (1696-1743). He entered Westminster School in 1733 and then he joined the Royal Navy in 1735 at the age of eleven. He was commissioned lieutenant on 31 October 1740. Promoted to commander on 16 September 1746 and to captain on 15 January 1747, he was elected Member of Parliament for Bury St. Edmunds, holding that seat until 1763, when he was elected Member of Parliament for Saltash, a seat he held until 1768. He commanded the frigate *Phoenix* at the Battle of Minorca in 1756. He commanded the 74-gun *Dragon* at Martinique and Havana. He retired from active naval

who were to Defend the Castles fled into the Woods, we march'd along the Beach, part of the Army Cross'd a little River to Coxemar,[7] lay on our arms this night, on the Beach, about 10 miles to the Eastward of the Havanna.

8th. The Army Cut a Road & March'd up the country about 6 Miles, to the village of Guanamacoa,[8] near it a large body of the Enemy's horse [call'd the Edinburgh Dragoons][9] were drawn up on a rising ground to Oppose us; they came down towards us full Gallop, but receiving a fire some of our advanc'd light Infantry, turn'd tail & scamper'd off as fast as they could, leaving a few Wounded Men behind; we march'd into Guanamaeoa, the Inhabitants had just deserted it; leaving all their Effects behind. The Spaniards sunk a large Ship of War a little way within the harbours Mouth of the Havanna. The Regim[t] of Edenburgh Dragoons were among the Spanish fled.

10th. March'd & invested the Mora Fort or Castle,[10] it lies on the East side at the Entrance of the Harbour, is built on the point of an High Rock & appears very Strong. Another ship of War sunk close to the first.

11th. The Light Infantry attack'd a Redoubt which the Enemy had erected on the Cavannos,[11] (hills on the same side with the Mora Fort, but farther within the Harbour;) they carry'd it with very little loss. in the Harbour were twelve Ships of the Line & a large two deck'd frigate. The Castle of Chorera[12] to the Westward of the Havanna was batter'd & taken possession of—

12th. the Enemy sunk another ship near the Harbour's Mouth.

service with the Peace of Paris in 1763, but remained in the Navy. He served as an Admiralty commissioner in 1771-1775. Succeeding his brother, he became 3rd Earl of Bristol on 13 March 1775 and was promoted to rear admiral of the blue on 28 April 1777, to rear admiral of the red on 23 January 1778, and vice admiral of the blue on 28 January 1778. He died in 1779. See also, *Oxford Dictionary of National Biography* and *History of Parliament*. http://www.historyofparliamentonline.org/volume/1754-1790/member/hervey-hon-augustus-john-1724-79

7 The fortification at Cojímar was situated on the west side of the small bay that is at the mouth of the Cojímar River.

8 Guanabacoa is a town, situated about 3.1 miles (5 km) southeast of Havana.

9 The words between brackets are an explanatory note in the margin. This a Spanish regiment, Los Dragones de Edimburgo.

10 El Morro or Castillo de los Tres Reyes Magos del Morro; 'The Castle of the Three Magi of the Rock'.

11 Spelled 'Cavannas Hill' on an English map of the siege David Syrett (ed.), *The Siege and Capture of Havana 1762*. Publications of the Navy Record Society, Vol.114 (London: Navy Records Society, 1970), p. 316). The hill is the site of the San Carlos de la Cabaña Fortress, which was built immediately after the war to prevent another occurrence of an attack from the landward side of El Morro.

12 Torreón de la Chorrera (Tower of la Chorrera), or Fuerte de Santa Dorotea de la Luna de la Chorrera, at the mouth of what was then called the La Chorrera River, now known as the Almendares River.

15th. Eight hundred Marines were landed at Chorera. [A very strong boom across the Harbou'rs mouth][13] Col°. How with the Grenadiers, light Infantry & Rangers, about 1200 Men, went from the army on the East Side & Encamp'd to the Westward of the Town.

19th. Began a Battery for Mortars near the Sea Side, against the Mora Fort.

22d. Open'd the Battery of two 13 inch & one 10 inch mortars with fourteen Royal Mortars: Began Battery for Howitzers On the left of the Mora to remove the Shipping, which were very troublesome to us.

23d. Erected another Battery on the Beach for the Royals nearer the Mora, as they were at two great a distance in the 1st Battery. several other batterys were erecting against the Mora & Shipping.

29th. before day break this Morning, the Enemy landed above 1000 Men from the Havanna, mostly Grenadiers, follow'd by a great many Negro's & Mullattas; as it was dark they penetrated a good way into the Wood before they were perceived, & had pass'd some of our advance'd Posts; they were met by a picket of 50 men [commanded by Capt Roger Spendlove[14] 43d Reg^t.][15] who attack'd and repuls'd them, they were soon dispers'd, & being Oblig'd to repass our posts, were very roughly handled. many were kill'd & some taken Prisoner, they lost near 200 Men. They came with a design to spike our Cannon, drawn on the road—ready for the Batteries; had brought instruments with them for that Purpose; They were met by our Men close at the Guns & several lost their lives under the Carriages. The Spaniards were in two Divisions, one party came by the Mora, the other by the White Road, these last soon went back again Without making any Attempt. Our loss, was about 20 men—

July 1st. Open'd two Batterys against the Mora, one of Eight, the other of four 24 Pounders, with two 13 Inch mortars. Three Men of War, the *Cambridge*[16] 90 Guns

13 The words between brackets are a note in the margin.

14 Roger Spendlove was born in England in 1725. He was first commissioned, oddly, in a free death vacancy as an ensign on 1 November 1740, in one of the five invalid companies that went with Anson's South Seas Expedition. On his return, he went onto British half pay when the survivors of those companies disbanded on 25 December 1743. He exchanged with purchase from half pay a commission as lieutenant in the 54th Foot in Minorca on 14 May 1744. The 54th Foot was renumbered the 43rd Foot in 1749 and he was promoted to captain-lieutenant in the 43rd Foot on 4 September 1754, probable as a purchase, vice a retirement. He was promoted to captain in the 43rd Foot on 9 April 1756, by purchase vice a retirement. He was promoted to brevet major on 23 July 1772 and to major in the 43rd Foot on 8 February 1775 by purchase, vice a retirement. He died on 9 July 1775 of wounds suffered on 17 June 1775 at Bunker Hill, after 34.3 years of service.

15 The words between brackets are a note in the margin.

16 The 80-gun, third rate *Cambridge* was built at Deptford to a design by Joseph Allin by successive master shipwrights John Holland, Thomas Fellowes, Thomas Slade, and Adam Slade between 1750 and 1756. She was commissioned in 1755 and served in the Western Squadron. In 1757, she was fitted as a flagship. She served in the 1759 attack on Martinique and Guadeloupe. In 1760, she was flagship for Rear Admiral Charles Holmes. She sailed

[Capt Goostree[17] he was kill'd in this action],[18] the *Dragon* 74 Guns, & *Marlborough* 66 Guns, lay before the Castle, some hours, but were order'd off, having lost many men & reciv'd much damage, without being able to hurt the Fort in the Least, As it lies on an Exceeding high Rock directly above them; howerever they drew the Enemys attention to that side, whilst we were opening our batterys, in which they were of great service. Our Eight gun battery with the two Mortars were within 200 yards of the Mora, did great Execution, dismounted their Guns & brought down their Walls very fast; the four gun battery was about 460 yards distance & had very good effect. [the Stirling castle was to have led & as she pass'd the Mora to have fir'd on it, and amus'd them whilst the other 3 ships came to their Moorings; but she let all the ships pass her & did not go nigh the fort, but steer'd off to Sea, & there Lay. the Captn W^m^. Campbell was broke.[19] A very Cowardly Action. & all the Army looking on. twas throught he would have been shot.][20]

2d. This Afternoon our Eight gun battery took fire, from our own Constant firing, the fascines being so exceeding dry by the Violent heat of the Weather, caught like tinder. we work'd hard to put it out.

3d. Early this Morning the first broke out afresh in the eight gun battery & Notwithstanding all our Endeavours to Extinguish it, whereby we lost a number of Men, it was render'd useless; we thought we had got the better of it & saved 2 Embrasures, but the fire had got two far into it; our men were oblig'd to Expose themselves openly on the Tops of the Merlons & in the Embrassures, to pull down the Parts that were on fire, the Enemy continually firing grape shot on them did much Execution; besides they took this oppertunity of repairing their breaches & mounted more Cannon thereby gaining a superior fire. we, at the Expense of many lives much lives, and under numberless disadvantages, erected three batteries

for Jamaica on 26 March 1760. After the Havana operation, she was paid off in 1762 and underwent a middling repair at Plymouth from 1762 to 1765. Recommissioned in 1770 for the Falklands dispute, she was paid off in 1771. Between periods of service as a prison ship, receiving ship, and guard ship, she was commissioned briefly in 1782 for the relief of Gibraltar, then for brief periods as a flagship in 1790, 1791, 1793, 1794, 1795-99, and 1801. She was paid off in 1802 and broken up at Plymouth in 1808. Length of gun deck166 feet, length of keel 137 feet inches, breadth 47 feet, depth of hold 20 feet, 1,615 58/94 tons bm.

17 William Goostrey was commissioned a lieutenant in the Royal Navy on 5 June 1744. He was promoted to commander on 12 December 1757, and to captain on 23 January 1759. He had taken command of *Cambridge* in 1760 and was killed in action on 1 July 1762 during the attack on Morro Castle, Havana.

18 The words between square brackets are a note in the margin.

19 James Campbell was commissioned a lieutenant in the Royal Navy on 19 July 1742. He was promoted to commander on 4 September 1744 and to captain on 26 January 1749. In 1762, he was appointed to command *Stirling Castle*. Hervey, who commanded the small attacking squadron, ordered Campbell in *Stirling Castle* to open the attack on El Morro, while *Dragon*, *Marlborough*, and *Cambridge* took up their pre-planned positions. When the first ship was in position, *Stirling Castle* was to retire. Campbell's failure to follow these orders led Hervey to request Campbell's court martial. The court was held on 14 August 1762 and dismissed Campbell from the service. See the Report of the Court Martial. TNA, ADM 1/5301.

20 The lines between brackets are a note in the margin

more, of four guns each from 24 to 32 Pounders, these batteries lay about 100 yards behind, the 8 Gun battery, which was now made into a line for Musketry. As we were Oblig'd to pick the Earth from between the rocks, here & there when we could find it, & then bring it in sand baggs, at a distance to our Batterys, made out Work go on slow. however having Compleated these, & added three Guns 24 & 32 Pounders, with two 13 inch Mortars, to our first four Gun Battery, we had then the superiority, and Effectually Silenc'd the Mora; but the Shipping in the Harbour gave us much disturbance, tho' our Howitzers frequently oblig'd them to Shift their Stations. Two of the Batterys of 32 Pounders were work'd by Our Sailors.

18th. Began our sap[21] towards the Mora; as there was not any Earth to be had here abouts, the Advances were made of Stufft gabions [22]& Cotton bags.

19th. Made a Lodgement on the Glacis, & Extended our Sap.

20th. Placed our Miners under the face of the Sea Bastion by a Narrow way running along the Edge of the Rock, this was the only place possible to get at the foot of the Wall.

21st. about 12 o'Clock this Night a Serjeant & 12 Men with an Engineer scaled the Wall near the Mine, a few Men who were asleep at that Place awoke, & ran to alarm the rest, the Serj[t]. & Party came down, were sent up again; but found the Enemy ready to oppose them, & came back, as this was only an Experiment, & not more than two Ladders could be apply'd, the attempt was dropp'd, could they have been properly supported at first, the Fort might have been Carry'd.

22d. the Spaniards made a Sally[23] from the Havanna with about 1800 Men, they landed in three different Divisions, at three different places, one came up close under the Mora, a second by the Spanish redoubt, a third came by the White road, & after a good deal of resistance, being oppos'd only by our small out Partys, were all beat back to their boats, leaving a Number of Dead behind, many were drowned or kill'd, Endeavouring to swim to a Large Boom they had a cross the Harbour, & some were taken Pris[nr]. in the Water. We had about 50 kill'd & Wounded. The Spaniards lost Near 400. When they saw their Men repuls'd & Pursued so close, they Cannonaded most furiously from the Punta,[24] Town, & Shipping; nor could we be angry with them; as they did not spare their own people, indeed it was hard to say which party they fir'd at. in the afternoon we had Truce to bury the Dead. we sunk a mine in the

21 To approach a fortress protected from shot by digging saps or trenches. Boscawen, *Louisbourg*, p. 419.

22 A gabion is wicker work that resembled a bottomless basket, three feet in diameter and four to six feet tall, used for building fieldworks. Once in place they are filled with stones or rocks. Boscawen, *Louisbourg*, p. 415.

23 A small force leaving a fortress to attack besiegers through stealth and surprise rather than strength. Boscawen, *Louisbourg*, p. 419.

24 La Puntal, the name of the fort on the west side of the entrance to Havana Harbour, opposite El Morro.

Counterscarp[25] to help to fill up the Ditch. That under the bastion goes on but slow, by reason of very large Stones which the miners meet with, & retards the Work. in this Sally Col°. Carlton was wounded in the arm.

26th. A Large Frigate was sunk near the Boom by Our Howitzers. Some batterys are began against the Town.

27th. Part of the Troops from North America Arriv'd; with Brigadier Burton; They were sent to Joyn Brig^dr^. How at the West Side.

28th. a Merchant Ship belonging to the Enemy deeply loaded, was set on fire by lightning in the upper part of the Harbour; in a very short time it blew up & sunk. It was said that this Ship was exceedingly Rich. [The Spaniards told us that most of the Plate money & other Treasure belonging to the Merchents & Gentry was aboard this Vessel & all lost—][26]

30th. Early this Morning a Floating Battery carrying two twenty four pounders came out of the Harbour, attended by two Boats, they fir'd a few rounds of Grapeshot at the Mouth of the Mine, but our Covering Party, ply'd them so warmly with small arms, that they were glad to get back. Between one & two o'Clock this day we sprung our mines, that under the Counterscarp was of no service, but that under the Bastion had great Effect, the Regiments & partys were all in readiness; the Breach would admit only one man a breast, but before the Enemy had time to recollect themselves, we storm'd the Fort & Carry'd it, driving the Spaniards from every part of the Ramparts, down into the Body of the Place, where above 300 threw down their Arms and were made prisoners; a Noble instance of British bravery & mercy; they had 300 kill'd some Endeavouring to get off in boats were mostly Either drowned, or kill'd in the boats. & out of 700 that were on the fort when we storm'd it, very few escap'd to the Havanna. The Marquis de Gonzales[27] was amongst the kill'd, & Don Lewis de Velesco,[28] Governour of the Mora, mortally Wounded. We had 2 officers & near 40 Men kill'd & wounded. The Spaniards when they saw their colours removed for the English, Cannonaded most Violently from the Town. Genl. Kepple[29] Mounted the breach with the Troops.

25 A counterscarp is the outer retaining wall of a fosse or ditch at the rear of a covered way. Boscawen, *Louisbourg*, pp. 413, 415.

26 The sentence in square brackets is a note in the margin.

27 Marquis de Gonzales was colonel and second in command of El Morro under Don Luis de Velasco.

28 *Capitán de Navio* Don Luis Vicente de Velasco e Isla was born in Cantabria in 1711. He joined the Spanish Navy at the age of 15. Early in his naval career, he saw action against the North African corsairs. In 1742, he captured a British frigate and sank another, and in 1746 captured a British 36-gun frigate. In 1754, he was given command of the 70-gun ship of the line *La Reina,* which he still retained in 1762 at Havana. In 1762, he was additionally made commander in chief and colonel of garrison at El Morro. He died on 31 July 1762 from wounds received.

29 The Hon. William Keppel was born in 1727, the third son of William Keppel, 2nd Earl of Albemarle (1702-1754) and a younger brother of Lieutenant General George, 3rd Earl of

Aug[st]. 1st. Began several Batterys on the Cavannos, against the Town, the Punta Fort, & Shipping. The Town fires on the Mora.

2d. The Town still continues to fire on the Mora, chiefly at the Cistern, to let out of the Water, as that is the scarcest article we have: a 74 Gun Ship is brought down & directs her fire against the Cistern.

3d. The 74 Gun Ships that fired at the Cistern was drove away by our Howitzers & went up the Harbour—

10th. Our batteries on the Cavannos being near ready to open, a Flag was sent to the Governour, with a sumons to Capitulate, he refus'd in a polite but resolute manner, & after detaining the officer with the Flag a long time in the Fields, fir'd before he reached our works. During the Cessation we could observe many People going from the town with Loads on their Backs.

11th. This Morning at day break we open'd all our Batterys consisting of 43 Peices of Cannon 24 & 32 pounders, with ten large Mortars besides small ones & kept up a most infernal fire; soon silence'd & Dismantled the Punta, & turn'd the fire of a ten Gun battery of 32 Pounders, work'd by Sailors, which play'd upon it, against the Town, we pull'd down the Merlons of this Battery & fired the Guns en Barbet.[30] about 2 oClock in the Afternoon the Spaniards hung out Flags, on the ships & in many parts of the Town, to Capitulate.

14th. Articles were Settled Yesterday & this day we took posession of the Punta Fort & Punta Gate of the Town, the Grenadiers took the Land Gate.

24th. The Spanish troops march'd out with the Honours of War & Embark'd on board Transports, our Grenadiers & a Brigade of the Army march'd into the Town when they march'd out.

Albemarle, and Admiral Augustus Keppel. William Keppel was commissioned an ensign in the Coldstream Guards and a lieutenant in the Army on 26 June 1744. He was promoted to lieutenant in the Coldstream Guards and captain in the Army on 25 June 1745, to captain-lieutenant in the 1st Regiment of Foot Guards and lieutenant colonel in the Army on 28 April 1751, to captain in the 1st Regiment of Foot Guards on 16 March 1752, to second major in the 1st Foot Guards and colonel in the Army on 21 July 1760. He was appointed colonel of the 56th Regiment of Foot on 17 December 1761. For the Havana expedition, he was made acting major general on 10 July 1762 with his promotion to major general confirmed on 10 July 1762. When Havana fell on 30 July 1782, he was appointed governor of the city. He was appointed colonel of the 14th Foot on 31 May 1765 then promoted to lieutenant general on 26 May 1772. He became colonel of the 12th Light Dragoons on 18 October 1775. He died in 1782.

30 En barbette is a term to describe guns that are elevated to fire over the top of a parapet, and not through embrasures.

Spanish ships of War taken at the Havanna[31]
Ships Guns Commanders
El Tigre[32] 70 Don Juan Ignacio Madariga; Marquis del real Transporta
El Enfanto[33] 70 Don Franciseo de Medina; Killed
El Soverano[34] 70 Don Juan de Postigo
La Reyna[35] 70 Don Lewis de Velasco (Governour and [blank space][36] Mortally wounded at the storming the Mora —)
El America[37] 70 Don Juan ~~de Colina~~ Antonia
El Aquilon[38] 70 El Marquis de Gonzales. Kill'd at the Storming the Mora
El Neptuno[39] 70 Don Pedro de Bermudas
El Asia[40] 60 Don Francisco Garyunta
La Europa[41] 60 Don Jose van Vincent
El Conquestado[42] 60 Don Pedro Castujon

---

31 British forces captured five Spanish 70-gun ships at Havana that they took back to England. All were added to the Royal Navy, rated as 74-gun ships, but none were armed or actively employed, except for the one employed as a hospital hulk. In addition, they brought three 60-gun ships back to England. See details in the notes below

32 The 70-gun *El Tigre,* also known as *San Lorenzo,* was built at Havana and launched in 1747. Taken into British service and renamed *Tiger,* she served as a hospital ship at Plymouth until sold in 1784. Length of gun deck 169 feet 3 inches, length of keel 136 feet 4 inches, breadth 51 feet, 1,886 17/94 tons bm.

33 The 70-gun *Infante,* also known as *San Luis Gonzaga,* was built at Havana and launched in 1750. Taken into British service, she was renamed *Infanta,* but saw no service and was sold in 1775. Length of gun deck 171 feet 6 inches, length of keel 137 feet 4 inches, breadth 51 feet 4 inches, depth of hold 22 feet 5 inches, 1,918 64/94 tons bm.

34 The 70-gun *El Soberano,* also known as *San Gregorio,* was built at Ferrol in 1755 (or possibly 1759). She was taken to Portsmouth, purchased by the Royal Navy, and renamed *Soverano,* but never commissioned. She was broken up at Portsmouth in 1770. Length of gun deck 175 feet, length of keel 143 feet 5 inches, breadth 49 feet 7 inches, depth of hold 21 feet, 1,875 33/94 tons bm.

35 The 70-gun *El Reina* was built at Havana in 1743. She was taken to Portsmouth, purchased by the Royal Navy, and named *Reyna* but never commissioned. She was sold in 1772. Length of gun deck 173 feet 2 inches, length of keel 141 feet 8½ inches, breadth 48 feet 7 inches, depth of hold 22 feet 1 inch, 1,779 14/94 tons bm.

36 Bamford may have intended to write in the blank space something to indicate that Velasco was also commander in chief and colonel of the El Morro garrison.

37 The 64-gun *El America,* also known as *Nuestra Señora de Belén,* was built at Havana in 1736. She was not taken into British service.

38 The 68-gun *El Aquílon,* also known as *San Damasco,* was built at Ferrol in 1754. Taken to England, she was brought into the Royal Navy and first renamed *Moro,* but a version of her original name, *Aquilon,* was restored just before she was broken up at Portsmouth in 1770. Length of gun deck 175 feet 3 inches, length of keel 143 feet 7 inches, breadth 49 feet 7½ inches, depth of hold 20 feet 5½ inches, 1,880 77/94 tons bm.

39 The 68-gun *El Neptuno,* also known as *San Justo,* was built at Ferrol in 1754. She was scuttled in 1762 to block the Havana harbour entrance.

40 The 64-gun *Asia* was built at Ferrol in 1752. She was scuttled in 1762 to block the Havana harbour entrance.

41 The 64-gun *Europa,* also known as *Nuestra Señora del Pilar,* was built at Havana in 1734. She was scuttled in 1762 to block the Havana harbour entrance.

42 The 60-gun *El Conquistador* was built at Carraca in 1758, she was brought back to Woolwich, where her name was slightly changed to *Conquestador,* and she was initially fitted to lie at

El St. Genaro[43] 70} No Commanders,
El St. Antonio[44] 70} lately launch'd at the Havanna
La Vinganza 24 guns Don Diego Argote
La Thetis 22 Don Joseph Portier
La Marte 18 Don Domingo Penechea

The *Neptuno, Asia,* & *Europa* were sunk a little way within the Entrance of the Harbour, besides these Ships of the Line they had a large Frigate, several Floating Batteries Each carrying two 24 Pounders, in the Harbour; & a strong boom, compos'd of a Prodigious chain, very Great Cables, & Monstrous beams well bound together with Iron, laid across the Entrance—

Aug^st^. 30th. The Transports with the Spaniards sail'd for Spain. After the Spanish Troops had Sail'd Our Whole Army except the 9th Regim^t^. which was at Guanamacoa, march into the Havanna & were quarter'd in the Spanish houses.

The Mora Fort or Castle was much Stronger than it was represented, or we Expected to find it, 'tis of a triangular Shape; to the Water 'tis built according to the Rock it stands on, but to the Land side tis Regular, having two Bastions with retir'd & low Flanks, an Excessive great ditch, covert way, & Glacis. The Parapet is entirely of Masonry 18 feet thick, but the Chief Strength is the ditch, which at the N, E, or Sea Bastion is 63 & ½ Feet Deep, sunk Perpendicular in the Solid Rock & between 40 & 50 feet deep at the Land Bastion, tis every where Extreamly broad, & as the Mora is built on a Rock tis impossible to beat down more of it than the Parapet, or fill up the Ditch; the face attack'd was as much destroyed as it could be, the Parapet was levell'd with the Rampart & they had no shelter either for themselves or Guns, Yet if the Mine had fail'd we should not have got in. Some Money found in the Mora was Distributed amongst the Troops that storm'd it. here were 62 peices of brass Cannon, & 31 Iron Cannon, two of the Brass Cannon were 15 feet Long 24 Pound^rs^. made in the year 1601. Three pieces 9½ feet long, made Anno 1555. Five peices for the low flanks 7½ inches bore & only 6 feet long. in the Mora are vast large Cisterns for Rain Water, & very Spacious Casmets. The Havanna is of no great Strength, tho'

---

the Nore. Commissioned in 1770 for the Falkland Island dispute, she was paid off in 1771. She was fitted in 1775 at Sheerness as a receiving ship to lie at the Nore. Recommissioned in in 1775, she was paid off in 1778. Recommissioned once again in 1779, she remained a receiving ship at the Nore until paid off in 1782. She was broken up at Chatham in 1782. Length of gun deck 155 feet 9 inches, length of keel 128 feet 6 inches, breadth 43 feet 3 inches, depth of hold 19 feet 3 inches, 1,278 51/94 tons bm.

43 The 60-gun *El St. Genaro* was built in Havana in 1761. Brought home by the Royal Navy, but she wrecked en route from Havana in the Downs in January 1763, before reaching port. Nearly identical to her sister ship, *El San Antonio* (see note below), her dimensions would have been similar.

44 The 60-gun *El San Antonio* was built at Havana in 1761. Taken to Portsmouth, the Royal Navy purchased her in 1764, kept her name as *San Antonio*, and rated her as a 64-gun third rate. Commissioned in November 1764, she served as guard ship at Portsmouth under six successive commanding officers until she was paid off in 1771. She was sold in 1775. Length of gun deck 159 feet 6 inches, length of keel 132 feet 2 inches, breadth 44 feet 6 inches, depth of hold 20 feet, 1, 392 12/94 tons bm.

Wall'd entirely round, & fortify'd to the Land Side with a number of bastions, & a ditch partly Wet, but the ground rises gradually from it to the Country, whereby you may see all the Wall at a little distance, the ditch is of no Depth, & the Masonry but indifferent.

The Punta Fort is an Irregular Square of four Bastions. it stands at the West side of the Harbour's Mouth, on a Point of rocks, about 300 yards from the Havanna, & opposite to the Mora, the Entrance of the Harbour between these two Forts being only about 500 yards Wide: the Punta is Weak, the Parapet but a single thin Wall & without a ditch. Yet it looks formidable from Sea, having 37 Pieces of Large Cannon Mounted found mostly Pointed that way. The Harbour is said to be as good as any in the World, the Entrance is Well defended by the Mora Fort, the Apostle's Battery 12 guns & the Shepherd's Battery 14 Guns, these lye on the East Side. on the West, by the Punta Fort, the Bastion S[t]. Joseph 18 Guns; several Flanks in the Water Line of the town & the Fuerga Fort, have all Cannon that bear upon the Harbour's Mouth.

In the Town of the Havana are a great Number of very good Houses, mostly built with Balconies after the Spanish Fashion; here are a great many Publick Edifices. all their churches & Chapples are extreamly gaudy, & some of them Rich, particularly the Jesuits which is Ornamented with much cost

The Island of Cuba is rich, & Fruitful, producing every thing Natural to the Climate in great abundance with very little trouble, & many things Spontaneously; On the Mountains grow great plenty of large fine Mohogeny; was the Island in the Posession of any other People, but those indolent ones who have it, it would be a most glorious Spot; Nor did we find the climate so unhealthy as the West India Islands are generally represented; —

Oct[r]. 25th. Three Transports, with Disabled men for Chelsea,[45] that lay at Anchor outside the Harbours mouth, were drove on shore by the Violence of the North wind to the Westward of the Town & Dash'd to peices; two or three People were lost, Gen[l]. Lafausill[46] who was in one of them with Difficulty was saved.

45 The Royal Hospital Chelsea, London, opened in 1692 for 'the relief and succour' of wounded soldiers.

46 John Lafausille was born in Ireland in 1703 and commissioned an ensign in Onslow's 8th Regiment of Foot on 6 July 1719. He was promoted to lieutenant in that regiment on 12 November 1726, to captain-lieutenant and major in the Army on 15 June 1743. Promoted to captain in the 8th Foot on 14 July 1743, he simultaneously held a commission, from 4 October 1745 to 2 July 1746, as captain in Montague's Ordnance Regiment of Foot raised during the Jacobite uprising. He was promoted to major in the 8th Foot on 17 February 1746 and to lieutenant colonel on 27 April 1749. Appointed colonel of the 66th Regiment of Foot on 24 August 1758, he was promoted to major general on 2 March 1761. He died from disease in the West Indies on 31 December 1762.

'View of the Mora Castle from the Beach on the West Side beyond the Punta'.

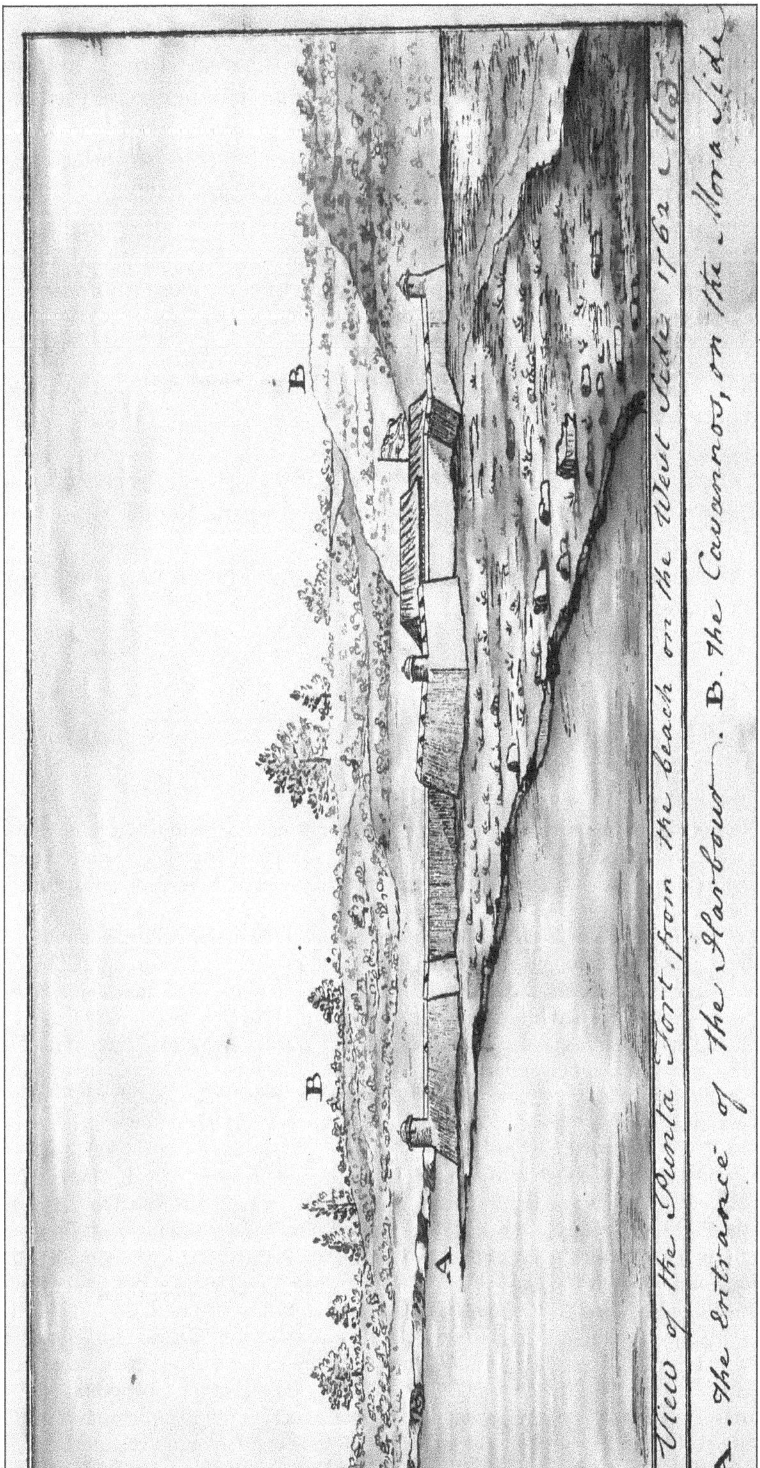

'View of the Punta Fort, from the beach on the West Side, 1762'.

Nov 4th. Admiral Pocock with a Part of the Fleet sail'd for England, the officers of Burton's[47] Grants[48] & some detachments from Corps[49] went at the same time, the Private men were drafted into the Regiments, that remain'd behind at the Havanna.

We had a report that the Spaniards intended to rise & put us all to Death, as our Garrison was now much weaken'd by Sickness having scarcely 700 Men that could do Duty; the Bishop was the Chief incendiary, who Endeavour'd to spirit up the People to this Massacre; Lord Albemarle had him seized & sent immediately off, in one of our Frigates, to St Augustine, not to return whilst we were in the Island.

1763
Jan^ry. 10th. By the Master of a Vessel who arriv'd here we had Advice that Peace was concluded between England France & Spain.[50]

15th. A Confirmation of the Preliminary Articles, for a general Peace, being settled, Was sent Express from Jamaica to the Havanna by Admiral Kepple.

22d. Lord Albemarle sail'd for England in the *Rippon*[51] Man of War. The Command devolv'd on his Brother Genl. Kepple.

---

47 Burton's 95th Regiment of Foot.

48 The 90th Regiment of Foot. Colonel Francis Grant took command of this regiment on 9 July 1762 in succession to Colonel Hugh Morgan, who had died on Martinique on 17 October 1761, but news of his death was not reported to Major General Keppel at Havana until 8 July 1762.

49 Freron's, later Fuller's, Corps. William Freron was appointed major commandant on 1 February 1762 of two companies of French Protestant prisoners raised to fight at Havana. The Corps had eight officers and 202 men. Freron died on 6 July 1762 and Major Thomas Alexander Fuller succeeded him. See Syrett, *Havana*, pp.126, 180, 183, 235, 244, 245.

50 In London, Parliament had accepted the preliminary arrangements on 8 December 1762; the final peace treaty was signed at Paris on 10 February 1763.

51 The 64-gun fourth rate *Rippon* was built at Woolwich to a design by Joseph Allin by successive master shipwrights Adam Hayes, Edward Allin, and Israel Pownoll, between 1752 and 1758. Commissioned in February 1758 under Captain Edward Jekyll, she served with Anson's fleet then sailed for the Leeward Islands and was at St. Pierre, Martinique, and Guadeloupe in 1759, also taking a privateer in that year. In 1760, she sailed to St Helena to escort the East Indies ships home. In 1761, she served in Buckle's squadron off Brest and was in the action against the French 64-gun *l'Achille* on 9 March 1761. She sailed for the West Indies on 5 March 1762 and was at Havana from 6 June 1762. On her return home, she was paid off in March 1763. She served as guard ship at Portsmouth until 1768, when she was fitted for sea and returned to service. She was at Boston, Massachusetts in 1786, in the Channel in 1770. From 1776 to 1780, she was in the East Indies, where she was in the Battle of Pondicherry on 10 August 1778. In 1781-82, she was in the Downs and North Sea squadrons. Paid off in 1783, she served was fitted as a receiving ship at Plymouth in 1787-1788. She was broken up at Plymouth in January 1808. Length of gun deck 155 feet 5 inches, length of keel 129 feet 4 inches, breadth 42 feet 6 inches, depth of hold 18 feet 7 inches, 1,242 56/94 tons bm, draught 11 feet 6 inches forward / 16 feet 6½ inches aft.

1763
April [By this time our sick began to recover very fast. The Disorders they Labour'd under Was occasion'd][52] more by the Excessive fatigues they underwent during the Siege, than from the inclemency of the Climate, The Winter was particularly Pleasant, frequently so cold that we were glad to sit at a Charcoal Fire. The Spaniards in general were polite & very Obliging, the better sort treated the English officers with very great Civility. [The Lowest Class of people at the Havanna are a mixture of the Moor, the Negro & Mulatta a base set—][53] A very handsome theatre was fitted up by the English Officers who Amus'd themselves, & entertaind the Town with some excellent Theatrical performances—

June 30th. Four Spanish Men of War & some Transports with troops on board Arriv'd at the Havanna, & brought Orders from the British Court for Delivering the Place up to the Spaniards; Our Troops were according order'd to Embark, the Detachment of the Royal & 3d. Battalion of Royal Americans were to take possession of East & West Florida.

July 6th. The Embarkation of the British Troops was finish'd & the Havanna restor'd to the Spaniards.

9th. Sail'd out of the Harbour. Since our troops were on board, the town has been every night Illuminated, Guns firing from all quarters of the Town, & fire works play'd off from every Steeple, in short for the three preceding Nights the Whole Town was in a blaze.

52 The first portion of this entry, shown here between brackets, begins as a continuation of the 22 October 1762 entry, but continues on the next page of the manuscript under April 1763. Based on its content, the editor has chosen to interpret it as belonging to the beginning of the additions to the document made in April 1763, and not part of the entry for 22 October 1762.

53 The sentence between brackets is a note in the margin.

8

West Florida: Pensacola and Mobile, 10 July 1763–2 December 1765

10th. Admiral Kepple with some Ships that did not get out Yesterday came out this day. Three of the Spanish Ships of war were drest. The 3d. Batt^{n}. of Royal Americans sail'd for Pensacola in West Florida. the rest of the Fleet steer'd towards Europe.

14th. The Detachment of the Royal[1] parted the Fleet & Sail'd for St Augustine in East Florida.

18th. The *Swift* Sloop of War[2] came into the Fleet & brought the Destination for the Army, the 9th. & 35th. Regim^{ts}. to go to Florida; the 22d. & 34th to Louisiana; the 48th. & 56th. to Ireland; the Rest of the Army to New York; We chang'd our Ship's at Sea, this took us up two days, as a great Part of the Regiments were on board the Spanish men of War taken at the Havanna, & were oblige'd to remove, into smaller ships.

21st. The Fleet separated the 9th. & 35th. sail'd for St Augustine, under convoy of the *Danae* Frigate.[3]

---

1 Four companies of 'The Royal' or 1st Regiment of Foot under Captain John Hedges, then Major Francis Ogilvie, were assigned to St. Augustine in East Florida. See Charles Loch Mowat. *East Florida as a British Province, 1763-1784* (Berkeley: University of California Press, 1943; reprinted Gainesville: University of Florida Press, 1964), p.6.

2 The 14-gun ship sloop *Swift* was built at Limehouse by John Greaves in 1762-1763 and completed at Deptford Dockyard in 1763. Commissioned in 1762 under Commander William Cornwallis she sailed for Jamaica on 13 May 1762. Under Captain Charles Lucas in 1765, she was paid off and given a small repair at Woolwich in 1765-1766. Recommissioned in 1766, she was in the Falkland Islands from 1766 to 1769 and then paid off. Repaired and refitted at Deptford, she recommissioned in 1769 and sailed for the Falkland Islands on 15 November 1769. She wrecked with the loss of three lives at Port Desire, Patagonia, on 13 March 1770. Length of gun deck 91 feet 5 inches, length of keel 74 feet 3 inches, breadth 26 feet 2½ inches, depth of hold 13 feet 3½ inches, 271 25/94 tons bm.

3 The 38-gun, fifth rate *Danae* was built at Le Havre in 1756-1757 to a design by Jean-Joseph Ginoux as the French 32-gun *La Danaé*. She was taken by the frigates *Southampton* and *Melampe* on 28 March 1759, and refitted at Portsmouth. Commissioned in 1759, she was stationed off Dunkirk in 1760 and in 1761, sailed for the West Indies as a convoy escort and took a prize. In 1762, she was in action off Gibraltar with a privateer. On 6 May 1762, she sailed with a convoy to the West Indies and was in Jamaica in January 1763. About March

28th. Met the *Renown*[4] Frigate, & the ships coming out of St Augustine, that carry'd the Royal in there. We came to an Anchor about 7 Leagues from the shore

29th. Weigh'd & Stood nearer in, anchor'd about 3 Leagues from the Town of St Augustine; small Vessels only can go over the Bar, which shifts & is very dangerous; the Road is a Wild, bleak place, quite open to the Ocean & every wind that blows, we left the 9th. Regt. at St Augustine, the Men of the Royal were drafted into it, the officers went for Europe.

Augst. 2d. Sail'd for Charles Town in South Carolina.

7th. Came to an anchor in the Harbour of Charles town; the Ship we sail'd in was not thought proper to prosecute the Voyage to Pensacola [She founder'd going to Europe],[5] we were oblig'd to take up two Transports & remain here till they were fitted for us, which detain'd us till October. Charles Town South Carolina is a very handsome Place, the streets regular & well laid out & the Buildings good; here are two very neat Churches.[6] The soil of this Country is mostly a dark fine sand, yet very fertile & provisions in General are Cheap.

Octr. 5th. Sail'd from the Harbour down to Rebellion Road.[7]

6th. Sail'd for Pensacola in compy. with the *Carey* & *Venus* Transports, on board the former was a Pilot for Pensacola, the Later had recruits for the 22d. & 35th. Regiments, the Albemarle was our Third Transport. We sail'd together till we came

---

1763, Captain Charles Leslie took command. She was paid off in October 1763 and broken up at Chatham in 1771. Length of gun deck 147 feet 6 inches, length of keel 123 feet 11 inches, breadth 37 feet 9½ inches, depth of hold 11 feet 4½ inches, 941 35/94 tons bm.

4 The 30-gun, fifth rate frigate *Renown* was built at Brest in 1744-1745 to the designs of François Guillaume Clairin Deslauriers as the French 8-pounder frigate *Renommée*. Taken as a prize on 29 September 1744, by the 44-gun *Dover*, she was refitted at Portsmouth and commissioned in 1748. *Renown* had a major influence on British frigate design. She initially served in the West Indies in 1748 and returned home in 1751. After a great repair in 1757-58, she was recommissioned and sailed for the Leeward Islands, where she participated in the Guadeloupe and Martinique operations in 1759. She was at Jamaica in 1760-61. Returning, she took two prizes off Morlaix and one off St Malo in 1762. Under Captain Frederick Maitland from 1762, she took troops to Portugal in 1762 and took a prize in the Channel in August 1763. Paid off in 1764, she was repaired at Woolwich and recommissioned in 1766 and sailed for the West Indies. She returned home in 1770 and was paid off, then broken up in 1771, length of gun deck 126 feet 2 inches, length of keel 103 feet 7 inches, breadth 34 feet 10½ inches, depth of hold 11 feet 8 inches, 669 53/94 tons bm.

5 The words within brackets are a note in the margin.

6 St Michael's Church, built between 1752 and 1761, which has some resemblance to London's St. Martin-in-the-Fields, designed by James Gibbs and still standing. St. Philips Church, built in 1751, was destroyed by fire in 1835 and rebuilt to a different design.

7 Rebellion Road. Probably a reference to the anchorage on the Atlantic coast near the mouth of the Stono River, a tidal channel located southwest of Charleston, South Carolina. In September 1739, the area around the Stono River was the site of the Stono Rebellion, the largest uprising of slaves in the British North American colonies before the American Revolution.

near the Windward Passage, when the *Carey*, & the *Venus* parted us; our Voyage proving long, our Water almost expended Our provisions running Short, & not having any Person on board acquainted with the Florida Coast, we steer'd for Port Royal in Jamaica.

Novr. 5th. Arriv'd at the Port Royal, here we found the *Venus* Transport, that had put in three days before us. by Order of Admiral Kepple who was Station'd here, we were supply'd with Water & Provisions, & thc Swift sloop was to convoy us to Pensacola.

10th. Sail'd in comp^{y}. with our Convoy & the *Venus*.

30th. Arriv'd at Pensacola, met the *Carey* Transport off the Mouth of the Harbour; by the Ignorance of the Man who pretended to be a Pilot, the ship had gone down almost as far as the Mouth of the Mississippi, & was oblig'd to beat up again. here we Landed, the Royal American Battalion that came here from the Havanna was reduc'd, the men were sent to the 22d Regiment, who were to go up the River Mississippi, to the Illinois Country.

Pensacola is only a single, Rotten Stockaded Fort without even a ditch & incapable of Defence, it is an oblong square'd & has one bastion at the N, E, angle, full of Embrasures, & another at ye S.W.

1764
May The 22d. Regiment came to Pensacola, they had been up the River Mississippi 22 days Voyage, when they were attack'd from the Banks by Indians & drove back, had they not met with this opposition, they would have been near 4 Months on their passage the Country lying above 1500 miles up the River & a Strong Current always running down.

Since our Arrival here we have finish'd a ditch & friez'd it, & have began a Strong Bastion at the N,W, angle which gives the Place at least the Appearance of Strength, the Work is done by the Soldiers who are pay'd for it. The Barracks & habitations the Governours house excepted, are miserable bark huts, that will neither keep out the Sun, rain nor Wind, & without Chimneys, the Spaniards us'd only a little Charcoal in a tub of Sand to keep them warm.

The Country is a Sandy barren Soil, [The sand in perfectly white & dry][8] the Woods mostly Pitch Pine, in the swamps are some good Cedars and Oak. The Land produces nothing, [Garden stuff may be rais'd but w^{t} much trouble][9] all our Fresh Provisions, Vegetables &c^{a} are brought from Mobile & Orleans & from our Nearest Settlements in America.

Aug. 8. the 22d. Reg^{t} went to Mobile to make a second attempt up the River Mississippi.

---

8 The words between brackets are a note in the margin.
9 The words between brackets are a note in the margin

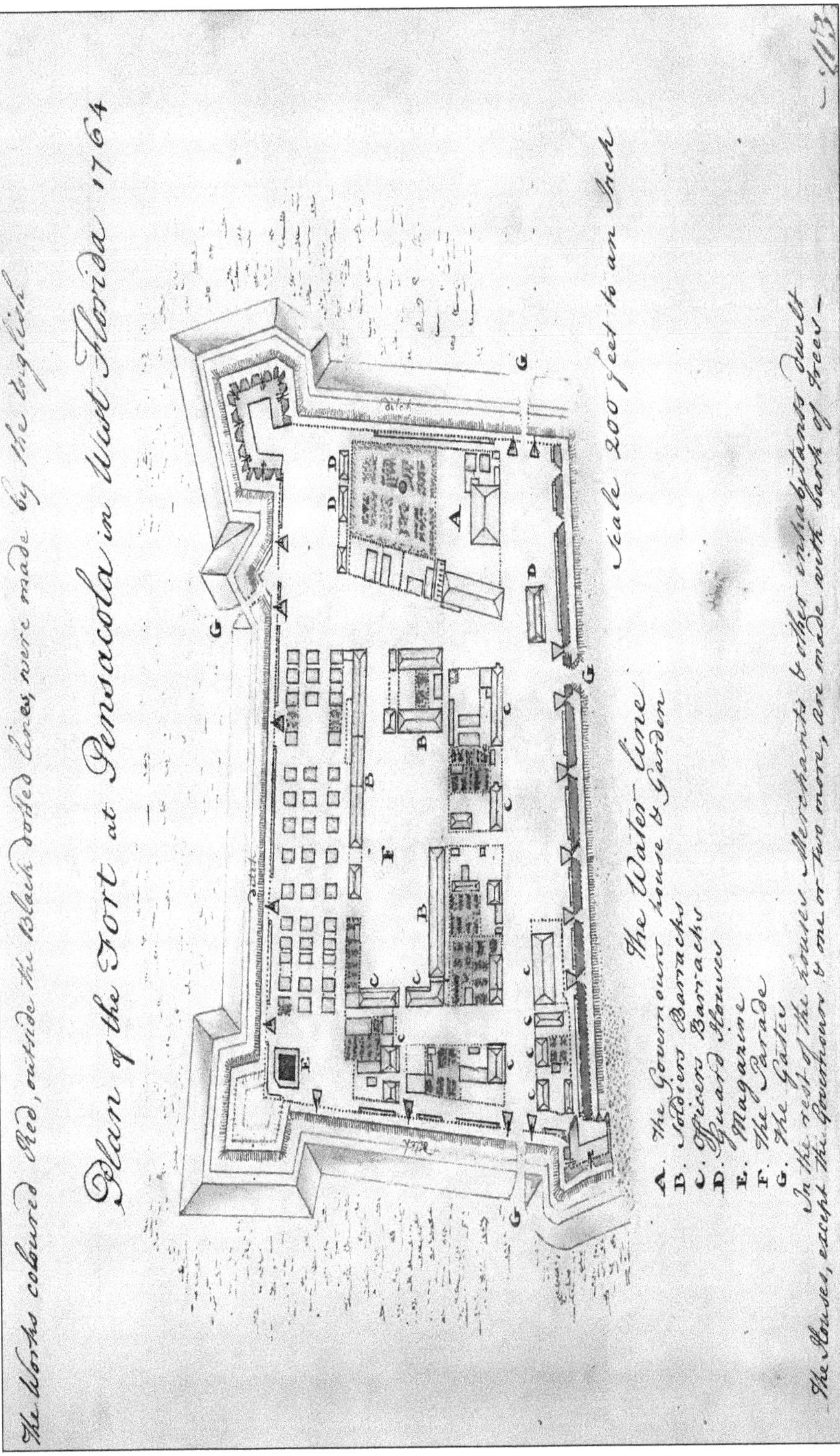

'Plan of the Fort of Pensacola in West Florida 1764'.

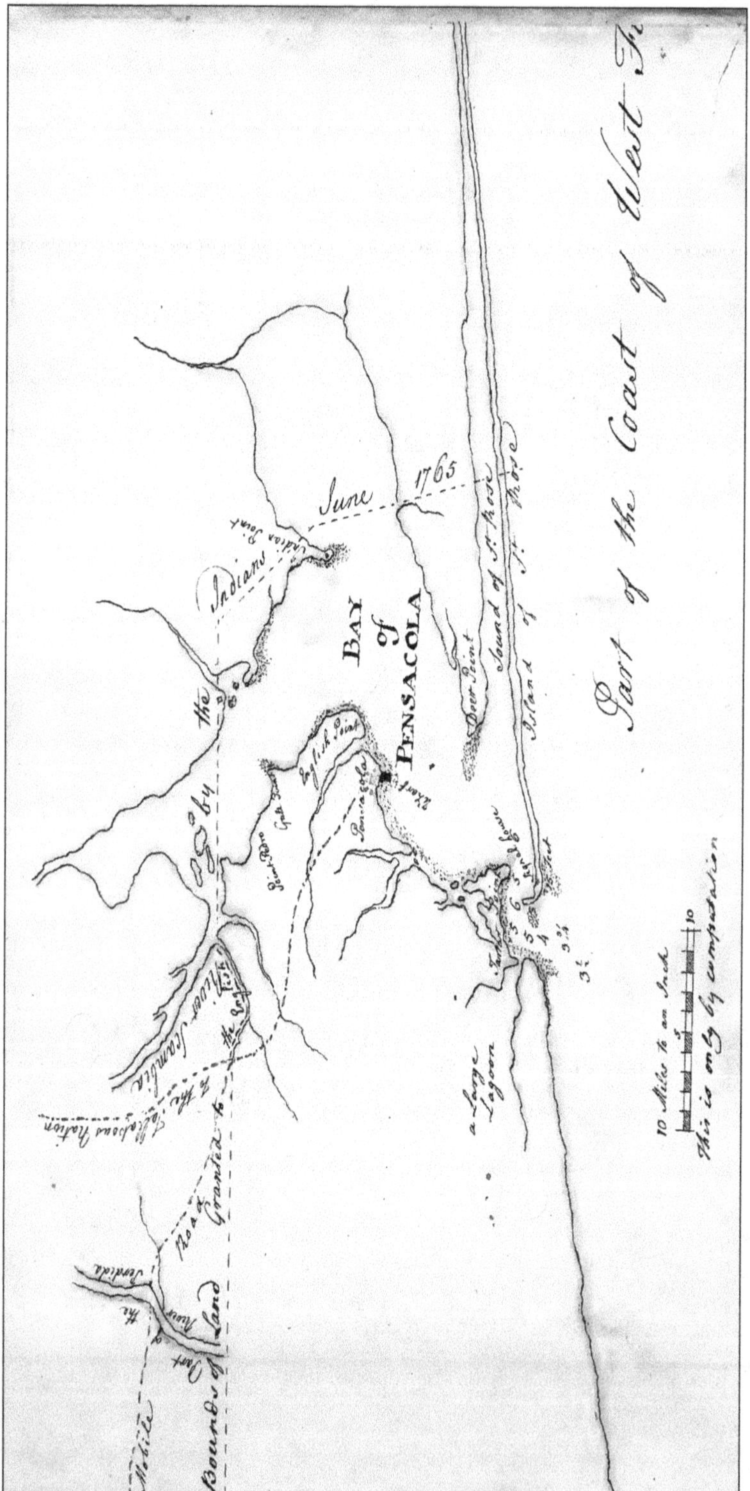

'Part of the coast of West Florida'.

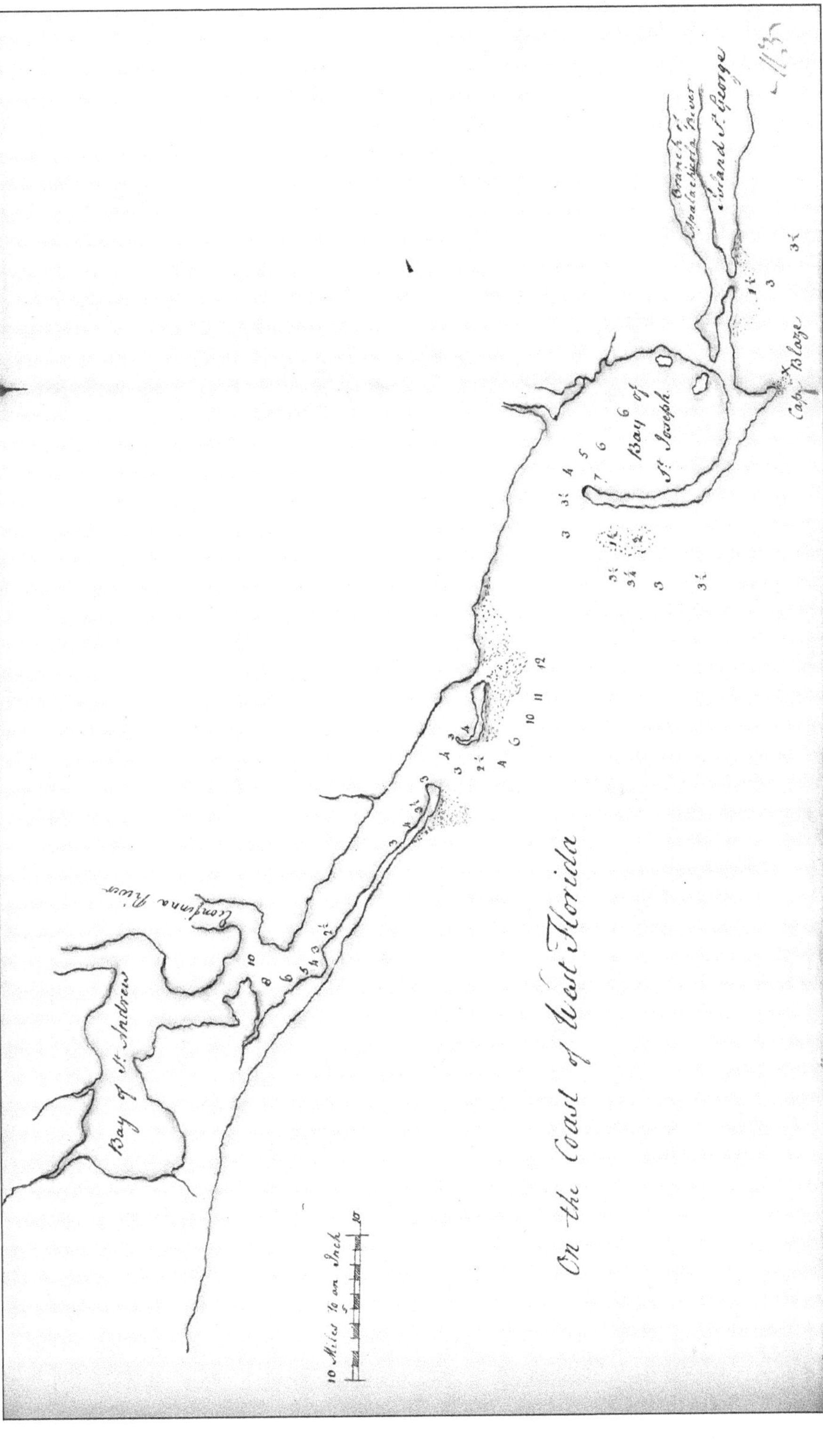

'On the coast of West Florida'.

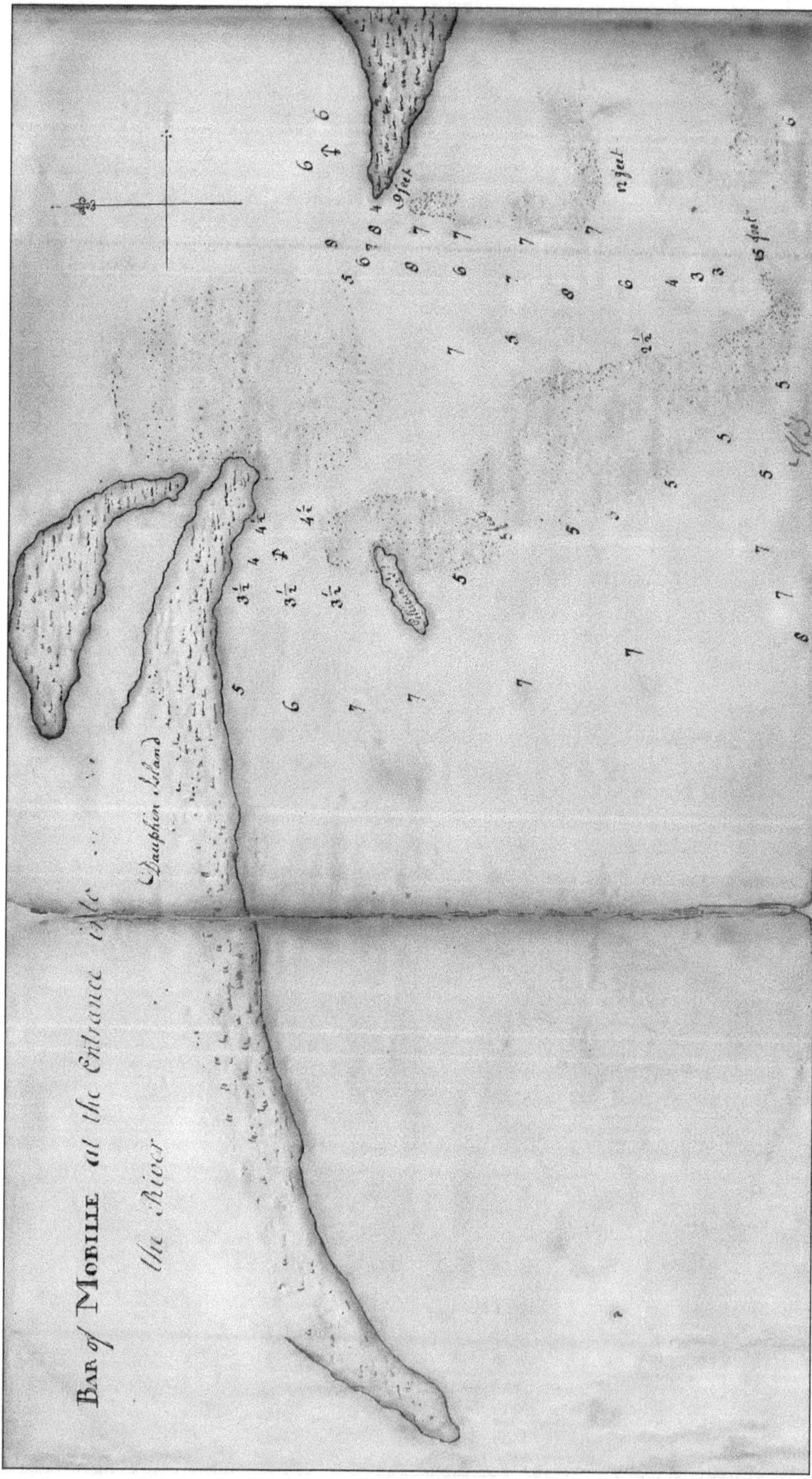

'Bay of Mobile at the entrance into the river'.

[Govr. Johnstone[10] quarrel'd with all the Millitary. he was a very bad Man.][11]

The town of Mobile lyes to the Westward of Pensacola about 70 Miles Distance, but bad traveling, the Way being Entirely through Woods, some Rivers are to be cross'd, which after a fall of rain are often impassible for two or three days together, in which time the traveler is oblig'd to lie in the Woods, as there are no habitations till he arrives at the side of the Bay opposite Mobile, where the French have some plantations, this part of the Bay is 9 Miles over. From Pensacola to Mobile is but 24 leagues by Water, which if an Opportunity offers, is the way Most people chuse to go. The town of Mobile is pleasant with several tolerable houses, it is situated on the Side of the Bay, which looks like a Narrow river by reason of a large Island lying before it. here are a Vast number of Alligators. The Country about this Place is much better than at Pensacola. The Fort is a pretty small square of four bastions, with Casmetts All of brick, a Ditch, covert way & Glacis Large Ships cannot go up farther than within three Leagues of the Town, but good Navigation for small Vessels. Mobile about the fall of the Year is Extreamly unhealthy, Occasion'd by the Marshes that lie about it on all sides, and, the Woods are cleared no farther than the Skirts of the Town, which must prevent a free Circulation of the Air, the disorders are Chiefly slow fevers & the fever & Ague, which it is very Difficult to get the Better of, & often proves fatal. At some few Miles distance are several pretty good farms, which are purchased by the English.

10 George Johnstone was born in 1730, the fourth son of Sir James Johnston, 3rd Baronet. As a boy, he went to sea in merchant ships and then entered the Royal Navy in 1746. He earned a reputation for bravery, but also one as a difficult person, challenging his commanding officer to a duel for not giving him his certificate for service. With the end of the war in 1748, he was unemployed, but passed his lieutenant's examination in 1749. He returned to the merchant service and was then recalled to the Navy as war approached again. He commissioned a lieutenant on 9 October 1755. He saw action in the Battle of Cap-Français in 1757, where he was praised for gallantry, but them got into a dispute with his admiral over prize money. In 1758, he demanded his captain be court martialed, but the Admiralty dismissed his request. Without a ship for a period, he was promoted to commander on 6 February 1760 and given command of a sloop, whose crew mutinied. After skillfully putting down the mutiny, he captured several prizes. Promoted to captain on 1762, he was given command of a frigate. His naval career ended in November 1763, when, through his friendship with the secretary to Prime Minister the Earl of Bute, Johnston was one of the four Scots named to be governors of the new British territories acquired at the Peace of Paris. Johnston became Governor of West Florida and immediately earned distinction by physically attacking a writer for *The North Britain* who had criticized Bute's appointments to these posts. Johnston arrived at Pensacola, the capital of West Florida, on October 1763 and made significant progress in creating the civil government, but immediately come into conflict with the commanders of British forces, who he thought should answer to him, not to the commander in chief, North America. He was recalled in 1767, when he attempted to start a war with the Creek Indians, contrary to the policy of promoting peaceful relations with Native Americans that the ministry in London had established. Returning to London, he entered politics and became successively Member of Parliament for Cockermouth in 1768-1774, Appleby in 1774-1780, Lostwithiel in 1780-1784, and Ilchester in 1786-1787. Additionally, he was a director of the East India Company from 1784 to 1787. He died in 1787.

11 The statement between brackets is a note in the margin.

The French bred a great many Cattle & rais'd much Stock, corn, & garden stuff about Mobile, but most of those Inhabitants have dispos'd of their plantations, sold off their Stock & retired to New Orleans.

Septr. The Beginning of this month the Wolf king of the Creek Nation of Indians came to Pensacola; gave to the English a large Tract of Country, near ten miles deep round this bay, & running the same distance from the Sea Side all up the Bay of Mobile till it comes opposite to that Town. The Wolf had 300 head Men Attending him.

[The Chickesaw Nation of Indians promis'd to conduct the English up the River Mississippi which they perform'd. their chief was call'd Matapiahá][12]

1765

June. The Mortar, a chief of the Alabama Indians, and a most inveterate Enemy to the English, came with a number of Savages, made Peace & confirm'd the grant the Wolf had given. [Many nations of Indians came to this Congress][13] The Climate here is Hot to Excess in Summer & cold for two or three Months in Winter; [when the N. West Winds set in Here, 'tis very cold & freezes hard—You may stand on Ice in the Morn^{s} & by 12 oClock tis so hot you can hardly bear your coat on][14] in this season the Indians bring in a little Venison, which is meer Carrion, & they sell it at a good Price, tho' the Deer are plenty about the Country, but they have so little food that they cannot fatten. Since the Arrival of the Governour & Civil branch, they have Mark'd out a Town outside the Fort & began to build a few Wooden Houses. But the country is so excessively barren that Notwithstanding any Encouragement, the Inhabitants will be hard push'd to subsist, instead of making fortunes, as several have come here with that View. The Indian Traders report, that about 200 Miles back in the Country, the Land is very good. but there the Indians inhabit. An engineer & Party from Mobile went up the River Mississippi, to Erect a Stockaded Fort on the Point of land form'd by the Junction of the River Ibérville[15] with the Mississippi, they buried most of the People who were there at Work, at last the Indians came, destroy'd the Stockades[16] & roll'd the Cannon into the River, this put an End to the Undertaking.[17] The Point was named Point Pitt, & the Fort to be call'd Fort Bute [NB, the Govr. was Johnstone, a Scotch Gent^{n}.][18]

12 The words between brackets are a note in the margin
13 The words between brackets are a note in the margin.
14 The information between brackets is a note in the margin.
15 When Piere La Moyne d'Iberville visited the area in 1699, the natives in the area showed him the waterway. It located about 115 miles (185 km) up the Mississippi River from New Orleans. It is not a river, but an 18-mile (29 km) long bayou, now called Bayou Manchac, that links the Mississippi River in the west with the Amite Rver, a tributary of Lake Maurepas, in the east.
16 A note in the margin repeats this information: 'the Indians destroy'd all Works and drove the People away'.
17 A Britsh fort stood at or near this site when the Spanish captured it in 1779.
18 The words between brackets are a note in the margin.

The 22d. Reg^t. rec^d. an Order to remain at Mobille & Wait the Arrival of Troops from England to relieve them, & the 34th. Regiment were Order'd to the Illinois; they set off for that Country about the Middle of June, they go all the Way in Large boats rowed by the Soldiers. The Chickesaws met them on the way & conducted them][19]

July 18th. The Transports from England with the 21st. & 35th. Reg^ts. Arrived at Pensacola the 21st. Reg to relieve the 22d at Mobile & the 31st. to Relieve the 35th. at Pensacola[20] [Whilst we were at Pensacola we buried 5 officers, Cap^tn. McKinnen,[21] L^t. Ormsby,[22] L^t. Lysagth,[23] L^t. Ferguson,[24] L^t. Crutchfield[25] —All of the fever & ague contracted at Mobile. very few of the Private men died][26]

19 The information between brackets is a note in the margin.

20 In her diary, Elizabeth Digby Pilot came with her husband, Captain Henry Pilot, when the 31st Regiment arrived at Pensacola. She recorded 'The Garrison (as it was called) was filled with the shattered remains of the 35th Regt, which has suffered severely during the War, and had gone to Pensacola to be relieved by troops from Europe. It was our unhappy fate to do this. What a contrast was presented between our fine healthy blooming men, and the poor emaciated soldiers of the 35th! Nor was this more striking than the joy they expressed at the prospect of going home, and the feelings of sorrow our men experienced at the wretched place they had come to'; Michelle Arentsen and Jennie Hurl-Eamon (eds.), 'Elizabeth Digby Pilot: Memoir', *JSAHR*, 96 (2018), Part I, p. 112.

21 Robert McKinnon was born 'in America'. He was commissioned a lieutenant in Pepperrell's new-raising 66th Foot on 19 September 1745. He went on to British half pay when the regiment disbanded on 15 May 1749. From half pay, he became a lieutenant in Shirley's new-raising 50th Foot on 28 December 1754, by a free augmentation vacancy. He became lieutenant in the second battalion of the 1st Regiment of Foot on 25 December 1756, free vice an augmentation. He was promoted to captain-lieutenant in the 35th Foot on 14 April 1759 by purchase. He was promoted to captain in the 35th Foot on 27 July 1759 by a free death vacancy. He died of disease on 31 May 1765, after 14.1 years' service.

22 Eubule Ormsby was born in Ireland. He was commissioned an ensign in the 35th Foot on 16 February 1756 by purchase vice an augmentation. He was promoted to lieutenant in the 35th Foot on 24 January 1758 by purchase vice a retirement. He died of disease on 1 October 1764 after 8.7 years' service.

23 Cornelius Lysaght was born in Ireland. While serving as a volunteer with the 46th Foot, was one of the young gentlemen sent from the regular army in 1757 to learn the 'ranging-discipline' with Rogers' Rangers. From Gentleman volunteer, he was commissioned ensign in the 35th Foot, 24 January 1758 by purchase. He was promoted to lieutenant in the 35th Foot on 11 June 1760 by purchase. He died of disease on 1 October 1764 after 6.7 years' service.

24 There was no Ferguson in any of the regiments in West Florida at this time. Bamford is likely referring to Robert Farquharson, who was commissioned an ensign in the 35th Foot on 31 July 1758 by purchase vice an augmentation. He was promoted to lieutenant in the 35th Foot on 30 August 1761 by purchase vice a resignation. He died of disease on 9 November 1764, after 6.3 years' service while in West Florida.

25 John Crutchfield was born in England. A gentleman volunteer, he was commissioned an ensign in Scotland in the new-raising 113th Regiment of Foot on 20 October 1761. He was promoted to lieutenant in the 113th Foot on 30 June 1762. He went onto British half pay when the regiment disbanded on 3 June 1763. He transferred as lieutenant to the 35th Foot on 19 March 1764. He died in 13 December 1765 after 3.4 years' service.

26 The information between brackets is a note in the margin.

25th. the 35th. Regiment Embark'd; the Transports with the 21st. went to Mobile bay, they got within 9 miles of the town, lay at a Place call'd Dog river,[27] where the men disembark'd, & march'd to Mobile. The 22d. Embark'd whilst they lay in the River of Mobile two of the Transports were struck with Lightning, & lost their Masts, this destain'd us a long time. The Harbour of Pensacola is Extreamly Fine with near four fathom Water on the Bar & Capable of Containing any Number of Ships, it Produces a great Variety of Excellent Fish, as Trout, Mullet, Carp of 30 pounds Weight, perch Reas, with several other kinds, & Oysters in the greatest plenty.

Many considerable rivers empty themselves into this Bay, Particularly the River Scambia,[28] which is reported to be large & Navigable to a great distance.

Whilst we lay in the Harbour, the 31st. Reg^t^. on Shore suffer'd very much by Sickness & were so reduc'd that they could hardly furnish a Corporal's Guard to do the Duty of the Fort. They have buried 3 officers and about 170 Men, women & Children—of Six officers Wives, five were dead & the Sixth narrowly excap'd; the 21st Regiment at Mobile were much in the same condition. about the Beginning of this Year a small Party of the Inhabitants of Pensacola went to the Bay of S^t^. Andrew near 40 Leagues to the Eastward of Pensacola to cut Cedar & if they found it worth while, to endeavour to make a Settlement there. They give a very good account of the Bay & land round it, say that it abounds with several sorts of Fish, & abundance of Turtle, that Cedar & Oak are in great Quanitys, but the Indians grew Jealous when they saw them building a Wooden house there, & oblig'd them to go away.

Septr. 17th. The Transports from Mobile having Joyn'd those at Pensacola, the Whole sail'd out of the harbour, 5 with the 22d. Reg^t^. on board, & four with the 35th.

28th. Made the Island of Cuba. stood in close, for the Havanna; we could Observe as we pass'd the Mora, that the Spaniards, have Made up the Breach, cut down the narrow way along the Rock, by which we got to the Wall, made embrasures where there were not any, & several other alterations in the Fort. We saw a large Work erecting where the Spanish redoubt stood, & another Work toward the White Road, so that they seem determin'd to defend that side Well. We could not perceive any Alteration on the West Side, Tho 'tis said they are building a strong Redoubt on Mount Gonzales.

27 The Dog River is a relatively shallow river about eight miles (13 km) long located in Mobile, County, Alabama. The river is influenced by the tide in Mobile Bay, the estuary on the northern Gulf of Mexico into which it discharges near Hollinger's Island. The French named it Rivière au Chien.

28 The Escambia River flows into the western end of Pensacola Bay at Escambia Bay. The name applies to the river within Florida. About 60 miles (97 km) upstream and the confluence of Escambia Creek about 1.2 mile (1.9 km) downstream from the present Florida-Alabama border, the river's name changes to the Conecuh River. Despite the change in name, the Escambia-Conecuh River is a single, 258-mile (415 km) long waterway that rises in southeastern Alabama.

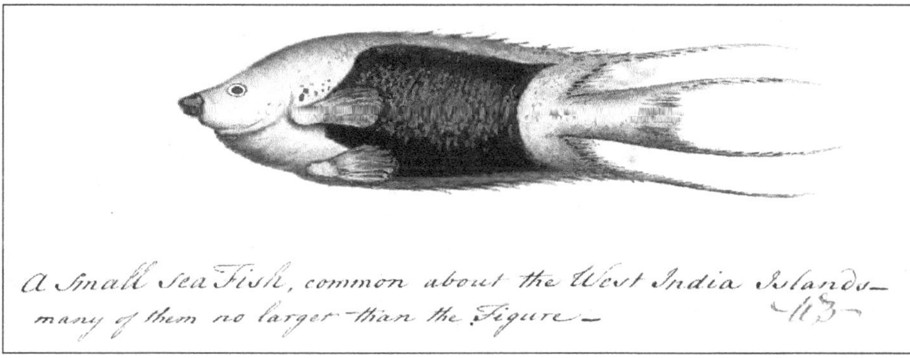

'A small sea fish, common about the West India Islands—Many of them no larger than the figure'.

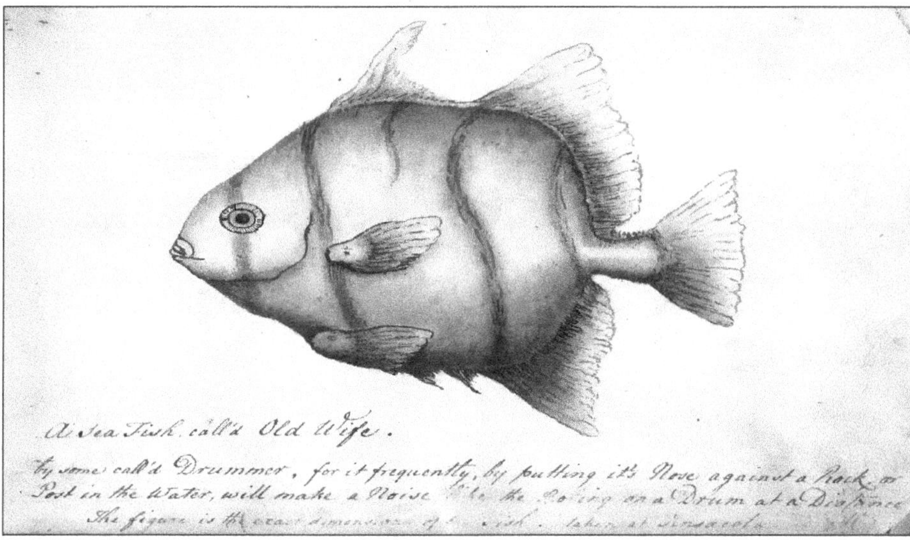

'A sea fish call'd Old Wife'. By some call'd Drummer, for it frequently by putting it's nose against a rock or Post in the water, will make a noise like the banging on a Drum at a distance. The figure is the exact dimensions of the fish. taken at Pensacola.

'Head of a Turkey Buzzard, or Carrion Crow, a fowl common in the West Indies. the Body & resembles very much a large brown turkey'.

Novr. 27th. Made the Lizard.[29] Penitus tota divises Orbe Brittanos.[30]

30th. Arriv'd in the Harbour of Portsmouth.

Decr. 2d. The feeble remains of our Worn out Regiment got on shore we buried a great many men at Sea & some in the Harbour, several were sent to the Isle of Wight [to Carrisbroke Castle][31] dreadfully afflicted with the Scurvy, such deep root had it taken by a long continuance on Salt Provisions without Vegetables, that a scratch on the leg was almost Certain Death, & the loss of the Joynt at least in the Hands; in such a corrupt State was their blood; we landed scarcely 100 Men. March'd to Chatham Barracks.

29 Lizard Point, Cornwall. The most southerly point in England (excepting the Isles of Scilly), it is a traditional point of arrival or departure at the western entrance to the English Channel.

30 A phrase from Virgil's first *Eclogue* in which Melibœus says: 'At nos hinc alii sitientis ibimus Afros, pars Scythiam et rapidum cretae veniemus Oaxen et penitus toto divisos orbe Britannos' or translated: 'But as for us, we turn our weary steps Some to parched Africa, to Scythia some, Or to Oaxes, the swift Cretan stream, Or distant Britain, cut off from the world'.

31 The words between brackets are a note in the margin marked for insertion here.

9

'A few Notes relative to the foregoing Journal'

Copy of Genl: Webb's Letter[1] to Col^{o}. Monro

Fort Edward Augst. 4th. [1757][2] 12 oClock at noon

Sir

I am directed by Genl Webb[3] to acknowledge the receipt of three of your letters, two bearing date about nine yesterday Morning, & one about Six in the Evening, by two Rangers, which are the only men that have got in here, except two yesterday Morning with your first, acquainting him of the Enemy being in sight. he has Order'd me to acquaint you he does not think it prudent (as you know his Strength at this Place) to attempt a junction, or to assist you till reinforc'd by the Militia of the Colonies, for the immediate [March][4] of which repeated expresses have been sent. One of our scouts brought in a Canadian Prisoner last night from the Investing Party, which is very large, & have possess'd all the grounds five Miles on this side of Fort

1 Bamford's transcription of this letter is the only surviving part of his journal that relates to the information that was in the eight missing leaves at the beginning of the document, including the regiment's experiences at Fort William Henry 1757. The 35th Regiment had arrived there in the spring of 1757 under Lieutenant Colonel Monro, who took command of the fort.

2 The letter is dated following the arrival of Montcalm's French forces and their attack on Fort William Henry. Munro surrendered the Fort on 8 August 1757.

3 Daniel Webb was born in Ireland in 1703 and purchased a commission as an ensign in the 1st Foot Guards on 20 March 1721. He was promoted to lieutenant in the 1st Guards and to captain in the Army on 16 April 1722. He left the 1st Guards on 20 May 1732 and purchased a commission as captain in Ligonier's 8th Horse, which Sir John Ligonier had made it the finest cavalry unit in the Army. He was promoted to major in the 8th Horse on 29 March 1742. He was present at the Battles of Dettingen and Fontenoy. Webb was promoted to lieutenant colonel of the 8th Horse on 27 May 1745 and placed in command, continuing to hold that position after the regiment was renumbered as the 4th Horse in 1751. Noticed by the Duke of Cumberland, he was promoted to colonel and placed in command of the 48th Regiment of Foot on 11 November 1755. Sent to North America in June 1756, he was ordered temporarily to command the British Army in North America until Major General Abercromby arrived and be the temporary replacement awaiting the arrival of Lord Loudoun. Webb was promoted to major general on 25 June 1759 and to lieutenant general on 19 January 1761. He was appointed colonel of the 8th King's Regiment of Foot on 22 May and colonel of the 14th Dragoons on 20 October 1722. He died in 1733. For further information, see, the *Oxford Dictionary of National Biography*.

4 The word between brackets are an interlineal note marked for insertion here.

W^{m}. Henry. The Number of the Enemy is very considerable, the Pris^{r}. says Eleven Thousand, & have a large Train of Artillery with Mortars, & were to open their Batteries [this][5] day. The General thought proper to give you this intelligence that in case he should be so unfortunate from the delays of the Militia not [to have it in his power][6] to give you timely Assistance, you might be able to make the best terms were left in your Power. The Bearer is a [~~Lieut of Putnam's Company of Rangers~~][7] Serj^{t}. of the Connecticut Forces, and if is happy enough to get in will bring advices from you. We keep continual Scouts going to endeavour to get in, or bring intelligence from you.

I am Sir with the heartiest and
most anxious wishes for your Welfare
your most Obedient
Humble servant
G: Bartman[8]
aid de camp

L^{t}. Col^{o}. Monro, or Officer commanding at Fort W^{m}. Henry

(Note the interlinings were in the original letter, except the words March & this)[9]

At the Action before Quebec 13th. Septr. 1759, Genl Wolfe was kill'd & Genl. Monckton dangerously Wounded, & carried off the Field, the Command devolv'd on Genl. [name blotted out] When the Battle was over, the French army being totally routed & disperse'd, & we in quiet Possession of the Field, the Rest of the Genl. Officers, went up to Genl. T[10] congratulating him on the success of the Day, & saying what Quebec must very soon be in our hands. Genl. T after some discourse, said it was an uncommon thing for a Victorious Army to retreat, Yet he did not know but it might be our Case: at Which Genl. Murray roar'd out, so as to be heard at a Considerable Distance, Retreat, Retreat; No, bleach our Bones here first, we won it & by G— we'll wear it. then Genl. T said, I do not say Genl. Murray that it will be so but such things have happen'd, Genl. M. swore again that it must not happen to us—Quebec capitulated in five days after—.

---

5 The word between brackets in an interlineal note marked for insertion here.
6 The words between brackets in an interlineal note marked for insertion here.
7 The name and unit between brackets has been crossed out but still legible.
8 George Bartman was the biological son of Thomas Hervey (1699-1775), brother of the 2nd Earl of Bristol. He was commissioned an ensign in the 17th Regiment of Foot on 20 August 1751. He was promoted to lieutenant in the new-rising 50th Foot on 17 September 1754, then he was made lieutenant in the in the second battalion of the 34th Foot. He served as aide-de-camp and assistant engineer to the commander in chief and governor of Massachusetts, William Shirley. With the strong recommendation of Henry Fox, the former Secretary of War, Secretary of State, and Paymaster General, Bartman was promoted to captain in the 44th Foot on 25 December 1756. He served as aide-de-camp to General Daniel Webb in 1757. Wounded in the action with the French at Fort Carillon (Ticonderoga) in July 1758, he died on 15 September 1758.
9 Bamford's parenthetical note to explain the insertions above.
10 Brigadier General George Townshend

28th. April 1760. Genl. Murray, seeing the second French Collumn coming against our Light Infantry, who had entirely dispers'd one Col^{mn}., order'd Major [Roger][11] Morris, who commanded the 35th. Reg^{t}. & were in the Reserve, to advance with the whole Reg^{t}. against that Collumn. but he thought proper to send the Grenadier Company only & stay behind himself with the rest of the Reg^{t}., whereas if he had Obey'd his Orders, & advanc'd with the Whole Reg^{t}., it, in all probability, would have decided the Battle in our favour. The Genl. next day gave it out in Orders, that whenever the 35th. Reg^{t}. was order'd out, the next Commanding Officer, should march out the Reg^{t}. & Major [Roger] Morris to stay in Garrison on & take charge of the Convalescents.

11 The name between brackets is a single note 'Major Roger Morris' marked for insertion in two places by a +.

Part II:

Memorials

10

Memorial for Promotion in 1765 and Commission as Captain, 1774

Letter from Captain Andrew Simpson, Commanding Officer, to Major General Thomas Gage, dated Pensacola, 8 March 1765, Forwarding the Memorials of Captain Simpson and Captain Lieutenant William Bamford, dated 2 March 1765.[1]

Sir,

I take this opportunity to acquaint you that Captn. Mackinen[2] Died the 1st. Instant, he has Injoy'd very little health since he has been here, and was Seiz'd six weeks ago with the Yellow Jandys which Carried him off. In regard to his Effects, as he died Intestate, I have ordered a Court of Inquiry, to take an Inventory of them, and shall sell them off at publick vendue, I shall call in his Debts, and Discharge them; making my self-accountable to his Relations for the overplus, after everything is paid, agreeable to the 1st. Article of the 17th. Section of the Articles of War.

Notwithstanding on the Death of Lieutenants Ormsby and Farquharson who likewise died intestate, Captn. MacKinen acted the same part to them, that I am doing in regard to him, but our Governor not satisfied with that insisted on appointing Executors for their effects and accordingly appointed Lieut. Robertson[3] the Engineer and one Macpherson[4] who is Secretary of

1 William L. Clements Library, University of Michigan, Gage Papers

2 Captain Robert McKinnon.

3 Archibald Robertson was born Scotland and became a practitioner-engineer in the Corps of Engineers on 17 March 1759. He was promoted to sub-engineer on 8 June 1763, to engineer extraordinary on 2 February 1775 (a rank retitled captain-lieutenant in 1782). Thereafter, he was promoted to brevet major on 3 August 1780 and to captain on 1 January 1783. Robertson resigned on 23 March 1786 after 27 years' service.

4 James Macpherson was born in 1736 in Kingussie, Inverness-shire, Scotland. He was educated at Inverness grammar school and Kings College, Aberdeen, in 1752. He began his career as a schoolmaster and turned to writing. In 1760, he published *Fragments of Ancient Poetry Collected in the Highlands of Scotland,* which purported to be his translations from ancient Gaelic poems. Continuing his writing, he published two epic poems, *Fingal* in 1761 and *Temora* in 1763, which he represented as translations of a third century Irish poet named Ossian. They were later shown to be largely his own fabrications. Macpherson dedicated the latter two works to Lord Bute, who obtained a pension for him and, in 1764, appointment as Colonial Secretary in West Florida. He served in West Florida for two years and returned home, where he became a writer and spokesman for the government for the next 16 years.

the Province, to be Executors for Lieut. Ormsby, who when he died was Pay Master to the Regim^{t}: his next demand was that all the Deceased Effects should immediately be given up to M^{r}. Macpherson, Consequently the Regiment's Books, Accounts, and Money, all which Captn. Mackinen most strenuously refused. I'm told that the Governor has taken out a Bill in Chancery against Captn, Mackinen. I expect that he will next fall upon me tho' no one Can pay more Regard to the Civil Law that my self, yet as I am Convinced, that without a Breach of the above mentioned Article of War, I cannot comply with his Request. I shall be happy to have your Excellency's approbation, as well as Opinion on this Subject.

The Governor is now at Mobile, and on his Return I have no other prospect, but that of being Involved in, Law Suits, for doing nothing more than what I think is my Duty.

Inclosed I send your Excellency the proceedings of a Court of Inquiry in regard to Commissary Watts, with Respect to the delivery of Goods to the Indians, likewise a Copy of Watts's daily book with an attested Copy of the merchants depositions.[5]

As to the Accounts of the publick Money laid out by Major Forbes[6] and Captain Mackinen for the use of the Garrison, Captain Mackinen's Publick and private affairs are so blended together, that it will take some time to bring them into any form, but as soon as possible I shall send them with the Vouchers or copies of them properly Certified. Major Forbes's Contingent Account was sent by Lieut Lundin.[7]

Among other works, he published the *Rights of Great Britain asserted against the claims of America* in 1776, and in 1779, a *Short History of the Opposition, but supporting the war against the American colonists.* He was also a partner in the *London Packet* and wrote news items on behalf of Administration to insert in the London papers, which Walpole described as 'Macpherson's daily column of lies'. He became interested in the East India Company. He wrote *A History of the East India Company* in 1779. He and his brother became the agents in England for the Nawab of Arcot. In 1780, the government arranged for him, at the cost of £4,000, to be Member of Parliament for Camelford. Apparently, the Nawab of Arcot paid the election costs in appreciation for political assistance. Macpherson held the seat until his death in 1796. See *Oxford Dictionary of National Biography* and *History of Parliament* http://www.historyofparliamentonline.org/volume/1754-1790/member/macpherson-james-1736-96

5 These documents are not present.

6 William Forbes was born in Scotland in 1721. He was commission an ensign in the second battalion of the 1st Regiment of Foot in Ireland on 15 December 1738, probably by purchase. He transferred in the same commission to the first battalion of 1st Foot in Ireland in 1741. He was promoted to 2nd lieutenant, in the first battalion of the 1st Foot on 10 May 1742 through a free augmentation vacancy. He was promoted to lieutenant in the first battalion of the 1st Foot on 19 May 1742, by purchase. He was promoted to captain in the second battalion of the 1st Foot in Scotland on 6 February 1748, by purchase vice a resignation. Reduced onto British half pay on 2 November 1748, he transferred from half pay as captain in the 46th Foot in Ireland on 11 February 1749. He was promoted to major in the 35th Foot on 31 October 1762 by purchase. Forbes retired on 25 December 1768 and died at Inverness on 27 March 1774 (*Scots Magazine*, March 1774).

7 James Lundin was born in Scotland in 1739. He was commissioned an ensign in the 35th Regiment of Foot on 28 July 1759 by purchase. He was promoted to lieutenant in the 35th

We are very much at a Loss at present for Money as the Artificers, as well as many of the Materials for the publick works, Remain unpaid for part of which Captain Mackinen has given promissory notes, which are now become due.

Captain Mackinen has likewise laid out a good deal of the Regiments Money, in Carrieing on the Works, I mean the Subsistence of the Regiment before the 24th. of August, we have had none since that time, I wrote to Mr. Blackwall a few days ago who is at Mobile, and one of the Contractors for supplying the Troops here with Money, but have not yet had his answer, not can the Officers get Money for bills, as there is none in the Place.

Mr Durnford[8] the Engineer intends to write to your Excellency by this opportunity, who will give you an Account of what Works have been Carried on since you last heard from Captn. Mackinen, for which I refer you to him.

Five days ago, the Detachment of artillery Arrived here from New York, they got a Ground on one of the keys near the Island of Providence,[9] which delay'd them some time, I shall take Care to send part of them to Mobile agreeable to your Excellency's Orders.

Foot on 7 March 1762 through a free death vacancy. He retired on 12 July 1773 and returned to the service as lieutenant in the new-raising second battalion of the Royal Highland Emigrants (later numbered as the 84th Regiment of Foot from 1779) on 14 June 1775, by raising for rank. He was promoted to captain-lieutenant in the second battalion of the 84th Foot on 11 December 1779 through a free death vacancy. He went onto British half pay when the battalion was disbanded on 2 February 1784. From half pay he became a lieutenant in the new-raising British Invalid Companies on 25 June 1790, of which fourteen companies were reduced on 25 December 1790, although their officers were continued on full pay. With his previous commission as lieutenant dated 25 June 1790, Lundin was commissioned in Captain Boleyn Douglas's new-raising Portsmouth Invalid Company, in 1793 and 1794.

8 Elias Durnford was born in England in 1739. He became a practitioner-engineer in the Corps of Engineers, on 17 March 1759. He was promoted to sub-engineer on 28 January 1762, to engineer extraordinary on 4 December 1770, to brevet captain on 25 May 1772, to engineer in ordinary on 26 March 1779 (a rank retitled captain in 1782), to lieutenant colonel on 15 December 1786, and to brevet colonel (a local rank in the West Indies) on 15 December 1793. He died at Tobago on 21 June 1794 after 35.4 years' service.

9 Given that the artillery detachment was coming from New York, this may possibly have been New Providence Island in the Bahamas rather than Providence Island off the coast of Honduras.

Lieu[t]. Hook[10] of the Royal Artillery has received orders from Major James[11] to repair to the Granades,[12] which he is to do by the first Opportunity.

I have the honor to transmit to your Excellency Memorials from Capt[n]. Lieut. Bamford, and Mr. Cockburn.

I send inclosed Returns for December, January & February— I am Your Excellency's Most Obedient Humble Servant,

And[w] Simpson[13]

Pensacola March 8th: 1765

P.S. Captain Mackinen Received your Excellency's Letters of the 16th and 26th of November.

To

His Excellency Gen[l]. Gage[14]

Since writing the above, Mr. Lundin Arrived here by whome I have the Honor of your Excellency's Letters of y[e]. 7th: 18th. and 24th. of January.

As the Garrison here has Labour'd under a very Great hardship, in having no allowance of either Fire or Candles, and from having few Men to bring home Wood, has put the Officers to very great expence. I hope

10 James Hook enlisted in the Royal Artillery as a matross in March 1749. He was commissioned at Havana from sergeant in the Royal Artillery to lieutenant-fireworker, Royal Artillery, on 19 October 1762, through a death vacancy. He was reduced onto Royal Artillery half pay on 25 April 1763. From half pay in 1768 he returned in his previous commission as lieutenant-fireworker. He died of disease on 25 December 1769.

11 Thomas James enlisted in the Royal Artillery as a matross on 12 August 1738. He was appointed a lieutenant-fireworker in the Royal Artillery 1 July1740. He was promoted to 2nd Lieutenant in the Royal Artillery on 27 April 1743, then to 1st lieutenant on 1 April 1744, to captain-lieutenant on 1 July 1746, to captain on 1 March 1755. His company served at Québec in 1759-60. He was appointed major, Royal Artillery, on 23 October 1761 and was in New York City from October 1764 to November 1765, during which time his house was pillaged by a mob. He was promoted to lieutenant colonel on 1 January 1771, to brevet colonel on 9 February 1779. He was appointed colonel-commandant, Royal Artillery, on 6 July 1780. He died at Blackheath on 6 March 1782 after 41.7 years' service as an officer.

12 Probably a reference to the island of Grenada in the West Indies, where the 70th Regiment of Foot was serving.

13 Andrew Simpson was born in Scotland in 1727. He was commissioned an ensign in the 55th (later 44th) Foot on 24 December 1747, by purchase vice a retirement. He was promoted to lieutenant in the 44th Foot on 26 June 1755 by purchase vice an augmentation. Subsequently, he was promoted to captain-lieutenant in the 44th Foot on 15 August 1758, a free death vacancy, then to captain in the 80th Foot on 16 August 1760 by purchase vice a resignation, to captain in the 35th Foot on 4 October 1760, free vice a resignation. He retired on 31 October 1770 after 22.8 years' service, when his regiment was in England.

14 General Thomas Gage (1721-1787), Commander-in-Chief, British Forces in North America, 1763-1774. See *Oxford Dictionary of National Biography*; John R. Alden, *General Gage in America* (Baton Rouge, Louisiana: Louisiana State University Press, 1948); John Shy, 'Thomas Gage: Weak Link of Empire', in George Athan Billias, (ed.), *George Washington's Opponents: British Generals in the American Revolution* (New York: William Morrow, 1969), pp. 3-38.

your Excellency won't disapprove of my drawing on Colonel Robertson,[15] for that purpose. I shall send an Exact Account of it in my next.

To His Excellency, The Hōnble Major-General Gage Commander in Chief of All His Majesty's Forces in North America &c, &c. &c^{a}.

The Memorial of Captain Andrew Simpson, Cōmanding the 35th: Regiment, Whereof Henry Fletcher Esqr: is Colonel, Sheweth,

That by the Death of Captain Mackinen there is a Vacancy in said Regiment.

That M^{r}. William Bamford is Captain-Lieutenant and has been a Commissioned Officer, upwards of twenty two years

That M^{r}. James Cockburn has been a Lieutenant since 1756, and is now the Eldest in the Regiment.

That both those Officers have always been present upon all Services, that the Regiment was engag'd in, either in North America or the West Indies.

Your Memorialist Therefore Prays That Your Excellency wou'd be pleased to appoint Captain Lieu^{t}. Bamford Captain; Lieu^{t}. James Cockburn Captain Lieutenant; and that the Succession of the other Commissions may go in the Regiment.

All Which is most humbly Submitted &c^{a}.

Andrew Simpson

Cap^{tn}. 35th. Reg^{t}.

Pensacola 2d March 1765.

To His Excellency Major General Gage Commander in Chief of His Majesty's Forces in North America, &c^{a}—

15 Colonel James Robertson was deputy quartermaster general in North America from 1758 to 1763, and barrack-master general in North America from 1765 to 1771. He was born in Scotland in 1717. He was commissioned In England as a 2nd lieutenant in the new-raising 2nd Marines on 29.November 1739 by raising for rank. He was promoted to 1st lieutenant in the 2nd Marines on 9 April 1741 through a free death vacancy, then promoted to captain in the 2nd Marines on 12 September 1745, by purchase vice a retirement. He went onto British half pay when the regiment disbanded on 9 November 1748. He transferred from half pay as captain to the 30th Foot in Ireland on 15 April 1749. Thereafter, he was promoted to major in the 38th Foot in the Leeward Islands on 23 December 1755, an augmentation vacancy, to major in the new-raising second battalion of the 62nd (later 60th) Foot on 26 December 1755, a free augmentation vacancy. Promoted to brevet colonel on 8 July 1758, he was appointed deputy quartermaster general in America. He was promoted to lieutenant-colonel in the 55th Foot, 29 October 1759, a free death vacancy. He transferred to lieutenant colonel in the 15th Foot at Québec on 25 February 1760, then exchanged to be lieutenant colonel in the 16th Foot at New York on 17 August 1768. He was made brevet colonel on 25 May 1772, then promoted to major general in America on 1 January 1776. He was appointed lieutenant colonel commandant of the second battalion 60th Foot, then dispersed in North America and the West Indies, on 11 January 1776. He was promoted to major general in the Army on 29 August 1777 and appointed colonel of the 16th Foot on 14 May 1778. He was became military governor of New York from March 1780 until April 1783. While serving in that office, he was promoted to lieutenant general 20 November 1782. Robertson died in Wimpole St, Cavendish Square, London, (*Gentelman's Magagzine*, March 1788), on 4 March 1788, after 48 years' service.

The Memorial of Captain Lieutenant Willm. Bamford, of His Majesty's 35th. Regiment

Sheweth

That your Memorialist has been a Commissioned Officer in said Regiment upwards of twenty two years, that he has never been Absent from the Regiment at any time, but constantly with it upon every Service wherein the Regiment has been Employ'd, both in North America and Else where.

That Notwithstanding your Memorialist's long & Severe Services, he was under the necessity of Purchasing the Captain Lieutenancy at an high Price, tho' he had been for some time the Eldest Lieutenant in the Regiment.

That as there is a Vacancy in the Regiment by the Death of Captain Mackinen, Your Memorialist humbly prays, that your Excellency will be pleased to appoint him Captain

Which is Humbly Submitted

Wm Bamford

Capt. Lieut. 35th. Regiment

William Bamford's Commission as Captain in the 40th Foot[16]

George R

George the Third by the Grace of God, King of Great Britain, France and Ireland, Defender of the Faith &c. To Our Trusty and well beloved William Bamford Esqr — Greeting

We reposing especial Trust and Confidence in Your Loyalty, Courage and good Conduct do by these Presents constitute and appoint you to be Captain of that Company whereof R. Martin Seymour[17] Esqr deceased was late Captain in Our Fortieth Regiment of Foot commanded by our Trusty & Wellbeloved Colonel Sir Robert Hamilton[18] Bar^{t}. — — — —

16 This document is folded and bound in at the end of the volume containing the 1776 diary at the Garratt Library, The Johns Hopkins University, Baltimore Maryland.

17 Robert Martin Seymour was born in England in 1747. He was commissioned an ensign in the 40th Regiment of Foot on 10 April 1764. He was promoted to lieutenant in the 40th Foot on 28 February 1766 by purchase vice a resignation, to captain-lieutenant in the 40th Foot on 28 April 1774 by purchase vice a retirement, and to captain in the 40th Foot on 14 January 1775 by purchase vice a retirement. He died 25 March 1775.

18 Sir Robert Hamilton, fourth Baronet Hamilton of Silvertonhill, was born in Scotland. He was commissioned an ensign in Minorca in the 18th Regiment of Foot on 16 July 1739 by purchase, He was promoted to lieutenant in the 18th Foot on 20 June 1744 by purchase vice a retirement, to captain in the 18th Foot on 31 August 1744 by purchase vice a retirement, to major 18th Foot on 14 December 1755 by purchase vice an augmentation, to lieutenant colonel in the 59th Foot in Ireland on 7 April 1759 by purchase vice a promotion to a colonelcy. Subsequently, he became colonel of the 108th Foot in Ireland on 17 March 1763. He went onto Irish half pay when the regiment disbanded on 31 March 1763. From half pay, he became colonel of the 40th Foot in Ireland on 20 March 1770. He was promoted to major general on 29 September 1775 and to lieutenant general on 29 August 1777, He died on 10 August 1786 in London.

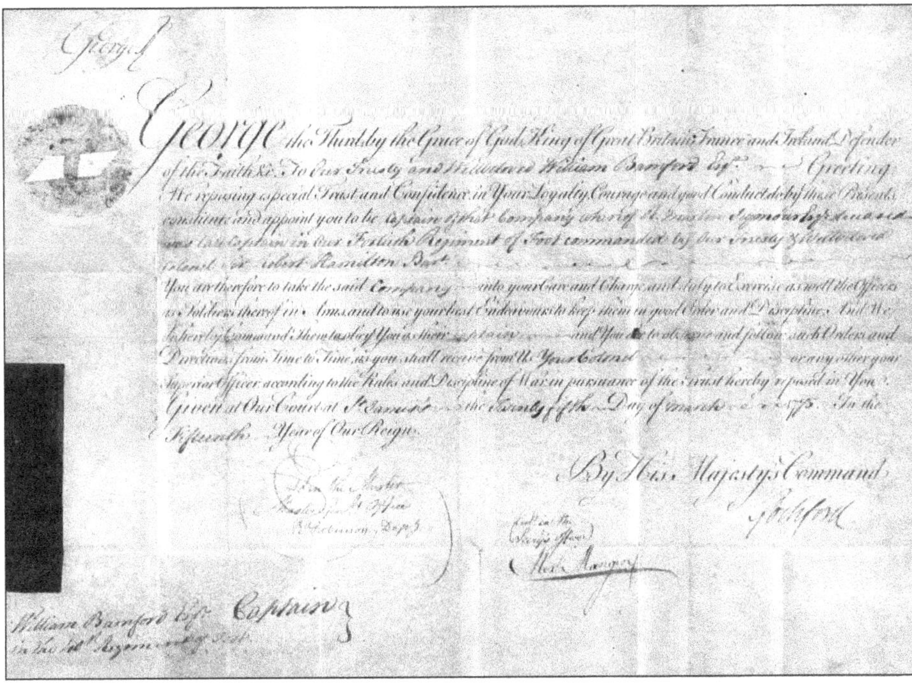

George R

George the Third by the Grace of God King of Great Britain France and Ireland Defender of the Faith &c. To Our Trusty and Wellbeloved William Bamford Esq. Greeting
We reposing especial Trust and Confidence in Your Loyalty, Courage and good Conduct do by these Presents constitute and appoint you to be Captain of that Company whereof [illegible] was late Captain in Our Fortieth Regiment of Foot commanded by Our Trusty & Wellbeloved Colonel Sir Robert Hamilton Bart.
You are therefore to take the said Company into your Care and Charge and duly to Exercise as well the Officers as Soldiers thereof in Arms and to use your best Endeavours to keep them in good Order and Discipline. And We do hereby Command Them to obey You as their Captain and You are to observe and follow such Orders and Directions from Time to Time, as you shall receive from Us Your Colonel or any other your Superior Officer according to the Rules and Discipline of War in pursuance of the Trust hereby reposed in You.
Given at Our Court at St James's the Twenty fifth Day of March 1775 In the Fifteenth Year of Our Reign.

By His Majesty's Command
Rochford

William Bamford Esq. Captain in the 40th Regiment of Foot

William Bamford's Commission as Captain in the 40th Foot.

You are therefore to take the said Company into your Care and Charge and duly to Exercise as well the Officers as Soldiers thereof in Arms, and to use your best Endeavours to keep them in good Order and Discipline. And We do hereby Command Them to obey You as their Captain—and You are to observe and follow such Orders and Directions from Time to Time, as you shall receive from Us Your Colonel—or any other your Superior Officer, according to the Rules and Discipline of War, in pursuance of the Trust hereby reposed in You.

Given at Our Court at St James's the Twenty fifth Day of March. 1775 in the Fifteenth Year of Our Reign

By His Majesty's Command
Rochford[19]
Entd in the Muster
Master Genls Office
Rd Robinson Depty
Entd in the Secry's Office
Alexr Manger
William Bamford Esqr Captain in the 40th Regiment of Foot.

19 William Henry Nassau de Zuylestein, 4th Earl of Rochford (1717- 1781) was Secretary of State for the Southern Department, 1770-1775.

Part III:

Journal, 1776

11

Charles Town and Boston, Massachusetts, 8 January–30 March 1776

[The preceding three pages, on two folios, are missing. The opening page, followed by the double page for the first week, 1 though 7 January, is missing, as is the left-hand page for the second week, 8 through 13 January. The surviving text starts with the remarks on the right-hand page for the second week.]

8. About 150 of the Rebells came over to the out parts of Charles Town set 2 Old houses on fire, took a Serg^{t} & 4 men & a woman (who contrary to Orders lay in those out houses) prisoners; it was between 8 & 9 oClock at night & very dark the Fortifications at Charles Town are only temporary, but strong, especially to the Neck of Land facing the Country; there it is hardly possible to force them.

13. its reported that ~~Marblehead~~ Falmouth[1] a little town to the Eastward was this day burn'd by one of our Men of War—Wants confirmation. [The town of Falmouth was burn'd by Capt. Wallace[2] in the *Rose* – 20 Gun ship][3]

Charles T^{n}. January 14th. to 20th. 1776
3d. Week.

14. Su. dull cold M^{g} N, blows exceeding sharp hard frost, w^{t} some snow this Eve^{g}— We hear that the Regim^{ts} from Gibraltar were spoke with at Sea, ou this side ye Western Isles—if that is fact they will soon arrive at Virginia.[4]

---

1 Falmouth is in Barnstable County, Massachusetts, on the southwestern tip of Cape Cod. It is located 77 miles (124 km) south-southeast of Boston.

2 James Wallace was commissioned a lieutenant in the Royal Navy on 11 March 1755. He was promoted to commander on 1 November 1762 and to captain on 10 January 1771. Knighted on 13 February 1777, he was made a colonel in the Royal Marines on 1 February 1793. He was promoted to rear admiral of the white on 12 April 1794, to rear admiral of the red on 4 July 1794, to vice admiral of the white on 1 June 1795. He was governor of Newfoundland in 1796-97, then promoted to vice admiral of the red on 14 February 1799, and to admiral of the blue on 1 January 1801. He died on 6 March 1803

3 The words between brackets are a note at the bottom of the page marked for insertion in this entry.

4 Lord North had proposed the idea of sending troops from Ireland to the southern colonies on 15 October 1775 and orders were given to the 15th, 37th, 53rd, 54th, and 57th regiments

15. M. hard frost—some Snow dull M^{g}. cold day p m, V[5] Snow—VII, rain

16. Tu. rain'd last N^{t} froze towards M^{g}. mild M^{g}. calm thaws— dull last N^{t} a few times of y^{e} Enemy remov'd part of the Abbatis[6] before y^{e} Lines, this M^{g} we repaired it Main G^{d} C : T :[7]

17. W. dull Moist foggy M^{g}. p.m. II heavy rain aft$^{n.}$ snow

18. Th. Severe frost last N^{t}. clear cold M^{g}. blows hard & cold w. Eve^{g}. Mild
About 7 this Eve^{g}. some of the Rebels Barr^{ks} were on fire to the W. of our Lines a Little way—

19. F. very hard frost last N^{t}. clear cold M^{g}. W. Reinforcem^{t} G^{d}. C. T.

20. Sa. very hard frost last N$^{t.}$ Bright cold M^{g}. W much Ice in the River.

Charles Town & Boston. January 21st. to February 3d. 1776[8]
4th Week.

21. Su. Warm bright M^{g}. very little W^{d}. N. XII blows fresh and cold—Eve^{g} snow
We hear that the Army under Lord Dunmore,[9] in Virginia, is repuls'd & routed; with a good many kill'd & several taken prisoners, & Lord Dunmore on board a Ship of War (he began too soon).

22. M. dull m^{g} N gentle Thaw

23. Tu. pleasant cool bright M. S. W. frost last N^{t} Main G^{d} C: T:

24. W. very fine warm bright M^{g} light w^{d} S. W. This Af^{t}. the Rebels Exercis'd about 1000 Men on an Hill opposite Charles Town—out of Shot.

---

to prepare for deployment, but they did actually sail from Ireland until January and February 1776. Three of the seven regiments at Gibraltar left there on 6-7 December and sailed for Portsmouth, England, where they disembarked in late December. No regiments came directly from Gibraltar to North America. See R.E. Burns, 'Ireland and British Military Preparations', *Cithara,* Vol.11 (1963), pp. 47-52.

5 Bamford uses Roman numbers to indicate the hour of the day.

6 Abatis. Obstacle comprising felled trees, branches intertwined, with trunks parallel to the enemy's line of advance. Boscawen, *Louisbourg*, p. 411.

7 This abbreviation probably indicates that Bamford had been assigned to the Main Guard in Charleston on this day.

8 The left-hand page is missing for the entries on 28-30 January and 1-3 February. This appears to be an error made at the time, as Bamford has changed the ending date at the top of the page to 3 February rather than on 28 January, thereby encompassing Week 5. The next pages start with Week 6

9 John Murray, 4th Earl of Dunmore, was born in 1730. He succeeded his father as Earl of Dunmore in 1756. He served as Governor of New York, 1770-1771, Governor of Virginia in 1771-1775, and Governor of the Bahamas, 1787-1796. He died in 1809

25. Th. dull M^{g}. pleasant N.—XII, bright warm sun Piquet G^{d}. The Detachm^{t} at Charles Town reliev'd. came from thence

26. F. snows very fast, cold M^{g}. W—

27. Sa. very severe frost last N^{t}. excessive cold day, freezes hard—N. W.—The Ink freezes in the Pen, as I write by the fire side. Piquet. A good deal of Snow on ye Ground.

Feb. 1. Admiral Graves[10] sail'd for England in the Preston.[11] Admiral Schuldam Commands.

Tho' the Cold here has sometimes been very severe, yet is it by no means equal to what I have experienced in Canada. An Arm'd Schooner belonging to the Rebels Run ashore & destroy'd by a Frigate.[12] two armed schooners were decoy^{d} off Shore by the *Nautillus*[13] one of y^{m} she sunk it self [a mistake they both escaped in a Snow Storm].[14]

several ships have lately arriv'd with provisions of different kinds, which have supply'd us very well, tho' dear.

We have lately had a confirmation of the news of the Defeat of the Rebel Army under Montgomery.[15]

Lee,[16] with a body of men went to N. York to endeavor to make the people coin ye plate, in order to hold out another year. those well affected to Govern^{t}. sent theirs on

10 Samuel Graves was born in 1713 and commissioned a lieutenant on 3 March 1740. He was promoted to captain on 11 September 1744, to rear admiral of the blue on 21 October 1762, rear admiral of the red on 18 October 1770, vice admiral of the blue on 24 October 1770. He was appointed commander in chief of the North American Station in July 1774 and was promoted to vice admiral of the white on 31 March 1775, to vice admiral of the red on 5 February 1776, and to admiral of the blue on 29 January 1778. He was superannuated in 1783 and died in 1787. See *Oxford Dictionary of National Biography.*

11 The 50-gun, fifth rate *Preston* was built at Deptford between 1751 and 1757 by successive master shipwrights Thomas Fellowes, Thomas Slade, and Adam Hayes. Commissioned in 1757, she served in the North Sea and the Mediterranean during the Seven Years War. Paid off in 1763, she was recommissioned in 1766 and served in the West Indies, then paid off in 1769. After repairs she was recommissioned in 1774, under Captain John Robinson as flagships for Vice Admiral Samuel Graves. She was in North American waters in 1774, then returned home in 1776. Under Captain Samuel Uppleby, she sailed again for North America on 6 May 1776. She participated in operations at New York and Rhode Island in 1776.

12 The armed schooner *Hancock*, Captain John Manley, was run ashore by the 14-gun sloop brig, *Hope*, Lieutenant George Dawson. *Hancock* was raised, repaired and cruised again.

13 Vice Admiral of the Blue Molyneux Shuldham served as commander-in-chief, North American Station from 27 January until July 1776, when he was relieved by Vice Admiral of the Blue Richard, Lord Howe.

14 The words between square brackets are a note in the margin marked for insertion here.

15 Brigadier General Richard Montgomery, Continental Army, had led an attack on the city of Québec and was killed during the attack on 31 December 1775. With his death, the attack fell apart and the American force retreated.

16 On 8 January 1776, General George Washington ordered Major General Charles Lee to go to New York, raising volunteers en route, to try to put the defences in the area on a better footing.

board the *Asia* Man of War,[17] & those on the contrary side hid Theirs they all refused parting w^{t}. Their plate, & Their paper money, even amongst themselves seems to be of very little Estimation, & was it not for the cloathing of ye Reg^{ts}. & ships coming w^{t}. Necessaries which they took, their Army would by this time have been quite naked. [to disarm the Well Affected in Long Island they did disarm most of the People][18]

Boston. February 4th. to February 10th. 1776
6th. Week.

4. Su. clear M^{g}. a little snow last N^{t}. not as cold as yesterday, W—
Clear'd Barrett[19] to this day charg'd for the Last fortnight £1/1—
Picquet G^{d}.

5. M. bright cold M^{g}. hard frost. W. rivers froze over—some firing from Charles Town last N^{t}. the Rebels fir'd from Coblers hill—small arms near the Mill.

XII blows very fresh. Rebels burn'd y^{e}. old Mill near Charles Town.

The Rebels are now at work erecting works at the Orchard opposite C. Town & cutting the Ice round the shore; it is said they are not near so numerous as they were; nothing but great fear, or meer necessity could oblige them, they should think, to endeavour to work at this most rigorous season.

A small Party from Charles Town went out & drove in 4 Bullocks belonging to the Rebels; one of our men was shot in the Neck.

6. Tu. high W^{d}. all last N^{t}. blows fresh and very cold this M^{g}. N. W. —XII, blows very hard. blew very hard & cold all day—hard frost.

Picquet G^{d}
To McLean a Doll^{r}—Lent—£4:8

7. W. clear, very cold, M^{g}. blows fresh N, W—hard frost—Eve^{g}. Mild—
We have an Acc^{t}. that Norfolk in Virginia is burn'd—

---

17 The 64-gun, third rate *Asia* was built to designs of Thomas Slade at Portsmouth by successive master shipwrights Edward Allin and Thomas Bucknall between 1758 and 1772. Work had stopped on the vessel after her launching on 16 May 1764 and she was laid up until June 1771, when work commenced again and she was completed in February 1772. Commissioned as a guard ship at Portsmouth, she participated in the Spithead Review on 22 June 1773. Under Captain George Vandeput, she sailed for North America on 10 June 1775. She served at New York and returned to England for repairs in 1777. In 1778, she sailed for the East Indies and Pondicherry. On her return home she was paid off in 1781. She was refitted and coppered at Chatham, then recommissioned briefly for service in 1782-83, and 1790. Recommissioned in 1793, she was with Jervis in the West Indies in 1794 and in home waters in 1795. In May 1796, she sailed for Halifax, Nova Scotia, where she served as flagship for Vice Admiral George Vandeput from 1798 to 1800. Paid off in 1800, she was recommissioned in 1801 for service in Pole's squadron, then paid off in 1802. She was broken up at Chatham in 1804. Length of gun deck 158 feet, length of keel 129 feet 6½ inches, breadth 44 feet 6 inches, depth of hold 18 feet 10 inches, 1,364 46/94 tons, draught 10 feet 2 inches forward / 16 feet 6 inches aft.

18 The statement between square brackets is a note in the margin.

19 Probably one of the soldiers in the 40th Regiment.

The Rebels say that have march'd 4000 men more to attack Quebec—

A Small Party of Rebels cross'd on the Ice & burn'd a Mill near Charles Town—

The News papers give an Acc^{t}. of their defeat at Quebec, w^{t}. Montgomery and his Aid de camp McPherson being kill'd & several taken Prisoner—they say only 100 kill'd & wounded—& 300 prisoners—

~~To Lt. Gason[20] 8 Dollars Lent—~~Paid——~~1:16~~

8. Th. dull Mild M^{g}. little W^{d}. S. W. XII, began to snow— p. m. IV, ceased to snow—very mild—

9. F. dull M^{g}. a good deal of Snow on ye Ground—calm & mild—Aft^{n} small rain thaws W^{d}. Variable

Piquet G^{d}.

10. Sa. rain'd heavily last N^{t}. with Squals—dull M^{g}. small rain & freeze as it falls W^{d}. very variable. XII, Thaws fast—p. m, II, very thick fog—N,W—

Boston. February 11th. to 17th. 1776
7th. Week.

11. Su. very hard frost last N^{t}. exceeding cold day blows hard N, W—freezes; Rivers shut up with Ice—

Paid Barret to this day, for ye last W^{k}. 10/6, Mess.

12. M. cold Bright M^{g}., hard frost, blows fresh N.W—

13. Tu. Bright cold M^{g}. hard frost little W^{d}, W—

Line Guard.

14 W. began to snow about 4 oClock this M^{g}. very thick snow. p m III ceas'd to snow. E—thaws—

Picquet G^{d}.

between 4 & 5 oClock this Morn^{g}. Maj^{r}. Musgraves light Infantry & Wemyss's Genad^{rs}. 6 Comp^{ys} cross'd the Ice to Dorchester & burn'd several [about 12][21] houses there & took some prisoners—6—We did not fire, a single shot. A Captains Guard posted there ran away

To M^{rs}. V—n 9 ^{d}. £ — 2/6

15. Th. dull M^{g}. thaws: very little W^{d}. N,W—XII S. W—a good deal of Snow on the G^{d}. warm day—p, m, VI, NW, freezes—

---

20 John Gason was commissioned an ensign in the 40th Regiment of Foot in Ireland on 12 December 1774 by purchase vice a retirement. He was promoted to lieutenant in the 40th Foot on 11 December 1775 by purchase vice a retirement, to captain-lieutenant in the 40th Foot on 16 October 1778 purchase vice a retirement, to captain in the 40th Foot on 6 March 1780, probably by purchase. He retired on 1 March 1782 after 7.3 years' service.

21 The words between brackets are an interlineal note.

16. F. Bright M^{g}. warm sun hard frost, NW—The Sun thaws the Ice very fast—
Piquet G^{d}.

17. Sa. a great deal of Snow last N^{t}. bright warm Sun this day—N—two Vessels w^{t}. provisions to the West Indies taken by the [blank] Capt Dawson[22]

Several Vessels w^{t} Coal & provisions for this garrison have lately Arriv'd.

The Soldiers often receive fresh provisions gratis, & are serv'd with food porter 3 times a week. The Crops that went out the 14th rec^{d} each man a pair of Shoes & Stockings.

~~To Lieut. G______n lent 3 Dollrs~~ Paid ~~13/6~~

Boston. February 18th. to 24th. 1776
8th. Week.

18. Su. extream hard frost, very cold, N,W. bright Sun
P^{d}. Barrett a Week's Messing 14/
Piquet G^{d}.

19. M. very hard frost & very cold, little W^{d}. bright sun—IX N,W— p. m. v E. freezes hard some of the Pris^{rs} which were taken 14th. from Dorchester were sent back to ye Rebels.

The Rebels are very busy at Phipp's farm,[23] making some strong Works, in appearance; it was on this Ground out light Infantry landed 9th Novr last & brought off some Cattle soon after which the [Rebels][24] erected a Redoubt, on the highest part—

it is reported that a second Action happen'd in Canada near Quebec in which the Rebels were totally routed —[False][25]

20. Tu. clear bright M^{g}. hard frost, S,W—

21. W. bright M^{g}. S.W, pleasant XII, Hazy. p,m, II dull & cold£thaws fast—

22. Th. very dull M^{g}. raw, Thaws, N,E, some small snow this aft^{n}—
~~Line Gd~~ Artillery Red^{t}. G^{d}.

23. F. clear M^{g}.—sun melts the Ice very fast. S,W.
Picquet G^{d}.

---

22 This may possibly be a reference to Lieutenant George Dawson, commanding the 14-gun *Hope*, a ship operating in the Boston area, but the capture reported is not found in William Bell Clark, William J. Morgan, et al (eds.), *Naval Documents of the American Revolution* (Washington: Government Printing Office, 1964).

23 David Phipps's farm was located on Phipps's Point, part of the eastern side of the town of Cambridge that protruded in to the Charles River.

24 The word in square brackets is Bamford's interlineal insertion.

25 Bamford has marked this statement with a bracket in the margin and written 'false'.

24. Sa. clear bright M^{g}. froze last N^{t}— N,W—XII cloudy E—A great deal of the Ice gone out of the Bays & rivers—

P^{d}. M^{rs}. Vaughan to 21st inst for washing 1: 1—

~~To Do Lent 2 & ½ Dollrs~~ P^{d}.-11:3

~~To Lt. G—n Lent 8 Dollars~~ Paid ~~11:/1/6—~~

Boston February 25th. to March 2d. 1776
9th. Week.

25. Su. dull, raw cold M^{g}. E—blows fresh—p. m. IX Sleet, froze as fast as it fell. Very slippery.

Picquet G^{d}.

the Rebels are still hard at Work at Phipp's farm,—

We are Erecting a battery for three 32 pounders, on Mount Whordom;[26] to play on the Works at Phipp's Farm—

26. M. dull raw M^{g}. blows fresh N.—X some rain thaws fast—

To En^{s}. [name blotted out][27] — Lent a Doll^{r} — P^{d}. £ 4:6

27. Tu. Froze last N^{t}. dull M^{g}. XI, began to rain rain'd all day—E—

28 W. bright M^{g}. blows fresh S,W—p.m, I rain several Showers of hail & rain this aft^{n}. Eve very cold—Snow—The Rebels seem to have finish'd their work at Phip's Farm—Work^{g}. Party

29. Th. froze hard last N^{t}. blows fresh this M^{g}. N,W, very cold & bright.

~~To Ct. Sm__e[28] — — — lent 18 Dollrs~~. Paid ~~£ 4: 1~~

---

26 Mount Whoredom was the western summit of Beacon Hill; in modern times it is known as the Mount Vernon neighborhood.

27 Only a few letters are legible, but it is likely Cheshire. Edward Cheshire was born in Ireland. He was commissioned an ensign in the 40th Foot in Ireland in 20 October 1774 by purchase vice a retirement, He retired on 6 May 1777. He returned to the service as an ensign in the Royal Leinster Provincial Regiment of Foot in Ireland on 28 April 1783, free vice a retirement. He was reduced with his regiment 1 October 1783 after 3 years' service.

28 It is likely this is John Graves Simcoe. Born in England in 1752, the son of Captain John Simcoe, Royal Navy. He was educated at Exeter Grammar School, Eton College, then spent a year at Merton College, Oxford, before being admitted to Lincoln's Inn. Settling on a military career, he was commissioned an ensign in the 35th Foot in England on 27 April 1770 by purchase vice a retirement. He served as adjutant from 27 March 1772 to 27 December 1775. He was promoted to lieutenant in the 35th Foot on 12 March 1774 by purchase vice a retirement, to captain in the 40th Foot at Boston on 27 December 1775 by purchase vice a retirement, to brevet lieutenant colonel in America on 23 June 1779, to brevet lieutenant colonel in the Army on 19 December 1781. He was simultaneously lieutenant colonel commandant of the provincial Queen's Rangers, but succeeded in his captaincy in the 40th only on 25 December 1782, the date on which the Queen's Rangers were taken onto the regular British establishment. In 1787, he published *A Journal of the Operations of the Queen's Rangers from the end of the year 1777 to the conclusion of the late American War*. He was promoted to brevet colonel on 18 November 1790, he entered politics and became Member

1. F. March[29] Blew Violently & froze excessive hard last N^{t}. exceeding cold M^{g}. high W^{d}. N,W—bright M^{g}. very cold all day.

2. Sa. hard frost, very cold M^{g}. N, W—was bright Eve^{g}. very mild & fine no frost this night about 1/2 past XI, the Rebels began to cannonade & bombard the Town from Phipps farm.

Line G^{d}.

about 1/2 past XI this Night the Rebels open'd a Mortar Battery at Phipps' farm; threw several shells into the Town, chiefly near Bacon hill.[30] We return'd a number into their Works; threw some to Mount Pisga.[31]

Boston. March 3d. to March 9th. 1776
10th. Week

3. Su. cold, cloudy M^{g}. N—X bright

D^{d}. w^{t} M^{rs}. Roberts 49—

Picquet G^{d}–

last night at ½ past XI, the Rebels began to fire shot & shells from Phipp's farm on the Town; & threw some shot & shells from Roxbury,[32] at the Lines, there was not the least mischief done. we fir'd many shots & shells at them from Barton's point.[33] the Rebels shells were 13 & 10 inches.

4.M. dull soft M^{g}. S, E—the Enemy fir'd many shot & shells last N^{t}. we return'd the Comp^{lts}—dull day thaws fast—

The Rebels threw up a Work on Dorchester hill. a Great deal of firing on both sides shots & shells—

~~To Lt C—r —lent 15 Dollrs. £2:5—~~ P^{d}.

5.Tu. Warm pleasant bright M^{g}. —Aft^{n}. cloudy very high W^{d}. this Ev^{g}. with rain storm continue all night—S, W—This M^{g}. Embark'd on board the Good intent[34] to

of Parliament for St. Mawes. From half pay be became colonel-commandant of the new-raising Queen's Rangers on 1 September 1791. In 1792, he resigned his seat in Parliament to become the first lieutenant governor of newly organized province of Upper Canada (now Ontario). Promoted to major general in 1794, he returned to England from Canada in poor health and resigned as lieutenant governor in 1798. He was promoted colonel of the 81st Foot, but exchanged that post shortly thereafter for the 22nd Foot. Promoted to lieutenant general, he died in 1806.

29 The characters '1. F. March' are written in red ink.

30 Beacon Hill in Boston.

31 Mount Pisgah, near Northborough, Massachusetts, is located about 50 miles to the west of Boston. Presumably, Bamford is indicating that they shot the cannon in a westerly direction without aiming at anything in particular.

32 Roxbury was a town located three miles south of Boston and a key location during the colonial period on the only road leading into Boston. It was incorporated into the city of Boston in 1868.

33 Barton's Point was located on the northwestern point of Boston on the south shore of the Charles River. It is no longer visible due to land reclamation.

34 *Good Intent*, a troop transport under the command of John Wiely, master.

attack ye Enemy at Dorchester last Night the Rebels threw up [Redoubts][35] on 2 of the Highest hills at Dorchester. Some Reg^{ts}. embark'd & fell down to the Castle[36] in order to Attack those new works but a very high W^{d}. with rain prevented the Action. No firing this night—

6. W. blows fresh S,W—p,m, VIII, very high W^{d}. this M^{g}. disembark'd, bad weather prevented the affair from going on last N^{t}—p.m. X, blew violently I believe the prevention was very lucky—

Picquet G^{d}

This M^{g}. the Reg^{ts}. who had embark'd yesterday were disembark'd this day & orders were given for the Army to hold themselves in readiness to embark at the shortest notice— busily employ'd in getting the Baggage on board—The Rebels fire only in the night— It was a Lucky circumstance that the Troops sent Down the River the 5th. did not debark, as in all probability few would have come back, as the Rebel works were guarded by 12,000 Men & had every thing in readiness to oppose us—

The Rebels had large Hogsheads fill'd with stones & several Barrels also, to roll down the hill on our Troops as they advanc'd; & the hill being very steep, they must have come with great Velocity, which would have broke our Ranks & put us into disorder, & the consequence might have been Fatal—

They had many Cannon in their Works on Dorchester hill.[37]

7. Th. blows hard S,W—pm, I pleasant & mild
Working Part^{y} at C.T. all this N^{t} {heavy guns, mortars & Shot & shells
To L^{t}. Carter[38] lent 8 Doll^{rs} — £1:16 —
To M^{rs} V-g-n lent 16 Doll^{rs}—£3: 12—
√To McLean lent a Doll^{r} — — — 4: 8

8. F. hazy M^{g} E. little W^{d}. p. m, II a shower of Snow hail & sleet—
Very busy in getting our Baggage on board Ship.

9. Sa. some rain this M^{g}. mild W—p,m. II a little rain N,W—

Boston. March 10th. to 16th. 1776
11. Week

10. Su. clear cold M^{g}. N,W, blows fresh

35 The word between brackets in an interlineal insertion.

36 Castle William, a British-held fortification on an island off the southeastern point of the Boston peninsula.

37 This paragraph of the entry, beginning with 'the Rebels had large . . .' appears on the next pair of manuscript pages in the remarks section for week 11, but appears to be a continuation of the remarks in week 10 for 6 March.

38 William Carter was born in Ireland in 1750). He was commissioned an ensign in the 47th Foot in Ireland on 5 June 1771, by purchase. Then, he obtained a commission as ensign in the 40th Foot on 20 February 1773, a free death vacancy. He was promoted to lieutenant, in the 40th Foot on 22 November 1775, a free augmentation vacancy. He retired on 27 October 1777 after 6.4 years' service.

A great deal of cannonad^{g} last N^{t}–

11. M. pleasant day little W^{d}. S.

12. Tu. dull M^{g}. very hazy blows fresh S,E—
the Rebels very busy at Dorchester hills—
a good deal of Cannonading last N^{t}.

13. W. froze hard last N$^{t.}$ clear cold M^{g}. N[39]

14. Th. snow Sleet & high W^{d}. S,E—

15. F. fine M^{g}. N,W, p.m. II E—XII. Under Arms to Embark, W$^{d.}$ came foul—E—

16. Sa. much rain last N^{t}—rains this M^{g}.

E. hazy moist day.

On board y^{e} *Spy* Nantasket road, March 17th. to March 23d. 1776.
12th. Week.

17. Su. [Embarked][40] This M^{g}. about VI, we Embark'd & retreated from Boston, the Rebels did not molest us—W—sailed down to King's Road did not leave a man behind.

This M^{g}. about 5 oClock the Garrison Got under Arms & Embark'd on board the Transports appointed to receive them; the Retreat was preform'd in 2 Divisions; & tho' the last division which remain'd on shore, after ye first was Embarked, consisted of but a few men, yet the Disposition was so good that the Rebels dare not give us the lease disturbance notwithstanding their great superiority of Numbers—a great many of the People of the Town, had embark'd w^{t}. their families & goods, & vessels were assign'd to carry them—The Rebels were told that if they gave us any Annoyance in our Embarkation, the Town of Boston should be set on fire; & everything was ready for that purpose—

18. M. pleasant day, E—blew hard Last N^{t}.

19. Tu. pleasant M^{g}—E—blew hard last N^{t}. this Day a good deal of Castle W^{m}. was blown up

20. W. pleasant M^{g}—S, sail'd down to Nantasket—this Ev^{g}. Castle W^{m} was destroy'd & ye 64th. Reg^{t}. Embark'd—

---

39 There is one more letter on this line, either an 'E' or a 'W', but it is illegible and only partially on the page.

40 The word between brackets is a note in the margin.

21. Th. blew very hard last Nt. Wt much snow & sleet—N.W—the Admiral wt. what Transports had not come down before, came this day down to Nantasket—

22. F. pleasant cool Mg—blew hard last Nt XII, cold—

23. Sa. blew very hard last Nt. wt. much rain & snow—N,W—blows hard this Mg—X, sun, p.m. XI. this Nt. got foul wt. the *America* Transport Ship, blows hard, soon got clear—

On board the *Spy.* Nantasket road. March 24th. to March 30th. 1776
13th. Week.

24. Su. blew very hard all last Nt. & blows extremely hard this Mg—hard Gale all day N,W—a Transport a shore on the Point of George Island[41]—
~~To Lt. G___n—lent—8 Dollrs.—~~ Pd ~~£ 1 - /6~~

25. M. blew most Violently all last Nt. more moderate & clear this Mg. N,E—several of ye small vessells sail'd out this Mg—the *Milford*[42] man of War arriv'd from Engd
Several small Vessels, on board which most of the Inhabitants wt. their Families & goods were Embark'd sail'd from Nantasket under convoy of 2 Men of War— This Evg. the *Milford* Man of War came in from England—

26. Tu. exceeding hard frost last Nt. very cold Mg—blows fresh—N,W—

27. [Sail'd][43] W. clear cold Mg. frost last Nt. p,m NW about III, this day the Fleet sail'd From Nantasket road about 90 sail for Hallifax in Nova Scotia. The Adml. sail'd wt. us.

41 George's Island is located in Quincy Bay of Boston Harbor, approximately 7.3 miles from Boston's Long Wharf in central Boston.

42 The 28-gun, sixth rate frigate *Milford* was built at Milford by Richard Chitty between 1757 and 1759. Commissioned in 1759, she took two privateers in 1761 and three more in 1762, before being paid off in 1763. She recommissioned again for the West Indies in 1763 and was paid off in 1766. Recommissioned in 1775, she sailed for North America under Captain John Burr on 20 January 1776. Under Commander Henry Mowatt from about June 1776, she operated in American waters. She had captured four American privateers before she returned to be refitted at Plymouth in 1778. She was present at the Battle of Ushant in 1778, was in Hardy's fleet, went to the relief of Guernsey and was with Reynold's squadron in 1779, served in Geary's fleet in 1780 and took a French frigate on 1780. Paid off in November 1780, she was sold at Woolwich in 1785. Length of gun deck 118 feet 3 inches, length of keel 97 feet 5 inches, breadth 33 feet 9 inches, depth of hold 10 feet 6 inches, 588 72/94 tons bm.

43 The word between brackets is a note in the margin.

about 2 oClock this aft^{n}. The Fleet about 90 sail—sail'd from Nantasket road, Admiral Schuldam in the *Chatham*,[44] & the *Centurion*,[45] & several Arm'd vessels sail'd W^{t} us,we steer'd for Hallifax

28. Th. clear M^{g}. Moderate N,W—fresh— Lat. 42°. 8′

29. F. high W^{d}. w^{t} a great swell N,W—Frost—very cold—roll'd very much—saw several Grampuses[46]

30. Sa. moderate M^{g}—hard frost—N, E—a small sloop made Signals of Distress Lat 42°—34

44 The 50-gun, fourth rate *Chatham* was built at Portsmouth by successive master shipwrights Peirson Wright and Edward Allin between 1752 and 1758. Commissioned in 1758, she took a prize in 1759 and was with Hawke in the actions at Quiberon Bay, and the blockade of Basque Roads. From 1760 to 1764, she was in the East Indies. Paid off in 1764, she underwent repairs at Portsmouth and was recommissioned in 1766 and sailed for the Leeward Islands, where she served as a flagship until 1769. Paid off in 1769, she underwent a middling repair, then was recommissioned in 1772, She returned to the Leeward Islands as flagship from 1772 to 1775. Paid off, she recommissioned in September 1775 under Captain Joe Raynor as flagship for Rear Admiral Molyneux Shuldham. She sailed for North America on 30 October 1775 and participated in operations at New York and Rhode Island in 1776. She remained in American waters until she returned home in 1778. In 1779, she operated in the Channel and the North Sea, and the Mediterranean, before returning to North America in 1780, where she participated in the Chesapeake battle in March 1781 and took several American privateers and a French frigate. Paid off in 1783, she was placed in ordinary at Plymouth. In 1791, she became a sheer hulk at Chatham, then a convalescent ship at Plymouth in 1793-1797, a receiving ship at Falmouth from 1800-1802, and a floating magazine at Plymouth from 1805. Her name was changed to *Tilbury* in 1810. She was broken up in 1814 at Chatham. Length of gun deck 147 feet, length of keel 123 feet ¼ inch, breadth 40 feet 3 inches, depth of hold 17 feet 8 inches, 1,067 37/94 tons bm.

45 The 50-gun, *Salisbury* class, fourth rate *Centurion* was built at Harwich by Barnard & Turner between 1771 and 1774, then completed at Chatham in 1775. Commissioned in July 1775 under Captain Richard Braithwaite, she sailed for North America on 25 October 1775. She participated at Rhode Island in December 1776. Later she participated in Howe's encounter with d'Estaing and the operations at St. Lucia in 1778, the Battle of Martinique in 1780, after which she returned home for repair. Following the American War, she had an active career in the East Indies from 1793 to 1804, when she was found to be infested with white ants. Fitted as a hospital ship, she sailed to Halifax, Nova Scotia, where she served from 1807. Hulked in 1817, she sank at her mooring in 1824 and was broken up in 1825. Length of gun deck 146 feet, length of keel 120 feet 2 inches, breadth 40 feet 5 inches, depth of hold 17 feet 3½ inches, 1,044 11/94 tons bm, draught 10 feet 8 inches forward / 15 feet 7 inches aft.

46 A Grampus is a cetacean of the dolphin family, but the word is also used to describe various other small cetaceans, such as Orca, killer whale, or pilot whale.

12

Halifax, Nova Scotia, 31 March–15 June 1776

On board The *Spy.* At Sea, March 31st. to April 6th. 1776
14th. Week.

31. Su. dull M^{g}. blows fresh S, E—X Sun—p. m. IV small rain, rain'd all ye aft^{n}. S,E Lat. 43°—

1. M. April.[1] rain & sleet, last N^{t}. cold M^{g}—sea runs high N,E—

2. [Anchored][2] Tu. pleasant calm M^{g}—XII pleasant Breeze. S,E—p. m, II made the Land of Nova Scotia IV saw the Light House of Cape Sambro[3] anchor'd about VIII in Hallifax Harbour

The Men of War & most of the Transports anchor'd this Ev^{g}. in Hallifax harbour.

3. W. Dull raw M^{g}. some rain S,E—aft^{n} rain

4. Th. rain'd all last N^{t}. & blew a storm S.S.E. X, ceas'd to rain blows fresh S.S.E— Several boats blown away from The Ships last N^{t}—

Last Night it blew a Storm & rain'd most Violently—The Light Horse were landed & the horses to be sent to Grass to Windsor (Pisaquid)[4] about 38 miles off & the men to be quarter'd there—

The Town of Hallifax does not seem to be much improv'd since I was here in 1759. The dock Yard is made very compleat. As the Town is not capable of containing all the Troops; it being mostly taken up w^{t}. the Inhabitants that came from Boston, the greatest part of ye Sol^{rs}. remain on board ship but are landed & excersized on the Hill above Hallifax in turn—

When we arriv'd at Hallifax all the fresh Lakes about the Country were froze over; & much Ice in the Streets of the Town—The Hills almost cover'd w^{t}. snow—

About Hallifax are many small Lakes at a few miles distance; all full of very fine Trout; in some of the small rivers you get Salmon, & at this Season innumerable quantities of Smelts, that run into the mouths of the rivers to Spawn. These lakes are

---

1 The characters '1. M. April' are written in red ink.
2 The word between brackets is a note in the margin.
3 Cape Sambro is located about 13 miles (21) km from Halifax harbor.
4 Fort Edward was located at Windsor.

entirely froze over in Winter, & on the Ice clearing away they are full of Trouts—in the Summer & fall, many of them are quite dry, yet on the [rain][5] water filling them, they have abundance of Trouts, tho' no communication with any other Water either lake or River, & 'tis Wonderful where The fish comes from—[6]

5. F. pleasant clear M^{g} light W^{d}

6. Sa. very pleasant day little W^{d}. N

On board The *Spy*. Hallifax harbour. April 7th. to 13th. 1776
15th. Week.

7. Su. pleasant calm M^{g}—warm XII S,E, cool

8. M. very fine bright M^{g}—little W^{d}. N—
√ to McLean lent a Doll^{r} - - - £ - 4 : 8—

9. Tu. very pleasant day—light W^{d}. S.E.

10. W. dull M^{g}. —very foggy Moist Day— part of the L^{t}. Drag^{s}. marched to Pisaguid or Windsor Aft^{n}. wet—SE—

11. Th. wet all last Night heavy Mist dull Misty M^{g}—SE—

12. F. very wet fog all day S.E—

13. Sa. clear M^{g}. blows fresh

On board the *Spy*. Hallifax Harbour. April 14th. to April 20th. 1776
16th. Week.

14. Su. pleasant Warm day S—

15. M. Snow this M^{g}. —XII Ceas'd, dull—N

16. Tu. clear M^{g}. cold N—very pleasant day—
√~~To Lt G—n for Rum Lent £ - 4 sh. 11~~

17. W. dull day cold—W.
√~~To Do.~~[7] ~~for Whiting &c. Lent £ - 9 sh.~~

5 The word in square brackets is an interlineal insertion.
6 This paragraph appears in the remarks section of Week 15, but appears to be a continuation of the remarks in Week 14.
7 Lieutenant Gason.

18. Th. dull Wet M^{g}. W, N,W—47th. Reg^{t}. order'd to embark— several ships from ye W. India Islands came in ye day w^{t}. some Ships of War—

19. F. cold M^{g}. clear blows fresh—
Several Ships from ye W. India Islands came in—Capt Wallace in y^{e}. *Rose*, 20 Guns, came in being drove away from her Station at Rhode Island by the Rebels, & we hear the *Glascow* 20 Guns[8] was attack'd by some Rebel Vessels two carrying 30 Guns [each][9] & was much damag'd, 5 ships attack'd y^{e} *Glasco* the smallest carry'd 16 Guns—[10]

List of the Ships that attack'd y^{e} *Glasco*[11]

Ships	Commanders	Guns		Men
		3lb^{s}	6lb^{s}	
Alfred[12]	Ad. Hopkins[13]	20	10	280

8 The 20-gun, later *Seaford* class sixth rate frigate *Glasgow* was built at Hull by John Reed in 1756 and 1757. Commissioned in 1757, she served in the Mediterranean in in 1757-1759, was in the West Indies and at Jamaica in 1760. She was in the Havana operation and the attack on Spanish shipping at Mariel, Cuba, in 1762, where she took two sloops. Paid off in 1763, she underwent a large repair and recommissioned in 1766. She served in North American waters in 1767 and was paid off in 1771. Recommissioned in 1771, she was in South Carolina in 1772-74, in Boston and New England, then in Jamaica in 1775-1776, where she fought her action with two ships of the Continental Navy on 6 April. Returning to Jamaica in 1779, she was burnt in an accident at Montego Bay 1 June 1779. Length of gun deck 109 feet 4 inches, length of keel 91 feet 2½ inches, breadth 30 feet 6 inches, depth of hold 9 feet 7½ inches, 451 89/94 tons bm.

9 The word between brackets in an interlineal insertion.

10 This engagement was the first battle for the American's Continental Navy under the command of Commodore Ezek Hopkins. Just returned from its first amphibious raid in the Bahamas on 3 March 1776, the American squadron encountered the *Glasgow* between Block Island and Newport, Rhode Island. *Glasgow's* escape under the skillful direction of Captain Tyringham Howe was one of the first of a series of ineffectual actions that led to the eventual dismissal of Ezek Hopkins as commander in Chief of the Continental Navy in 1778.

11 The following list is written in the remarks section for week 17

12 The 24-gun *Alfred* was built at Philadelphia as the merchant ship *Black Prince* in 1774, she was acquired by the Continental Navy on 4 November 1775 and commissioned on 3 December 1775. Alfred was the first American warship to fly the national flag of the new republic. She served as the flagship for Commodore Ezek Hopkins's expedition to New Providence, 17 February-7 April 1776, then went on to capture a number of prizes. Two years later, she was captured by the 20-gun *Ariadne* and 14-gun *Ceres* off Barbados on 9 March 1778. Taken into British service with the name, *Alfred*, she was commissioned in October 1778, then paid off in July 1780 and sold. She initially carried 24 9-pounder guns, later reduced to 20 9-pounder guns. She had a complement of 220 men. 440 tons.

13 *Alfred* was commanded by Captain Dudley Saltonstall and served as the flagship for Commodore Ezek Hopkins. There were no admirals in the Continental Navy, although Hopkins was designed as commander-in-chief of the Continental Navy, theoretically on an equal footing with George Washington as commander in chief of the Continental Army. Ezek Hopkins was born in Rhode Island in 1718. He commanded merchant ships for the brown family of Rhode Island and had been a successful privateer during the French and Indian War. In October 1775, Rhode Island appointed him a brigadier general to command the military forces of Rhode Island. On 22 December 1775, the Continental Congress appointed him commander-in-chief of the Continental Navy, although having no prior

Columbus[14]	C. Whipple[15]	18	10	280
Andrew Doria[16]	C. Dunn[17]	20	8	160
Cabbot[18]	C. Dunn Jr[19]	18	8	150

naval experience. Hopkins's ineffective leadership led to Congress censuring him on 12 August 1776, although he retained command until 2 June 1778 and Congress terminated his commission

14 The 24-gun *Columbus* was built at Philadelphia as the merchant ship *Sally* in 1774. The continental Navy acquired the ship in November 1775 and was commissioned on 4 January 1776. On the expedition to New Providence, she became the first Continental Navy ship to capture a British vessel, when she took the 6-gun schooner *Hawk* on 4 April 1776. After participating in the *Glasgow* affair, she captured five more vessels before a British squadron chased her ashore and burned her at Point Judith, Rhode Island. She carried 18 9-pounder guns and 10 6-pounder guns with a complement of 220 men. 200 tons.

15 Captain Abraham Whipple was born in Rhode Island in 1733. He had been a merchant ship captain for the Brown family of Rhode Island, and had been a successful privateer captain during the French and Indian War in 1772. He was the key leader in the *Gaspee* Incident in 1772. In 1775, he Rhode Island General Assembly appointed him commodore of the Rhode Island State Navy, whose flagship, the sloop *Katy*, he brought into the Continental Navy with him when he was commissioned a captain in that service on 22 December 1775. After commanding *Columbus*, he commanded the 28-gun frigate *Providence.* During the defence of Charleston, South Carolina, in 1779-80, he was taken a prisoner. He died in Marietta, Ohio, in 1819.

16 The 14-gun brig *Andrew Doria* was built as the merchant ship *Defiance.* Purchased by the Continental Navy in November 1775, she was converted at Philadelphia and commissioned in January 1776. After participating in the New Providence raid and the *Glasgow* affair, she received the first foreign salute to the American flag at St. Eustatius on 16 November 1776, she was in the defence of Delaware Bay operation in October-November 1777 and subsequently burned at Red Bank, New Jersey, to prevent capture on 21 November 1777. She carried 14 9-pounder guns, had a complement of 112 men.

17 Bamford's information is incorrect. *Andrew Doria* was commanded by Captain Nicholas Biddle.

18 The 14-gun brig *Cabot* was built as the merchant brig *Sally.* The Continental Navy acquired the vessel in November 1775 and commissioned her in 1776. She was the first to fire on *Glasgow* and was damaged in the action. Following this action, she took seven prizes. On 26 March 1777, the 28-gun frigate *Milford* took *Cabot* as a prize off Nova Scotia. The first Continental Navy ship captured by the Royal Navy warship, she was brought into the Royal Navy under the same name. In British service, she was commissioned in June 1778, initially as an armed ship, she participated in the relief of Jersey and the action in Cancale Bay, and served in the Channel and the North Sea in 1779. In 1781, she escorted a Baltic convoy and was in the Battle of Dogger Bank on 5 August 1781. Paid off in 1781, she was sold on 25 June 1783. Length of gun deck 74 feet 10 inches, length of keel 58 feet 7 inches, breadth 24 feet 8 inches, depth of hold 11 feet 4 inches, 186 15/94 tons bm. She originally carried 14 6-pounders, later reduced to 14 4-pounders. She had a complement of 80 men.

19 Bamford's information is incorrect. *Cabot* was commanded by Captain John Burroughs Hopkins, the son of Commodore Ezek Hopkins. Born in 1742, he became a merchant ship captain and commanded one of the long boats involved in the 1772 *Gaspee* affair. He was commissioned one of the first captains in the Continental Navy on 22 December 1775. He died in 1796.

Providence[20]	C. Hazard[21]	16	6	118
		---	--	---
		92	42	988
				92
				42
				134 guns

The *Glasco* rec[d] but little damage ----
3 Row Gallies, 50 Men Each }
those Gallies were not at the Attack } 650 Men

20. Sa. clear cold M[g]. N,W— this M[g]. the 47th. Reg[t]. sail'd for Quebec
at Exercise on Citadel Hill
To L[t]. Carter lent — 2 Doll[rs] – 9 sh.

On board the *Spy*. Halifax Harbour April 21st. to April 27th. 1776
17th week.

21 Su. Bright Mild M[g].
Maj[r] Grant[22] now L[t] Col[o] came in from his Expedition which was to Georgia[23] where they retook some Vessels which had been detain'd by the Rebels & took four prizes

20 The 12-gun sloop *Providence* was built in Providence, Rhode Island, by John Brown as the merchant vessel *Katy*, possibly before 1765. She is known to have been a voyage to Surinam in 1769 and, in 1770 and 1772, went on whaling voyages. In 1775, she was initially chartered by the Rhode Island Committee of Safety and then purchased by the State of Rhode Island in October 1775 to serve as the flagship of the Rhode Island Navy under Commodore Abraham Whipple. In late November 1775, she sailed to Philadelphia with seamen for the Continental Navy and was immediately taken into the Continental Navy and renamed *Providence*. She was commissioned on 9 January 1776 under Captain John Hazard. She captured or burned some 15 ships in 1776. Just a month after the *Glasgow* incident, temporary Captain John Paul Jones took command, remaining in the post until September. During the Penobscot River expedition in July-August 1779, she was blow up in the river to prevent capture on 14 August 1779. She carried 90 men. She was initially armed with 12 4-pounder guns, and later in 1776 carried 12 6-pounders. In 1779, she carried 6 6-pounders, 6 4-pounders and 22-pounders.

21 Captain John Hazard was commissioned a captain in the Continental Navy on 9 January 1776. Hazard was accused of neglect of duty following the *Glasgow* incident and dismissed from the service on 9 May 1776.

22 James Grant was born in Scotland in 1733. He was appointed a surgeon in the first battalion of the 36th Regiment of Foot in England on 27 April 1756 by purchase vice a resignation. Thereafter, he was commissioned an ensign in the Earl of Eglintoun's new-raising 62nd (later 77th) Foot in Scotland on 12 January 1757. He was promoted to lieutenant in the 77th Foot on 19 August 1758 in a free death vacancy, to captain-lieutenant in the 77th Foot on 6 May 1762 by purchase vice a resignation, to captain in the 77th Foot on 5 August 1762 through a free death vacancy, to captain in the 40th Foot on 17 August 1762 in Cuba in a free vacancy vice a resignation. Subsequently, he was promoted to major in the 40th Foot on 12 December 1770 by purchase vice a retirement, and then lieutenant colonel in the 40th Foot on 11 December 1775, by purchase vice a promotion to a colonelcy. He was killed in action on 27 August 1776 in the Battle of Long Island, after 20.3 years' service.

23 In late December 1775, Major Grant had been ordered with 175 men on board two transport ships to proceed to Georgia to obtain rice, peas and other provisions for feeding

Laden w^{t} rice: A Disagreement between him & ye Capt of y^{e} *Scarborough*,[24] who would not assist him lost two of ye prizes. The *Hallifax* Pacquet arriv'd Govr Legge[25] to go to England. Com^{dre} Arbuthnot appointed Lt Governour.[26]

A Report was current that the Rebels had taken Quebec, not confirm'd, & unlikely.

22. M. dull M^{g}. X Snow—much snow this day E—blows hard—

23. Tu. blows fresh N,W—cold—cloudy
~~To Lt. G n for Beef & Johnson £ - 15 9~~

24. W. blows hard & cold N,W—
To Mr Bullard[27] this date—

25. Th. very pleasant & Calm M^{g}—XI cloudy, cool blows fresh N,W—
To M^{r}. Vaun lent a Doll^{r}. — — — 1: 16—

26. F. wet, blowing, cold M^{g}.—E—rain'd all day—& a great part of this N^{t}—

27. Sa. dull M^{g}.—N—blows fresh—
This aft^{n}. the *Spy* Transport fell down to ye Eastern Battery w^{t}. 5 comp^{ns} 40th on board

Eastern Battery Near Hallifax. April 28th. to May 4th. 1776
28th. Week.

28. Su. pleasant day—N,W. light W^{d}—part of the 40th. Reg^{t}. landed this day at the Eastern Batt^{ry}. to remain till further Orders—it lies Opposite Hallifax. very pleasant.

Eight Comp^{ys}. of 40th. Reg^{t}. wore landed at the Eastern Battery—it lies on the East side of the Harbour of Hallifax opposite George's Island—The Battery has been a long time demolish'd & the house almost in ruins, but was fitted up in some manner for our reception—

---

the Army during the winter. The transports were escorted by *Scarborough* and the schooner *Hinchinbrook*. See Clark, Morgan, et al (eds.), *Naval Documents of the American Revolution*, Vol.3, pp. 238, 254, 764, 992, 994; Vol.4, pp. 24, 60, 152, 167, 170, 186-87, 206, 207, 223-24, 246, 247, 344, 345, 371, 459, 460, 674, 1223, 1292,1437.

24 Captain Andrew Barkley, Royal Navy.

25 Francis Legge (c. 1719-1783), Governor of Nova Scotia, 1773-1776.

26 This paragraph appears in the remarks page for week 16, but is dated 21 April.

27 Mr Bullard has not been unidentified. From subsequent entries, he appears to have been either an agent or a banker. The 40th Foot had retained William Montgomery in Dublin as its agent in 1771 until 1775, when the regiment left Ireland. From that point, the 40th Foot employed Cox & Mair in Craig's Court, London, as its agent. The 40th Foot remained with Cox & Mair, and their successors, until 1786. There was no regimental agent called Bullard during the period between the years 1744 and 1793, but it is possible that a Mr Bullard could have been employed by Cox & Mair's, or he may possibly have represented a private bank or other firm tht provided financial services to individual Army officers.

A report, the Quebec was taken by the Rebels—'tis not probable. This was in the Philadelphia Newspapers with many particulars of the Affair some people seem to Credit it. I do not—

29. M. very pleasant day—S—the Rest of ye 40th. Reg^{t}. landed at ye Eastern Batt^{y} The Grend^{rs}. & L^{t}. Infantry Comp^{ys} did not land.

30. Tu. fine clear Warm M^{g}. 20 Trouts small in a little river about ½ mile E. of ye Battery—p. m. began to rain— continued all day

1. W. May[28] rain'd all last N^{t}. rains heavily this M^{g}—S. Rain'd all day, sometimes thick fog.

2.Th. clear cold M^{g}. N,W— 2 doz^{n}. Trouts in the Above mention'd River

3. F. dull M^{g}. N,E, —Much Snow this Aft^{n}

4. Sa. clear cold M^{g}. N,W—p. m. II began to rain 2 doz^{n}. 9 trouts—ye Same river—

Eastern Battery. May 5th. to May 11th. 1776
19th. Week.

5. Su. very pleasant day—S,W—Some Strong Redoubts are begun on the Hills above Hallifax.[29]

6. M. dull day—N,W—aft^{n}. a little Snow.

7. Su. bright cold m^{g} N.W. little W^{d}—

8. W. clear, bright M^{g}. S,W. little W^{d}— 20 Trouts. as before

9. Th. rain this M^{g}—S—moist foggy day

10. F. Foggy M^{g}.—Calm—XII, clear Sun S,W—

11. Sa. bright M^{g}. blows fresh. NW— Doz^{n}. & ½ Trouts herring size in a lake about 3 miles from Eastern Battery—NE—

Eastern Battery. May 12th. to May 18th. 1776
20th. Week.

12. Su. blows fresh—flying clouds, W—

28 The characters '1, W. May' are written in red ink.
29 This statement in the remarks section is undated by opposite the entry for 5 May.

13. M. calm M^{g}. X, S.W. fresh W^{d}. Clear Sun—
The Greyhound[30] Brought the Pacquet—A Transport w^{t}. part of 46th. Reg^{t}.—arriv'd— 2 doz^{n}, 10 Trouts, larger herring size mostly; ye Last lake
A Great promotion of Genl Officers.
To M^{rs} V—n lent 8 Doll^{rs}. £1: 16 —

14. Tu. clear, bright. M^{g}—blows fresh S,W— 12 Trouts in ye Last ment^{d}. lake.
From Capt. Green—[31]

15. W. Some rain last N^{t}. foggy M^{g}. IX, clear'd, hot sun— 2 doz^{n}. Trouts in ye same lake

16. Th. pleasant M^{g}. dull, XII Cloudy, cold, & windy N.W—with some rain. Aft^{n}. pleasant 1 doz^{n}. & 1/2 Trouts as above

17. F. pleasant M^{g}—calm IX light W^{d}. S,W. XII very cold— 10 Trouts as before
From Mr Bullard—by Mr Fitzgerald—[dated][32] Feb^{ry}. 26th.
A Report prevail'd that the Rebels had got a second drubbing at Quebec, wherein about 800 were kill'd & 500 taken prisoners—wants confirmation.
We heard that Genl. Clinton's Army from the South has orders to joyn us at N, York—

30 The 28-gun sixth rate frigate *Greyhound* was built at Bucklers Hard by Henry Adams between 1771 and 1773 and completed at Portsmouth on 1 January 1776. Commissioned under Captain Archibald Dickson, she sailed for North America on 5 April 1776. In 1779, she was refitted at Sheerness and sailed again for North America on 4 June 1779. She took three American privateers in 1779-1780, participated in the Penobscot Expedition in 1779, at the Battle of Martinique in 1780, in the actions of 15 and 19 June 1780, with Rodney at New York in September 1780. In 1781, she sailed as escort with the Oporto trade, and on 16 August 1781 wrecked on the South Sand off Deal. Length of gun deck 124 feet 2 inches, length of keel 102 feet 8 ⅞ inches, breadth 33 feet 7½ inches, depth of hold 11 feet, 617 83/94 tons bm.

31 Charles Green was born in 1749 at Gibraltar, one of three sons of Ensign, ex-Sergent Major, Christopher Green of the 37th Foot, then in the Minorca garrison. Charles entered as a Cadet at the Royal Military Academy, Woolwich, in 1760, but is described in the War Office Succession Book as a Volunteer when first commissioned. From gentleman volunteer, he was commissioned an ensign in the 31st Foot in the East Florida/Gulf Garrison on 10 August 1765, a free death vacancy. His regiment was the one that relieved Bamford's 35th Regiment at Pensacola. Bamford and Green would have previously met between 18-25 July 1765 at Pensacola. Green was promoted to lieutenant of the 31st Foot on 23 November 1769, a free vacancy vice a resignation. He served as adjutant from 20 July 1773 to 1 June 1777) and was promoted to captain-lieutenant in the 31st Foot on 3 November 1774 by purchase vice a retirement. Sunbsequently, he was promoted to captain in the 31st Foot on 18 January 1775, a free death-vacancy, to brevet major on 19 March 1783, to major in the 31st Foot on 25 February 1788 by purchase vice a retirement, to lieutenant colonel in the new-raising 95th Foot in England on 30 Octber 1793, a free augmentation vacancy. He was to be knighted in May 1803 and created Baronet of Milnrow, Yorkshire in December 1805; was made colonel of the 16th Foot in August 1808 and colonel of his father's old 37th Foot in Feb 1814, dying a full general in 1831.

32 The word in brackets is an interlinear insertion.

A Letter from Capt. Green says, some of ye 33d. & [blank] have Joyn'd Gen. Clinton.

18. Sa. pleasant M^{g} rather cold—blows fresh, S,W.
From Mr Bullard, by Pacquet. D^{td}. Decr. 12th. 1775

Eastern Battery. May 19th to May 25th 1776
21st. Week.

19. Su. pleasant day.
The Soldiers who serv'd last campain at Boston have each rec^{d}. a pair of Shoes & Stockings a woolen cap, & a quantity of Tobacco, [illegible insertion] a donation from the People of England; & the Women who lost their Husbands, or were otherwise objects of Charity, rec^{d}. for themselves & Children each a pair of shoes & stockings a Charity Rais'd by the English as some recompense for their sufferings. The officers had 1 p^{d}. superfine Tobacco given them; & the Sold^{rs}. got a quantity of Cheese—besides the above—The officers had a present of 10 Gall^{ns}. of Rum each—The Merchants sent 100 pipes of Madeira to be dispos'd of amongst the officers, at prime cost, about 29£ a pipe.
Tis S^{d}. The Army under Gen Clinton are sent for to Joyn Gen Howe—[33]

20. M.

21. Tu. pleasant day S,W— 10 Trouts—as above

22. W. very wet M^{g}—XI clear'd fine day

23. Th. pleasant day, W & SW—

24. F. pleasant day N,W— Bit very much with black flies, face in Lumps. 6 doz^{n}. 8 Trouts in a River near Laurence Town[34] an innumerable Quantity of smelts—

25. Sa. calm warm M^{g}—X S,W, cool—

Eastern Battery. May 26th. to June 1st. 1776
22d. Week.

26. Su. rain'd all day

27. M. pleasant day—little W^{d}

28. Tu. foggy moist day

33 The paragraph above is undated and written in the remarks section for week 21.
34 Lawrencetown, Halifax County, Nova Scotia, is located on the eastern shore about 5 miles (8 km) from the entrance to Halifax harbour.

L^{t}. Carter drew provisions to ye day inclu^{d}.

29. W. foggy M^{g}–Aft^{n}. Pleasant
~~To Lt. Gason lent £14 : 8 : 4~~

30. Th. bright warm M^{g}—calm—XII brisk W^{d}. S.W—pleasant day
The *Niger*[35] from Quebec Arriv'd

The *Niger* from Quebec Arriv'd, brought word, that Genl Burgione w^{t}. the Forces had got to Quebec & that the Rebel Army on their Arrival had broke up in the greatest precipitation, on the arrival of most of the 29th. Reg^{t}. at Quebec they were immediately landed with them & what Genl. Carlton could muster up in the Garrison, making in all about 1000 men he sallied out, to attack the Rebels, who had 4000 men, besieging the Town [on][36] which the Rebels fled in the greatest Confusion, leading their tents [cannon, mortars,][37] Ammunition & stores behind them; nor did they stay to Eat their dinners, which were just dress'd; a Subaltern's party got Gen$^{l.}$. Thomas's dinner;[38] a welcome repast—The Rebels had lain before Quebec 5 months—This is a severe check to the Rebels, as all their hopes of succeeding, or prolonging the War, depended on their taking Quebec, whereby they become masters of All America—

To L^{t}. Carter lent 8 Doll^{rs}. £1 : 16—

31. F. bright Warm M^{g}—calm—X light W^{d}. NW
at exercise on the Cittadel hill

35 The 32-gun fifth rate *Niger* was built at Sheerness by Joseph Harris in 1758-59. Commissioned in 1759, she served in the Channel in the Bay of Biscay and the Chanel in 1759, was in the Quiberon Bay operation in 1760 and took several prizes in 1762. In 1764, she served off the coast of Scotland, then sailed for Newfoundland in 1766, where she remained until returning home in 1769. In the Mediterranean in 1770, she was paid off in 1772 and given a large repair at Deptford. Recommissioned in July 1775 under Captain George Talbot, she sailed for North America on 24 September 1775. In 1777-1780, she was in the West Indies. Paid off in 1783, she underwent several repairs and eventually was recommissioned in 1790. She was in Howe's fleet at the Glorious First of June in 1794, the Battle of Cape St Vincent in 1797, and en flûte in the operation in Egypt in 1801. Reclassed as a 28-gun sixth rate in 1804 she was armed with carronades. Laid up at Portsmouth in 1808, she became a prison hospital. Renamed *Negro* in 1813, she was sold at Portsmouth in 1814. Length of gun deck 125 feet, length of keel 103 feet 4 inches, breadth 35 feet 2 inches, depth of hold 12 feet, 679 67/94 tons bm.

36 The word between brackets is an interlinear insertion.

37 The words between brackets are an interlinear insertion.

38 John Thomas was born in Massachusetts in 1724 and studied medicine with Dr. Tufts in Medford, Massachusetts. In 1774, he recruited volunteers for the 2nd Massachusetts Regiment and served as colonel of it. The Massachusetts Assembly appointed him brigadier general in February 1775, leading his troops in the siege of Boston. In June 1775, the Continental Congress appointed him a brigadier general in the Continental Army. To assuage his disappointment in not being made major general, he was made the senior brigadier general in the Continental Army. He fortified Dorchester Heights in 1776. After the death of General Montgomery, he took charge of the invasion of Canada. Following the repulse of the American force at Québec, he died of small pox during the retreat at Chambly on 18 June 1776.

[1. Sa.] dull M^{g}. [June].[39] Brisk W^{d} S—some rain this Aft^{n}— 3 Sallmon & 50 Trouts, some large, as last

~~To Lt. Gason — — — 4 : — 10¾~~

L^{t}. Gason Gave me a Bill on his mother for what he was in Debt to me.

L^{t}. Gason Gave me a bill on his mother in Dublin for 20£ Irish. I have given him the amount of that sum in Cash June 1st 1776, which settles accounts. Sent ye Bill to Mr Bullard, by C^{t} McLean 8th inst.

Eastern Battery. June 2d. to June 8th· 1776
23d. Week.

2. Su. heavy rain all day S,W—high W^{d}.
To Mr Bullard—sent a Bill for £20—Irish

3. M. dull M^{g}. N—10 Trouts in the little brook to ye E—of ye Battery ½ mile—
To Wm V—n 2 doll^{rs}. £ - 9 - 4

4. [Embarked][40] Tu. some rain this M^{g}—Aft^{n}. Wet—
Embark'd on board the *Spy* Transport

5. W. blows fresh N—cool day caught a great number of Flat fish—
To L^{t}. Carter lent— — — 8 doll^{rs}. — — —1 : 16 —

6. Th. pleasant day S.W— caught some flat fish & Cod

7. F. rain'd all day—S,W—very thick fog Ev^{g}— caught some flat fish & some cod—

8. Sa. Dull M^{g}—N—XI rain, rain'd all day with fog—& high W^{d}—The Howe saild for Europe.
Some flat fish.
Wrote by C^{t}. McLean to Mr Bullard—by ye Howe Ship—

> A Ship with part of the 42d. Reg^{t} arriv'd. To Mr. Bullard — by C^{t}. McLean who went in y^{e} *Howe* Transport 8th. Inst. —
> [Mine][41] dated 2d Sent 20£

---

39 On this line '1. Sa.' and 'June' are written in red ink.
40 The word between square brackets is a note in the margin.
41 The word in square brackets is an interlinear insertion.

The part of the 29th. Reg^t. got to Quebec 6th. May. They went in the *Surprize* Frigate,[42] the *Isis*,[43] & Sloop *Martin*.[44] The 5th. of December the Rebels under Montgomery & Arnold invested Quebec 31st. they assaulted the Town in two places one under Cape Diamond headed by Montgomery; the other attack was lead by Arnold,[45] & came by St. Rocque. They were repuls'd in both Places, Montgomery was kill'd, & Arnold wound'd—the Rebels lost between 6 & 7 hundred men & between 40 & 50 officers

---

42 The 28-gun sixth rate *Surprise* was built at Woolwich by successive master shipwrights William Grey and Nicholas Phillips between 1771 and 1775. Commissioned in February 1775 under Captain Robert Linzee, she sailed for Newfoundland on 23 May 1775, then was at the relief of Québec in 1776. She took two American privateers in 1776 and returned to Newfoundland in 1777 and 1778, taking another privateer in 1778. She returned for refitting at Portsmouth in 1779. She recommissioned in 1779, returned to Newfoundland in 1779 and 1781, took six privateers in 1779-80, and another six in 1781-82. Paid off in 1782, she was sold at Woolwich in 1783. Length of gun deck 120 feet 6 inches, length of keel 99 feet six inches, breadth 33 feet 6 inches, depth of hold 11 feet, 593 89/94 tons bm.

43 The 50-gun, fourth rate *Isis* was built by John Henniker & Co, at Chatham between 1772 and 1774 and completed at Chatham Dockyard in 1776. Commissioned in October 1775 under Captain Charles Douglas, she sailed for North America on 7 March 1776 and participated in the relief of Québec in May 1776. She returned to England, then went back to North America and participated in the Delaware operation in October 1777 and in 1778 was at Sandy Hooke, in Howe's action with d'Estaing, in the Leeward Islands, and at St. Lucia, returning home and was paid off in 1779. After a small repair, she recommissioned in 1780. She sailed for India in 1781 and was at Porto Playa and, as part of Hughes's squadron, was in the battles of Sadras, Providien, Negapatam, and Trincomalee in 1782, at the Battle of Cuddalore in 1783. She returned home in 1783 and was paid off in 1784. After a great repair, she recommissioned in 1794. She participated in the Battle of Camperdown in 1797 and the Battle of Copenhagen in 1801. In 1802-1806, she was flagship at Newfoundland, returning again in 1808. After service in the North Sea in 1809, she was broken up at Deptford in 1810. Length of gun deck 146 feet, length of keel 119 feet 8¼ inches, breadth 40 feet 7½ inches, depth of hold 17 feet 6 inches, 1,050 65/94 tons bm.

44 The 14-sloop *Beaver* class sloop *Martin* was built at Cuckold's Point, Rotherhithe, by John Randall in 1760-61 and completed in 1761 at Deptford. Commissioned in 11761, she was with Hawke's fleet in 1762, sailed for Africa and the Leeward Islands in 1763, where she remained until 1767. After a small repair at Sheerness, she recommissioned in 1767 and sailed for North Carolina and was paid off in 1772. After being fitted at Chatham, she was recommissioned in 1775 and sailed for Newfoundland. Under Commander Henry Harvey, she was at the relief of Québec in 1776, after which she returned to the Newfoundland station. Refitted in 1780, she was in the Downs in 1780 and returned to the Leeward Islands and Jamaica in 1782. Paid off in 1784, she was sold at Deptford in 1784. Length of gun deck 96 feet 11 inches, length of keel 80 feet 1 inch, breadth 26 feet ½ inch, depth of hold 12 feet 6 inches, 288 82/94 tons, bm.

45 In 1775, Arnold was elected captain of a Connecticut militia company. Proposing an attack on Ticonderoga, Massachusetts made him a colonel. When Congress decided to make a second attack on Québec in 1775, he was passed over for command, but obtained a commission as colonel in the Continental Army after suggesting to Washington that he take a group by a wilderness route. Wounded in the leg during the attack, he was promoted to brigadier general for reaching Québec. Retreating from Quebec, he was briefly governor of Montréal before it was retaken by British forces, He retreated further to Lake Champlain, after participating in many operations, and he defected from the Americans and was made a brigadier general in British service in 1781. He remains a controversial figure in history.

kill'd Wounded & taken. The Garrison had one Lieut. Of the Navy, 4 Rank & file kill'd & 13 wounded—2 died since[46]

On board the *Spy* at Sea, June 9th. to June 15th. 1776
24th. Week.

9. Su. dull, cold, Windy M^{g}—N—cold day

10. [Sailed] M. very cold blowing M^{g}—N—sail'd out of the Harbour of Hallifax caught Many Codd at the mouth of the Harbour & a little below Georges Isle

Course SbE.

About XII This day, The signal for sailing was made & the fleet sail'd out as fast as They could get under way—lay to off the Harbour's mouth, till IX at night & Then made Sail, steering to the S^{t}

Admiral Shuldam, in the *Chatham*, Commanding the Navy Genl. Howe the Army—with about 160 Sail of Shiping of all sorts.

The Centurion brings up ye Rear—

The Two Battalions of Marines, Highland Emigrants & Fencible American Corps, about 3000 men were left in N: Scotia

I fear our leaving Hallifax, without some certainty of Lord Howe's fleet being near, which I do not find there is, will prove rather premature What can we do at York w^{t}. our small Army—only make the Rebels, draw their Forces there, to oppose us, & throw up works as they did at Boston perhaps it may be for the better it did turn out much so.

11. Tu. pleasant M^{g}. almost calm, N,W—bright M^{g}. We scarcely see The Land—Aft^{n}. W

C—SbE—

12. W. very foggy M^{g}. W,S,W, cold—XII clear'd—

C—SbW. Lat. 42° 59′

13. Th. pleasant M^{g}. cool—S,W—clear—XII, N,W, light breeze—

C—SbW— Lat—41°. 42′

14. F. bright Warm M^{g}—light Wind E—

C—W½S Lat. 41° 23′

15. Sa. Something hazy This M^{g}. Tumbling Seas little W^{d}. W.S.W,

Lat. 41° 4′

Paid for our Sea Store £6:13.3

46 The undated paragraph above appears in the remarks section of Week 23.

13

New York Bay and Staten Island, 16 June 1776–17 August 1776

On board The *Spy* at Sea, June 16th. to June 22d. 1776
25th. Week.

16. Su. hazy to Windward—S,S,E—some Ships that lost the Fleet last N^{t}. joyn'd this M^{g}– XII, W^{d}. began to rise—aft^{n}. blew hard
Lat. 40°— 4′

17. M. blew exceeding hard all last N^{t}. S,S.W. with heavy showerz of rain—heavy squalls all day—Af^{n}. w^{d}. abated very foggy—S.S.W—
No Obs^{n}.

18. Tu. Dull Moderate M^{g}. cool S,S,W—
Lat. 41°— 4′

19. W. dull M^{g}. light W^{d}. Warm. IX sometimes Sun—
Lat 40°. 35′

20. Th. warm bright M^{g}. NNW—lay to from VIII till Eve^{g}. then made Sail— Sam. Taylor went on board y hospital Ship some Ships y^{t}. parted Comp^{y}. Joyn'd—
Lat. 39°— — 40′

21. F. bright Warm M^{g}. light breeze N,E, caught a few Rudder fish w^{t}. a hook & line—C—WbN.
Lat 39°—33′

22. Sa. bright Warm day light breeze E—were Told y^{t}. one of the Rebels privateers had attack'd one of our Transports—false. C—W—

On board The *Spy*. at Sea. June 23d. to June 29th. 1776
26th Week.

23. Su. bright Warm M^{g}. light Breeze E,S,E. pm, I, almost calm. VIII, light Breeze SbyE were told y^{t}. L^{d}. Howe w^{t}. ye Fleet had arriv'd at N. York & made a landing—false.

Lat 39°—58′

24. M. Very Warm M^{g}. light W^{d}. SbE—bright caught many Rudder fish, some large
Lat. 39°—49′

25. Tu. calm, hot, bright M^{g}. —XII light Air
Lat 39°—58′

26. W. very hot, little W^{d}. XII light breeze
Lat. 39°—56′

27. Th. calm M^{g}.—XII, a light breeze N,E—hot day—
Lat 39°—57′

28 F. hot M^{g}. pleasant light Gale E. XII a little rain caught many Rudder fish large, with hook & line Aft^{n}. dull—
Lat 39°—51′—
The *Liverpool*[1] Frigate came into our Fleet—saluted the Admiral

29. Sa. light breeze W, SW—This M^{g}. about VI made the Land, call'd never sink[2] in the Jerseys—p. m., II Anchor'd in Sandy hook about 25 Miles from N York—About 6 o'Clock this M^{g}. made the Land, call'd never sink, in the Jerseys; to the southward of Sandy hook—

About 2 oClock This day we came to an Anchor in Sandy hook—Admiral Lord Howe had not got in nor any Troops, except a few of Frazer's Highlanders—Genl. Howe arriv'd here some days ago in the Greyhound frigate, which left our fleet at Sea, the rest of our fleet are coming in—

The Rebels took 4 ships of Frazer's Highlanders; march'd the Men through Long Island, playing the Rogue's march before Them—this by here say only.

---

1 The 28-gun, sixth rate, *Coventry* class frigate *Liverpool* was built at Liverpool by Gorill & Pownall in 1756-1758. Commissioned in 1758, she served in Boys's squadron off Dunkirk and took three privateers in 1759. In 1760, she sailed for the East Indies and returned to serve off Brest in 1762, where she captured a privateer in 1762 and another in 1764. She sailed for The East Indies in 1763, and, with the news of the impending peace, was paid off in 1764. After a great repair at Woolwich, she recommissioned in 1767 and sailed to Newfoundland in 1767, and to the Mediterranean in 1768. Paid off in 1772, she underwent a large repair at Chatham and recommissioned in in 1775 under Captain Henry Bellew. She sailed for North America on 14 September 1775 and took the Continental warship *Warren* on 26 August 1776. She returned to England, then sailed again for North America on 9 May 1777. She participated in the Delaware operation in October 1777. She wrecked in Jamaica Bay, Long Island, New York, on 11 February 1778. Length of gun deck 118 feet 4 inches, length of keel 97 feet 7¼ inches, breadth 33 feet 8½ inches, depth of hold 10 feet 6 inches, 589 85/94 tons bm.

2 Navesink is an area within Monmouth County, New Jersey that includes the Atlantic shoreline just to the south of Sandy Hook. In 1665, a patent for a tract of land in East Jersey, called the Monmouth or Navesink Patent, was given for a triangular shaped area that extended from Sandy Hook to the mouth of the Raritan River, upstream approximately 25 miles (40 km), and then southeast to Barnegat Bay.

On Board the *Spy*, Sandy hook, June 30th to July 6th 1776
27th. Week.

30. Su. very hot M^{g}. calm, XI, pleasant breeze
[1. M.] hot M^{g}. [July][3] IX. Pleasant air—were told that the Rebells had got a drubbing at S^{t}.John & were driven out of Canada with great Loss—weigh'd Anchor, work'd up Nearthe Narrows.
Weigh'd anchor about 7 ev^{g}. from Sandy hook & Work'd up to Gravesend near ye Narrows 18 miles from N Y —

2. Tu. this M^{g}. weigh'd but ye W^{d}. coming a head, soon came to anchor—some ships Pass'd the Narrows, several shott were fir'd—

3. [Landed][4] W. this M^{g}. the first line of Our Army landed on Staaten Island. Ev^{g}. work'd higher up the River, &, about 11 at Night Most of our army was landed.
Landed on Staaten Island

4. Th. the Troops march'd to their several Cantonements round the Island—40 Quarter'd on the road between Richmond & Amboy from much firing this M^{g}—of great Guns, very hot day
March'd to our several cantonements round Staaten Island—The People (a few who had fled from their Habitations excepted) seem very glad at our coming amongst them; & supply us with provisions at reasonable rates—we march'd about 12 miles from ye Landing Place[5]—to A—Woglam's several people from long Island & some from the Jerseys came in—
'Tis most Wonderful that people who might be & were extreamly happy, should give up such delightful habitations to run wantonly into Rebellion, & They know not for what—but that they are led a stray by a Set of designing iniquitous Men—
Genl. Washington Com^{ds}. in N York & its said has about 30,000 Men W^{t}. him—
The Prickly pear grows in great plenty on this Island, but very low & small & almost without prickles.

5. F. dull M^{g}. X cleard hot day
Many of the Inhabitants came to meet us.

6. Sa. hot, mov'd our Quarters, father to ye left nearer Amboy ferry—
To McLean a Doll^{r} £ — 4:8

3 On this line, the characters '1.M.' and 'July' are written in red ink.
4 The word 'landed' is written vertically in the margin with each letter above the next.
5 The landing place was on the north shore of Staten Island. After landing, Bamford's unit marched about 12 miles to the residence of Abraham Woglom (1759-1780), located on Staten Island's south shore—in an area of the island that is today known as Rossville. The Woglom residence was along the shore of the present-day Arthur Kill waterway. The editor thanks Dr. Phillip Papas for this information. Woglom is a simplification of the family's Dutch surname: van Woggelum.

Staaten Island—July 7th. to July 13th. 1776
28th. Week.

7. Su. very hot day. Got a small portmantua [illegible words crossed out] from on board.

Piquet G[d].

The Militia of the Island near 400 men assembled at Richmond & took y[e]. Oaths&c[a]. to his Majesty—

We hear that Gen[l]. Burgoyne has cros'd the Lakes [I believe not],[6] & taken Gen[l]. Thomas & his Garrison at Fort Edward Prisoners [S[t]. John's rather I suppose.][7] —

8. M. hot M[g]. brisk W[d]. N,W— caught a small fish commonly call'd a Sea horse, in a Net tis a small fish, w[t]. an head like an horse & crest—

9. Tu. very hot day almost calm. its said Gen[l]. Washington has left N. York w[t]. about 30,000 Men; & gon to Kings bridge, about 14 miles from York where he is Entrenching—[8]

10. W. very hot day—brisk W[d]. N,W—

Piquet G[d]—

11. Th. dull M[g]— some heavy rain, + Lightning & Thunder

6 The words between brackets are an interlineal note above the underlined words preceding it.

7 The words between brackets are an interlineal note above the underlined words preceding it.

8 This entry from the 'Remarks' page is undated, but has a small line at that top that separates it from the preceding entry that is placed under 7 July and also seems to link it to the entry on the facing page for 9 July 1776.

12 F. very hot day. 2 comp^{ys}. mov'd to ye Left— Two men of war [*Phenix*[9] & *Rose*][10] (& some transports) [no transports][11] went up the North River much firing of Cannon as they pass'd the Town—

Lord How w^{t}. a part [small part] [no part][12] of his Fleet came into the Hook—he sail'd after ye Fleet from England, a few days—(The 17th. Light Dragoons we hear are landed—17th not arriv'd—[13]

There are so many Stories circulated that 'tis impossible to know what to depend on—indeed most of y^{m} are false—

Lord Howe did not sail till 4 days after his fleet, & put into Hallifax— & came in here Without any of his fleet.

'Tis said Gen. Washington is gone South to fortify Philadelphia—false—he is at N York—

13. Sa. dull M^{g}— L^{t}. Hasset[14] 10th was wounded, in endeavouring to prevent a boat passing — — — he died next M^{g}.

Staaten Island—July 14th. to July 20th. 1776
29. Week.

14. Su. very wet M^{g}. Calm—X W. rains. pm 111 rains W^{d}. N. E. blows fresh—Some firing last N^{t}. towards Elizabeth Town Point—IV ceas'd raining—dull

---

9 The 44-gun, fifth rate frigate *Phoenix* was built at Limehouse by John & Robert Batson in 1758-59 and completed at Deptford Dockyard in 1759. The ship was commissioned in 1759 under the brief command of Captain HRH Prince Edward Augustus. Later in 1759 under Captain Christopher Bethell, the ship was in Boys's squadron of Dunkirk and in the blockade of Basque Roads. In 1762, she captured the French 24-gun *La Folle*. She sailed to the Mediterranean, Africa, and the West Indies in 1763. She sailed on a mission to Algiers in 1765, and was on the coast of Africa in 1766-1768 before being paid off in 1771. After a great repair at Portsmouth, she recommissioned in 1775 under Captain Hyde Parker, who remained in command until 1780. She sailed for North America on 14 September 1775 and was in the New York operation in 1776, the Hudson River action on 9 October 1776, at Sandy Hook on 22 July 1778, the action between Howe and d'Estaing on 11 August 1778, and at Savannah in December 1778. Refitted at Plymouth in 1779, she was with Harvey's fleet, and the relief of Guernsey in September 1779. She sailed as escort for the West Indies convoy on 25 December 1779 and later foundered in a hurricane off Cuba on 4 October 1780, with her crew being saved. As later remeasured: length of gun deck 140 feet 9 inches, length of keel 116 feet 10¾ inches, breadth 37 feet 1 ⅜ inches, depth of hold 16 feet, 856 41/94 tons bm.

10 The ship names between brackets are in a note at the bottom of page marked for insertion here.

11 The words between brackets are an interlineal note above the underlined words preceding it.

12 The two sets of brackets are successive corrections to the original entry and are written above the words 'a part'. The words 'no part' appear to be the latest correction.

13 The underlined words are a later correction.

14 John Blennerhassett was commissioned an ensign in the 10th Regiment of Foot at Québec on 6 February 1772 and died of his wounds on 14 July 1776, after 4.4 years' service. George Inman, comp., 'Losses of the Military and Naval Forces Engaged in the War of the American Revolution', *The Pennsylvania Magazine of History and Biography*, 27 (1903), p.178, records that 'Lieutenant Blennerhassett' was killed on Staten Island, but War Office records do no show that he was promoted to lieutenant. An undocumented note in the possesion of J.A. Houlding records that he was known to have been killed by a hidden sniper.

Muster'd this M^{g}.

15. M. some rain last N^{t}. pleasant M^{g}. cool W^{d}. N,E—XII, W.

Carrigan of C^{t}. Duffs[15] com^{py}. was stabb'd by Northington—being got upon his Wife—died in ½ hour

NB Northington after stabbing Carrigan stabb'd his wife & then stabb'd himself & attempted to throw himself again on his bayonet. (he wounded himself & wife slightly)—

Some Tenders which went avove ye Town w^{t}. the men of war came down; to have more ships sent up, as the Country people come in so fast that the Ships are all full which went up—wants confirmation. false.

We are told a flag of Truce was sent into York by Lord How, to know if the People would accept of his Majesty's Clemency—they have desir'd 3 days to give their answer—They saluted ye boat. going in & returning. This the report [lie][16] of the Day—

We hear the Purport of the Flag was to tell the Rebels if they destroy'd York, as it was said they determin'd to do, that we would carry fire & Sword, through the provinces concern'd in burning it.

The Ships as they went up Above the Town cannonaded a Camp of ye Rebels & kill'd a great many men; for they were order'd under Arms to see the ships sunk by their Batteries.

16. Tu. bright M^{g}.

√ To McLean a Doll^{r}. lent — — £ — 4 : 8

17. W. bright M^{g}. pleasant Am—

18. Th. grey M^{g}. cool & pleasant—E—

19. F. bright M^{g} blows fresh—W—

20. Sa. very calm M^{g}—hot—XII light W^{d}. S,W—

a body of the Rebels w^{t}. colours flying red, blue, green, & yellow, march'd down towards Amboy ferry.

---

15 James Duffe was born in Scotland in 1734). He was commissioned an ensign in Drumlanrig's new-raising regiment in the Scots-Dutch Brigade on 2 June 1747 and went onto Dutch half pay when the regiment disbanded in 1749. From the Scots-Dutch brigade as a lieutenant he became a lieutenant in Scotland in the Earl of Eglintoun's new-raising 62nd (later 77th) Foot on 11 January 1757. He was promoted to captain in the 77th Foot on 19 October 1762 in a free death-vacancy. He went onto British half pay when the regiment disbanded on 10 April 1764. He transferred from half pay as captain in the 40th Foot in Ireland on 28 February 1766. He was promoted to brevet major on 29 August 1777 and retired on 26 January 1780, after 21.2 years in British service.

16 The word 'lie' is written above the underlined word 'report'.

The Report now is, that Genl Burgoyne has cut 1500 of the Rebels to pieces at Fort S^{t}. Johns & that Lt Col.^{o} Paterson Adj^{n}. Genl.,[17] went into N. York w^{t}. a Flag of Truce ye last confim'd—

Many deserters come in.

our ships That sail'd above ye Town were at first well supply'd by the country people, which Genl. Washington being told of sent 3 New England Reg^{ts}. up which put a stop to y^{r} being further supply'd—

Staaten Island, July 21st. to July 27th. 1776
30th. Week.

21. Su. hot bright M^{g}.—calm—XII light W^{d}. E—some showers this day

Several Ships are seen coming in they are 7 ships from Boston w^{t}. part of the R^{l} Highlanders & Frazers Batt^{n}— they put in to Boston, landed at the Lighthouse, drove away the Rebels & brought off the Flag—

22. M. hot day E—

Same comp^{ys} of the Rebels, marched from Amboy towards Elizabeth town. I suppose they were reliev'd by those that march'd last Saturday—

28. Tu. hot M^{g}. Calm X S,E— An officer & 12 men of ye Rebels landed near the Quarters of 10th. Reg^{t}. to take off 2 sentrys posted by the waterside, the sentrys fir'd on them kill'd the officer ye Rest ran to y^{r}. boat & made off—

24. W. hot M^{g}. light W^{d}. S,W—p. m. VIII very heavy rain w^{t}. a great deal of Lightening & Thunder—the Rebels much alarm'd in the shower y^{e}. beat to Arms, in y^{r}. cantonem^{ts}. in ye Jerseys

25. Th. hot M^{g}. little W^{d}. N—p.m. II pleasant cool breeze N,W—

---

17 James Paterson was born in Scotland in 1732. He was commissioned 2nd Lieutenant in the 7th Marines on 17 May 1744 by purchase vice an augmentation. He was promoted to 1st Lieutenant in the 7th Marines on 22 November 1746 by purchase vice a retirement. He went onto British half pay when the regiment disbanded on 3 November 1748. He transferred from half pay as lieutenant in the 31st Regiment of Foot in England on 18 March 1748/49. He was promoted to captain in the new-raising 18th Company of Marines on 18 July 1755, then became captain in the 19th Foot in England on 25 August 1756 in a free augmentation vacancy. He was promoted to major in the 19th Foot on 24 November 1761 by purchase vice a retirement. Thereafter, he was promoted to lieutenant colonel in the 63rd Foot in Guadeloupe on 15 June 1763 by purchase vice a retirement. He was promoted to brevet colonel on 29 August 1777, then to major general on 20 November 1782. He became colonel of the 28th Foot on 13 July 1787 and died 6 July 1789 after 44.7 years' service. Here and subsequently, Bamford refers to Paterson as adjutant general. On 18 April 1776, General Sir William Howe appointed Paterson 'Adjutant General of the army under his command, & he is to be obeyed as such'; see Benjamin Franklin Stevens (ed.), *General Sir William Howe's Orderly Book at Charlestown, Boston and Halifax, June 17, 1775 to 1776 26 May.* (London: B.F. Stevens, 1890, reprint, Port Washington, NY: Kennikat Press, 1970), pp.254-55. I am grateful to Professor Gregory J.W. Urwin for this reference.

Some Sloops belonging to the Inhabitants of Staaten Island, were fir'd on by the Rebels as they pass'd Amboy [from a Battery there][18] we were returned the Comp^{t} which they did not expect & Kill'd & Wound'd a good many people—They did not know we had cannon against them.

26. F. very hot M^{g}. X pleasant breeze N—A N York newspaper has some remarkable Expressions such as—the insidious Court Of Great Britain—what the People are to expect from the clemency of their late King & the Prayers for the King chang'd for this Common Wealth.

Two sloops pass'd Amboy, the Rebels did not molest them; they suffer'd too much yesterday—& did us no hurt—They fir'd small Arms At the Sloops, from the Shore all along the River, tho' the shot could not reach them—

Tis said, a manifesto is to be publish'd offering a General pardon to all the Americans who will return to their Allegiance, & if they Labour under any real Grievance, they shall be redress'd—can such Terms be REJECTED—

The Rebels have several small Encampm^{ts} on the Jersey shore, opposite to our Quarters.

A report from the Rebels that Genl Clinton was defeated at Charles Town—partly confirm'd—

27. Sa. very hot calm M^{g}—XII, light W^{d}. S,E— some Ships came into ye Hook. They were some prizes brought in by y^{e} *Liverpool* Frigate.

Staaten Island July 28th. to Augst. 3d. 1776
31st. Week.

28. Su. very hot calm M^{g}—Aft^{n}. light W^{d}. S,E.

reported y^{t}. Genl Burgoyne died near Albany of a bilious fever—y^{t}. Parts of Lord Howes fleet are coming in—y^{t}. a flag of Truce was sent in from N York contents not transpir'd—All Lies—

29. M. Close dull M^{g}. very sultry—XII light W^{d}. S this N^{t}. very heavy rain, W^{t}. most Violent Lightning & Thunder Several Ships coming in—

The 17th. Light Dragoons from Hallifax & part of the 1st. Division of the Hessians are come in—reported that L^{d}. Sterling a Maj^{r}. Genl. in the Rebel service was among the Kill'd at Amboy, 25th. inst:[19]—Lt Drag^{s}. Landed—

18 The words between brackets are an interlinear insertion.

19 William Alexander was born in New York City, the son of a lawyer. Between 1756 and 1759, he claimed the dormant earldom of Stirling as the eldest son of the first earl's paternal grandfather. The House of Lords denied the claim in 1762, but William Alexander continued to style himself as Lord Stirling. At the outbreak of the American Revolution, he became a colonel in the New Jersey militia. In 1776, the Continental Congress commissioned him as a brigadier general. He commanded the 1st Maryland Regiment in the Battle of Long Island in August 1776 and was captured. On his release, he was promoted to major general and fought at Trenton, Brandywine, Germantown, and Monmouth. In 1781, he commanded the Northern Army on the Hudson River during the Franco-American Yorktown campaign. He died in 1783.

30. Tu. close hot M^{g}. W—X bright very hot. XI pleasant breeze N— A [total][20] Eclipse of the moon, very plain & fine.

To McLean a Doll^{r}. lent — — — — £ — 4 : 8

31. W. very hot calm M^{g}. The Light Drag^{ns}. Landed on Staaten Is^{ld}.—

1. [Th.] very hot M^{g}. [August.][21]

Violent Lightning Thunder & Rain y^{s} N^{t}. Gen. Clinton from Carolina Arriv'd

Genl Clinton w^{t}. the Army [8 Regim^{ts}.][22] from Charles Town S^{h}. Carolina Arriv'd—The ships got a good drubbing. C^{t}. Scott[23] kill'd Sr Peter Parker[24] Wound^{d}. & several others kill'd & wound'd, the Army were not Land^{d}.—Two 50 gun ships were lightned, to get over the Bar and attacked the ye Batteries w^{t}. their upper deck guns only, ye Lower being taken out—Quere, were not Frigates nearly Equal—

The *Acteon*[25] & *Sphinx*[26] ran foul & went aground the former was burn'd by ye Captain without Orders—he was try'd, but acquitted—The Ships did not go within

---

20 The word between brackets is an interlineal insertion…

21 On this line the characters '1. Th.' and 'August' are written in red ink.

22 The information between brackets is an interlineal insertion.

23 Captain Alexander Scott, Royal Navy, commanded the 50-gun, fourth rate *Experiment.* He was wounded, not killed. Having lost his left hand, he relinquished command on 30 June and was sent home. Scott had been commissioned a lieutenant in the Royal Navy on 14 March 1770, then promoted to commander on 15 March 1770, and to captain on 25 April 1776, He was promoted to superannuated rear admiral on 9 July 1794 and died in 1811.

24 Peter Parker was born in 1721, joined the Royal Navy at early age, and was commissioned a commander on 17 March 1735. He was promoted to captain on 6 May 1747 and retired from the service in 1763. Knighted in 1772, he returned to the Navy in 1773 and was promoted to rear admiral of the blue on 20 May 1777, to rear admiral of the white on 23 January 1778, and to rear admiral of the red on 29 January 1779. He was made a general of the marines in 1779, then promoted to vice admiral of the blue on 29 March 1779 and to vice admiral of the white on 26 September 1780. Created a baronet on 13 January 1783, he became Member of Parliament for Seaford from 1784 to 1786, then Member of Parliament for Maldon from 1787 to 1790. He was promoted to admiral of the blue on 24 September 1787, to admiral of the white on 12 April 1794, and to admiral of the fleet on 16 September 1799. He died in 1811. See *Oxford Dictionary of National Biography* and *History of Parliament.* http://www.historyofparliamentonline.org/volume/1754-1790/member/parker-sir-peter-1721-1811

25 The 28-gun, sixth rate frigate *Acteon* was built at Woolwich by William Gray and completed by Nicolas Philips in 1772-1775. Commissioned on 19 June 1775 under Captain Christopher Atkins, she sailed for North America on 29 August 1775, but ran aground on the Shingles Bank off Poole. Docked for repairs, she sailed again for North America in January 1776 with the convoy going to Charleston, South Carolina. During the operations against Charleston, she grounded during the attack on Fort Sullivan on 29 June 1776 and was burnt to avoid capture. Length of gun deck 120 feet 6 inches, length of keel 99 feet 6 inches, breadth 33 feet 6 inches, depth of hold 11 feet ½ inch, 593 89/94 tons bm.

26 The 20-gun sixth rate *Sphinx* was built at Portsmouth by Edward Hunt in 1773-1775. Commissioned in 1775 under Captain Anthony Hunt, she sailed for North America on 23 February 177. After serving with Parker's squadron at Charleston in 1776, she took two American privateers in 1777. In 1778, she was with Howe during his encounter with d'Estaing on 11 August 1778. In 1779, she was in the Leeward Islands and captured a 32-gun French warship off Martinique. She paid off in 1780 and underwent a middling repair at Deptford. Recommissioned in 1783, she sailed for the Mediterranean and paid off in 1786. Undergoing a middling and great repair, she recommissioned in 1790. She was in the East

a mile of the Batteries, tho' they might have got within a few Yards of them. seems bad conduct—the *Glasco* Pacquet was burn'd. The Rebels had a Battery on Sulivans Island at the mouth of the River—ye bugbear to ye Men of War.

The Pilot ran the *Acteon, Sphynx* & *Syren*[27] aground the attack was 28th. June. L^t^. Pike[28] of y^e^ *Active*[29] kill'd. Capt Morris[30] lost his right arm & died—

2. F. cool M^g^. W.

3. Sa. pleasant cool M^g^. N,W—

Staaten Isl^d^. August 4th. to August 10th. 1776
32d. Week.

4. Su. hot calm M^g^.—XI light W^d^. S,W Many Ships this day come in—Rec^d^. my Abstract from the Paymaster—to 24th: inst. Shea 40th. Deserted. [he][31] Swam across ye River

Indies in 1795, with Elphinstone at the surrender of the Dutch Fleet in Saldanha Bay in 1796, at the capture of Foul Point, Madagascar, in 1796, and at the Cape of Good Hope in 1797-1799. Thereafter, she was placed in ordinary and eventually broken up in 1811. Length of gun deck 108 feet, length of keel 89 feet 7 ⅜ inches, breadth 30 feet 1 inch, depth of hold 9 feet 8 inches, 431 37/98 tons bm.

27 The 28-gun sixth rate *Enterprise* class frigate *Siren* was built at Chatham by Henniker & Co. in 1771-1773, and completed at Chatham Dockyard in 1775. She commissioned in August 1775 under Captain Tobias Furneaux and sailed for North America 9 November 1775. After serving in the Charleston operation in 1776, she grounded off Point Judith, Rhode Island, on 6 November 1777. She was abandoned under the fire from shore with 15 killed and 20 wounded. Length of gun deck 120 feet 10 inches, length of keel 99 feet 7½ inches, breadth 33 feet 9 inches, depth of hold 10 feet 9 inches, 603 40/94 tons bm.

28 Richard Pike was commissioned a lieutenant in the Royal Navy on 18 December 1774. He was killed in action. The list of ships and vessels in sea pay for June 1776 (TNA, ADM 8/52, printed in Clark et al (eds.), *Naval Documents*, vol. 5, p.1363), lists him as Edward Pike, but Syrett and DiNardo identify him as Robert Pike.

29 The 28-gun sixth rate *Coventry* class frigate *Active* was built at Rotherhithe by Thomas Stanton & Co. in 1757-58 and completed at Deptford Dockyard in 1758. She served in Howe's squadron in 1758 and sailed for the Mediterranean in 1759. Then, was in Jamaica in 1763 and was paid off in 1769. After repairs at Sheerness, she recommissioned in 1771 and was in the West Indies in 1771, the Leeward Islands in 1772 and North American waters in 1773. Paid off in 1774, she recommissioned in 1775 under Captain William Williams and sailed from Cork to North America on 12 February 1776. She joined Parker's squadron at Charleston, and thereafter sailed for Jamaica in 1777. In August 1778, she was dismasted in a hurricane and taken as a prize by the French. Brought into the French Navy as *L'Active* she remained in French service until condemned at Brest in 1794. Length of gun deck 118 feet 4 inches, length of keel 97 feet 5 ⅜ inches, breadth 33 feet 10½ inches, depth of hold 10 feet 6 inches, 594 87/94 tons bm.

30 John Morris was commissioned a lieutenant in the Royal Navy on 10 July 1755. He was promoted to commander on 7 January 1771, and to captain on 15 October 1775. Morris had commissioned the newly built 50-gun fourth rate *Bristol* on October 1775 and with the broad pennant of Commodore Peter Parker had sailed for North America on 12 February 1776. Morris lost his right arm in the action against Sullivan's Island on 18 June 1776 and died on board the hospital ship *Pallas* on 2 July 1776.

31 The word between square brackets is an interlinear insertion.

5. M. hot M^{g}. S,E— several Ships coming in—of L^{d}. Howe's fleet. caught some Eels—several Transports Arriv'd, with [part of] the Guards Hessian & Highlanders—

'Tis said—that the Rebels had fitted out a Fire ship, to destroy the 2 ships which went above N. York; they came down w^{t}. some scows w^{t}. Cannon & a Number of boats, to attack the Ships; the *Phenix* which lay highest up in ye River Let them come very near her; them open'd and soon sunk the Fire ship [&][32] some of the Scows; in the confusion, the remainder of the boats & scows fell down to the *Rose*, who got between them & the shore, & drove them to the opposite side where they took refuge in an house, C^{t}. Wallace of the *Rose* landed his Marines, beat them from the House, set it on fire, & brought off a Number of Cattle—

The *Liverpool* Frigate has brought in a Prize worth 10,000 £ —silks & rich Goods from Holland.

6. Tu. hot M^{g} brisk W^{d}. S,W—

7. W. very hot foggy M^{g}.—VII clear and very hot S,W—X Exceedingly hot, little W^{d}.S— XII pleasn^{t}. breeze E—some heavy rain This Ev^{g}.

8. Th. dull close M^{g}. very sultry [&][33] calm—

9. F. close hot day W^{d}. Variable

10. S. hot day pm, II pleasant W^{d}. E—

Staaten Isld. August 11th. to August 17th. 1776
33d. Week.

11. Su. close dull M^{g}.—some showers, S,W much Lightning Thunder & Rain this Eve^{g}—

A report, that Genl Burgoine has got as far as Albany—wants confirmation—& I Fear he never will get to Albany

12. M. cloudy M^{g}. Cool, W—A number of L^{d}. Howe's fleet came in—

Lord Dunmore w^{t}, a Fleet from Virginia bringing about 1500 men came in; among those are many negroes.

~~To Enn C—h—re~~[34] ~~lent 10 Dr.~~—P^{d}. — ~~£ 2 6:8~~

13. Tu. very hot bright M^{g}. little W^{d}. W— caught a fish call'd a Sheep's head, & some black fish. like Tench—

14. W. hot M^{g}. little W^{d}. E— caught some black fish—Ships continue to come in—

32 The word between square brackets is an interlinear insertion.
33 The word between square brackets is an interlinear insertion.
34 Ensign Edward Cheshire.

15. Th. rain'd all last N^{t}., very wet M^{g}.—E— X, ceased to rain, cloudy—several drizling showers this day— The Hessians landing to Encamp—
To Maj^{r}. Bradstreet,[35] lent 40 Doll^{rs}. P^{d}. 9: 6:8

16 F. close cloudy M^{g}—heavy showers, last N^{t}—W. Observ'd the Rebels marching towards York w^{t}. 2 peices of Cannon & 5 Cover'd Waggons; Escorted by about 50 men, on the Jersey side—heard they were leaving Amboy—some Showers this Eve^{g}.
To Maj^{r}. Bradstreet 10 Doll^{rs}. P^{d}. £2.. 6.. 8
{in all 50 Doll^{rs}. due me by ye Maj^{r}} P^{d}.

26th March 1777 rec^{d}. the above 50 Doll^{rs}. from L^{t}. Doyle[36] on Acct. of Maj^{r}. Bradstreet & at same time p^{d}. him 9/7 charg^{d}. on Acct of Murray Dead of my Co—

17. Sa. a good deal of rain last N^{t}. showers this M^{g}—N,W—IX soaking rain—
Sent 200 Doll^{rs} to be lock'd up on board the *Wm & Mary* by Maj^{r} Bradstreet. Note the Major put them on board the *Spy*. The Major gave me these 200 Doll^{rs} back again.

35 Samuel Bradstreet was born in England in 1734. He was commissioned an ensign in the 40th Foot on 27 March 1753 by purchase vice a resignation. He was promoted to lieutenant in the 40th Foot on 29 June 1755in a free vacancy vice an augmentation, to captain in the 40th Foot in 10 November 1761 by purchase vice a resignation, to major in the 40th Foot on 11 December 1775 by purchase vice a promotion to a colonelcy. He died of disease on 10 December 1779, while the regiment was in Antigua, after 26.7 years' service.

36 John Doyle was born in Ireland in 1756, He was commissioned an ensign in the 48th Foot in Ireland on 14 March 1771. He was promoted to lieutenant in the 48th Foot on 17 September 1773 by purchase vice a retirement. He exchanged to lieutenant in the 40th Foot in Ireland on 1 March 1775, then resigned on 24 October 1778 to take up provincial commission on 26 May 1778 as captain in the loyalist Volunteers of Ireland. He was promoted to major in the Volunteers of Ireland on 15 March 1782, a corps taken onto the regular British Establishment in 1782 as 105th Foot. He went onto Irish half pay when the 105th Foot disbanded on 31 January 1784. From half pay, he was promoted in Ireland to lieutenant colonel commandant of his own new-raising 87th Foot on 18 September 1793.

14

Long Island, 18 August 1776–14 September 1776

Staaten Isl^{d}. & Long Isl^{d}: August 18th. to August 24th. 1776
34th. Week.

18. Su. heavy rain all last N^{t}. very wet M^{g}. NE. much cannonading this M^{g}. towards York—The two Men of War came down into ye Fleet from their Station above the Town.

19. M. wet last N^{t}. wet M^{g}. X ceas'd raining Aft^{n}. pleasant. A Comp^{y}. of ye Hessian Troops Encamp'd close by our Quarters, we remov'd—

20. Tu. This M^{g}. at IV The 8 Comp^{s}. of the 40th. Reg^{t}. march'd from Their cantonem^{ts}. To the Landing place & Embark'd on board y^{e} *Wm. & Mary*—The Troops march'd from their several cantonements & Encampm^{ts}., & Embark'd on board their ships—

21. W. Rain last N^{t}. pleasant M^{g}. little W^{d}.
The Embarkation was finish'd & the Order of Landing given out—

22. Th. raind w^{t} Lightning & Thunder last N^{t}.
This day about IX M^{g}. our Army landed on Long Isl^{d}. at a place call'd Gravesend,[1] without opposition, some of ye L^{t}. I^{y}. march'd into ye Country—
The Army Landed on Long Island about IX this M^{g}. without Opposition. The L^{t}. Infantry push'd into the Country & got as far as flat Bush about 6 miles from the Landing Place.

23. F. pleasant M^{g}.—Landing Artillery, Stores, &c^{a}.
Various Reports, none to be depended on
Piquet G^{d}. Advanc'd—

1 Gravesend is on the southwestern end of Long island. It was one of the first Dutch settlements of New Netherlands, then one of the six chartered towns of King's County in the colony of New York. Today, it is a neighborhood in the New York City borough of Brooklyn.

24. Sa. Warm M^{g}. some rain last N^{t}— 'tis reported y^{t}. the Hessians, hang'd 3 Rebels which they took Prisoners,—contradicted.

Several Bullocks were landed which came from England—So poor they can scarcely stand—

There has been much firing between our Advanc'd Parties & the Rebels who keep in y^{e}. Woods—we have had 3 or 4 kill'd & a few Wounded—We took some prisoners—

Long Isl^{d}. August 25th. to August 31st. 1776
35th. Week.

25. Su. very heavy rain last N^{t}. dull M^{g}.—W— about 4000 Hessians came over from Staaten Isl^{d}.

26. M. Much Lightning & Thunder last N^{t}. gloomy day— March'd from ye Ferry Cantonem^{ts} about IX this Eve^{g}.

the 4th. & 6th. Brigades [under Genl Grant][2] march'd from their cantonem^{ts}. about IX at N^{t}. they March'd towards Brookline Ferry, the York Comp^{ys}. march'd on y^{r}. Flanks; surpriz'd some [small][3] posts of the Enemy on the road & took some prisoners. Maj^{r} Byrd taken.[4]

27. [Battle][5] Tu. fine M^{g}.— About VII this M^{g}. a sharp action w^{t}. the Rebels. they were defeated—we lost but a few Men & some officers, Coll^{o} Grant[6] of 40th. Reg^{t} Kill'd—

About VII in the M^{g}. we discover'd the Enemy drawn up on an hill [on our right Flank];[7] our Advanc'd Guard was fir'd upon from an Orchard; the Enemy were soon drove from thence; & we march'd to gain the Hills, the Enemy firing on us from the Woods, when we had possessed the Heights, the enemy pour'd A very heavy fire upon us from the woods, we drove them into the thickest part, & there kept them in awe as we found they had great Numbers conceal'd in the woods, we did not think it prudent to pursue them, but drew up on the Heights & lay on our Arms. About one the L^{t}. Infantry & G^{ds}. w^{t}. part of G^{l}. Howe's Army [from Flatbush][8] having

---

2 The words between brackets are an interlinear insertion.

3 The word between brackets is an interlinear insertion.

4 In is not clear from the context whether Major Byrd was an American or a British officer. If he were British, it is likely that this is John Bird, who was born in England in 1729. Bird was commissioned an ensign in the 19th Foot in Flanders on 23 May 1746, by purchase. He was promoted to lieutenant in the 19th Foot on 24 April 1755 by purchase vice a resignation, He served as adjutant from 14 April 1756 to 11 August 1759. Promoted to captain-lieutenant of the 19th Foot on 11 August 1759, probably by purchase, vice a retirement, he was subsequently promoted to captain in the 19th Foot on 15 July 1761, by purchase, then promoted to major of the 19th Foot on 26 May 1769 by purchase vice a retirement, to lieutenant colonel of the 15th Foot in Ireland on 13 January 1776 by purchase shortly before the regiment embarked for America. He was killed in action on 4 October 1777 at Germantown, after 31.4 years' service.

5 The word 'Battle' is written in the margin next to the date.

6 Lieutenant Colonel James Grant.

7 The words between square brackets are an interlinear insertion.

8 The words between square brackets are an interlinear insertion.

march'd to attack them by a road on the Right began to cannonade & attack w^{t}. small Arms, the Rebels finding themselves attack'd on both sides, after a good deal of resistance being very hard press'd gave way & ran in great confusion some were drown'd endeavoring to cross to a Mill on the opposite side; we took a number of Pris^{rs}. & kill'd a great many Men—the Enemy say they had 11,000 men to attack us, besides reinforcem^{ts}. y^{t}. came during ye Action—they Lost above 3000 Men—numbers are deserting. Our Loss very trifling—50, kill'd 260 Wounded a number of them slightly.

28. W. very pleasant M^{g}. Aft^{n}. rain—a great deal of Firing this Aft^{n}. Cannon & Musquetry

We got near 2000 head of Cattle which the Rebels would have drove off—

29. Th. gloomy M^{g}.

We began a Work to play on one of the Rebels Redoubts—call'd Putnam Fort—

30. F. This M^{g}. our Army Took Posession of the Enemy's works on this Isl^{d}. they having abandon'd them. & governours Isl^{d}—their chief works are near Brookline[9]—they went off in great hurry—

31. Sa. the Army March'd & Encamp'd on the Ground opposite N York & some went still more to the height—beyond Bedford—

Genl. Ld Stirling, Genl Sulivan, & a great number of officers are pris$^{rs.}$ with us—Maj^{r} Genl. Wogan[10] a Pris^{r}. w^{t}. us—we took 4 Brass field pieces, & the Ammunition—

We are since told that the Rebels had 18,000 or 19,000 men against us the 27th—

Long Isl^{d}. September 1st. to September 7th. 1776
36th Week.

[1. Su.][11] hot M^{g}. we hear that the Rebels are going from N York in ye Greatest hurry—They have strong Works behind N. York, towards Kings bridge[12]—

The Works which the Enemy Abandon'd are very Numerous & Strong; Redoubts & Lines either friez'd or pallisadoed & abatti round the Whole, [with][13] a communication from one to the other—One Work which they call Fort ~~Green~~ Putnam[14] is

9 i.e., Brooklyn

10 Brigadier General John Sullivan was the American general who was captured at Long Island.

11 The characters '1.Su.' are written in red ink.

12 King's Bridge was a bridge that Frederick Philipse, the major landowner in the area, built over the Spuyten Duyvil Creek in lower Westchester County in 1693. The bridge was part of the Boston Post Road, connecting Boston and New England with New York City. The Spuyten Duyvil Creek, or Harlem River, is a tidal estuary that delineates the northern end of Manhattan Island. The original site of the bridge was on a section of the creek that was re-rerouted and filled in during the late 19th century, but is roughly parallel to present-day 230th Street in the northwest section of the Bronx in New York City.

13 The word between square brackets in an interlineal insertion.

14 This fort, originally named Fort Putnam, was an earthwork built in 1776 under the direction of Major General Nathanael Greene of Rhode Island. Located in the area now called South

a round Redout rais'd high, w^{t}. a round Cavallier in the Center; it overlooks a large extent of Country—but of no strength against Cannon—when the Rebels abandon'd their Works, 30th. Augst. it was a very Thick fog in the M^{g}. they took that oppertunity to go off, went in great hurry & confusion, leaving several things behind; we had began approachs towards Their highest Redoubt—

The Rebels are throwing up a number of works on N York Isl^{d}. we are erecting Works opposite to them near Hell gates.[15]

Three Delegates[16] came from the Congress, but had the Insolence to Expect to treat [& be acknowledg'd][17] as Delegates from a separate power that had no Dependence on England—they would not be received as such & return'd Back.

When we beat the Rebels at Brooklyn, the 27th why were we not allow'd to pursue them when most numbers of them, panick struck, had thrown away their Arms, & fled in the greatest confusion, but we were stop'd to look at their Works which had not Men in them—I fear this may be set down among our other Blunders to prolong the war—

Tis most undoubted that had we taken the Advantage of this conquest at Brooklyn we might easily have put an End to the Rebellion, but perhaps our [blank space] do not think they have made sufficient fortunes.[18]

2. M. hot day.

This N^{t}. about XII, a number of our Flat boats, & a frigate [the *Rose*][19] pass'd theTown & went up E. River

Much firing of Cannon—

3. Tu. hot day, several Cannon fir'd this M^{g}—

4. W. hot day, brisk W^{d}—cannonading on both sides—

5. Th. pleasant cool M^{g}. Cannonading but seldom Aft^{n}. a great deal of Cannonading between the *Rose* Frigate & the Rebels from N York Isl^{d}.—

Advanc'd Picquet—

6. F. cool M^{g}. very little firing this day—

7. Sa. some rain last N^{t}—small thick rain this M^{g}. aft^{n}. fair & cool—

Brooklyn just south of the Brooklyn Navy Yard at Wallabout Bay, it faced the lower part of Manhattan across New York Harbor.

15 Hell Gate is a narrow tidal strait that connects the East River with Long Island Sound.

16 On 11 September 1776, Benjamin Franklin, John Adams, and Edward Rutledge met with General Howe at The Conference House at the southwestern tip of Staten Island. The American refused to accept Howe's offer of peace in exchange for withdrawing the Declaration of Independence.

17 The words between brackets are an interlineal insertion.

18 This paragraph is written at the bottom of the left-hand page facing the remarks section on the right-hand side. The editor has interpreted it as a continuation of the remarks on the facing page, rather than their beginning.

19 The ship's name in square brackets in an interlineal insertion.

Long Isl^{d}.—September 8th. to September 14th. 1776
37th. Week.

8. Su. some firing last N^{t}. rain this M^{g}—XI clear'd
Open'd a Batt^{y}. at Hell gates against the Rebels Strong redoubt, which they call a Fort—
√To McLean— — — —2 Doll^{rs}. lent— — — £ — 9 : 4

9. M. much firing of Artillery all day—Very hot day—
Our Batt^{rs}. near Hell gates, do not seem to have the desir'd Effect—as we are inform'd—
The Rebels have made N York Isl^{d}. a complicated peice of Fortification—have a Strong Redoubt near hell gates, against which our Batt^{ys}. are erected— & Breast Works all round the Isl^{d}. near the Water Edge, w^{t}. Batt^{ys}. at convenient distances & a great Number of Very Strong Red^{ts}. on the Higher grounds—

10. Tu. VIII began to rain—many showers this day—no firing this M^{g}—Many of our Flat boats pass'd the Town last N^{t}.

11. W. some rain last N^{t}. dull M^{g}. cool—
Our L^{t}, Infantry has taken possession of two Isl^{ds}. near Hell gates, Bahama[20] & Montresor's Islands—[21]

12. Th. cool M^{g}. much cañonading all M^{g}—'tis said the Hessians have taken an Isl^{d}. whereon the Rebels had a Batt^{y} of 3 Guns—

13. F. calm M^{g}— hot—XII, pleasant cool W^{d}—cloudy— This Aft^{n}. 4 Ships of War pass'd the Town & sail'd up the East River. The *Phenix*, *Roebuck*[22]

14 Sa. some rain this M^{g}. close & Sultry—

---

20 Great Barent's Island, now co-joined with Randall's Island, was renamed Ward's Island in 1784. Until the 1960s, there was a channel between the two islands called 'Little Hell Gate'.

21 Montresor's Island, owned by John Montresor from 1772 to 1783, lies in the East River at the mouth of the Harlem River. It is now known as Randall's Island.

22 The 44-gun, fifth rate *Roebuck* was built at Chatham by successive shipwrights Joseph Harris and William Gray to a design by Sir Thomas Slade in 1770-1774 and completed at Chatham in 1775. Commissioned in July 1775 under Captain Andrew Snape Hammond, she sailed for North America on 4 September 1775 and participated in the New York and Hudson River operations in 1776, then in 1777 was in the Delaware operations, took the South Carolina Navy brig *Defence*, and the Continental Navy sloop *Sachem*. In 1778, she was at Sandy Hook and in Howe's encounter with d'Estaing. In 1779, she took two American privateers and in 1780 was in the Charlestown operation, where she was flagship for Vice Admiral Marriott Arbuthnot. She took three prizes in 1781-82 before being paid off in 1783. In 1788-90, she recommissioned as a hospital ship, then served as a troop ship from 1793 until 1802. Thereafter, she served as a guard ship and floating battery, serving successively at Woolwich. Leith, and Yarmouth. She was broken up in 1811. Length of gun deck 140 feet, length of keel 115 feet 9 inches, breadth 37 feet 9 inches, depth of hold 16 feet 4 inches, 879 26/94 tons bm.

15

New York, 15 September 1776–31 December 1776

N: York Isl[d]—September 15th. to September 21st. 1776
38th. Week.

15. [Landed][1] Su. very hot day. Landed on N York Isl[d]. without opposition— lay on our Arms this Night, the Rebels went off in great hurry, from the Town towards Kings Bridge—

This M[g]. about V we march'd from our Encamp[mt]. near Bedford to the shore near where we Embark'd in flat Boats & landed at Kip's bay[2] without opposition, the Ships drew up Close to the Shore, & kept up a very hot Cannonade for some time before the boats row'd towards the Shore; the Enemy had breast works all along the shore, & numberless redoubts on the Higher Grounds—The Rebels quit their Batt[y] at Hell gates—We found that our Batt[ys] had greater Effect than we Expected, for most of the Guns in the Rebels Red[t]. are wounded & the face of the Batt[y] in ruins—they left 4 guns in the Red[t]. near Hell gates one [12 P[dr].][3] not spiked. Got possession of N York.

16. M. last N[t]. very cold—cool M[g]—no tents—a Sharp Skirmish between some of our Advanc'd Troops & the Rebels in y[e] Woods, we had <u>many</u> [91][4] Wounded very few kill'd [10 kill'd][5] —encamped near Hornshook,[6] on y[e] Common—

Our Advanced L[t] Infantry were fir'd on by the Rebels, a smart skirmish Ensued, the Highland Batt[rs]. march'd to support the L[t] Inf[y]. the Enemy after a great deal of Firing were beat off w[t]. much loss, but our men Advanc'd too far, when the Enemy fir'd on them w[t]. grape from 3 field pieces they brought w[t]. them, & kill'd some of

---

1 The word between brackets in a note in the margin.
2 Kip's Bay was an inlet on the east side of Manhattan Island, New York, where two streams entered the East River. The landing took place near the foot of present-day East 33rd Street.
3 The information between brackets is an interlinear insertion.
4 The number between brackets in an interlineal insertion.
5 The information between brackets in a note in the margin.
6 American forces had built a 9-gun star shaped earthwork battery at Horn's Hook beginning in February 1776, opposite Hell Gate and the islands in the East River near it. It was located near the present-day intersection of 89th Street and East End Avenue. In 1794, Archibald Gracie leveled the works and built a mansion, now the official residence of the mayor of New York City.

our men. we had a good many Wounded—but nothing to What might expected from so long & hot a fire—Pris^{rs}. say the Rebels had 8,000 men Engag'd—

17 Tu. Very wet M^{g}—p,m, I Cleared— No tents—built Wigwams— We cannot learn the loss of the Enemy—The Deserters tell us Genl. Thomas is killed— w^{t}. many Men—

18. W. hot sun—got our Tents— Moved our Encampm^{t}. about ½ mile to the Front—very rough Ground—much Labour to clear it—Deserters & Pris^{rs}. come in daily—

19. Th. hot sun— Advanc'd Piquet—

20. F. pleasant M^{g}. cool W^{d}—

This day a man on the Advanc'd picquet was shot through the Hand. (I think by himself) his hand was cut off—he said the Wood was full of ye Enemy he s^{d}. false

21. Sa last N^{t}. about XII, some Villians set the town of N York on fire; it burn'd Violently till X this M^{g}, seems to be something got under—it blew fresh all N^{t}.—w^{t}. some rain—four of The Villians who were caught in the fact—were hang'd up by the Heels, & put to death. several were taken & put in prison—in many parts of the Town combustibles were found conceal'd, ready to be set on fire. a large part of the Town, was consumed, about XII, the Fire was stop'd—near a fourth part of the Town is destroy'd—last night the Town of N York was set on fire & about a fourth part of it consumed—This was done by some disafected people who were suffer'd to remain in the Town, after the Rebel Army quitted it; 'tis said they were left on purpose.

N. York Isl^{d}. September 22d. to September 28th. 1776
39th. Week.

22. Su. bright hot M^{g}— Nathan Hales,[7] a Capt. in ye Rebel Army, & a Spy. was taken by Maj^{r} Rogers;[8] X this M^{g}. hang'd—he had several Papers w^{t}. acc^{ts}. of our Force &c^{a} he confess'd he was a spy—many deserters come in—

7 Nathan Hale was born in Connecticut in 1755. He graduated from Yale College in 1773 and became a school teacher in New London, Connecticut. He joined a Connecticut militia unit in 1775 and was elected a lieutenant. He accepted a commission in the 7th Connecticut Provincial Regiment. On 1 January 1776, the Continental Congress gave Hale a commission as captain in the successor unit to Connecticut regiment, the 19th Regiment of Foot of the Continental Army. While the 19th Foot was serving in New York, Hale volunteered on 8 September 1776 for the spying mission to report on British movements behind the lines. He was ferried from Norwalk, Connecticut, across to Long Island on 12 September and was apprehended in a tavern at Flushing Bay, Queens. At the age of 21, he was executed by hanging on 22 September 1776, probably in the Artillery Park next to the Dove Tavern that was near the present-day intersection of 66th Street and Third Avenue in New York City.

8 Major Robert Rogers, then of the Queen's Rangers, and earlier of Rogers' Rangers of the French and Indian War.

A Body of Our Troops march'd from their Encampment & Embark'd on board flat boats—it is said to make a descent in the Jerseys, but the W^{d}. blowing fresh & coming about contrary, they disembark'd & march'd back to their encampments—

23. M. hot day almost calm—

This M^{g}. about IV 200 Rebels under the Command of a Maj^{r}. came down from Kings Bridge, in boats to take possession of Montresors Island—ye Maj^{r} & about 50 land^{d} a Capt^{s} Picq^{t}. attack'd y^{m} beat y^{m}. off kill'd some & took ye Maj^{r}. & 14 men prisn^{rs}.

The Above s^{d}. Troops embark'd this day about 2 oClock & landed at Paulus Hook in ye Jerseys without opposition—most of them return'd in y^{e}. eve^{g}— the 57th. Reg^{t}. remained—

The 57th. Reg^{t}. attack'd a Redoubt which the Rebels had on an hill above their post & carried it w^{t}. very little resistance; there were 3 Guns in the Work, which our Men turn'd on ye Enemy as soon as they took it—

24. Tu. pleasant M^{g}. walk'd to N York, it's a deserted Place—about a 5th. part of the Town consum'd—scarcely any of the Inhabitants, in Town—

25. W. pleasant day, very cool M^{g}—To W^{m} U—n — lent 2 Doll^{rs}. ——— £ — 9 : 4

26. Th. warm M^{g}—hot day got my small Portmantua from on board y^{e} *Wm & Mary*.

27. F. very cool M^{g}— dull—XII very hot sun—Some Cannonading at Powlers hook[9] this M^{g}—

Genl. Prescott Exchang'd for Genl Sullivan[10]

28. Sa. Very cool Bright M^{g}—brisk W^{d}.—A note from Col^{o}. Paterson—went to wait on him, could not meet him—

The Rebels took all the Bells out of the Churches to cast into cannon & all the Leads even from the Windows to cast into bullets—

The Rebels took the bells out of the Steeples, to cast into cannon, & the Leads which held up the Sashes of the Windows to make ball of. They even took down the Kings Statue[11] for the same purpose, imagining it had been Lead, but were deceiv'd.

---

9 Paulus Hook, New Jersey. Located one mile across the Hudson River from Manhattan. In 1776, the American built a fort here, along with others on the west bank of the Hudson, to guard the natural approach from New York City to New Jersey.

10 General Howe had proposed the prisoner exchange, which the Continental Congress approved on 4 September 1776. Following the American seizure of Montréal in 1775, Richard Prescott, then a brigadier general attempted to escape with the 7th Regiment of Foot down the St. Lawrence River. The advancing American forces under Montgomery seized Prescott at Sorel in November 1775 and held him as a prisoner of war. British forces captured Brigadier General John Sullivan at Flatbush Pass during the Battle of Long Island on 27 August 1776.

11 The 8-foot high 4, 000 pound (1,800 kg) gilded equestrian statue of King George III in Roman Dress by Joseph Wilton stood on an 8-foot high marble plinth in Bowling Green at the southern end of Broadway in New York City. Captain Oliver Brown and a group

one Scoundrel [Dyking][12] had the Impudence to kick the Head about the street. Tis almost incredible to think that this Rebellion should be so universelly diffus'd over our Colonies, & that a few wicked designing men could have such [art &][13] influence, & carry their Point in opposition to some of the first men on the Continent. & that Many of Sence & affluence, who had nothing to fear and scarcly any thing to wish, & whom no change could hardly better, should be led into so Idle, Vague, & Wanton a scheme. This May open their Eyes [that][14] they may see their Error, & avoid so desperate an undertaking for the Future—But I fear the old Hatred for Kings & the seeds of Sedition are so thickly sown among them, that it must be thrash'd out of them.

New England has poyson'd the Whole—[15]

N: York Isl^{d}. [& York Town][16]—September 29th. to October 5th. 1776
40th Week.

29. Su. dull M^{g}. some small rain—Work^{g}. Party

30. M. blew hard last N^{t}. fresh W^{d}. this M^{g}. rec^{d} a very genteel Letter from Col^{o}. Paterson, A.G., offering me the Town Majorship of York—Accepted—

1. [Tu.] Yesterday [October][17] appointed Town Major of New York[18]—Several Reg^{ts}. 4th. Brigade chang'd their Encampment came to dwell in N York

---

of 40 members of the Sons of Liberty pulled the statue down on 9 July 1776. It was made of an alloy of lead, tin, copper, and antimony. The protective fence for the statue from 1773 still stands in the park. The Museum of the American Revolution in Philadelphia made a replica of the Statue in 2016. See *New York Times*, 21 October 2016. https://www.nytimes.com/2016/10/21/nyregion/toppled-statue-of-king-george-iii-to-ride-again.html and Alexander J. Wall, 'The Equestrian Statue of George III ...' *Quarterly Bulletin of the New York Historical Society*, (July 1920). https://ia802905.us.archive.org/26/items/equestrianstatue01wall/equestrianstatue01wall.pdf

12 The word between brackets in an interlineal insertion.

13 The word between brackets in an interlineal insertion.

14 The word between brackets in an interlineal insertion.

15 This paragraph appears in the remarks section for Week 40, but appears to be a continuation of his comments in the remarks section of Week 39, despite a large unused Space for remarks in Week 39.

16 The words between brackets are an insertion. Bamford uses the term 'York' or 'York Town'" for New York City.

17 On this line the characters '1. Th.' and 'October' are written in red ink. In the margin the name 'York' is written vertically in black ink with each letter over the next.

18 Bamford's appointment as town-major was announced in the *London Gazette,* 28 January 1777 (Issue 11740), p. 3. This published notice of promotions and appointments from the War Office was dated 27 January 1777 and included Bamford's name in a section headed 'Staff Officers in North America'. Along with Bamford's appointment as Town-Major of New York, Sergeant-Major Thompson of the 37th Foot was appointed Town-Adjutant of New York, and Lieutenant Michael Seix of the 64th Foot was appointed Barrack-Master of New York.

2. W. pleasant day a little Windy—got an house in Fair street—near St Paul's Church[19]—
To McLean a Doll^{r}. lent ———————— £ — 4 : 8

3. Th. Windy dull M^{g}—Ev^{g}. some rain—

4. F. Some rain last N^{t}—dull M^{g}—XI clear'd pleasant—

5. Sa. dull day—blew hard last N^{t}—
To M^{r} V—n 6 Doll^{r} lent [£] 1 : 8 —

N York— October 6th. to October 12th. 1776
41st. Week.

6. Su. dull M^{g}–

7. M. Bright Pleasant M^{g}— 2d. & 6th. Brig^{ds}. cross'd to Long Isl^{d}. to march to Jamaica—57th. Rg^{t}. at Paulus hook

8. Tu. pleasant day.

9. W, Warm bright M^{g}—hot day
Began My Washing w^{t} M^{rs} McLean—

10. Th. hot Mg—XII, cool—Aft^{n}. some rain
To M^{r} V^{n}. lent 4 Doll^{rs}———— £ — 18 : 8

11. F. very cold day—This Ev^{g}. great Part of the Army embark'd on board boat & went up the [E.][20] River above Kings bridge, where they Landed

Genl Burgoyne gave the Rebels a compleat drubbing on Lake Champlain destroy'd most of the Craft they had on the Lake by their own Acc^{ts}. & that their Army retir'd to Ticonderoga—The Enemy acknowledge in their Acc^{ts}. that they have lost a large schooner, 3 Gallies, 8 Gondaloes—[21]

---

19 St. Paul's Chapel stands in lower Manhattan in New York City at 209 Broadway, between Fulton and Vesey Streets. Built in 1766, it was modelled after St, Martin's-in-the-Fields, London. In the 18th century, St. Paul's was located in a field North of the main part of New York City and designed was to serve as a chapel of ease for the main parish church, Trinity Church, at Wall Street and Broadway. When the 1698 Trinity Church was destroyed in the 1776 New York City fire, St. Paul' served as the main Anglican Church in New York until the new Trinity Church building was consecrated in 1790. St Paul's Chapel is the oldest surviving public building in continuous use in New York City.

20 The abbreviation between brackets is an interlineal insertion.

21 The above paragraph from the remarks page in week 41 notes that it refers to 11 and 12 October.

Genl Howe w^{t}. a large Part of the Army embark'd on board boats &c^{a}. & went up the River above Kings bridge; East River—Lord Percy[22] commands on York Island in Genl Howe's Absence.

12. Sa. cold day

New York October 13th. to October 19th. 1776
42d. Week.

13. Su. pleasant day—Part of ye 16 L^{t}. Drag^{ns}. went over to L. Island.

14. M. Very pleasant day some Ships Arriv'd w^{t}. recruits prov^{n} &c^{a}.

15. Tu. very fine day—

16. W. pleasant day

17. Th. heavy rain last N^{t}. moist M^{g}.

18. F. some rain last N^{t}. blows fresh—Part of the Hessian fleet arriv'd
The Rest of the Fleet arriv'd aft^{n}—
[The fleet which brought the Hessians brough recruits for our Army][23]

---

22 Hugh, Earl Percy was born Hugh Smithson in England in 1742, the son of Sir Hugh Smithson, 4th Baronet, and Lady Elizabthe Seymour, Baroness Percy. In 1750, when his father, Sir Hugh Smithson, became the 2nd Earl of Northumberland by special remainer on the death of his maternal grandfather, the 7th Duke of Somerset, Smithson, by Act of Parliament, took the name of Percy for his heirs. From 1750 until 1766, Sir Hugh's son, Hugh, was styled Lord Warkworth. As Lord Warkworth he was educated at Eton in 1753-58, and graduated from St. John's College, Cambridge in 1760. He was commissioned an ensign in the 24th Foot in England on 1 May 1759 in a free death vacancy, then promoted in England to captain in the Hon. John Craufurd's new-raising 85th Foot on 6 August 1759 and then to lieutenant colonel commandant of his own new-raising 111th Foot in England on 16 April 1762. He went onto British half pay when the regiment was disbanded on 28 May 1763 and became member of Pariament for Westminster, a seat he held until 1776, when he succeeded his mother as Baron Percy. He married the daughter of Lord Bute in 1764 and was promoted to brevet colonel on 26 October 1764 as ADC to the King Geroge II. In 1766, when his father was created the 1st Duke of Northumberland (third creation), he was styled Earl Percy. From half pay he became colonel of the 5th Foot on 7 November 1768. Lord Percy led the relief column on the day of Lexington & Concord in April 1775 and was promoted to major general on 29 August 1775, to lieutenant general in America on 1 January 1776 and to lieutenant general in the Army on 29 Auust 1777, to captain & colonel of the 2nd Troop of Horse Grenadier Guards on 1 November 1784, reduced when the Troop was disbanded on 25 June 1788, but remained on the list of General Officers and still there in 1794. In 1786, he succeeded to his father's title and became the 2nd Duke of Northumberland. He was lord lieutenant of Northumberland from 1786 to 1799 and 1802 to 1817, and Vice Admrial of Nothumberland, 1786-1817. He died in 1817.

23 The sentence between brackets is a note at the bottom of the page marked for insertion with this entry.

19. Sa. blew very hard all last N^{t}. cold M^{g}. XII Clear sun—

NYork October 20th. to October 26th. 1776
43d. Week.

20. Su. very fine day

21. M. very fine day M^{g}. Windy— The Pacquet[24] from England arriv'd, was attack'd in Lat: 20 by a Rebel Privateer & Had a smart Engagem^{t}. lost ye Mast^{r} & 5 Men kill^{d}; had 9 wound^{d}.

22. Tu. fine mild day
This day the Forreign Troops, which came in ye 18th. went up the River in flat Boats &c to Genl. Howes Army—

23. W. pleasant M^{g}—

24. Th. very fine day

25. F. fine Weather

26. fine day

NYork October 27 to November 2d. 1776
44th. Week.

27. Su. fine day 22d. Reg^{t}. march'd at IV this M^{g}. to our advanc'd lines—much firing up the River—towards Genl Howe's Army
Our Advance'd Batt^{ns}—march'd more forward

24 The packet *Harriot* had a passage from England of 6 weeks and 5 days.

The Firing up the River was against the *Repulse* & *Pearl*[25] Frigates from Forts—Washington[26] on York Island & Constitution[27] on the Jersey side they did no damage. A Detachment of our Army has driven the Rebels from White Plains in Westchester county—

28. M. Moist fogy Mg. The Liberty Pole[28] this Mg. taken down, it was all cas'd with Iron & so for 5 feet under ground—in ye Action yesterday, we had 10 kill'd & woundd—

Lord Percy made an Excursion with the part of the Troops under his command towards the Enemys works, took possession of some posts nearer the Enemy—had only a few men wounded ~~&ca~~ 10 kill'd & woundd— [29]

29. Tu. fine day.

N.B. the Liberty pole was at the Door of Bridewell—[30]

We hear that Genl Howe had a Smart Action with the Rebels, we had 4 offrs. kill'd 5 wound'd & about 120 Men kill'd & woundd— & the Rebels lost great numbers. & that the Hessians attack'd Fort independance[31] & carried it with little loss—

The 4th. Brigade Emark'd to Joyn Genl Howe's Army above Kingsbridge—

Since Our Army went above Kingsbridge there has been Many Movements made there, & much firing wt. loss on both sides—however we always gain our point—

---

25 The 32-gun, fifth rate, *Niger*-class frigate *Pearl* was built by successive master shipwrights John Lock and Edward Allin at Chatham Dockyard in 1761-1762. Commissioned in April 1762, she served repeatedly on the Newfoundland station from 1764 to 1772, after which she was paid off. Following a Small repair at Portsmouth in 1772-1773, she recommissioned in November 1775 and sailed for North America in March 1776 under Captain Thomas Wilkinson. She took the 16-gun American sloop *Lexington* on 20 December 1776. Wilkinson died in mid-February1777 and was succeeded by Captain the Hon. George Keith Elphinstone, who on 1 July 1777 took the American schooner *Mosquito*. She was subsequently in Howe's action with d'Estaing in August 1778, at St Lucia in 1778, and the Battle of Cape Henry in March 1781. She remained in active service until 1804, became a receiving ship in 1814 and was renamed *Prothée* in 1825. She was sold in 1832. Length of gun deck 125 feet ½ inch, length of keel 103 feet 4 ⅜ inches, breadth 35 feet 3 inches, depth of hold 12 feet, 683 16/94 tons bm, draught 8 feet 10 1.2 inches forward / 14 feet 4 inches aft.

26 Fort Washington was located near the northern end of Manhattan Island and on the island's highest point. British and Hessian forces took 2,818 prisoners as well as supplies. After this action, the fort was named Fort Knyphausen, the site is now Bennet Park on Fort Washington Avenue, between 183rd and 185th Streets in Washington Heights, Manhattan.

27 Fort Constitution

28 The Sons of Liberty first erected a Liberty Pole in front of Army Barracks at City Hall Park in New York in 1766. It was removed by British authorities on five separate occasions.

29 This entry on the right-hand page is dated 27-28 [October].

30 Bridewell was the municipal prison in New York, located at City Hall Park. Construction began in 1768, but it was not complete in 1776. Nevertheless, during the years between 1776 and 1783 prisoners of war were kept in the unfinished building.

31 Fort Independence was constructed by the Americans on the heights between the old Boston and Albany Post Roads on Manhattan. The breastworks were started in June 1776, forming a rough parallelogram with bastions at two angles enclosed a stone barracks, magazine, and tents. It was abandoned by the Americans in October 1776 and subsequently occupied by Hessian troops. The fortification was evacuated and destroyed September 1779. The site is now a New York State Park

30. W. cool day. We hear that Col°. Carr[32] of 35th is dead of his Wound too true—he rec^d^. his Wounds 28th—

31. Th a great deal of rain last N^t^. very wet M^g^.

1. F: very cold November[33] day— we hear Our Troops have got possession of Kings Bridge—

2. Sa. very hard frost this M^g^—cold day, bright we hear the Rebels have abandon'd their Works at King's bridge & left 72 peices of Cannon behind—

This day Got an Order for a Cord of Wood.

the Rebels have Abandon'd their Lines at Kings bridge & left 72 peices of Cannon behind them—they burn'd their Barr^ks^—by Accounts from several Officers we had a noble opportunity at White Plains of destroying the Rebel Army, & of consequence putting an End to the War, but We do not seem to be in any great hurry to gain so Wish'd for an Event—for this [is][34] the second great Oppertunity we have let slip—is it through incapacity, or by design of our C— that so many great oppertunitys are let slip, I am—inclin'd to Adopt the latter—

O thou Spirit of the Great Wolf[35] the More I see, the more I think of thee, & the more I revere they most Sacred Memory—

Quando inveniendus Parem[36]

N York November 3d. to November 9th. 1776
45th. Week.

32 Robert Carr was born in England in 1732. He was commissioned an ensign in the 24th Foot in England on 26 January 1751 by purchase vice a retirement. He served as quartermaster from 11 February 1756 to 8 August 1759, and was promoted to lieutenant in the 24th Foot on 31 March 1756 by purchase vice an augmentation. He was promoted to captain-lieutenant in the 24th Foot on 1 December 1758 probably by purchase. He was promoted to captain in the 24th Foot on 12 July 1759 by purchase, to major in the 24th Foot in 17 April 1769 by purchase vice a retirement, to lieutenant -colonel in the 35th Foot on 5 March 1775 by purchase vice a retirement. He was killed in action at White Plains on 28 October 1776 after 25.7 years' service.

33 The number 1 and November are written in red ink.

34 The word in square brackets is an interlineal insertion.

35 A reference to Major General James Wolfe (1727-1759), under whom Bamford had served at Québec.

36 The above entry is on the remarks page of the following week, Week 45, but clearly refers to the entry in Week 44, where the remarks page was already full. Bamford's words are a variation on: '*quando ullum invenient parem*' a line that derives from Quintus Horatius Flaccas or Horace (65 BC-5 BC), *Carminum* (Odes), Book I, Carmen XXIV *Ad Virgilium*, lines 6-8: '*Cui pudor & justitiae soror incorrupta fides nudaque veritas quando ullum invenient parem*' translated as 'When shall Reverence and the sister of Justice, untainted Honour, and naked Truth, ever find one to be his peer?'

3.Su. cold bright M^{g}. cold day.The 71st. Reg^{t} at Montresor's Island, embark'd landed on the Main & Encamp'd at Morrissania[37]

4. M. very pleasant day—light frost

5. Tu. light frost very fine day

6. W. light frost very fine day [Late][38] Capt. Evelyn 4th. Reg^{t}. buried, died of his Wounds[39]

7. Th. light frost very fine day

8. F. dull M^{g}. raw—X cleard fine day

9. Sa. pleasant day.

N York November 10th. to November 16th. 1776
46th week.

10. Su. fine Warm day frosty M^{g}

11. M. dull Hazy Mg.—pm II began to rain rain'd Heavily all the Ev^{g}.

---

37 Morrisania was the 2,000-acre Manor of the Morris family located in modern day South Bronx, New York City. The Morris family included two very prominent participants in the rebellion; Lewis Morris (1726-1798), the 4th Lord of the Manor and a delegate from New York to the Continental Congress who signed the Declaration of Independence, and his half-brother, Gouvernor Morris (1752-1816), who signed the Articles of Confederation and the U.S. Constitution. Another half-brother, who had inherited the land and then sold it to Gouvernor Morris in 1787, was Staats Long Morris (1728-1800), an Army officer. He had been promoted to brigadier general in 1763, to major general in 1778, and to general in 1797 and was colonel of the 61st Regiment of Foot from 1778-1800, and governor of the garrison at Québec, 1797-1800.

38 The word between brackets is an insertion in the margin.

39 William Glanville Evelyn was born in England in 1742 the son of a clergyman. He was commissioned ensign in the 50th Regiment of Foot in England on 29 March 1760, probably by purchase, vice an augmentation, He was promoted to lieutenant in the 50th Foot on 23 May 1761 by purchase. Reduced onto British half pay on 14 April 1763, he exchanged from half pay as lieutenant in the 4th Foot in England on 15 July 1767. He was probably the 'Glanville Evelyn' who on 13 December 1769 was appointed lieutenant in the infantry of the Honourable East India Company's forces in the Madras Presidency, but who resigned the appointment on 17 January 1770, thereby aborting the transfer. He was promoted to captain in the 4th Foot, 16 October 1772, by purchase vice a retirement. In 1774, he was asked to look after a kinsman in the 4th Foot: the teenage Ensign George Evelyn Boscawen (1758-1808), third Viscount Falmouth, the third but only surviving son of Admiral Edward Boscawen and his wife, Francis Glanville. Evelyn's letters on this subject have been published. See G.D. Scull (ed.) *Memoir and Letters of Captain W. Glanville Evelyn of the Fourth Regiment . . . , 1774-1776* (Oxford: Printed for Private Circulation by James Parker, 1879). Evelyn died on 6 November 1776 of wounds suffered on 18 October 1776 in a skirmish near Pell's Point, New York, after 12.4 years' service.

12. Tu. blew very hard & rain'd much last N^{t}. windy day but fair

13. W. hard frost last N^{t}—pleasant M^{g}—
To Serg^{t} Barret 2 Doll^{rs} £ — 9 : 4

14. Th. pleasant day. frosty M^{g}—

15. F. hard frost last N^{t}—dull p,m, I rain.

16. Sa. pleasant bright M^{g}—frosty much Cannond^{g}. up the River, suppose at Fort Washington. The cannonading was at the Lines beyond Fort Washington—& at this side
To Morrison 4 doll^{rs} — — — —£ — 18 : 8
16th Genl Howe attack'd the Lines of Fort Washington on the side of Kingsbridge, when L^{d}. Percy Made an Attack on Those on the Side of New York, both succeeded & the Fort was surrender'd, we kill'd a great [many][40] men & took 2600 Prisoners—in the fort were 32 peices of ~~heavy~~ Cannon & 2 brass Mortars

N York November 17th. to November 23d. 1776
47th Week.

17. Su. pleasant day, but very cool—hard frost
The Rebels abandon'd their 2 Forts Constitution & Lee, in the Jerseys upon theApproach of our Troops, & went off towards Philadelphia. We got their Cannon, mortars, tents &c^{a}—
As we go forward into the Country the Rebels fly before us, & when we come back, they always follow us, 'tis almost impossible to catch them. They will neither fight, nor totally run away—but they keep at such a distance that we are always abve a days March from them—We seem to be playing Bo peep—
√To Millikin — — — 4 Doll^{rs}. ————————£ — 18 : 8
√To Corp^{l} McKinnen a Dl^{r} — — — — 4 : 8

18. M. pleasant day, cool hard frost

19. Tu. very pleasant day cold M^{g}—frost

20. W. A good deal of rain last N^{t}. soft dull M^{g}— A large body of our Troops cross'd to the Jerseys, Very early—much cannonad^{g}. at a distance
To McLean a Doll^{r}. ———— ——— 4 : 8

21. Th. hazy Mg. X small rain moist day
To Mr Thompson 3½ Jo^{r}. 24 Dol^{rs}. £5 : 12 —

40 The word between brackets is an interlinear insertion.

22. F. very pleasant M^{g}. XI, hazy w^{t}. small rain, some rain last N^{t}—rain'd heavily All this Ev^{g}.

Genl Howe came to York this evening—

23. Sa. pleasant M^{g}. Grey, rain last N^{t}. rain'd very much all this Ev^{g}—

NYork November 24th. to November 30th. 1776

48th. Week.
24. Su. a great deal of rain last N^{t} dull M^{g}—[3d 5th][41] Brigades embark'd for an Expedition; Under Genl Clinton & Lord Perçy & G^{l}. Prescott.

25. M. pleasant M^{g}. fine day, dull— [part of y^{e}][42] 5th Brigade Embark'd; & [two][43] Brig^{des}. of Hessians

25. Our Troops Advanc'd into the Jerseys got possession of Hackingsack and Newark

26. Tu. very wet day.

Tis conjectur'd that the Expedition Under Genl. Clinton is for Rhode Island—

27. W. rain'd all last N^{t}. wet M^{g}— Aft^{n}. fair

To McLean	3 Doll^{rs}.	— — — — —	£— 14 —
To McKinzie	a Doll^{r}	— — — — —	4: 8

28. Th. pleasant day. The 1st Brigade of British came into N York to winter Quarters—

29. F. very pleasant M^{g}—pm VII Rains very heavily—

30. Sa. rain'd heavily all last N^{t}. wet M^{g}— pm III ceas'd raining—

A Proclamation was Issued by Lord Howe & Genl. Howe, offering every protection to those who would come in & only promise, not to take up Arms themselves nor oblige others to take up Arms against the King, & that their properties should be secur'd for them—Sure such terms Offer'd when we are in the height of success must induce Those deluded Rabble to seize so fair & Easy an Opportunity of reinstating themselves in the happiness they once Enjoy'd. The Proclamation holds good for 60 days—Those who remain in Arms after the Expiration of the Time—deserve no mercy—

We hear the Rebels have Besieg'd Fort Cumberland, Nova Scotia, at the Head of the Bay of Fundy—

N. York December 1st to December 7th 1776
49th. Week.

---

41 It appears that Bamford first wrote '3d Brigade', then corrected it by adding '5th' underneath '3d' with an open brace connecting the two and adding an 's' to Brigade.

42 The words between brackets are an interlineal insertion.

43 The word between brackets is an interlineal insertion that repeats the same word that had been removed.

[1. Su.][44] Mild day

The Ships in which our Troops Embark'd sail'd up the East River toward the Sound—

2. M. very sharp, cold M^{g}. cold day

Our Troops have got as far as Brunswick[45] The Rebels are retreating very fast towards Philadelphia—Where we hear the Congress have summon'd All ranks of Men to assemble for its Defence—

Since the Publishing the Proclamation the 30th. Utl^{o}—great numbers of People in the Jerseys have come in & taken the benefit, got Certificates & taken quiet possession of their Habitations. Too great an Indulgence for their past behavior[—Villains—][46]

We got a Very great quantity of Stores at Brunswick flour, Beef &c^{a}.

The Rebels ran away in the greatest hurry—

3. Tu. dull M^{g}—X began to rain, continued till XII. —pm VII began to rain

4. W. rain'd all last N^{t}. very wet M^{g}—aft^{n}. dry—

To Mr Bullard w^{t}. a 20£ Bill 2d. copy—

To Mr Toler—by the Tamer—

5. Th. Pleasant day—The Reg^{t}. of Waldeck[47] went over to Amboy in the Jerseys—The Hessians came into NYork to Quarters.

Genl Howe went from York to the Jerseys—

6. F. very fine day.

To Ens^{n}. Chessire, by Serj^{t} Davis, on Acct. of comp^{y}—dep 24 £5 : 12 —

To Serj^{t} Boutcher — by D^{o} — 4 Doll^{rs} — — — — — — — — — 18 : 8

All accounted for WB

7. Sa. pleasant day.

The Hessians took the Guards, G^{l} Stirnns Brig^{de}—[48]

Detachment of the 14th. Reg^{t}. drafted—

The Expedition which sail'd under G^{l}. Clinton arriv'd at Rhode Island 7th. & Landed—without opposition 8th. several Persons had fled from the Town of Newport & other parts of the Island—

N York December 8th. to December 14th. 1776
50th. Week.

---

44 The information between square brackets is written in red ink.

45 In New Jersey.

46 The word 'Villains' and the dashes on either side of it are written in red ink.

47 The Third English-Waldeck Regiment was an auxiliary regiment provided by Friedrich Karl August, Fürst zu Waldeck und Pyrmont.

48 *Generalmajor* J.D. von Stirnn commanded this Brigade of Hessian troops.

8. Su. Dull M^{g}. some rain—X clear'd very fine day—We hear our Troops are on their March to Trent Town,[49] —where the Rebels say [they][50] intend Opposing their passage over the Delaware

9. M. very fine day.

Mr Brindley a commissary riding with his servant near Elizabeth Town, 5 scoundrels ran out of a ~~Wood~~ [house][51] & fir'd after them, wounded him in 3 places & 3 shott went through the servants cloaths; wanton cruelty—

To Mrs Moore lent 3 Doll^{rs}. — — P^{d}. — — £ — 14 —

To D^{o}. — D^{o}. 5 Doll^{rs}. — — P^{d}. 1 : 3 . 4

To M^{rs} V — A Guinea Washing 1 : 1 —

10. Tu. Sharp frost this M^{g}—fine day. The 2d. Brigade came down from Fort Lee in ye Jerseys, they came in ships, did not disembark

11. W. very hard frost, dull cold day—pm X some snow— the 2d Brigade sail'd for Amboy in the Jerseys—

12. Th. A little snow on the G^{d}. this Mg—cold—The snow soon disappear'd & the weather grew very warm—The Part of the 7th. Reg^{t}. that were prisoners came in & some few of the 26—

13. F. an Exceeding fine day, bright & Warm—gave up a Room in my house

14. Sa. clear cold day, blows fresh hard frost last N^{t}—The 6th. Reg^{t}. drafted—

NYork December 15th, to December 21st. 1776
51st. Week.

15. Su. very cold day, hard frost last N^{t}.

We hear the Mighty Genl Lee is taken Prisoner—by a party of L^{t}. Dragoons[52]

We hear that the Rebels who had besieg'd Fort Cumberland in the Bay of Fundy Nova Scotia, were obliged to raise the Siege w^{t}. great Loss, & that Capt Dawson[53] has taken Brig of 16 Guns, call'd the *Washington*—in the Bay of Fundy—

to M^{r} M^{c} — — — — — — — — — — — — — — — — — — £ — 6 —

49 Trenton, New Jersey.

50 The word in brackets is added in the margin.

51 The word in brackets is a correction, written over the crossed-out word.

52 Lieutenant Colonel William Harcourt and a party from the 16th Light Dragoons captured Major General Charles Lee, Continental Army, at Widow White's Tavern in Basking Ridge, New Jersey, on 13 December 1776.

53 Commander George Dawson, Royal Navy, commanding the 14-gun sloop brig *Hope*. Dawson had been promoted from Lieutenant to Commander on 13 May 1776. It was reported in late December 1776 that Dawson had captured the armed brig *Independence*. See Clark, Morgan et al (eds.) *Naval Documents of the American Revolution*, Vol. 7, p.619.

16. M. very pleasant day.

Mr Lee Was ~~yesterday~~ [this day][54] brought into Brunswick Escortd by Lt. Infantry Dragoons & Grenadiers

Our Army in the Jersey went into Cantonemt.

We hear that great disputes have arose at Boston, that one party is for applying to His Majesty's Commissioners for peace & the other party opposing it, they fell to blows & call'd in the Assistance of their Privateer men, & that some lives were lost in the squabble—Partly true—

17. Tu. very cold Mg—hard frost—Gen Howe Arriv'd from the Jerseys

18. W. frost cold day

19. Th. very cold day—hard frost

20. F. began to snow very early this Mg. Snow & sleet all day

A Battn. of Hessians march'd [to][55] Fort Kniphausen to relieve a Battn. of Hn. Grendrs. who go over to the Jerseys

21 Sa. A good deal of snow on the Gd. this Mg. snow'd till X. The Hessian's Barrks. in broadway was on fire this Mg. soon put out—

The *Scarborough* wt. part of the Fleet from Halifax came in yesterday Evg.

Within these few days several Ships have arriv'd from Ireland & Hallifax with provisions & stores &ca—

N. York December 22d. to December 28th. 1776
52d. Week.

22. Su. clear Mg. very hard frost
23. M. cold Mg. hard frost
To N Mc ————3 Dollrs ————£—14—
Clear'd McLean to 27th. incluce.

24. Tu. very cold Mg hard frost
A Quartr. Cask of Wine from Mr Dumaresque

25. W. moderate soft Mg.—XII. dull—some Ships from Hallifax Arriv'd

26. Th. some snow last Nt—very, cold, wet windy Mg— blows very hard—Aftn —very high Wd. with cold drifting snow—

27. F. clear Mg. hard frost, the streets are all a sheet of Ice—Accts from the Jerseys unfavourable, that a body of the Hessians Are cut off—by the Rebels—true

54 The words between brackets are written above the preceding, crossed out word.
55 The word between square brackets is an interlineal insertion.

The Rebels attack'd Trentown with about 7000 men, where Col°. Rahl[56] commanded a Brigade of Hessians, & by some misconduct suffer'd himself to be nearly surrounded, without making any disposition for Securing his retreat, he had about 100 kill'd & wounded, & 700 with him~~self~~ & many officers taken prisoners, — The Rebels got 6 peices of cannon & 15—colours—between 4 & 500 of the Hessians who were with Col°. Rahl, made a good retreat to Col°. Donop's[57] Post.

Col°. Ralh died a few days after~~wards~~ of his Wounds—The Hessians Officers say his death's a lucky circumstance for him, for had he Liv'd he must have been broke with Infamy—at Least—

28. Sa. very cold Mg.— dull—XII began to snow—
To Mr Bullard, wt. 3d. copy of 20£ bill from Mr Gason—

N York December 29th. to 31st.—
52d. Week.[58]

29. Su. very fine day, hard frost
This Rebellion is most obstinately persisted in, nor do I see that We take proper steps to put an End to it for by our continual blunders, which the Enemy never fail to take advantage of, we seem more to Encourage than dishearten them. I wish our mismanagement may not produce Effects fatal to Great Britain & I greatly fear our neglects are Wilfil & that in the End we shall loose this Country.[59]

30. M. pleasant cold day frost

31. Tu. fine Mg. —XII dull Thaw—gentle—The Weather thus far has been very mild we have not [had][60] any severe weather of Any kind ; very little snow, & but gentle Frost—it has been most favourable for our Military Opperations—

O Lord God I praise thy holy Name for that thou hast been pleased to protect me in the day of danger

Accept my thanks Gracious God—
WB.

[This Book became my property after my dearly beloved Father obtained it through a friend at Bannagher[61] after the Death of his uncle William Bamford JBrd–][62]

---

56 Colonel Johan Gottlieb Rahl at the Battle of Trenton.

57 Count Carl Emil Ulrich von Donop.

58 Bamford numbered both the week of 22-28 December 1776 and the partial week of 29-31 December 1776 as the 52nd week. Presumably, he started another diary on 1 January 1777, but it has not been located.

59 His paragraph is not dated, but is placed opposite the entry for 29 December 1776 on the facing 'Remarks' page.

60 The word between brackets in an interlineal insertion.

61 Banagher is a town in the Irish Midlands, located in Leinster on the western edge of County Offaly on the River Shannon. It was a garrison town from the 17th century through the mid-19th century.

62 This inscription is written on the otherwise blank last page of the volume.

Notes on Financial Transactions, 1776[1]

	√To Murray		£ — 2 : 18
3.	√To McKay		2 : 4
15.	√To H Kinleys at Charles Town		: 6
23.	√to Rhodes	a Doll^{r}	9 : 4
March 6.	√To Kenney	a Doll^{r}	4 : 8
8.	√To M^{rs}. Fisher	2 Doll^{s}	9 : 4
18.	√To Serj^{t} Davis	2 Doll^{s}	9 : 4
	√To John Gordon	2 Doll^{s}	9 : 4
	√To M^{rs}. Guthrae	a Doll^{r}	4 : 8
	√To M^{rs}. Dickenson	a Doll^{r}	4 : 8
	√To Fitzhenry	a Doll^{r}	4 : 8
	√To M^{rs}. Read	a Doll^{r}	4 : 8
April 15th	√To Serj^{t}. Heath	a Doll^{r}	4 : 8
June 4.	√To Corp^{l}. Fisher	2 Doll^{rs}	9 : 4
5.	√To Serj^{t} Davis	4 Doll^{s}	18 : 8
	√To Corp^{l}. McKinnen	6 Doll^{s}	£1 18 : 8
	√To Corp^{l}. Fisher	2 Doll^{s}	9 : 4
	√To Connor	2 Doll^{s}	9 : 4
	*~~To Reed~~	~~2 Dolls~~	~~9 : 4~~
	√To Guthrie	2 Doll^{s}	9 : 4
	√To Gordon John	2 Doll^{s}	9 : 4
8	√To M^{rs} [illegible]	a Doll^{r}	4 : 8
	√To Read	A Doll^{r}	4 : 8
	√To McKinzie	½ Doll^{r}	2 : 4
	√To Rankin		2 —

1 These fragmentary financial notes appear on both sides of the first folio of the 1776 diary. They complement similar entries that are strewn though the document under particular dates.

Due to me by Capt. Wemyss[2]

for Conroy		£ 2 : 10
for Bond		£1 — : 2¼
for Fitzhenry		£1 8 : 7½
at 4 / 8 the Doll^r		£2 11 : 7¾
Rec^d the Above WB		

Due to me by Capt. Simcoe —

For Reed		£1 —
For McGowen		2 : 9¾
At 4 / 8 the Doll^r	Paid	£1 2 : 9¾

Due to me by Capt Wolfe[3]

For McKinley	Paid	£ — 7 : 1¼

2 James Wemyss was born in Scotland in 1748) and commissioned in Ireland an ensign in the 40th Foot on 6 August 1766 by purchase vice a retirement. He was promoted to lieutenant in the 40th Foot on 1 April 1767 by purchase vice a resignation, to captain in the 40th Foot on 14 March 1771 by purchase vice a retirement. He was appointed ADC to Major General James Robertson on 14 May 1776 and to Major General William Tryon on 20 April 1777 and was also made major-commandant on 5 May 1777 of the loyalist Queen's American Rangers, but resigned on 14 Octover 1777 to resume his appointment as ADC. He was to major in the 63rd Foot at New York on 10 August 1778 in a free vacancy vice a retirement. He was promoted to brevet lieutenant colonel 22 August 1783 and to lieutenant colonel in the 63rd Foot on 20 August 1787 by purchase vice a retirement. He retired on 31 July 1789 after 23 years' service. See Walter Dornfest, *Loyalist Officers* (Jefferson: McFarland, 2011), p. 355.

3 William Wolfe was born in Ireland in 1751, where he was commissioned an ensign in the 40th Foot on 15 March 1768 by purchase vice a retirement. He was promoted to lieutenant in the 40th Foot on 12 December 1770 by purchase vice a retirement. He was subsequently promoted captain in the 40th Foot on 5 March 1775 by purchase vice a retirement. Wolfe was killed in action on 20-21 August 1777 in the night action at Paoli, Pennsylvania, after 9.5 years' service.

Appendix

Service Biographies of Officers in the 35th Regiment of Foot, 1757-1765, and in the 40th Regiment of Foot, 1776, Listed in Order of Regimental Rank.[1]

Key to Abbreviations:

Adjt = Adjutant
AL = Army List
b. = born
Bgde = Brigade
BHP= British Half Pay
BL Addit. Ms = British Library, Additional Manuscript
Bn = battalion
bvt = brevet
Cmdnt = commandant
Col = colonel
comm = commission
coy = company
dd = cied
dd-vacancy = vacancy by death
disb = disbanded
Ens = ensign
Estb = establishment
Expd = expedition
Ft = Foot
GB - British
Gen = general
HP = Half Pay
IHP = Irish Half Pay
Ire. = Ireland
kia = killed in action
Lieut = lieutenant
Lieut Col = lieutenant-colonel

1 This appendix has been graciously provided by Dr. J. A. Houlding from his currently unpublished *Database of Georgian Military Officers*. The database ends in 1794 and does not include information on careers after that date.

Maj = major
New raising = a unit being raised and organized.
QM = Quartermaster
R.Amers. = Royal American Regiment
rgt = Regiment
Sct. = Scotland
unk = unknown
WO = War Office records
X'd = an officer exchanged, rather than simply moved from A to B.
2/1st Ft = The first number indicates the battalion, the second the regiment

List of Officers in the 35th Regiment in 1757

Lieut Colonel:

Geo. Monro (Ire., b.1700): first commissioned as Lieut, 11th Ft, 19.8.18; retired onto BHP, 17.3.35/6; X'd from HP as Capt, 35th Ft (in Ire.), 27.9.37; Maj, 35th Ft, 18.8.47; Lieut Col, 35th Ft, 4.1.49/50; dd 3.11.57 at Albany, NY

Major:

Henry Fletcher (Sct., b.'24): Ens, 5th Foot, 2.5.39, a probable purchase; to Lieut, 37th Foot, 13.3.40/41, purchase vice an augmentation; to Capt, 2nd Foot, 20.9.45, a dd-vacancy; to Major, 35th Foot, 25.12.55, purchase vice an augmentation; Lieut Col, 35th Foot, 16.2.58, a free dd-vacancy; bvt Col, 20.6.62; Col, 35th Foot, 10.8.64, a free dd-vacancy; Maj Gen, 25.5.72; Lieut Gen, 29.8.77; Gen, 12.10.93; died on or shortly before 17.3.1803 (after 63.9 years' service).

Captains:

John Maunsell (Ire., b.'24): Ens, 39th Foot, 23.5.42, a free augmentation vacancy; 2nd Lieut, 39th Foot, 30.4.46, free vice a retirement; Lieut, 39th Foot, 25.8.49, purchase vice a resignation; to Capt, 35th Foot, 5.1.50/51, purchase vice a resignation; to Major, 77th Foot, 17.9.60, purchase vice a resignation; to Major, 3/60th Foot, 20.3.61, free vice a promotion to a colonelcy; to Major, 35th Foot, 30.9.61, free vice a resignation; to Lieut Col, 72nd Foot, 31.10.62, a free dd-vacancy; exchanged to Major, 27th Foot, 10.12.62; exchanged onto the Irish HP List, 2.8.65 (after 23.2 years' service), his regt at Trois Rivières 'and its dependencies'; bvt Col, 29.8.77; Maj Gen, 19.10.81; still on HP List in 1794 .

Thomas Collins: 2nd Lieut, 21st Foot, 22.4.45, by purchase; to Lieut, de Grangue's new-raising 60th Foot, 21.1.40/41; Capt-Lieut, 60th Foot, 29.10.45, purchase vice an augmentation; Capt, 60th Foot, 24.7.46, by purchase; onto Irish HP List when regt disb, 2.12.48; from HP as Capt, 35th Foot, 12.3.54, by purchase; resigned 14.4.59; dd at Boston, Mass., 22.5.66.

John Conyngham: Ens, 35th Ft (in Ire.), 13.3.40/41, purchase vice an augmentation; 2nd Lieut, 35th Ft, 14.5.42, a free augmentation vacancy; Lieut, 35th Ft, 29.10.45, purchase vice an augmentation; Capt, 35th Ft, 7.4.55, purchase vice a resignation; retired 24.1.58 (after 16.9 years' service).

George Fletcher: Ens, 35th Foot, 6.6.41, purchase vice an augmentation; 2nd Lieut, 35th Foot, 15.5.42, free vice an augmentation; Lieut, 35th Foot, 29.10.45, free vice an augmentation; Capt, 35th Foot, 8.4.55, purchase vice a resignation; kia before Québec, 27.7.59 (after 18.2 years' service).

William Bellew (Eng., b.'15): Ens, 35th Foot, 14.3.33/34, by means unknown; Lieut, 35th Foot, 1.5.42, purchase, vice an augmentation; Capt-Lieut, 35th Foot, 11.12.52, a free dd-vacancy; Capt, 35th Foot, 16.2.56, purchase vice a resignation; retired 5.10.60 (after 26.6 years' service), his regt in Québec and Montréal.

Charles Ince (Scot., b.'22): Ens, 35th Foot, 1.6.39, a free dd-vacancy; 2nd Lieut, 35th Foot, 10.5.42, free vice an augmentation; Lieut, 35th Foot, 10.3.42/43, a free dd-vacancy (and Adjt., 12.3.54 to 9.4.56); Capt-Lieut, 35th Foot, 16.2.56, free vice a resignation; Capt, 35th Foot, 24.2.56, purchase, vice a resignation; dd 28.4.60 of wounds suffered at Ste. Foy (after 20.9 years' service).

John Ormsby (Ire.): Ens, Richbell's new-raising 61st Foot, 23.5.42, by raising for rank; 2nd Lieut, 61st Foot, 27.12.44, a free dd-vacancy (and Adjt, 30.7.45 to 20.11.47): Lieut, 61st Foot, 26.2.45/46, free vice an augmentation; Capt, 61st Foot, 20.11.47, purchase vice a resignation; onto Irish HP List when regt disb, 1.12.48; from HP as Capt, 35th Foot, 24.2.56, free vice a resignation; retired 9.11.64 (after 15.3 years' service), his regt in West Florida (Pensacola and Mobile).
(* a note in a WO list of officers seeking preferment in 1755-56 recorded that he was recommended in 'Mr. Conway's Paper', and had 'Served 13 years & purchased his Compy.' – BL Add.MS 73,594, f.128).

Capt-Lieutenant:

Luke Gardiner (Ire.): 2nd Lieut, 5th Foot, 16.5.42, a free augmentation vacancy; to Lieut, 35th Foot, 29.10.45, free vice an augmentation; Capt-Lieut, 35th Foot, 24.2.56, free vice a resignation; Capt, 35th Foot, 24.1.58, purchase vice a retirement; resigned 30.8.61 (after 19.3 years' service), his regt in Staten Island, NY, shortly to embark for Barbados.

Lieuts:

Maurice Herbert (Ire., b.'30): 2nd Lieut, 35th Foot, 1.11.45, a free augmentation vacancy; Lieut, 35th Foot, 24.1.52, purchase vice a retirement; Capt-Lieut, 35th Foot, 27.7.59, by purchase; resigned 7.4.60 (after 14.5 years' service), his regt in Québec.

John De la Vallé: Ens, 35th Foot, 25.5.42, a free augmentation vacancy; 2nd Lieut, 35th Foot, 29.10.45, free vice an augmentation; Lieut, 35th Foot, 11.12.52, by purchase; exchanged onto GB HP List, 16.11.64 (after 22.5 years' service), his regt in West Florida (Pensacola and Mobile); name removed from the HP List in 1786, for reasons unknown.

Thomas Jetherill: Ens, 35th Foot, 26.5.42, a free augmentation vacancy; 2nd Lieut, 35th Foot, 29.10.45, free vice an augmentation; Lieut, 35th Foot, 12.3.54, a free dd-vacancy; exchanged onto GB HP List, 12.8.64 (after 22.2 years' service), his regt in West Florida (Pensacola and Mobile); died on HP, 13.4.75.

Edward Cane (Ire., b.'32): 2nd Lieut, 35th Foot, 25.2.45/46, purchase vice a resignation; Lieut, 35th Foot, 7.4.55, purchase vice a resignation; Capt-Lieut, 35th Foot, 11.6.60, by purchase; to Capt, 43rd Foot, 8.4.62, a free dd-vacancy; Major, 43rd

Foot, 10.7.75, a free dd-vacancy; retired 8.10.75 (after 29.7 years' service), his regt at Boston, Mass

(* according to Levinge, *Forty-Third*, p. 301) he was 'the founder of the house of Cane, army agents, Dublin', a business begun in 1777).

Richard Baillie (Ire.): Ens, 35th Foot, 23.5.42, a free augmentation vacancy; 2nd Lieut, 35th Foot, 29.10.45, free vice an augmentation; Lieut, 35th Foot, 3.9.47, purchase vice a resignation; reduced onto Irish HP List, 3.12.48; exchanged from HP as Lieut, 35th Foot, 8.4.55 (and Adjt., 9.4.56 to 24.3.57); Capt-Lieut, 35th Foot, 24.1.58, purchase vice a retirement; Capt, 35th Foot, 14.4.59, purchase vice a resignation; retired onto Irish HP List, 13.3.64 (after 15.5 years' service), his regt in West Florida (Pensacola and Mobile); still on Half-Pay List in *1794 AL*.

James Belcher: Ens, 35th Ft29.10.45, purchase vice an augmentation; 2nd Lieut, 35th Ft, 21.12.46, a free dd-vacancy; Lieut, 35th Ft, 8.4.55, purchase vice a retirement; resigned 24.1.58 (after 12.3 years' service).

William Bamford (Ire., b.'28): Ens, 35th Foot, 10.3.42/43, probable purchase, a dd-vacancy; 2nd Lieut, 35th Foot, 26.2.45/46, free vice an augmentation; Lieut, 35th Foot, 16.2.56, purchase vice a resignation; Capt-Lieut, 35th Foot, 25.12.62, purchase vice a resignation; bvt Capt, 25.5.72; to Capt, 40th Foot, 25.3.75, a free dd-vacancy; retired 15.10.78 (after 35.6 years' service), his regt at New York.

Thomas Brown (Ire.): Ens, 35th Foot, 2.5.50/51, a free dd-vacancy; Lieut, 35th Foot, 16.2.56, purchase, vice a promotion to a colonelcy; to Capt, 83rd Foot, 17.6.61, purchase vice a retirement; onto Irish HP List when regt disb, 6.6.63; from HP as Capt, 13th Dragoons, 2.6.70, purchase vice ?; retired 14.3.72 (after 13.9 years' service), his regt in Ireland.

Charles Gore (Ire.): Ens, 35th Foot, 5.11.45, purchase vice an augmentation; reduced onto Irish HP List, 3.12.48; exchanged from HP as Ens, 35th Foot, 24.1.52; Lieut, 35th Foot, 24.2.56, purchase vice a resignation; Capt-Lieut, 35th Foot, 7.4.60, purchase vice a resignation; Capt, 35th Foot, 11.6.60, a free dd-vacancy; dd 5.6.62 (after 13.4 years' service), his regt on board the fleet approaching Havana.

Gabriel Maturin (Ire., b.'30): Ens, 35th Foot, 24.1.52, a free dd-vacancy; Lieut, 35th Foot, 12.4.56, free vice an augmentation; Capt, 35th Foot, 9.11.64, purchase vice a retirement; exchanged to Capt, 31st Foot, 17.6.67; dd of pneumonia at Boston, Mass. (after 22.9 years' service) while serving as secretary to Lieut Gen the Hon. Thos. Gage.

Theophilus Blakeney (Ire., b.'34): Ens, 35th Foot, 12.3.54, by purchase; Lieut, 35th Foot, 13.4.56, free vice an augmentation; Capt, 35th Foot, 30.8.61, purchase vice a resignation; retired 20.3.72 (after 18.0 years' service), his regt in England.

Hon. Richard Allen (Ire., b.'34): Ens, 35th Foot, 8.4.55, purchase vice a retirement; Lieut, 35th Foot, 14.4.56, free vice an augmentation; Capt, 35th Foot, 5.10.60, purchase vice a retirement; Major, 35th Foot, 25.12.68, purchase vice a retirement; Lieut Col, 35th Foot, 25.12.72, purchase vice a retirement; retired 5.3.75 (after 19.9 years' service), his regt at Cork, about to embark for America.

William Widdrington: Ens, 35th Foot, 4.1.49/50, purchase vice a resignation; Lieut, 35th Foot, 14.4.56, purchase vice an augmentation; kia at Havana, 24.7.62 (after 12.6 years' service).

William Hamilton: from Scots-Dutch Bgde (his career untraced there) as Lieut, 35th Foot, 15.4.56, a free augmentation vacancy (and QM, 24.2.57 to 27.7.59);

kia before Québec, 27.7.59 (after 3.3 years in the British service), in what Amherst referred to as 'the affair . with Otway's Regt', that is Wolfe's recon. up the Montmorency River.

James Cockburne (Ire., b.'29): Gentleman volunteer made Ens, 44th Foot, 26.6.55, a free augmentation vacancy; to Lieut, 35th Foot, 26.11.56, free vice an augmentation (and Adjt., 25.3.57 to 27.3.72); Capt, 35th Foot, 13.4.67, purchase vice a retirement; Major, 35th Foot, 13.1.76, purchase vice a retirement; Lieut Col, 35th Foot, 30.10.76, a free dd-vacancy; cashiered 3.6.83 (after 27.9 years' service), his regt in the Windward Islands.

(* Loudoun described him as 'a very good Officer Putt in [the 35th] to Improve the Regt fitt for an Adjutant' [Pargellis, *Military Affairs*, 281]).

James Sinclair (Scot., b.'36): Ens, 47th Ft (in N.S.), 2.7.55, a free augmentation vacancy; to Lieut, 35th Ft, 28.11.56, a free augmentation vacancy; to Lieut, 22nd Ft (at NY), 8.3.57, a free augmentation vacancy; to Capt, 45th Ft (in the Canadian Maritimes), 10.3.61, purchase vice a resignation; retired 8.9.68 (after 13.2 years' service)

James Field (Eng., b.'43): Ens, 48th Foot, 28.6.55, a free dd-vacancy; to Lieut, 35th Foot, 29.11.56, free vice an augmentation; to Capt, new-raising (in Scotland) 108th Foot, 20.10.61, by raising for rank; onto Irish HP List when regt disb, 31.3.63; exchanged from HP as Capt, 44th Foot, 30.6.66; bvt Major, 29.8.77; retired 31.1.78 (after 19.4 years' service), his regt at Philadelphia.

Thomas Comberford (Ire.): a Troop QM, 12th Dragoons, already there in 1752, made Ens, 35th Ft, 16.2.56, purchase vice an augmentation; Lieut, 35th Ft, 15.12.56, purchase vice an augmentation; to Lieut, Gage's new-raising (in America) 80th Ft, 25.12.57, a free augmentation vacancy; kia 8.7.58 in the attack on the field fortifications at Carillon (after 2.5 years' service).

Thomas Fortye: Ens, Shirley's new-raising (in New England) 50th Foot, 17.12.54; Lieut, 50th Foot, 25.11.55; onto GB HP List when regt disb, 7.3.57; from HP as Lieut, 35th Foot, 8.3.57; exchanged onto GB HP, 19.3.64; exchanged from HP as Lieut, 75th Foot, 23.7.78; onto HP when regt disb, 10.5.83 (after 14.1 years' service); name removed from the HP List in 1786, for reasons unk.

Wm. Frederick Phillips: Ens, 35th Ft, 16.2.56, purchase vice a resignation; Lieut, 35th Ft, 16.5.57, a free augmentation vacancy; resigned 15.12.58 (after 2.8 years' service).

Ensigns:

William Brown (Ire., b.'35): Ens, 35th Foot, 16.2.56, purchase vice a resignation; Lieut, 35th Foot, 31.7.58, a free dd-vacancy; Capt, 35th Foot, 3.2.69, purchase vice a retirement; dd 17.7.75 (after 19.4 years' service), his regt at Boston, Mass.

William Mason: Ens, 35th Foot, 16.2.56, purchase vice a promotion to a colonelcy; Lieut, 35th Foot, 24.1.58, purchase vice a resignation; kia on the Plains of Abraham, 13.9.59 (after 3.6 years' service).

Eubule Ormsby (Ire.): Ens, 35th Foot, 16.2.56, purchase vice an augmentation; Lieut, 35th Foot, 24.1.58, purchase vice a retirement; dd of disease, 1.10.64 (after 8.7 years' service), his regt in West Florida (Pensacola and Mobile).

Nicholas Weld (Ire.): Ens, 35th Foot, 16.2.56, purchase vice a resignation; Lieut, 35th Foot, 15.12.58, probable purchase, vice a resignation; dd of disease 7.3.62 (after 6.1 years' service), his regt at Martinique.

Thomas Armstrong (Ire.): Pte, 6th Drags, made Ens, 35th Foot, 9.4.56, a free augmentation vacancy; resigned 6.4.70 when appointed Fort Major at Dartmouth, England; exchanged from Dartmouth to Lieut, Irish Invalid Coys., 23.1.79; onto Irish HP List when Coys reduced, 24.6.83 (after c. 27 years' service as a commissioned officer); dd on half pay at an unknown date in 1792.

William Anne Skinner (b. at Rotterdam, '36): Ens, 35th Foot, 10.4.56, a free augmentation vacancy; Lieut, 35th Foot, 27.7.59, by purchase; resigned 14.9.61; returned to the service as Lieut, new-raising Freron's Corps, 1.2.62; onto GB HP List when Corps disb, 19.1.63; exchanged from HP as Lieut, 35th Foot, 3.9.66; retired 14.11.70 (after 10.6 years' service), his regt in England; appointed to the East India Company's forces as a Cadet, in 1.71 and made Ens in the army of the Bengal Presidency on 1.1.73, but resigned 20.1.75.

Colin Campbell #5 (Scot., b.'36): Ens, 35th Foot, 11.4.56, a free augmentation vacancy; Lieut, 35th Foot, 27.7.59, a free dd-vacancy; Capt-Lieut, 35th Foot, 28.6.75, a free dd-vacancy; Capt, 35th Foot, 17.7.75, a free dd-vacancy; Maj, 35th Foot, 9.4.89, probable purchase vice a retirement; same in 1793…

Charles Portis: QM, 35th Foot, 9.4.56 (to 23.2.57), a free augmentation vacancy; Ens, 35th Foot, 1.12.56, probable purchase, vice an augmentation; Lieut, 35th Foot, 25.9.59, a free dd-vacancy; dd 15.11.62 (after 6.6 years' service), his regt in Cuba.

Robt. Bayard (NY,b.'39): Ens, Pepperrell's 51st Ft (Mohawk R. / Oswego), 7.1.56, probable purchase, vice a resignation; onto GB HP when regt disb, 7.3.57; from HP as Ens, 35th Ft, 8.3.57, a free augmentation vacancy; to Lieut, Gage's new-raising (in America) 80th Ft, 26.12.57; X'd to Lieut, 4/60th Ft (in Champlain – Hudson corridor), 16.7.58; to Capt, 2/60th Ft (at Quebec), 18.4.59, purchase vice a resignation; to Maj, 1/60th Ft (dispersed in N. Amer.), 4.10.65, purchase vice a resignation; X'd in same comm. later in 1765 to Maj, 2/60th Ft, in Champlain – Hudson corridor); retired 17.3.69 (after 13.3 years' service).

Chaplain:

Edward Whitty (Eng., b.'20): Chaplain, 35th Foot, 9.2.50, by means unknown; exchanged to Chaplain, 47th Foot, 20.5.67; retired 9.9.75 (after 25.6 years' service), his regt in Boston, Mass.

Surgeon:

Thomas Wilkins b.'13): Surgeon, 35th Foot, 22.3.47/48, purchase vice a resignation; resigned 1.6.62; returned to the service as Master Apothecary, Havana Hospital, 1.7.62, by means unknown; reduced onto GB HP List, 25.12.63 (after 16.7 years' service); still on HP in 1794.

New Entrants in 1758:

Major:

Roger Morris (Eng., b.'27): Gentleman volunteer made 2nd Lieut, 21st Foot, 1.5.45, by purchase; to Capt, 59th/48th Foot, 13.9.45, purchase vice a resignation; retired on full pay, 6.6.57; returned to the service as Major, 35th Foot, 16.2.58, a free dd-vacancy; to Lieut Col, 47th Foot, 19.5.60, a free dd-vacancy; resigned 15.6.64 (after 19.2 years' service), his regt in Ireland. (* in May 1757, Surgeon Richard Huck certified that Morris 'labours under such a Complication of Diseases, as will render him forever incapable of performing the Duties and supporting the Fatigues of a military Life' [Pargellis, *Loudoun*, p.327]).

Lieut:

James Abercromby #2 (Scot., b.'41): Ens, 44th Foot, 25.12.56, free vice a resignation; to Lieut, 35th Foot, 26.3.58, free vice an augmentation; to Capt, 42nd Foot, 5.5.62, purchase vice a resignation; reduced onto GB HP List, 18.3.63; exchanged from HP as Capt, 3rd Foot, 15.5.65; bvt Major, 29.8.77; bvt Lieut Col, 19.2.83; to Capt, late Capt Alex. Martin's North British Invalid Coy., 9.6.86, a free dd-vacancy; bvt Col, 1.3.94; dd at an unknown date in 1804.
(** third son of the Gen. James Abercromby defeated by Montcalm at Carillon in 1758).

Ensigns:

Wareham Browne (Ire., b.'33): Ens, 35th Foot, 24.1.58, purchase vice a resignation; Lieut, 35th Foot, 7.4.60, purchase vice a resignation; dd 27.9.62 (after 4.6 years' service), his regt in Cuba.

Cornelius Lysaght (Ire.): Gentleman volunteer made Ens, 35th Foot, 24.1.58, purchase vice a retirement; Lieut, 35th Foot, 11.6.60, by purchase; dd of disease, 1.10.64 (after 6.7 year service), his regt in West Florida (Pensacola and Mobile).
(** CL, a volunteer serving with the 46th Foot, was one of the young gentlemen sent from the regular army in 1757 to learn the 'ranging-discipline' with Rogers' Rangers (Rogers, *Journals*, 56-9).

Robert Farquharson: Ens, 35th Foot, 31.7.58, purchase vice an augmentation; Lieut, 35th Foot, 30.8.61, purchase vice a resignation; dd of disease, 9.11.64 (after 6.3 years' service), his regt in West Florida (Pensacola and Mobile).

Colin Campbell #11 (Scot., b.'36): Ens, 35th Foot, 23.8.56, probable purchase, vice an augmentation; Lieut, 35th Foot, 5.10.60, purchase vice a retirement; Capt-Lieut, 35th Foot, 17.7.75, a free dd-vacancy; Capt, 35th Foot, 22.11.75, free vice an augmentation; exchanged onto GB HP List, 20.6.87 (after 28.9 years' service), his regt in England; still on HP in 1793.

John French (Ire., b.'37): QM, 55th Foot, 18.6.57 (to 15.12.58), a free augmentation vacancy; to Ens, 35th Foot, 15.12.58, purchase vice a resignation; Lieut, 35th Foot, 14.9.61, purchase vice a resignation; reduced onto GB HP List, 19.7.63; exchanged from HP as Lieut, 13th Dragoons, 12.11.67; Capt, 13th Dragoons, 12.12.70, purchase vice a retirement; retired 14.1.75 (after 13.2 years' service), his regt in Ireland.

New Entrants in 1759:

Capt-Lieutenant:

Robert McKinnon (b. 'in America'): Lieut, Pepperrell's new-raising 66th Foot, 19.9.45, by raising for rank; onto GB HP List when regt disb, 15.5.49; from HP as Lieut, Shirley's new-raising 50th Foot, 28.12.54, a free augmentation vacancy; to Lieut, 2/1st Foot, 25.12.56, free vice an augmentation; to Capt-Lieut, 35th Foot, 14.4.59, purchase vice a resignation; Capt, 35th Foot, 27.7.59, a free dd-vacancy; died of disease, 31.5.65 (after 14.1 years' service), his regt in West Florida (Pensacola and Mobile).

Ensigns:

John de Bruyères (Eng.): Ens, 35th Foot, 27.7.59, a free dd-vacancy; to Lieut, 56th Foot, 5.10.62, a free dd-vacancy; reduced onto GB HP List, 6.9.63 (after 4.1 years' service), his regt just arrived home in Ireland from Cuba; dd on HP at unknown date in 1786.

James Lundin (Scot., b.'39): Ens, 35th Foot, 28.7.59, by purchase; Lieut, 35th Foot, 7.3.62, a free dd-vacancy; retired 12.7.73; returned to the service as Lieut, new-raising 2Bn, R. Highland Emigrants (numbered 84th Foot from 1779), 14.6.75, by raising for rank; Capt-Lieut, 2/84th Foot, 11.12.79, a free dd-vacancy; onto GB HP List when Bn disb, 2.2.84; from HP as Lieut, new-raising British Invalid Coys., 25.6.90 (which fourteen Coys were reduced on 25.12.90, although their officers were continued on full pay); Lieut in previous (25.6.90) commission in Capt. Boleyn Douglas's new-raising Portsmouth Invalid Coy., in 1793; same in 1794.

Hunt FitzGerald (Ire., b.'35): Gentleman volunteer made Ens, 35th Foot, 25.9.59, a free dd-vacancy; Lieut, 35th Foot, 4.5.62, purchase vice a retirement; Capt, 35th Foot, 20.3.72, purchase vice a retirement; bvt Major, 12.6.82; resigned at an unknown date in 1785 (after c.25.8 years' service), his regt in the Leeward Islands.

(* he was one of the eight gent volunteers who led the 'forlorn hope' that secured the path up the cliffs onto the Plains of Abraham on 13.9.59)

Quartermaster:

John Wicks; QM, 35th Foot, 27.7.59, a free dd-vacancy; resigned 30.10.61 (after 2.3 years' service), the regt in Staten Island, shortly to embark for Barbados.

New Entrants in 1760:

Major:

Thomas Addison (b. In America): Capt, Gooch's new-raising Regt of Foot, 9.6.40; onto GB HP List when regt disb, 24.10.42; from HP as Capt, 28th Foot, 25.6.44, free vice an augmentation; to Major, 35th Foot, 19.5.60, a free dd-vacancy; resigned 30.9.61 (after 19.8 years' service), his regt in Staten Island, shortly to embark for Barbados.

(* in a list of officers of late Gooch's examined by a Board of Gen'l Officers on 12.1.43/4, he was described at Gooch's raising as 'a Gentleman residing upon his Estate in Maryland' who was 'wounded upon the Attack of Fort Lazare', VMHB, 30 [1922], 9).

Captain:

Andrew Simpson (Scot., b.'27): Ens, 55th/44th Foot, 24.12.47, purchase vice a retirement; Lieut, 44th Foot, 26.6.55, purchase vice an augmentation; Capt-Lieut, 44th Foot, 15.9.58, a free dd-vacancy; to Capt, 80th Foot, 16.8.60, purchase vice a resignation; to Capt, 35th Foot, 4.10.60, free vice a resignation; retired 31.10.70 (after 22.8 years' service), his regt in England.

Ensigns:

Nathaniel Weld (Ire., b.'41): Ens, 35th Foot, 7.4.60, purchase vice a resignation; Lieut, 35th Foot, 24.7.62, a free dd-vacancy; retired 27.11.70 (after 10.6 years' service), his regt in England.

Edward Candler (Ire., b.'41): Ens, 35th Foot, 11.6.60, by purchase; to Lieut, 48th Foot, 12.8.62, a free dd-vacancy; Capt, 48th Foot, 11.1.69, by means unk; retired 14.1.75 (after 14.6 years' service), his regt in the Windward Islands.

Hugh Scott #1 (Ire., b.'43): Ens, 35th Foot, 5.10.60, purchase vice a retirement; to Ens, 28th Foot, 21.10.61, free vice a removal to the Invalids; Lieut, 28th Foot, 23.10.62, a free dd-vacancy; left the army for reason unknown, 6.11.69 (after 9.1 years' service), his regt in Ireland.

New Entrants in 1761:

John Maunsell (see previous list, p. 322) returned as Major.

Ensigns:

James Lyon (Sct., b.'41): Surgeon's Mate (regt untraced) made Ens, 35th Ft, 30.8.61, purchase vice a resignation; Lieut, 35th Ft, 27.9.62, a free dd-vacancy; reduced onto GB HP, 19.7.63; X'd from HP as Lieut, 7th Ft (in Scot.), 3.2.69; to Capt, 35th Ft, 31.10.70, purchase vice a retirement; dd 27.6.75 of wounds suffered on 17.6.75 at Bunker Hill (after 8.3 years' service).

Samuel Calderwood: Gent Volunteer with 60th Ft made Ens, 35th Ft, 14.9.61, probable purchase, vice a resignation; Lieut, 35th Ft, 15.11.62, a free dd-vacancy; dd 17.11.62 (after 1.2 years' service).

Quartermaster:

Edward Parker (Eng., b.'28): QM, 35th Ft, 30.10.61 (to 19.1.63), free vice a resignation; Lieut, 35th Ft, 17.11.62, a free dd-vacancy; reduced onto GB HP, 19.7.63; from HP as Lieut, 32nd Ft (in St. Vincent), 25.12.70, a free augmentation vacancy; Capt-Lieut, 32nd Ft, 27.9.75, purchase vice a retirement; to Capt, 65th Ft (at Halifax?), 5.7.76, a free augmentation vacancy; to Capt, 31st Ft (at Quebec), 10.9.76, a free augmentation vacancy; retired 30.4.88 (after 19 years' service).
(* considering his age he was likely an NCO, but this not noted in the WO register)

New Entrants in 1762:

Major:

Wm. Forbes (Scot., b.'21): Ens, 2/1st Ft (in Ire.), 15.12.38, probable purchase: transferred in same comm. to 1/1st Ft (in Ire.) in 1741; 2nd Lieut, 1/1st Ft, 10.5.42, a free augmentation vacancy; Lieut, 1/1st Ft, 19.5.42, by purchase; to Capt, 2/1st Ft (in Scot.), 6.2.47/8, purchase vice a resignation; reduced onto GB HP, 2.11.48; X'd from HP as Capt, 46th Ft (in Ire.), 11.2.48/9; to Maj, 35th Ft, 31.10.62, by purchase; retired 25.12.68; dd at Inverness, 27.3.74 (*Scots Mag*, Mar 1774).

Captain:

Charles Ruxton (Ire., b.'26): Gent Volunteer made Ens, 1/1st Ft (in Flanders), 17.5.48, a free dd-vacancy; reduced onto GB HP, 2.11.48; from HP as Ens, 2/1st Ft (in Ire.), 24.1.52, a free dd-vacancy; to Lieut, 28th Ft (in Ire.), 16.2.56, purchase vice an augmentation; to Capt-Lieut, 40th Ft (in Cuba), 15.5.62, probable purchase; to Capt, 35th Ft, 5.6.62, a free dd-vacancy; reduced onto GB HP, 19.7.63; from HP as Capt, 35th Ft, 25.12.65, a free augmentation vacancy; X'd onto GB HP, 13.4.67; from HP as Capt, own new-raising Irish Invalid Coy., 18.7.76; reduced onto Ire HP when five of the ten Irish Invalid Coys disb, 24.6.83 (after 20.2 years' service); still on HP in 1793

Capt-Lieutenant:

Vernon Hawley: Ens, Sir John Bruce Hope, Bt.'s 60th Ft (in Ire.), 2.11.45, purchase vice an augmentation; 2nd Lt, 60th Ft, 26.8.48, by purchase; onto Irish HP when regt disbanded, 2.12.48; from HP as Lt, 43rd F (in Ireland), 16.2.56, purchase vice an augmentation; to Capt-Lt, 35th Ft, 8.4.62, by purchase; resigned 25.12.62 (after 10 years' service).

Lieuts:

Henry Jenkins (Eng., b.'44): Lieut, 35th Ft, 2.4.62, purchase vice an augmentation; Capt, 35th Ft, 22.8.70, purchase vice a retirement; retired 25.7.75 (after 13.4 years' service).

Montfort Browne (Ire., b.'33): Lieut, Capt Wm. Rickman's new-raising (in Eng.) North American Independent Coy, 7.3.60; in same comm. when his Independent Coy. And eight others amalgamated (in S.Carolina) in 3 - 5.61 to form Ralph Burton's 95th Ft; to Lieut, 35th Ft, 4.5.62, vice a resignation; reduced onto GB HP, 19.7.63 (after 3.4 years' service); resigned his HP in 1.66.

(* appointed Lieut-Gov of West Florida in Jan '66, and acting Gov there from Feb '67; Gov of Bahamas, '74 to Mar '76, and Nov '78 to late '79; provincial comm. as Col, loyalist Prince of Wales' American Regt; onto Provincial HP List when regt disb, 25.10.83; dd 31.3.85 [Dornfest, *Loyalist Officers*, 49].

Hugh Massey (Ire., b.'48): Ens, 27th Ft (in Cuba), 1.8.62, probable purchase; to Lieut, 35th Ft, 25.12.62, purchase vice a resignation; Capt-Lieut, 35th Ft, 22.11.75, a free augmentation vacancy; Capt, 35th Ft, 4.1.77, a free dd-vacancy; retired 23.6.89 (after 26.9 years' service).

Surgeons:

George Hugonin: Surg., 35th Ft, 1.6.62, probable purchase, vice a resignation; dd 11.10.62 (after 0.4 years' service).

Edward Bray (Eng., b.'31): Surgeon's Mate (regt untraced) made Surg., 90th Ft (in Cuba), 15.7.62, by means unk.; to Surg., 35th Ft, 11.10.62, a free dd-vacancy; dd 17.1.74 (after 11.6 years' service).

New Entrants in 1763:

Quartermaster:

John Southwell: QM, 35th Ft, 19.1.63, purchase vice a resignation; retired 19.10.66 (after 5.3 years' service).

New Entrants in 1764:

Lieut Colonel:

Thomas Hall: Cornet, 8th Drags (in Eng.), 19.3.46/7, purchase vice a resignation; Lieut, 8th Drags (in Ire.), 10.12.55, purchase vice a resignation; to Capt, 16th Ft (in Ire.), 27.4.56, a free augmentation vacancy; to Capt, new-raising (in Eng.), 2/12th Ft, 27.8.56 (and remained with 2nd Bn when it was regimented in 1758 as the 65th Ft); bvt Lieut Col, 25.4.60, as Deputy Adjt Gen; retired 24.11.62; returned to regtl service as Lieut Col, 35th Ft, 17.8.64, by purchase; X'd onto GB HP, 22.2.68; bvt Col, 25.5.72; Maj Gen, 29.8.77; from HP as Col, 79th Ft (in Eng), 8.1.79; onto GB HP when regt disb, 5.2.84; from HP as Col, 3rd Ft, 10.4.86; same in 1793 .

(* in an internal WO list of 1755-56 of officers seeking promotion he was recommended by Lord Granby, adding that he was 'provided in Ireland' [BL Add.MS 73,594, f.117]).

Captain:

Robt. Sherwood (Eng., b.'39): Ens, 51st Ft (on Rochfort exped.), 4.10.57, a free augmentation vacancy; Lieut, 51st Ft (in Germany), 27.8.59, a free dd-vacancy; to Capt, 35th Ft, 13.3.64, purchase vice a retirement; Maj, 35th Ft, 25.12.72, purchase vice a retirement; retired 12.3.74 (after 16.4 years' service).

Lieuts:

John Crutchfield (Eng.): Gent Volunteer made Ens, new-raising (in Scot.) 113th Ft, 20.10.61; Lieut, 113th Ft, 30.6.62, free vice a supersession; onto GB HP when regt disb, 3.6.63; X'd from HP as Lieut, 35th Ft, 19.3.64; dd 13.12.65 (after 3.4 years' service).

Wm. Ramsay (Scot.,b'40): Gent Volunteer with army in America made Ens, 4/62nd Ft (R.Amers.), 7.12.56, a free augmentation vacancy; Lieut, 4/60th Ft (R.Amers.), 26.7.58, a free dd-vacancy; reduced onto GB HP, 24.8.63; X'd from HP as Lieut, 35th Ft, 12.8.64; to Capt-Lieut, 14th Ft; (in Va.), 10.12.75, by purchase; Capt, 14th Ft, 24.10.76, a free dd-vacancy; bvt Maj, 18.11.90; same in 1793 .

James Hughes: Ens in the Pennsylvania Regt, 4.12.57, and Lieut there, 17.3.59; to Ens, 44th Ft, 16.8.60 (in Quebec), free vice a resignation; to Lieut, 35th Ft, 9.11.64, purchase vice a retirement; X'd onto GB HP, 3.9.66; X'd from HP as Lieut, 1/60th Ft (widely dispersed in N.Amer.), 9.10.67; retired 4.4.72 (after 10.6 years' service in the regulars).

Josias Taylor: Lieut, new-raising (in GB) 110th Ft, 19.10.61; onto GB HP when regt disb, 1.6.63; X'd from HP as Lieut, 35th Ft, 16.11.64; X'd onto GB HP, 4.5.67; from HP as Lieut, new-raising (in Eng.) 72nd Ft, 21.12.77; retired 6.4.80 (after 6.4 years' service).

Ensign:

Robt. Gray (Ire., b.'45): Ens, 35th Ft, 9.11.64, a free dd-vacancy; retired 30.4.70 (after 5.4 years' service.

New Entrants in 1765:

Captains:

Chas. Ruxton (see above) returned as Capt.

Wm. Gaule (Eng., b.'38): Ens, 17th Ft, 24.7.59 (in Champlain/Hudson corridor), probable purchase, vice a dismissal; Lieut, 17th Ft, 8.4.62, purchase vice a resignation; X'd onto GB HP, 15.3.64; from HP as Capt, 35th Ft, 31.5.65, a free dd-vacancy; Maj, 35th Ft, 12.3.74, purchase vice a retirement; retired 13.1.76 (after 15.2 years' service).

(* included in an internal WO list of 1763-64 of officers 'desirous of being put on full Pay', his application supported by 'Mr. Stephenson & very strongly by Mr. Grenville for a Company any where' [BL Add.MS 73,594, f.24])

Ensigns:

Wm. Bard (New Jersey,b.'40): Ens, 80th Ft (at the Western Posts), 8.9.61, probable purchase, vice a resignation; onto GB HP when regt disb, 1.11.64; from HP as Ens, 35th Ft, 23.2.65, a free dd-vacancy; Lieut, 35th F, 12.7.73, purchase vice a retirement; kia 17.6.75 at Bunker Hill (after 13.5 years' service).

John Lewis (America, b.'50): Ens, 35th Ft, 23.2.65, a free dd-vacancy; retired 22.2.69 (after 4 years' service).

Richard Cribb (Eng., b.'48): Ens, 35th Ft, 13.12.65, by means unk.; Lieut, 35th Ft, 3.2.69, purchase vice a retirement; X'd onto GB HP, 27.8.72; from HP as Capt, new-raising (in Eng.) 79th Ft, 12.1.78; Maj, 79th Ft, 12.1.80, a free dd-vacancy; dd of disease, 2.11.80, the regt in Jamaica (after 9.5 years' service).

List of Officers in the 40th Regiment of Foot in 1776

Lieut Colonels:

James Grant (Scot., b.'33): Surg., 1/36th Ft (in Eng.), 27.4.56, purchase vice a resignation; to Ens, the Earl of Eglintoun's new-raising (in Scot.) 62nd/77th Ft, 12.1.57; Lieut, 77th Ft, 19.9.58, a free dd-vacancy; Capt-Lieut, 77th Ft, 6.5.62, purchase vice a resignation; Capt, 77th Ft, 5.8.62, a free dd- vacancy; to Capt, 40th Ft, 17.8.62 (in Cuba), free vice a resignation; Maj, 40th Ft, 12.12.70, purchase vice a retirement; Lieut Col, 40th Ft, 11.12.75, purchase vice a promotion to a Colonelcy; kia 27.8.76 in battle of Long Island (after 20.3 years' service).

Thomas Musgrave (Eng., b.'38): Ens, 3rd Ft (in Eng.), 31.12.54, purchase vice a retirement; Lieut, 3rd Ft, 21.6.56, purchase vice a departure for the Invalids; to Capt, 64th Ft (in Eng.), 20.8.59, purchase vice a dd-vacancy; bvt Maj, 23.7.72; Maj, 64th Ft, 17.8.74, purchase vice a promotion to a Colonelcy; to Lieut Col, 40th Ft (at NY), 28.8.76, a free dd-vacancy; bvt Col, 18.4.82, as ADC to the King; to Col, new-raising (in Eng.) 76th Ft, 25.12.87; Maj Gen, 28.4.90;; same in 1793 .

Major:

Samuel Bradstreet (Eng., b.'34): Ens, 40th Ft (in N.S.), 27.3.53, purchase vice a resignation; Lieut, 40th Ft, 29.6.55, free vice an augmentation; Capt, 40th Ft, 10.11.61, purchase vice a resignation; Maj, 40th Ft, 11.12.75, purchase vice a promotion to a Colonelcy; dd of disease 10.12.79, the regt in Antigua (after 26.7 years' service).

Capts:

James Duffe (Scot., b.'34): from Scots-Dutch Bgde as Lieut, the Earl of Eglintoun's new-raising (in Scot.) 62nd/77th Ft, 11.1.57; Capt, 77th Ft, 19.10.62, a free dd-vacancy; onto GB HP when regt disb, 10.4.64; X'd from HP as Capt, 40th Ft (in Ire.), 28.2.66; bvt Maj, 29.8.77; retired 26.1.80 (after 21.2 years in British service).

(* He was Ens, Drumlanrig's new-raising Regt in the S-D Bgde, 2.6.47; onto Dutch HP when regt disb in 1749).

James Wemyss (Scot., b.'48): Ens, 40th Ft (in Ire.), 6.8.66, purchase vice a retirement; Lieut, 40th Ft, 1.4.67, purchase vice a resignation; Capt, 40th Ft, 14.3.71, purchase vice a retirement; to Maj, 63rd Ft (at NY), 10.8.78, free vice a retirement; bvt Lieut Col, 22.8.83; Lieut Col, 63rd Ft, 20.9.87, purchase vice a retirement; retired 31.7.89 (after 23 years' service).

(* appointed ADC to Gen James Robertson on 14.5.76 and to Gen. Wm. Tryon on 20.4.77; was also made Maj-Cmdnt on 5.5.77 of the loyalist Queen's American Rangers, but resigned on 14.10.77 to resume his appointment as ADC to Robertson [Dornfest, *Loyalist Officers*, 355)

Wm. MacLean (Scot., b.'40): Ens, the Earl of Eglintoun's new-raising (in Scot.) 62nd/77th Ft, 10.1.57; Lieut, 77th Ft, 18.9.58; to Lieut, 40th Ft (in Cuba), 24.7.62, a free dd-vacancy (and Adjt, 16.6.70 to 1.4.73); Capt-Lieut, 40th Ft, 1.4.73, purchase vice a retirement; Capt, 40th Ft, 28.4.74, purchase vice a retirement; retired 6.5.76; returned to the service as Capt, new-raising (in Scotland) Sutherland Regt of Fencible Men, 8.10.79; reduced with the regt, 8.5.83 (after 23.6. years' service); dd 14.8.88 'at Craighon, Sutherlandshire' (*Scots Mag*, Sept 1788).

Wm. Montgomery (Ire., b.'53): Ens, 40th Ft (in Ire.), 15.8.66, a free dd-vacancy; Lieut, 40th Ft, 16.12.68, purchase vice a resignation (and QM, 18.1.70 to 13.11.75); Capt-Lieut, 40th Ft, 14.1.75, purchase vice a retirement; Capt, 40th Ft, 22.11.75, purchase in an augmentation; Maj, 40th Ft, 6.3.80, a free dd-vacancy; kia 6.9.81

in the attack on Fort Griswold during Arnold's raid on New London, Conn. (after 15.1 years' service).

Wm. Wolfe (Ire., b.'51): Ens, 40th Ft (in Ire.), 15.3.68, purchase vice a retirement; Lieut, 40th Ft, 12.12.70, purchase vice a retirement; Capt, 40th Ft, 5.3.75, purchase vice a retirement; kia 21.9.77 in the night action at Paoli (after 9.5 years' service).

Wm. Bamford (Ire., b.'28): Ens, 35th Ft (in Ire.), 10.3.42/43, probable purchase, a dd-vacancy; 2nd Lieut, 35th Foot, 26.2.45/46, a free augmentation vacancy; Lieut, 35th Ft, 16.2.56, purchase vice a resignation; Capt-Lieut, 35th Foot, 25.12.62, purchase vice a resignation; bvt Capt, 25.5.72; to Capt, 40th Ft (in Ire.), 25.3.75, a free dd-vacancy; retired 15.10.78 (after 35.6 years' service), his regt at New York.

Edward Eyre (Ire., b.'35): Ens, 28th Ft (in Ire.), 3.6.52, purchase vice a resignation; to Lieut, new-raising (in Eng.) 58th/56th Ft, 2.1.56; to Capt, Maj-Cmdnt John Deaken's new-raising (in GB) 110th Ft, 18.10.61; onto GB HP when regt disb, 1.6.53; from HP as Capt, 40th Ft (at Boston), 15.8.75, a free augmentation vacancy; bvt Maj, 29.8.77; bvt Lieut Col, 19.2.83; X'd onto GB HP, 1.6.85 (after 20.8 years' service); same in 1793 .

John Edward Adlam (Eng., b.'46): Ens, 40th Ft (at NY), 30.9.61, purchase vice a resignation; Lieut, 40th Ft, 28.9.62, purchase vice a resignation; Capt-Lieut, 40th Ft, 22.11.75, by purchase; Capt, 40th Ft, 11.12.75, purchase vice a promotion to a Colonelcy; bvt Maj, 19.3.83; Maj, 40th Ft, 12.9.87, purchase vice a promotion to a Colonelcy; same in 1793 .

John Graves Simcoe (Eng.,b'52): Ens, 35th Ft (in Eng.), 27.4.70 (and Adjt, 27.3.72 to 27.12.75), purchase vice a retirement; Lieut, 35th Ft, 12.3.74, purchase vice a retirement; to Capt, 40th Ft (at Boston), 27.12.75, purchase vice a retirement; bvt Lieut Col (in America), 23.6.79; bvt Lieut Col (in Army), 19.12.81; bvt Col, 18.11.90; from HP as Col-Cmdnt, new-raising (in Eng.) Queen's Rangers, 1.9.91; same in 1793 .

(* he was simultaneously Lieutenant Colonel Commandant, the provincial Queen's Rangers, but succeeded in his captaincy in the 40th only on 25.12.82, the date on which the Queen's Rangers were taken onto the regular British Estab.)

Robt. Mostyn (Welsh, b.?): Ens, 65th Ft (in Ire.), purchase vice a retirement; Lieut, 65th Ft, 7.11.74, purchase vice a retirement; to Capt, 40th Ft, 6.5.76 (in N.S.), purchase vice a retirement; retired 1.10.78 (after 10.3 years' service).

Capt-Lieut:

Wm. Harris (Eng., b.'46): Ens, 40th Ft (in Cuba), 6.10.62, by means unk.; Lieut, 40th Ft, 15.3.68, (and Adjt, 1.4.73 to 24.5.76), purchase vice a retirement; Capt-Lieut, 40th Ft, 28.12.75, purchase vice a promotion to a Colonelcy; Capt, 40th Ft, 21.9.77, a free dd-vacancy; bvt Maj, 18.11.90; same in 1793 .

Lieuts:

Richmond Webb (Eng., b.'50): Ens, 40th Ft (in Ire.), 12.11.67, purchase vice a retirement; Lieut, 40th Ft, 16.8.70, purchase vice a retirement; retired 14.3.77 (after 9.3 years' service).

(* in an internal WO list of the later 1760s of applicants for ensigncies he was recommended by 'His Father late Col. R. Webb' [BL Add.MS 73,594, f.67])

Wm. Hamilton (Eng., b.'54): Ens, 40th Ft (in Ire.), 3.6.70, by means unk; Lieut, 40th Ft, 28.4.74, purchase vice a retirement; Capt-Lieut, 40th Ft, 6.3.80, by purchase; Capt, 40th Ft, 8.9.81, by purchase; X'd onto GB HP, 30.11.89 (after 19.5 years' service); same in 1793 .

John Moore (Ire., b.'54): Ens, 40th Ft (in Ire.), 12.12.70, purchase vice a retirement; Lieut, 40th Ft, 20.10.74, purchase vice a retirement; Capt-Lieut, 40th Ft, 8.9.81, by purchase; retired 10.6.83 (after 12.5. years' service), his regt in NY.

Norman Uniacke (Ire., b.'51): Ens, 40th Ft (in Ire.), 28.1.71 purchase vice a retirement; Lieut, 40th Ft, 12.12.74, purchase vice a retirement; retired 16.1.77 (after 6 years' service), the regt in NY.

Hon. James De Courcy (Ire.,b'54): Ens, 40th Ft (in Ire.), 17.12.72, a free dd-vacancy; Lieut, 40th Ft, 14.1.75, purchase vice a retirement; retired 7.3.80 when appointed Lieut-Gov of Tilbury Fort; from Tilbury as Lieut, one of fourteen new-raising British Invalid Coys, 25.6.90 (and remained on full pay when these Coys all reduced on 25.1.91); to Lieut, Capt Chas. Murray's new-raising Alderney Invalid Coy, in 1793 (in previous 25.6.90 commission); same end 1793 .,
(* badly wounded at Brandywine on 11.9.77)

John Doyle (Ire., b.'56): Ens, 48th Ft (in Ire.), 14.3.71, by means unk.; Lieut, 48th Ft, 17.9.73, purchase vice a retirement; X'd to Lieut, 40th Ft (in Ire.), 1.3.75; resigned 24.10.78 to take up provincial commission of 26.5.78 as Capt in the loyalist Volunteers of Ireland; Maj, Volunteers of Ireland, 15.3.82 (a corps taken onto the regular Brit Estab in 1782 as 105th Ft); onto Ire HP when 105th disb, 31.1.84; from HP as Lieut Col Cmdnt, his own new-raising (in Ire.) 87th Ft, 18.9.93; same end 1793 ...
(* was a brother of Welbore Ellis Doyle)

Theodore Morrison (Sct., b.'55): Ens, 40th Ft (in Ire.), 28.4.74, purchase vice a retirement; Lieut, 40th Ft, 5.3.75, purchase vice a retirement; to Capt, 45th F (at NY), 30.10.77, purchase vice a retirement; X'd onto GB HP, 28.2.85 (after 10.9 years' service); same in 1793 ...

Alex. Philip Forbes (Scot., b.'56): Ens, 40th Ft (in Ire.), 14.5.74, purchase vice a retirement; Lieut, 40th Ft, 1.5.75, purchase vice a retirement; to Capt, 2/60th Ft (at Quebec), 26.9.87, by raising men for rank in an augmentation; to Capt, 18th Ft (at Gib), 2.6.88, free vice a dismissal; dd 20.3.93 (after 18.6 years' service).

Charles Bourke (b?): Lieut, Maj-Cmdnt the Hon. John Nairne's new-raising (in GB) 109th F, 20.10.61; onto GB HP when regt disb, 10.6.63; from HP as Lieut, 40th Ft (at Boston), 15.8.75, a free augmentation vacancy; X'd onto GB HP, 12.5.79 (after 5.4 years' service); same in 1793 ...

Wm. Carter (Ire., b.'50): Ens, 47th Ft (in Ire.), 5.6.71, by purchase; to Ens, 40th F, 20.2.73, a free dd-vacancy; Lieut, 40th Ft, 22.11.75, a free augmentation vacancy; retired 27.10.77 (after 6.4 years' service).

James Bontein (Scot., b.'52): Ens, 40th Ft (in Ire.), 31.8.74, probable purchase vice a retirement; Lieut, 40th Ft, 23.11.75, purchase vice an augmentation; Capt, 40th Ft, 25.12.82, purchase vice a resignation; reduced onto GB HP, 24.6.83 (after 8.8 years' service); same in 1793 ...

John Gason (b?): Ens, 40th Ft (in Ire.), 12.12.74, purchase vice a retirement; Lieut, 40th Ft, 11.12.75, purchase vice a retirement; Capt-Lieut, 40th Ft, 16.10.78, purchase vice a retirement; Capt, 40th Ft, 6.3.80, probable purchase; retired 1.3.82 (after 7.3 years' service).

John Forbes (Scot., b.'55): Ens, 40th Ft (in Ire.), 14.1.75, purchase vice a retirement; Lieut, 40th Ft, 28.12.75, purchase vice a promotion to a Colonelcy; Capt, 40th Ft, 1.10.78, purchase vice a retirement; X'd onto GB HP, 30.4.90 (after 15.2 years' service); same in 1793 …

Ensigns:

Edward Cheshire (Ire.): Ens, 40th Ft (in Ire.), 20.10.74, purchase vice a retirement; retired 6.5.77; returned to the service as Ens, Royal Leinster Provincial Regt of Ft (in Ire.), 28.4.83, free vice a retirement; reduced with his regt, 1.10.83 (after 3 years' service).

Robt. Arbuthnot (Scot., b.'58): Ens, 40th Ft (in Ire.), 14.1.75, purchase vice a retirement; to Lieut, 65th Ft (in N.S.), 24.5.76, purchase vice a retirement; to Lieut, 31st Ft (at Ile-aux-Noix), 10.9.76, a free augmentation vacancy; Capt, 31st Ft, 27.2.88, purchase vice a retirement; same in 1793 …

Richard Barber (b?): Ens, 40th Ft (in Ire.), 5.3.75, purchase vice a retirement; Lieut, 40th Ft, 16.1.77, purchase vice a retirement; kia 11.9.77 at Brandywine (after2.5 years' service).

James Campbell (Scot., b.'54): Ens, 40th Ft (in Ire.), 1.5.75, purchase vice a retirement; Lieut, 40th Ft, 14.3.77, purchase vice a retirement; retired 20.4.85 (after 10 years' service), the regt in Eng.

Bernard Denis (b?): Ens, 40th Ft, 15.8.75 (at Boston), a free augmentation vacancy; Lieut, 40th Ft, 12.9.77, a free dd-vacancy; dd 17.5.76 (after 3.8 years' service), the regt in St.Lucia.

Henry Wm. Smyth (Eng., b?): Ens, 40th Ft (at Boston), 22.11.75, a free augmentation vacancy; Lieut, 40h Ft, 30.10.77, purchase vice a retirement; dd 9.9.81 of wounds suffered on 6.9.81 in the attack on Fort Griswold during Arnold's raid on New London, Conn. (after 1.1 years' service).
(* a son of the Revd. John Smyth, rector of St. Giles in the Fields).

Charles Roberts (Eng., b.'58): En, 40th Ft (at Boston), 23.11.75, probable purchase, vice an augmentation; to Lieut, 57th Ft (at NY), 18.8.78, purchase vice an augmentation; same in 1793

Thomas Tydd (b. ?): Ens, 40th Ft (at Boston), 24.11.75, purchase vice an augmentation; X'd onto GB HP, 27.2.78 (after 2.3 years' service); same in 1793 …

Charles Monck (Eng., b.'56): Ens, 40th Ft (at Boston), 28.12.75, purchase vice a promotion to a Colonelcy; to Lieut, 45th Ft (at NY), 10.10.76, purchase vice a retirement; X'd onto GB HP, 22.8.83 (after 7.7 years' service); same in 1793 …

George Browne (b?): Ens, 40th Ft (at Boston), 8.2.76, purchase vice a promotion to a Colonelcy; retired 27.5.77 (after 1.3 years' service).

George Craigie (Scot., b.'61): Ens, 40th Ft (in N.S.), 24.5.76, purchase vice a retirement; Lieut, 40th Ft, 12.5.78, purchase vice a retirement; Capt, 40th Ft, 26.1.80, purchase vice a retirement; dd 8.9. 81 of wounds suffered on 6.9.81 during Arnold's raid on New London, Conn. (dd after 5.3 years' service).

James Drummond (Scot., b.'56): Ens, 40th Ft (at NY), 10.10.76, purchase vice a retirement; to Lieut, 43rd Ft (at Rhode Is.?), 10.8.78, purchase vice a retirement; Capt, 43rd Ft, 17.1.87, purchase vice a retirement; Maj, 43rd Ft, 2.12.93, purchase vice an augmentation; Lieut Col, 43rd Ft, 31.12.93, purchase vice an augmentation …

Chaplain:

George Thomson (Eng., b?): Chapl, 40th Ft (in N.S.), 24.2.28/29, by means unk.; retired 21.12.82 (after 53.9 years' service).

Quartermaster:

James Carmichael (b?): QM, 40th Ft (at Boston), 13.11.75 (to 17.5.79), purchase vice a resignation; Ens, 40th Ft, 17.5.79, by purchase; retired 27.4.81 (after 5.4 years' service).

Surgeon:

Alex. Mackenzie (Scot., b.'42): Surg, 40th Ft (in Ire.), 14.3.72, a free dd-vacancy; dd at St. Lucia on unk. date in 8.79

Bibliography

Manuscripts

John Carter Brown Library, Brown University, Providence, Rhode Island, USA.
Codex Eng 41: [Seven Years' War Journal of the Proceedings of the 35th Regiment of Foot.]

The John Work Garrett Library, the Sheridan Libraries, Johns Hopkins University, Baltimore, Maryland, USA.
LC 22: The Diary of William Bamford, 1776.

West Sussex Record Office, Chichester, West Sussex, UK.
RSR: Records of the Royal Sussex Regiment.

William L. Clements Library, University of Michigan, Ann Arbor, Michigan, USA.
Gage Papers: Memorial of Lieutenant William Bamford.

Contemporary Newspapers

Pennsylvania Gazette.

Unpublished Theses

Odintz, Mark Frederick, 'The British Officer Corps, 1754-1783.' (2 volumes. PhD thesis, University of Michigan, 1988.)

Databases

Houlding, J.A., *Database of Georgian Military Officers, 1714-1793.* [Unpublished]

Books and Articles

Anon., 'Bamford's Diary: The Revolutionary War Diary of a British Officer,' *Maryland Historical Magazine*, vol. 27 (1932), pp. 240-59, 296-314; vol. 28 (1933), pp. 9-26.

Andrews, Robert J., ed. *The Journals of Jeffrey Amherst. 1757-1763* (East Lansing: Michigan State University Press, 2015).

Arentsen, Michelle, and Jennie Hurl-Eamon (eds.), 'Elizabeth Digby Pilot: Memoir of an Eighteenth-Century Officer's wife during his Service in North America,' *Journal of the Society for Army Historical Research*, vol. 96 (2018), Part I, pp.110-130; Part II, pp.213-230.

Baugh, Daniel. *The Global Seven Years War, 1754-1763* (London: Pearson, 2011).

Boscawen, Hugh. *The Capture of Louisbourg, 1758* Campaigns & Commanders, vol.27 (Norman: University of Oklahoma Press, 2011).

Burns, R.E. 'Ireland and British Military Preparations for War in America in 1775,' *Cithara*, Vol.11 (1963), pp.42-60.

Clark, William Bell, William J. Morgan, et al (eds.), *Naval Documents of the American Revolution* (Washington: Government Printing Office, 1964-present).

Dornfest, Walter T. *Military Loyalists of the American Revolution: Officers and Regiments, 1775-1783* (Jefferson, North Carolina: McFarland, 2011).

Gilbert, A.N. 'Law and Honour among Eighteenth Century British Army Officers,' *Historical Journal*, vol.19 (1976), pp.75-85.

Graham, Gerald S. *The Walker Expedition to Quebec, 1711*. Publications of the Navy Records Society, vol. 94 (London: Navy Records Society, 1953).

Grenier, John. *The Far Reaches of Empire: War in Nova Scotia, 1710-1760*. Campaigns & Commanders, vol. 16 (Norman: University of Oklahoma Press, 2008).

Guy, Alan J. *Oeconomy and Discipline: Officership and Administration in the British Army, 1714-63* (Manchester: Manchester University Press, 1985).

Houlding, J.A. *Fit for Service: The Training of the British Army 1715-1795* (Oxford: Clarendon Press, 1981).

Inman, George (comp.), 'Losses of the Military and Naval Forces Engaged in the War of the American Revolution', *The Pennsylvania Magazine of History and Biography*, 27 (1903), pp.176-205.

John Carter Brown Library, Brown University. *Annual Reports, 1901-1966*. (Providence, Rhode Island: The John Carter Brown Library and the Colonial Society of Massachusetts, 1972).

Martineau, Gerald D. *A History of the Royal Sussex Regiment: a History of the Old Belfast Regiment and the Regiment of Sussex, 1701-1953* (Chichester: Moore & Tillyer, 1953).

Matthew, H. C. G., and Brian Harrison (eds.), Oxford *Dictionary of National Biography: from the Earliest Times to the Year 2000* (Oxford: Oxford University Press, 2004).

Middleton, Richard (ed.), *Amherst and the Conquest of Canada: Selected Papers from the Correspondence of Major-General Jeffrey Amherst while Commander-in-Chief in North America from September 1758 to December 1760*. Publications of the Army Records Society, Vol.20 (Thrupp: Sutton Publishing Limited for the Army Records Society, 2003).

Odintz, Mark F. 'Charles Heathcote and the 35th Regiment' *Journal of the Society for Army Historical Research* 65, no. 263 (1987), pp.183-84.
Pargellis, Stanley (ed.), *Military Affairs in North America, 1748-1765: Selected Documents from the Cumberland Papers in Windsor Castle* (New York and London: D. Appleton-Century Company, Incorporated, 1936).
Robson, John. *Captain Cook's War & Peace. The Royal Navy Years, 1755-1768* (Barnsley: Seaforth Publishing, and Annapolis: Naval Institute, 2009).
Roche, Lieutenant de Vaisseau Jean-Michel, *Dictionnaire des Bâtiments de la Flotte de Guerre Française de Colbert à nos Jours* (Landerneaux: Privately printed for the editor at Presses d'Cloître-Imprimeur, 2013).
Scull, G.D. (ed.), *Memoir and Letters of Captain W. Glanville Evelyn of the Fourth Regiment (King's Own,) From North America, 1774-1776* (Oxford: Printed for Private Circulation by James Parker, 1879).
Shy, John. *Toward Lexington: The Role of the British Army in the Coming of the American Revolution* (Princeton: Princeton University Press, 1965).
Silverstone, Paul H., *The Sailing Navy, 1775-1854.* The U.S. Navy Warship Series (New York: Routledge, Taylor & Francis Group, 2006).
Smythies, Captain Raymond R. H. *Historical Records of the 40th (2nd Somersetshire) Regiment* (Devonport: A. H. Swiss, 1894).
Stacey, C.P., *Quebec, 1759: The Siege and the Battle.* Edited and with new material by Donald E. Graves (Montreal: Robin Brass Studio, 2014).
Starbuck, David R. *Massacre at Fort William Henry* (Hanover, NH: University Press of New England, 2002).
Syrett, David, and R.L. DiNardo, (eds.), *The Commissioned Sea Officers of the Royal Navy, 1660-1815.* Publications of the Navy Records Society, Occasional Publications, No. 1 (Aldershot: Scolar Press for the Navy Records Society, 1994).
Syrett, David (ed.), *The Siege and Capture of Havana 1762.* Publications of the Navy Record Society, Vol.114 (London: Navy Records Society, 1970).
Syrett, David (ed.), *The Rodney Papers: Selections from the Papers of Admiral Lord Rodney,* Volume 1, 1742-1763. Publications of the Navy Record Society, Vol.148 (London: Ashgate for the Navy Records Society, 2005).
Winfield, Rif, *British Warships in the Age of Sail, 1714-1792: Design, Construction, Careers and Fates* (Barnsley: Seaforth Publishing, 2007).
Winfield, Rif, and Stephen S. Roberts (eds.), *French Warships in the Age of Sail, 1626-1786: Design, Construction, Careers and Fates* (Barnsley: Seaforth Publishing, 2017).

Online Resources

Dictionary of Canadian Biography. http://www.biographi.ca/en/
Dictionary of American Naval Fighting Ships. https://www.history.navy.mil/research/histories/ship-histories/danfs.html
History of Parliament online. https://www.historyofparliamentonline.org/
Oxford Dictionary of National Biography. http://www.oxforddnb.com/

Index

From Reason to Revolution series – Warfare 1721-1815

http://www.helion.co.uk/published-by-helion/reason-to-revolution-1721-1815.html

The 'From Reason to Revolution' series covers the period of military history 1721–1815, an era in which fortress-based strategy and linear battles gave way to the nation-in-arms and the beginnings of total war.

This era saw the evolution and growth of light troops of all arms, and of increasingly flexible command systems to cope with the growing armies fielded by nations able to mobilise far greater proportions of their manpower than ever before. Many of these developments were fired by the great political upheavals of the era, with revolutions in America and France bringing about social change which in turn fed back into the military sphere as whole nations readied themselves for war. Only in the closing years of the period, as the reactionary powers began to regain the upper hand, did a military synthesis of the best of the old and the new become possible.

The series will examine the military and naval history of the period in a greater degree of detail than has hitherto been attempted, and has a very wide brief, with the intention of covering all aspects from the battles, campaigns, logistics, and tactics, to the personalities, armies, uniforms, and equipment.

Submissions

The publishers would be pleased to receive submissions for this series. Please contact series editor Andrew Bamford via email (andrewbamford18@gmail.com), or in writing to Helion & Company Limited, Unit 8 Amherst Business Centre, Budbrooke Road, Warwick, CV34 5WE

Titles

No 1 *Lobositz to Leuthen. Horace St Paul and the Campaigns of the Austrian Army in the Seven Years War 1756-57* Translated with additional materials by Neil Cogswell (ISBN 978-1-911096-67-2)

No 2 *Glories to Useless Heroism. The Seven Years War in North America from the French journals of Comte Maurés de Malartic, 1755-1760* William Raffle (ISBN 978-1-1911512-19-6) (paperback)

No 3 *Reminiscences 1808-1815 Under Wellington. The Peninsular and Waterloo Memoirs of William Hay* William Hay, with notes and commentary by Andrew Bamford (ISBN 978-1-1911512-32-5)

No 4 *Far Distant Ships. The Royal Navy and the Blockade of Brest 1793-1815* Quintin Barry (ISBN 978-1-1911512-14-1)

No 5 *Godoy's Army. Spanish Regiments and Uniforms from the Estado Militar of 1800* Charles Esdaile and Alan Perry (ISBN 978-1-911512-65-3) (paperback)

No 6 *On Gladsmuir Shall the Battle Be! The Battle of Prestonpans 1745* Arran Johnston (ISBN 978-1-911512-83-7)

No 7 *The French Army of the Orient 1798-1801. Napoleon's Beloved 'Egyptians'* Yves Martin (ISBN 978-1-911512-71-4)*

No 8 *The Autobiography, or Narrative of a Soldier. The Peninsular War Memoirs of William Brown of the 45th Foot* William Brown, with notes and commentary by Steve Brown (ISBN 978-1-911512-94-3) (paperback)

No 9 *Recollections from the Ranks. Three Russian Soldiers' Autobiographies from the Napoleonic Wars* Translated and annotated by Darrin Boland (ISBN 978-1-912174-18-8) (paperback)

No 10 *By Fire and Bayonet. Grey's West Indies Campaign of 1794* Steve Brown (ISBN 978-1-911512-60-8)

No 11 *Olmütz to Torgau. Horace St Paul and the Campaigns of the Austrian Army in the Seven Years War 1758-60* Translated with additional materials by Neil Cogswell (ISBN 978-1-911512-72-1)

No 12 *Murat's Army. The Army of the Kingdom of Naples 1806-1815* Digby Smith (ISBN 978-1-912390-09-0) (paperback)

No 13 *The Veteran or 40 Years' Service in the British Army. The Scurrilous Recollections of Paymaster John Harley 47th Foot – 1798-1838* John Harley, with notes and commentary by Gareth Glover (ISBN 978-1-912390-25-0) (paperback)

No 14 *Narrative of the Eventful Life of Thomas Jackson. Militiaman and Coldstream Sergeant, 1803-15* Thomas Jackson, with notes and commentary by Eamonn O'Keeffe (ISBN 978-1-912390-12-0) (paperback)

No 15 *For Orange and the States! The Army of the Dutch Republic 1713-1772. Part I: Infantry* Marc Geerdinck-Schaftenaar (ISBN 978-1-911512-15-8)*

No 16 *'Men who are Determined to be Free': The American Assault on Stony Point 15 July 1779* David Bonk (ISBN 978-1-912174-84-3)*

No 17 *Next to Wellington. General Sir George Murray. The Story of a Scottish Soldier and Statesman, Wellington's Quartermaster General* John Harding-Edgar (ISBN 978-1-912390-13-7)

No 18 *Between Scylla and Charibdys: The Army of Friedrich August II of Saxony, 1733-1763. Part I: Staff and Cavalry* Marco Pagan (ISBN 978-1-912174-89-8)*

No 19 *The Secret Expedition: The Anglo-Russian Invasion of Holland 1799* Geert van Uythoven (ISBN 978-1-912390-20-5)

No 20 *'We Are Accustomed to do our Duty' German Auxiliaries with the British Army 1793-95* Paul Demet (ISBN 978-1-912174-96-6)

No 21 *With the Guards in Flanders. The Diary of Captain Roger Morris 1793-95* Peter Harington (ISBN 978-1-911628-15-6) (paperback)

No 22 *The British Army in Egypt 1801. An Underrated Army Comes of Age* Carole Divall (ISBN 978-1-911628-17-0)*

No 23 *Better is the Proud Plaid. The Clothing, Weapons, and Accoutrements of the Jacobites in 1745* Jenn Scott (ISBN ISBN 978-1-911628-16-3)*

No 24 *The Lilies and the Thistle. French Troops in the Jacobite '45* Andrew Bamford (ISBN 978-1-911628-17-0)*

No 25 *A Light Infantryman With Wellington* Gareth Glover (ed.) (ISBN 978-1-911628-10-1) (paperback)

No 26 *Swiss Regiments in the Service of France 1798-1815. Uniforms, Organisation, Campaigns* Stephen Ede-Borrett (ISBN 978-1-911628-12-5)*

No 27 *For Orange and the States! The Army of the Dutch Republic 1713-1772. Part II: Cavalry and Specialist Troops* Marc Geerdinck-Schaftenaar (ISBN 978-1-911628-13-2)*

No 28 *Fashioning Regulation, Regulating Fashion. Uniforms and Dress of the British Army 1800-1815 Volume I* Ben Townsend (ISBN 978-1-911628-09-5)

No 29 *Riflemen. The History of the 5th Battalion 60th (Royal American) Regiment, 1797-1818* Robert Griffith (ISBN 978-1-911628-46-0)

No 30 *The Key to Lisbon. The Third French Invasion of Portugal, 1810-11* Kenton White (ISBN 978-1-911628-52-1)

No 31 *Command and Leadership. Proceedings of the 2018 Helion & Company 'From Reason to Revolution' Conference* Andrew Bamford (ed.) (ISBN 978-1-911628-53-8)

No 32 *Waterloo After the Glory. Hospital Sketches and Reports on the Wounded After the Battle* Michael Crumplin and Gareth Glover (ISBN 978-1-911628-48-4)

No 33 *Fluxes, Fevers, and Fighting Men. War and Disease in Ancien Regime Europe 1648-1789* Pádraig Lenihan (ISBN 978-1-911628-51-4)

No 34 *'They Were Good Soldiers'. African-Americans Serving in the Continental Army, 1775-1783* John U. Rees (ISBN 978-1-911628-54-5)*

No 35 *A Redcoat in America. The Diaries of Lieutenant William Bamford, 1757-1765 and 1776* Edited and Annotated by John B. Hattendorf (ISBN 978-1-911628-47-7)

* indicates 'Falconet' format paperbacks, page size 248mm x 180 mm, with high visual content including colour plates; other titles are hardback monographs unless otherwise noted.